Metropolitan College of NY
Library - 7th Floor
60 West Street
New York, NY 10006

Catastrophe and Philosophy

Catastrophe and Philosophy

Edited by
David J. Rosner

LEXINGTON BOOKS
Lanham • Boulder • New York • London

Published by Lexington Books
An imprint of The Rowman & Littlefield Publishing Group, Inc.
4501 Forbes Boulevard, Suite 200, Lanham, Maryland 20706
www.rowman.com

6 Tinworth Street, London SE11 5AL, United Kingdom

Copyright © 2019 by The Rowman & Littlefield Publishing Group, Inc.

The author wishes to thank The William Andrews Clark Memorial Library, University of California, Los Angeles, for permission to reproduce the three Hobbes frontispieces included as Figures 8.1, 8.3 and 8.4, and to thank Library Special Collections, Charles E. Young Research Library, UCLA, for permission to reproduce the three Callot plates included as Figure 8.2.

All rights reserved. No part of this book may be reproduced in any form or by any electronic or mechanical means, including information storage and retrieval systems, without written permission from the publisher, except by a reviewer who may quote passages in a review.

British Library Cataloguing in Publication Information Available

Library of Congress Cataloging-in-Publication Data Available

ISBN 978-1-4985-4011-7 (cloth: alk. paper)
ISBN 978-1-4985-4012-4 (electronic)

∞™ The paper used in this publication meets the minimum requirements of American National Standard for Information Sciences—Permanence of Paper for Printed Library Materials, ANSI/NISO Z39.48-1992.

Printed in the United States of America

Contents

Acknowledgments — ix

Introductory Essay: Catastrophe and the Limits of Understanding — xi
David J. Rosner

PART I: THE ANCIENT WORLD

Preface — 3

1. Catastrophe and Enlightenment: The Genesis of Buddhism's First Noble Truth — 7
   Jeidong Ryu

2. The Missing God: Voices of Despair and Empathy in the Book of Lamentations — 19
   Sarah Katerina Corrigan

3. Patterns of Post-Catastrophic Thought in Ancient China: The Growth of Philosophy After the Warring States Period — 31
   Kwon Jong Yoo

4. Athens in Ruins: Plato and the Aftermath of the Peloponnesian War — 43
   John Ross

PART II: THE MIDDLE AGES/RENAISSANCE

Preface   57

5   Augustine's Anti-Catastrophe   61
    Steven Cresap

6   Civilizational Trauma and Value Nihilism in Boccaccio's
    Decameron   71
    David J. Rosner

7   The Search for Stability in Chaotic Times: Niccolo Machiavelli   89
    Diana Prokofyeva

PART III: MODERNITY I: EARLY MODERN PERIOD

Preface   105

8   Three Catastrophes and One Philosopher: Atrocious
    Wars and the Political Ideas of Thomas Hobbes   107
    David Wilkinson

9   "A New Philosophy Calls All into Doubt": The
    Epistemological Crises of Early Modernity (and why
    they matter now)   137
    David J. Rosner and Steven Cresap

10 The Metaphysics of Catastrophe: Voltaire's *Candide*   151
    Carsten Meiner

PART IV: MODERNITY II: HIGH MODERNITY

Preface   167

11 Nietzsche and the Catastrophe of 19th-Century
    Democracy   171
    Phil Washburn

12 Ludwig Wittgenstein—Philosophy in the Twilight
    of the Habsburgs   191
    John Ross

13 Atonality in Music and the Upheavals of High
    Modernity   205
    Robert Quist

14	Toynbee and the World Wars Catastrophe: From the Philosophy of History to the Comparative Study of Civilizations *David Wilkinson*	219
15	Catastrophe and Decadence in *The Great Gatsby* *Peter W. Wakefield*	239
16	Deep Silence in the Holocaust Stories of Tadeusz Borowski *Nancy M. Reale*	253

PART V: POST-MODERNITY

Preface		281
17	States of Exception and the Problem of Detention in Post-9/11 American Jurisprudence *David A. Chalfin*	283
18	Swords of Damocles: An Essay on Catastrophe and Globalization *Pedro Geiger*	309

PART VI: CONCLUSION

Concluding Postscript		321
19	Primary Life Orientations and Philosophical Response to Catastrophe *Marek J. Celinski*	323

Index	339
Contributor Bios for *Catastrophe and Philosophy* *David J. Rosner (editor)*	343

Acknowledgments

This book has come to fruition through the work, help, and inspiration of many people. I would like to first thank the numerous chapter contributors who good-naturedly wrote various drafts and revisions for this project. I am also grateful to Metropolitan College of New York, which has provided me with a collegial work environment. Deb Spohnheimer helped with the daunting technical aspects involved in compiling an edited volume. Thanks also to Lexington's Jana Hodges-Kluck for being a knowledgeable, patient, and professional editor and to Trevor Crowell, also of Lexington, for his high level of competence and impressive attention to detail. I would like to acknowledge Joseph Drew and the editors of *Comparative Civilizations Review* for permission to reprint my (now slightly revised) paper "Civilizational Trauma and Value Nihilism in Boccaccio's *Decameron*" (Fall, 2015) and also DeGruyter Publishing, for permission to reprint Carsten Meiner's essay "The Metaphysics of Catastrophe—Voltaire's Candide," which first appeared as a chapter in C. Meiner and K. Veel (eds.) *The Cultural Life of Crises and Catastrophes* (DeGruyter, 2012). Thanks also to Phil Washburn of NYU, not only for the eminently reasonable comments he has provided me with regard to this volume, but for the generous editorial and philosophical assistance he has provided me over the years. Peter Wakefield of Emory University also read the manuscript and provided helpful and thoughtful advice. Nathan Mainster helped with proofreading a number of the papers in this book. Thanks also to Manikandan Kuppan for his patience and cheerfulness during the production process. I finally wish to express my appreciation to my wife Carol for all her love and forbearance.

Introductory Essay
Catastrophe and the Limits of Understanding
David J. Rosner

WHY THIS BOOK? PHILOSOPHY, LIFE'S EXTREMES, AND THE PROCESS OF "SENSE-MAKING"

What happens to values systems when the order of things is radically and suddenly disrupted? In such cases—for example, a tsunami that unexpectedly kills thousands in a few minutes, or a genocide that occurs over a number of years, such as the Holocaust—such upheavals do not merely change the fabric of everyday life. They actually upend a culture's long-standing values and assumptions, while leaving no new value systems in their place. The resulting epistemological and moral anomie (Cf. Durkheim)[1] can itself be viewed as trauma, a dislocation which leaves individuals and sometimes even entire civilizations bereft regarding life's most basic questions. Fundamental questions of meaning are raised, but the old answers no longer are convincing; long established paradigms have been rejected, and no new answers or explanatory frameworks are forthcoming. There is only cosmic silence.

If people can't make sense out of their world, this undercuts a fundamental feature and purpose of the human mind. Catastrophes are catastrophes not only because they bring widespread death and destruction in their wake, but also because they fundamentally challenge this basic "sense-making" feature of the human mind and our need for a meaningful world.[2]

One of humankind's primary sense-making activities has traditionally been philosophy. Yet little has been written focusing specifically on how many key developments in philosophy and the history of ideas arose out of larger crises and catastrophes (e.g., wars, plagues, natural disasters, etc.). This will be subject of the present volume. By examining developments in philosophy and the history of ideas through this specific lens, the book will aim to reveal commonalities between radically different times and places, to identify fundamental behavior patterns in relation to crises, as well as to help situate a number of these central philosophies in proper and historical and cultural context. This is a different approach to studying the history of philosophy, and one that seems increasingly relevant today, as the entire human race currently faces a number of existential catastrophes such as environmental degradation, global warming, overpopulation, the threat of nuclear conflagration, and widespread economic upheaval.

This new way of reading the history of philosophy and the history of ideas is based on the fact that catastrophe is not just a part of life; it is a very large one. Catastrophic events—such as nuclear plant meltdowns, natural disasters, terrorist attacks—can occur without warning and thus subtly underlie everyday life—somehow always looming as possibilities in the background or even just around the corner. Moreover, trauma in the wake of catastrophe results not only from the emotional pain of witnessing mass death, destruction, and dislocation, but also from our inability to adequately comprehend or make sense of it all. Our conventional explanations are suddenly seen to be woefully inadequate. New explanatory frameworks and concepts, sometimes even new first premises, are required. This is where philosophy comes in. This book explores the genesis of different philosophies and shows how, in many contexts and with different thinkers, individuals, and societies tried to make sense out of catastrophe and reorient themselves in its aftermath. However, catastrophic events also raise the disturbing question of the apparent randomness and amorality of life—and reconciling ourselves to this possibility is no easy task. Often sense-making seems impossible; in this connection Nietzsche writes of our deep need to postulate a meaning to events that is simply not present in them.[3] Yet this is itself a philosophical speculation upon the origins of nihilism, and it sets the stage for Nietzsche's dramatic alternative framework that grows out of it.

We acknowledge that this particular hermeneutic of reading philosophy through catastrophe is clearly not the only way to approach the subject—but we are offering it here as a unique and different perspective. And whether or not one agrees with this particular perspective, it is evident first that catastrophe raises a number of very serious philosophical questions, and second that out of trauma and catastrophe have often come different philosophies and worldviews, many of which have set the cornerstone for the gradual reorientation of individuals and societies.[4] Yet before proceeding further, we now must ask ourselves: in the aftermath of catastrophe, exactly how does the actual process of attempted sense-making occur? The phenomenology of this process will now be explored in greater detail.

CATASTROPHE AND THE PHENOMENOLOGY OF MORAL ANOMIE

The philosophers Edmund Husserl and Alfred Schutz formulated "the phenomenology of the life-world" as the sum total of our assumptions and beliefs that comprise the natural attitude. The psychologists R. Janoff-Bulman and J. Kauffman call this "the assumptive world" and analyze trauma in terms of "the loss of the assumptive world." Kauffman writes: "the assumptive world concept refers to the assumptions or beliefs that ground, secure, or orient people, that give a sense of reality, meaning or purpose to life."[5] Kauffman quotes C.M. Parkes in this regard: "The assumptive world is the only world we know and it includes everything we know or think we know. It includes our interrelation of the past and our expectations of the future, our plans, and our prejudices. Any or all of these may need to change as a result of changes in the life-space."[6] The assumptive world is thus the "ordering principle"[7] for the construction of an intelligible livable human reality. This refers not merely to beliefs about the empirical world (that the sun will rise in the morning) or the social world discussed by Schutz (the assumed roles of ourselves and others in a shared social reality) but to the very cognitive assumptions and psychological beliefs that render the world intelligible. When events transpire in such a way that these assumptions no longer seem to hold, there is a very real sense in which the world is "unlivable." Thus this "loss of the assumptive world" results not only in a sense of moral anomie and epistemological aporia, but also actually constitutes in and of itself a form of psychic trauma.[8]

Anthropologists and sociologists (Eliade, Berger, Geertz) have emphasized the notion that crises constitute actual moments in human consciousness during which the world no longer makes sense. These thinkers theorized that such aporia is psychologically untenable for most human beings. Geertz writes that "most men . . . are unable to leave unclarified problems of analysis merely unclarified . . . any chronic failure of one's explanatory apparatus . . . tends to lead us to deep disquiet."[9] Because of this, religious explanations (e.g., theodicies) have been formulated as a "nomos" that puts life's seemingly random events into an intelligible order, thus staving off the untenable idea of life and human suffering being ultimately random and amoral.[10] What exactly is the primal fear being referred to here? Geertz writes further:

> "The . . . opacity of certain empirical events, the . . . senselessness of intense or inexorable pain and the . . . unaccountability of . . . iniquity all raise the uncomfortable suspicion that perhaps the world, and hence man's life in the world, has no genuine order at all—no . . . regularity . . . no moral coherence. And the religious response to this suspicion is in each case the same: the formulation . . . of an image . . . of . . . genuine order in the world."[11]

What is unacceptable to human beings is not that the principles which constitute the moral order elude us when we are confronted with the cruelty of reality. Rather the unacceptable is the possibility that no such principles exist or ever existed. We need it to be that life's sufferings admit of an answer in principle, "that this elusiveness be accounted for, that it not be the result of the fact that there are no such principles, explanation or forms, that life is absurd and the attempt to make moral, intellectual or emotional sense of experience is bootless."[12]

Catastrophes reveal cracks in the moral scaffolding of a society, as if the bottom is pulled out from under a house of cards. Yet when a society's foundations are gone, what happens in the interim? What happens when what is experienced is a sense of moral anomie—as discussed in Durkheim's work, "a-nomic" literally referring to a lack of a (moral) law? Eventually a new value system is proposed to take the place of the old one, now rejected or disintegrated. But catastrophes raise the even more disturbing issue: did the moral foundations collapse or did the catastrophe simply lay bare the brutal fact that there was never any such set of existent values in the first place?[13]

As mentioned earlier, it is precisely this specter of an amoral, indifferent universe that is raised in the aftermath of catastrophe. A tsunami that kills thousands in minutes and destroys entire villages wholesale doesn't distinguish between those who are just and those who are unjust. This is alluded to as early as the Biblical book of Job. Job's friends try to put Job's sudden affliction into the traditional explanatory framework of theodicy and the existence of a coherent moral order. Job's friends are scandalized by his statement that effectively denies the existence of such a moral order: "It is all one: he destroys wicked and blameless alike."[14] And yet Job's lament here describes exactly how such things often appear to us.

There is also an epistemological component to consider. This is suggested by the work of Alastair MacIntyre, as well as the literature on "the assumptive world" discussed above. An epistemological aporia comes to the fore when traditional frameworks of explanation and prediction have been upended; one can no longer events in a logical or meaningful order or context, or predict future events with confidence.[15] "We seek regularity, stability, order and constancy in our surroundings."[16] We "rely on the stability of the world and the regularity of others' behavior and responses. We learn how to anticipate what will happen next and what will result from our actions."[17] Irene Smith Landsman describes what happens when we experience events, like catastrophes, that don't fit our preexisting explanatory schemas, and how this often leads to a crisis of meaning. She explains, through the use of Piaget's language, how "there is new information to be assimilated or accommodated. Either an event must be interpreted and explained in such a way to fit our schemas, which is a difficult and painful task, or our schemas must be altered, an even more daunting task."[18] She also discusses the common phenomenon of denial—the ultimate (and most desperate) way of reinterpreting an event in order to preserve our original coherent and livable world.

But it is not "only or even mainly, sudden eruptions of extraordinary events which engender in man the disquieting sense that his cognitive resources may prove unavailing."[19] According to Geertz, "more commonly it is a persistent, constantly re-experienced difficulty in grasping certain aspect of nature, self and society."[20] Suffering is part of everyday life for all human beings, not just victims of extreme trauma. According to the Buddha, suffering is the first noble truth of existence. Birth, sickness, sorrow, lamentation, pain, grief, and death are all inescapable features of the human condition. This is what Marc Epstein called "The Trauma of Everyday Life." Many try to deny this truth through refusing in various ways to admit their vulnerability and through other kinds of inauthentic behavior. In fact, society doesn't allow us the psychic space in which to properly process suffering and loss, experiences we confront every day in small and large ways. Epstein writes of the "rush to normal"—how pain is best not dwelled upon, as people are soon encouraged to "get over it."[21] But, even given this, phenomenon such as catastrophes challenge further (and more dramatically) our limited ability to process life events. There is no ability to deny or equivocate when a tsunami unexpectedly takes thousands of lives in a matter of minutes. With their seemingly random, large-scale onslaughts of indiscriminate death and suffering, and their attendant amoral quality, catastrophes suddenly throw our primal sense of cosmic anomie into even sharper relief.

DEFINITIONS

The emphasis in this book will not be upon the physical manifestations of a given disaster, be it the Lisbon earthquake or the pointless loss of life in World War 1, or the devastating economic meltdown of Weimar Germany. It will instead confine its examination to the transformations of the inner life of a culture following such crises, rather than the external causes. Catastrophes and crises, as defined by Carsten Meiner and Kristen Veel, constitute "disruptions of order."[22] The authors stipulate further that catastrophes and crises "differ in temporality - a catastrophe usually constitutes a sudden event, whereas a crisis stretches over a longer period of time"[23] but both "describe the uprooting of the existent."[24] By this definition, a massive, deadly earthquake constitutes a "catastrophe," while the more gradual destruction (physical and spiritual) of the 1500s Wars of Religion constitutes a "crisis."

One might furnish counterexamples to these definitions—for example, the Holocaust, which occurred over a period of years, would perhaps be more accurately classified as a catastrophe than a crisis. Perhaps this genocide was a human catastrophe that resulted from the underlying (moral, economic and political) crisis of Weimar Germany. And given these definitions, there are also a few chapters in this book that might come under the rubric of crises rather than actual catastrophes. Yet the commonality of all these developments is that they radically challenged the most basic assumptions of a civilization. They also required the reassessment and reconfiguration of these assumptions. What forms does the "uprooting of the existent" take in the everyday lives and philosophical outlooks of those that witness, survive, or experience crises and catastrophes?

AIMS AND SCOPE

A number of books and papers have been written about traumatic events that uproot people's lives—natural disasters, deaths of loved ones, being oneself diagnosed with a fatal illness, etc.[25] The present book looks at different philosophical ideas that arose out of these catastrophes, seeking both to extrapolate such disorientations to larger social complexes—cultures and/or civilizations, and to put these upheavals into larger perspective. For example, how did World War I affect European consciousness such that so much of the art of the interwar period exhibited increased tendencies toward fragmentation, distortion, and the dissolution of classical norms? How and why did a disoriented interwar Germany turn for leadership to Hitler, after the trauma of the loss of the war, the humiliation of the Versailles treaty, a deepening economic crisis, etc.? Can there be such a thing as civilizational trauma, in which an entire civilization loses its bearing until it somehow finds new ways to orient itself?[26] We know that individuals experience trauma. Can we extrapolate this to say that civilizations also can experience trauma in the wake of catastrophe? I believe we can do this.[27] For example, this is precisely what is conveyed in the following quote by Hermann Hesse, written in Weimar Germany during the bitter aftermath of World War 1:

> "In the years since the outbreak of the World War . . . one can already without exaggeration identify the death and dismantling of the culture into which the elder among us were raised as children and which then seemed to us eternal and indestructable . . . in times like the present, the demand for new formulations, new interpretations, new symbols, new explanations is infinitely great. . . . For even those who are superficial . . . still have the primary need to know that there is meaning to their lives. And when they are no longer able to find a meaning, morals decay, and private life is ruled by wildly intensified selfishness and an increased fear of death. All of these signs of the time are clearly legible, for

those who care to see . . . Irreplaceable things have been lost and destroyed forever; new, unheard of things are being imagined in their place."[28]

There are some very recent examples we could give as well. Taking our cue from Giorgio Agamben's *States of Exception*, let us consider the large-scale questioning of assumptions currently occurring (in different ways) in the US since 9/11. These questions have been cast into especially stark relief during the rise and current reign of the Trump administration, but the process began earlier, with the commencement of "the war on terror" in its many forms. Regarding the U.S. Constitution, is it ever permissible during "states of exception" to ban members of a certain religious group from entering the country? What about moral issues regarding increased use of surveillance, ethnic profiling, etc.? Do such measures entail morally problematic violations of privacy? And even if they do, could such violations still be justified during "states of exception"?[29] Many such conversations are currently being held across the country, revealing how "terror" and the "war on terror" have indelibly changed not only our way of life in the United States, but also our most basic ideas of the kind of nation we are, the values we embody, and the sort of country we would like to be. Many other examples could be furnished displaying similar statements, at different times and places in history when so many struggled with the lived experience of catastrophe, disaster, political upheavals, or civilizational disintegration.[30]

These examples raise the larger question of the relation between the individual and the collective. There are obvious differences between the two, because what is true of the individual is not necessarily always true of the collective. And while collectivities are comprised of individuals, we often observe how "the whole is equal to more than the sum of its parts." An example is an ethos or a zeitgeist—such a description can be true of a collectivity but not an individual.

The ideas of a few influential people can also seep into the collective consciousness without this process being understood as such by many individuals. Many peasants during the early modern period didn't understand the complexities of the scientific revolution. But maybe a subtle sense of cosmic uncertainty stemming from this questioning of the culture's basic assumptions began to slowly work its way into the collective consciousness and became part of the ethos of the period. Today, many of the instabilities, cultural shifts, and political pendulum swings occurring in the West may constitute aftershocks from the upheavals of the 1960s. Our society is now trying to reorient itself, undergoing a process of assimilating these upheavals and the attendant backlashes, and in stops and starts, integrating them into a new framework. Sometimes this process doesn't work smoothly. Civil wars and such can sometimes result from a failure of this sort of reorientation.

There is another, more positive side of catastrophe that we will also see analyzed in this volume, and we have just alluded to it. While often the results are negative, as in the movement toward fascism mentioned earlier, sometimes, this state of aporia may engender a new value system, a more positive perspective attempting to counteract or explain the crises that happened. Sometimes these new value systems have helped point toward catharsis, a new psychological resilience, or a sense of spiritual renewal.[31] Hopefully this book can also provide a number of philosophical perspectives that help can us adapt to catastrophe. These perspectives may be able to teach us how to revise previously held assumptions and routines, and also provide the guidelines to seek the (internal and external) resources to reorient ourselves to more effectively face life's challenges. Catastrophe can thus serve an adaptive purpose in our lives by forcing us to address undiscovered or ignored issues. Yet the process can only be adaptive if we are able to take an authentic stance—to face the truth about the situation, acknowledge the cognitive dissonance it has created, withstand the tension caused by this dissonance and gather the strength and insight to seek out the resources (cognitive, emotional, social, spiritual and material) to help put the experience in broader context and ultimately create new meaning in the catastrophe's aftermath.[32] Admittedly this is not an easy process, and perhaps is simply impossible for many people who unfortunately remain shattered and paralyzed by the apparent brutality that sometimes characterizes our earthly existence.

In light of these analyses what might be some positive prospects for hope and renewal? How did philosophies that grew out of crises help people find new paths to better, deeper, or more authentic lives? How did philosophies that arose from the ruins help mark the way toward civilizational progress? We will look at the various ways thinkers reacted to these catastrophes, in forms both destructive, positive, and perhaps even both at the same time. The latter phenomenon suggests that the very same event seen as a positive development from one perspective might simultaneously be considered a tragedy from another. Such perspectival matters thus reflect the subtlety of these questions and how they can be difficult to sort out.

CRITICAL CONSIDERATIONS

There are some objections one might offer against my approach in this book. In Frank Kermode's *The Sense of an Ending* Kermode argues that our views of crisis "are contemporary ways of making sense of the world, of giving it an intelligible order." That is, Kermode strikes a somewhat skeptical tone about the objective reality of crises, arguing how "crisis is a way of thinking about one's moment, and not inherent in the moment itself."[33] Kermode argues that the human condition occupies an intermediary position—every human being is born and dies "in the middle of things." Kermode's discussion elaborates on the "fictions" or coherent patterns we impose on an essentially transitory, disordered universe. Notions of crisis, catastrophe or apocalypse imply a coherent ending point to history and thus help to make sense out of things; they "make possible a satisfying consonance with the origins and with the middle,"[34] allowing us to impose some sense of order upon chaos and thereby "humanize the common death."

One might also ask: is it overdetermined to connect the formation of philosophies with environmental considerations to this degree? Many of the world's pivotal ideas came about during periods of relative tranquility, for example, Hume inventing skepticism in his armchair.[35] Yet, for every school of thought that flourished in a time of relative calm, there are many others thinkers whose work can only be fully understood as a response to crisis.[36] Not every significant development in philosophy and the history of ideas can be seen as the product of an epistemological upheaval or cultural crisis, but many certainly have been, and these connections warrant critical reflection. These developments will therefore be the subject of this book. Moreover, ideas often seep into the general culture in gradual, subtle ways, even if people do not realize it. As mentioned previously, religious fundamentalism has spread throughout the US since the upheavals of the 1960s and 1970s, in large part as a result of the aporias generated during these times, even though this may not be realized by many of the fundamentalists themselves.

Perhaps it has always seemed to observers that a given society is in crisis—such is the nature of human history and historical perception.[37] Yet if one lived in Lisbon before the 1755 earthquake and miraculously survived it, how would this event alter one's perspective? Everyday life in Lisbon would appear more precarious, fragile and fleeting after this event than before. Living through catastrophe alters the way one sees the world, it changes our views about what matters and what does not, and it affects how one formulates an answer to larger philosophical and spiritual questions.

One might also object to the premise of the book by arguing that philosophers strive to elucidate universal features of the human condition that exist independent of time, place, and particular events. Take, for example, Hobbes' conception of the state of nature, which presumably applied (and applies) to all human beings prior to entering into the social contract. Should we see Hobbes' theory as a response to the English civil war, or should we consider it independent of historical context? Hobbes would say the state of nature is the state we are all in when authority is removed, regardless of the political circumstances. Yet perhaps it could be both. Hobbes' pessimistic conception of human life as violent, "nasty, brutish and short," may have been influenced by the turbulent times in which he lived; moreover his discussion of monarchy as the best form of government could constitute a prime example of the search for political stability during a time when these were in short supply. Thinkers do not and cannot ever operate in a context-free vacuum.[38]

Regarding methodological considerations, even though the focus here is on different philosophies arising out of catastrophe, the reader will notice that this collection of essays doesn't deal only with philosophers in the narrow academic sense of that term. There are a number of essays in this collection focused primarily on literary works, musical compositions, religious texts, and legal cases. The volume is in this sense interdisciplinary. But all the essays illustrate a single overarching problem in moral philosophy and value theory in that they all are studies in how cultures, when set adrift in the wake of catastrophe, require a new value system or moral framework to reorient them in the future. I take my cues here from thinkers like Martha Nussbaum and others who have argued that works of literature and art can speak effectively to philosophical and moral concerns—at times perhaps more effectively than conventional theoretical works of philosophy themselves.

Finally, I have not limited the scope of this work to developments of Western European culture, but rather have tried to approach the subject from a more global perspective. Catastrophes, and philosophical reactions to them, have come about in all times and places, and it is instructive to learn about them. But there are a significant number of philosophies arising out of catastrophe that have not been covered in this book. Some of these might even constitute serious omissions. While this is a limitation, it is also unavoidable, considering the vastness of the book's topic. Hopefully the reader will still find the essays within edifying and the volume a good starting point for future investigations.

NOTES

1. Emile Durkheim, *Suicide* (New York: Free Press, 1951).
2. Regarding the larger issue of "sense-making" see Frank Kermode, *The Sense of an Ending: Studies in the Theory of Fiction* (Oxford: Oxford University Press, 1968). See also A. W. Moore, *The Evolution of Modern Metaphysics: Making Sense of Things* (Cambridge, UK: Cambridge University Press, 2014).
3. Friedrich Nietzsche, *Will to Power*, trans. Walter Kaufmann and R. J. Hollingdale, ed. Walter Kaufmann (New York: Vintage/Random House, 1968), 9–13.
4. This book looks at catastrophe more or less through the lens of the history of philosophy/intellectual history, from ancient times to the present. For another interesting theoretical perspective on catastrophe, see also Nitzan Lebovic and Andreas Killen, eds., *Catastrophes: A History and Theory of an Operative Concept* (Berlin: DeGruyter, 2014).

5. Jeffrey Kauffman, ed., *The Loss of the Assumptive World*, 2. See also Ami Harbin, *Disorientation and Moral Life* (Oxford: Oxford University Press, 2016), 2ff.

6. Colin Murray Parkes, "Psycho-Social Transition: A Field of Study," *Social Science & Medicine* 5, no. 2 (1971) as quoted in Kauffman, *Loss of the Assumptive World*, 2.

7. Kauffman, 2.

8. Ronnie Janoff-Bulman, *Shattered Assumptions* (New York: Free Press, 2002).

9. Clifford Geertz, "Religion as a Cultural System," in *The Interpretation of Cultures* (New York: Basic Books, 1973), 100.

10. See Peter Berger, *The Sacred Canopy* (NewYork: Image/Doubleday, 1967).

11. Geertz, "Religion as a Cultural System," 108.

12. Ibid.

13. See Patrizia McBride, *The Void of Ethics: Robert Musil and the Experience of Modernity* (Evanston, IL: Northwestern University Press, 2006).

14. Book of Job: 9:22, *Oxford Study Bible*.

15. Alasdair MacIntyre, "Epistemological Crises, Dramatic Narrative and the Philosophy of Science," in *Why Narrative? Readings in Narrative Theology*, ed. Stanley Hauerwas and L. Gregory Jones (Eugene, OR: Wipf & Stock, 1997), 138–57.

16. Thomas Attig, "Questionable Assumptions about Assumptive Worlds," in *The Loss of the Assumptive World*, ed. Jeffrey Kauffman (New York: Brunner-Routledge, 2002), 60.

17. Ibid., 59.

18. Irene Smith Landsman, "Crises of Meaning in Trauma and Loss," in *The Loss of the Assumptive World*, ed. Jeffrey Kauffman (New York: Brunner-Routledge, 2002), 18.

19. Geertz, 102.

20. Ibid.

21. See Marc Epstein, *The Trauma of Everyday Life* (New York: Penguin, 2014).

22. Carsten Meiner and Kristen Veel, eds., *The Cultural Life of Catastrophes and Crises* (Berlin: DeGruyter, 2012), 1.

23. Ibid.

24. Ibid.

25. See also Havi Carel, *Illness: The Cry of the Flesh* (Durham, UK: Acumen Publishing, 2013).

26. See Cornelius Castoriadis, *A Society Adrift*, trans. H. Arnold (New York: Fordham University Press, 2010).

27. For interesting analyses regarding individual and mass trauma, see also Marek Celinski and Kathryn Gow, eds., *Individual Trauma: Recovering from Deep Wounds and Exploring the Potential for Renewal* (Hauppauge, NY: Nova Science Publishers, 2012) as well as Marek Celinski and Kathryn Gow, eds., *Mass Trauma: Impact and Recovery Issues* (Hauppauge, NY: Nova Science Publishers, 2012).

28. See Hermann Hesse, "The Longing of Our Time for a Worldview" (1926), in *The Weimar Sourcebook*, ed. Anton Kaes, Martin Jay, and Edward Dimendberg (Berkeley: University of California Press, 1994).

29. See Giorgio Agamben, *States of Exception*, trans. Kevin Attell (Chicago: University of Chicago Press, 2005).

30. See also Piotr Sztompa, *The Sociology of Social Change* (Oxford and Cambridge, MA: Blackwell, 1993) and "The Trauma of Social Change: A Case of Post-Communist Societies," in *Cultural Trauma and Collective Identity*, ed. Jeffrey C. Alexander, et al. (Berkeley: University of California Press, 2004).

31. See Therese A. Rando, "The Curse of Too Good a Childhood," in *The Loss of the Assumptive World*, ed. Jeffrey Kauffman (New York: Routledge, 2002), 178.

32. This framework for resilience was suggested to me by Marek Celinski, and is explained in further detail in his chapter at the end of this book. Thanks also to Dr. Celinski for reading this introduction and offering valuable comments.

33. See Leo Bersani, "Variations on a Paradigm," a review of Frank Kermode, *The Sense of an Ending*. www.nytimes.com/books/00/06/25/specials/kermode-ending1.html.

34. Bersani, *passim*.

35. I am indebted to my colleague Steven Cresap for this thought.

36. This connection could be implicit rather than explicit. For example, Heidegger's work, although he steadfastly considered it to be a completely objective and context-independent investigation into "being" in itself, subtly reflects jarring shifts in European culture from its earliest beginnings, despite his best efforts to deny it.

37. Skepticism regarding crisis discourse itself is presented in Janet Roitman, *Anti-Crisis* (Durham, NC: Duke University Press, 2013).

38. I am indebted to Phil Washburn for this consideration.

BIBLIOGRAPHY

Agamben, Giorgio. *States of Exception*. Translated by Kevin Attell. Chicago: University of Chicago Press, 2005.

Attig, Thomas. "Questionable Assumptions about Assumptive Worlds." In *The Loss of the Assumptive World: A Theory of Trauma and Loss*, edited by Jeffrey Kaufmann, 55–70. New York: Brunner-Routledge, 2002.

Benjamin, Walter. "On the Concept of History." Translated by Dennis Redmond. https://www.marxists.org/reference/archive/benjamin/1940/history.htm.

Berger, Peter. *The Sacred Canopy*. New York: Image/Doubleday, 1967.

Bersani, Leo. "Variations on a Paradigm." *New York Times*, June 11, 1967. https://archive.nytimes.com/www.nytimes.com/books/00/06/25/specials/kermode-ending1.html.

Carel, Havi. *Illness: The Cry of the Flesh*. Durham, UK: Acumen, 2013.

Castoriadis, Cornelius. *A Society Adrift*. Translated by H. Arnold. New York: Fordham University Press, 2010.

Celinski, Marek and Kathryn Gow, editors. *Individual Trauma: Recovering from Deep Wounds and Exploring the Potential for Renewal*. Hauppauge, NY: Nova Science Publishers, 2012a.

Celinski, Marek and Kathryn Gow, editors. *Mass Trauma: Impact & Recovery*. Hauppauge, NY: Nova Scientific Publishers, 2012b.

Durkheim, Emile. *Suicide*. New York: The Free Press, 1951.

Epstein, Marc. *The Trauma of Everyday Life.* New York: Penguin, 2014.
Geertz, Clifford. *The Interpretation of Cultures.* New York: Basic Books, 1973.
Harbin, Ami. *Disorientation and Moral Life.* Oxford: Oxford University Press, 2016.
Hesse, Hermann. "The Longing of Our Time for a Worldview." In *The Weimar Sourcebook,* edited by Anton Kaes, et al. Berkeley: University of California Press, 1994.
Janoff-Bulman, Ronnie. *Shattered Assumptions.* New York: Free Press, 2002.
Kaes, Anton, Martin Jay and Edward Dimendberg, editors. *The Weimar Sourcebook.* Berkeley: University of California Press, 1994.
Kauffman, Jeffrey, editor. *The Loss of the Assumptive World: A Theory of Trauma and Loss.* New York: Brunner-Routledge, 2002.
Kermode, Frank. *The Sense of an Ending: Studies in the Theory of Fiction.* Oxford: Oxford University Press, 1968.
Landsman, Irene Smith. "Crises of Meaning in Trauma and Loss." In *The Loss of the Assumptive World*, edited by Jeffrey Kaufmann, 13–30. New York: Brunner-Routledge, 2002.
Lebovic, Nitzan and Andreas Killen, editors. *Catastrophes: A History and Theory of an Operative Concept.* Berlin: DeGruyter, 2014.
MacIntyre, Alisdair. "Epistemological Crises, Dramatic Narrative and the Philosophy of Science." In *Why Narrative? Readings in Narrative Theology*, edited by Stanley Hauerwas and L. Gregory Jones, 138–57. Eugene, OR: Wipf & Stock, 1997.
McBride, Patrizia. *The Void of Ethics: Robert Musil & the Experience of Modernity.* Evanston, IL: Northwestern University Press, 2006.
Meiner, Carsten and Kristen Veel, editors. *The Cultural Life of Catastrophes and Crises.* Berlin: DeGruyter, 2012.
Moore, A.W. *The Evolution of Modern Metaphysics: Making Sense of Things.* Cambridge, UK: Cambridge University Press, 2014.
Nietzsche, Friedrich. *Will to Power.* Translated by Walter Kaufmann and R. J. Hollingdale. Edited by Walter Kaufmann. New York: Vintage/Random House, 1968.
Oxford Study Bible. Oxford: Oxford University Press, l992.
Parkes, Colin Murray. "Psycho-Social Transition: A Field of Study." In *Social Science and Medicine* 5, no. 2 (1975): 101–15.
Rando, Therese. "The Curse of Too Good a Childhood." In *The Loss of the Assumptive World*, edited by Jeffrey Kaufmann, 171–192. New York: Brunner-Routledge, 2002.
Roitman, Janet. *Anti-Crisis.* Durham, NC: Duke University Press, 2013.
Schutz, Alfred and Thomas Luckmann. *The Structures of the Life World.* Evanston, IL: Northwestern University Press, 1973.
Sztompa, Piotr. *The Sociology of Social Change.* Oxford and Cambridge, MA: Blackwell, 1993.
Sztompa, Piotr, Jeffrey C. Alexander, Ron Eyerman, Bernhard Giesen, and Neil J. Smelser. "The Trauma of Social Change: A Case of Past Soviet Societies." In *Cultural Trauma and Collective Identity*, 155–95. Berkeley: University of California Press, 2004.

Part I
THE ANCIENT WORLD

Preface

The Ancient World

The first section of this book will deal with philosophical reactions to catastrophe in the ancient world. While we cannot research all the philosophical reactions to the many disasters that happened during ancient times, this section of the book will feature, among other things, an analysis of philosophical schools and changing perspectives which grew out of the devastation of the Peloponnesian War and the Warring States period in China.

In ancient Greece during the aftermath of the Peloponnesian War, an important theme raised by the tyrant Thrasymachus in Plato's *Republic* is that of moral relativism. How do crises raise the specter of the absence of any absolute values? Thrasymachus' emphasis on power as the sole criterion of morality, combined with similar themes in other works of this time (cf. Thucydides' "The Melian Dialogue") also reveal the morally corrupting effects (and the inevitable and tragic coarsening of the fabric of society) that war brings. Both texts stressed "a new ruthlessness, with a newly anarchic employment of power, and a new disrespect for . . . tradition."[1] Motivated also in part by the execution of his teacher Socrates, Plato spent the rest of his life attempting to argue for some "conduct of affairs that might eliminate the confusion and gross error that he saw around him."[2] Many of these themes—moral relativism, skepticism regarding absolute moral values, abuses of power and authority, still apply today, perhaps even in starker terms.

However, Plato's *Republic* with its emphasis on eternal truth has often been taught merely as an argument for an ideal state, a state by chance entailing extreme moral realism as its conceptual foundation. It is not always explained that Plato's philosophical apparatus was put forth to a considerable degree as a reaction to the catastrophe of the Peloponnesian War. The war resulted not merely in the military defeat of Athens, but also in the tragic defeat of the spiritual ideals of Athens, elaborated so eloquently in the past by Pericles in his *Funeral Oration*. In this sense, the backdrop of moral crisis can provide us not only with greater understanding of Plato's motivation as a philosopher but insight also into the particular trajectory of his thought. Plato abandoned the fleeting, transient world of "sights and sounds" for a supposedly eternal realm of truth, not subject to "coming into being and passing away." Understanding this way of dealing with the trauma and brutality of his violent times lends insight into this basic theme in Platonic thought. The war was not the only motivation for Plato's writing, nor is this the only way to understand his work, but we believe that this perspective does shed important light on Plato's lived world and some of his philosophical assumptions.

We will also examine some philosophical outgrowths of the Warring States Period in ancient China. Confucianism featured the doctrine of Filial Piety, which turns our eyes back toward earlier generations. The family as the fundamental unit of civilization was also highlighted in Aristotle's *Politics*, illustrating the universality of this truth. This implicit traditionalism of Confucius' thought (radical at the time) served to ground Chinese society in a more solid and enduring value system. This might not be the only way to understand Confucius, but it highlights how one outcome of the chaos of this period was a renewed urgency in the search for social and political stability and how Confucius' thought fits into this equation. If we accept this interpretation, we thus see how catastrophes took different forms, with the philosophical reactions to these catastrophes also manifesting themselves in various ways.

Yet can we meaningfully extrapolate lessons from ancient times to our contemporary situation? After all, these ancient civilizations had different value systems than ours and saw the world from a very different viewpoint. For example, contemporary students of *The Iliad* sometimes have trouble understanding the behavior of the Homeric heroes until they understand that this was a civilization fundamentally motivated by a warrior code or "cult of honor." And what of texts originating from the complete other side of the world? Can such radically different civilizations with such different languages, cultural norms, behavior codes and religions, truly communicate intelligibly to one another?

Just as the proposition "$2 + 2 = 4$" is true in all times and places, human nature itself does not change (nor has it changed) over time and place. Human beings still feel anger, gratitude, lust, shame, joy, and despair, just as they always have. Such thought processes and emotions are universal, not dependent upon time or place. While it may not always have been the exact same sort of event to occasion these responses, being human involves a sufficient number of universal truths and commonalities. These ancient works from all over the world still have the power to communicate these truths to us in the here and now, especially as we in the 21st-century struggle to deal with catastrophes of our own.

NOTES

1. Rex Warner, *The Greek Philosophers* (New York: Signet, 1958). Another interesting text in this regard is Simone Weil, *The Iliad or the Poem of Force* (Wallingford, PA: Pendle Hill, 1981).
2. Warner, *The Greek Philosophers.*

BIBLIOGRAPHY

Confucius. *Analects*. Translated by D. C. Lau. New York: Penguin, 1993.
Plato. *Republic*. Translated by A. Bloom. New York: Basic Books, 1968.
Warner, Rex. *The Greek Philosophers*. New York: Signet, 1958.
Weil, Simone. *The Iliad or the Poem of Force*. Wallingford, PA: Pendle Hill, 1981.

Chapter 1

Catastrophe and Enlightenment
The Genesis of Buddhism's First Noble Truth
Jeidong Ryu

INTRODUCTION

Buddhism is based upon four noble truths about suffering, taught by the Buddha and practiced by the Buddhist community. The first noble truth is the truth about the existence of suffering, the second the truth about the cause of suffering, the third the truth about the cessation of suffering, and the fourth the truth about the path toward the cessation of suffering. All four noble truths are focused upon suffering and its solution, which might reflect the Buddha and his early followers' facing a serious catastrophe during their lifetimes.

In the fifth century, approximately the time during which the Buddha lived and died, the Indian subcontinent was facing a thoroughgoing crisis in several dimensions. Due to technological advancements with the introduction of iron tools, the rapid growth of big cities facilitated the establishment of a few great kingdoms, with minor tribal societies being absorbed into their dominion. Mavis Fenn summarizes the situation succinctly:

> The changes were multiple. The development of the iron plow allowed for the intensification of agriculture. Many people were displaced from the land and forced to move into the newly emerging cities. These cities often provided a breeding ground for disease and violence. While agriculture flourished, ownership of the land devolved into the hands of individual families. Politically, there was a shift from an oligarchic tribe/clan system to a system of kingship. Trade flourished, guilds were established, and a banking system developed. The newly emergent mercantile class had money but little status, as the established order had no place for them.[1]

In addition to such drastic and rapid changes, the ideological stability of the sacrifice-oriented Brahmanism was now seriously challenged. The proper performance of sacrifices became regarded as no more than a certain way of securing earthly or heavenly happiness, possibly influenced by the rise of the notion of samsara (rebirth or transmigration in wandering). At best, the performance of sacrifices guaranteed happiness only for a limited span of future time, beyond which it was feared continuous rebirth would weaken their magical power. At worst, the radical change of social conditions following the displacement of many people from the land due to the intensification of agriculture—including their downgrading from farmers to pariahs and the unpredictable unfolding of life as a result of rampant disease and violence in the newly developing cities—made the expected efficacy of sacrifices questionable. This situation constituted a serious upheaval—it basically broke the stability and predictability of life regarding social status and regarding class and gender as described in the sacrificial texts of the established Brahmanic tradition.[2] Moreover, this crisis engendered serious philosophical debates about personal identity, as well as the nature of change and suffering in a radically transient unpredictable world. The crisis in Indian civilization thus provided fertile ground for the questioning of basic assumptions about life and its meaning. Hence,

> While we cannot enter the minds of the people at the time, it is not difficult to speculate about how these rapid technological, social, and political changes may have affected people psychologically. We thus see how themes of identity and the nature of change and suffering are central in the philosophical debates of the time, as are ideas regarding the proper construction of society.[3]

In short, the Indian civilization was in grave peril of facing a major catastrophe in both material and spiritual dimensions. As to the overall characteristics of the crisis of the period, Mavis Fenn writes,

> Our sense of identity and the comfortableness with which we accept our beliefs and practices as self-evident is rarely faced with scrutiny until we encounter those who believe and practice differently. Our encounter with *the other* frequently provokes us to contemplate who we are, what we believe, and why we do so. This need for clarification and distinction from others is not confined to individuals who may travel cross-culturally, but occurs on the larger scale as well. The differing values held by those indigenous to the Ganges Valley and those who immigrated, bringing Vedic religion with them, produced an often contentious discussion about ultimate truth, highest value, and the nature of what it meant to be human, both individually and collectively. It was that discussion that shaped and formed the foundations and outlines of Hinduism, Jainism, and Buddhism. Indeed, many Buddhist concepts were consciously conceived in contrast to Vedic thought.[4]

In the midst of such uncertainty and insecurity, the Buddha searched for a solution to these problems not through military or political engagements but through a thorough probing of the mind. His focus was confined to what can be controlled by his own decisions, producing an unwavering peace of mind. Of course the problem of change and permanence is fundamental to philosophy, especially ancient philosophy (cf. the pre-Socratic thinkers Heraclitus and Parmenides in the West). But for the Buddha, reflecting on this problem was not just an intellectual exercise. Indeed, for the purposes of this volume on catastrophe and philosophy, it is especially interesting how the Buddha not only witnessed the process of change and its catastrophic effects on his specific culture, but also specifically connected it to the problem of human suffering generally and discussed its alleviation through the cultivation of certain habits of mind.

THE BUDDHA'S UNYIELDING MIND IN HIS RECOGNITION OF SUFFERING AS THE FIRST NOBLE TRUTH

The first noble truth of Buddhism is suffering. The uniqueness of Buddhism is its initial emphasis on suffering as the fundamental truth about the world. Is this a pessimistic starting point? Some argue we should presuppose the initial good state of the world if we hope to improve the present bad state of the world, since the correction of the bad state needs an initial good state of the world. This is a presupposition of theodicy in Christianity and other theistic traditions. But this metaphysical assumption of an original or fundamental state of the world is alien to early Buddhism, even though it creeps into the Buddhist tradition later on. This is clear insofar as the Buddha keeps a distance from metaphysical questions about the world and personal identity.[5]

The Buddha lived in a period of full catastrophe, which required not a theoretical or metaphysical concern but a practical treatment. His recognition of catastrophe might have been influenced by the rapid changes of the fate of states and people due to frequent wars and the spread of diseases. He felt deep distress facing this catastrophic situation, desperately wishing to be liberated. So he chose to leave his palace and wandered Northeastern India for six years, seeking the way of liberation. His response to his father trying to persuade him to stay at the palace before his leaving home illustrates his concern about this. "My Lord, if you cannot give me these four boons—Freedom from misfortune and the terrors of sickness, old age, and dying—Then I request of you another boon. Please listen, Your Majesty: I wish that, after I die, I will not have to take rebirth again."[6]

His father, of course, could not guarantee such freedom at the palace. Buddha's desperate quest required a fully devoted life as a wandering mendicant. He would not be satisfied by compromised solutions. This strict attitude continued until his own enlightenment under the Bodhi tree. In the meantime, Alara Kalama and Uddaka Ramaputta, the two famous contemporary yogic teachers, tried to persuade him to stay within their group, guaranteeing that he would be their next leader. The Buddha, however, perceived that their practices could not guarantee absolute freedom from suffering.[7]

If he had a limited vision of freedom, he might have been persuaded to stay in the palace or with the yoga leaders. But his ambition was so high that he could not be satisfied by a fleeting experience of mental joy that the practice of yogic exercise can give. He did not seek the mere experience of freedom, but sought absolute freedom from suffering. Through his long wanderings, he realized that any path preached by the contemporary wandering teachers would be ephemeral and fleeting.

All such paths were only ways of conditioning our mind to be blind to actual realities of the world, securing a temporary happiness for a secluded mind. These practices thus only aggravated the existing suffering. He was sure that only the proper observation of actual realities in their deepest dimensions would produce the freedom he sought. In order to be healed, we should be able to feel the world's suffering. The perception of suffering is necessary in order to recognize a problem that needs to be solved. He realized that clinging to any phenomena, with their fleeting nature, might obstruct his arriving at absolute freedom. Steven Emmanuel writes,

> The Buddha's spiritual journey toward enlightenment was driven not only by his personal experience of suffering, but also by his profound empathy for the suffering of the world. This empathy was only deepened by his enlightenment experience, which confirmed in a direct way that everything in the world, including suffering, exists in a condition of interdependence.[8]

Over and above visible phenomena, the Buddha saw the reality of dharmas as higher principles that govern changes of phenomena. He focused especially upon the moral dimensions of the dharmas as the principles of managing human relationships. He recognized rightful living as the only way to reach absolute freedom from suffering.[9] Therefore, as the fourth noble truth, he proposed the eightfold path of rightful living that is composed of: right view, right intention, right speech, right action, right livelihood, right effort, right mindfulness, and right concentration.[10] In short, the eightfold path was a way of living a fully awakened life in the face of catastrophic realities, thereby also deepening our consciousness of suffering.

For him, the more awakened you are, the more suffering you perceive in your life and the world surrounding you. This awakening is fostered by the realization that there is no fixed self. Our self is the result of the combination of diverse conglomerations, the combination changing incessantly. As a stream of these combinations, we must be aware that the encounter between ourselves and our surrounding environments causes all kinds of suffering.[11] This is especially true when we cling to the notion of a fixed self on the basis of greed. This clinging causes our perspectives to be fixated on material objects in a way so as to cause more suffering, obstructing our correct observation of the phenomena facing us.

THREE KINDS OF SUFFERING

Thus, the Buddha distinguishes three kinds of suffering according to the degree of the depth of our understanding. The first is suffering as suffering. Walpola Rahula explains this suffering as follows.

> All kinds of suffering in life like birth, old age, sickness, death, association with unpleasant persons and conditions, separation from beloved ones and pleasant conditions, not getting what one desires, grief, lamentation, distress—all such forms of physical and mental suffering, which are universally accepted as suffering or pain, are included in *dukkha* as ordinary suffering (*dukkha-dukkha*).[12]

This is the most common form of suffering that all of us instantly recognize.

The second is suffering due to change, which is more difficult to recognize since its recognition requires our inference, not our direct perception. Walpola Rahula explains as follows: "A happy feeling, a happy condition in life, is not permanent, not everlasting. It changes sooner or later. When it changes, it produces pain, suffering, unhappiness. This vicissitude is included in *dukkha* as suffering produced by change (*vipariṇāma-dukkha*)."[13]

Here, we see that even happiness is included in suffering due to change. The Buddha, as we observed above, could not be satisfied with a happy feeling because it is fleeting.

The third is suffering due to conditioning, which is the most difficult to recognize since its recognition requires our profound intuition of ourselves. About this suffering, Walpola Rahula emphasizes it as "the most important philosophical aspect of the First Noble Truth" that "requires some analytical explanation of what we consider as a 'being', as an 'individual', or as 'I',"[14] adding the analytical explanation of the five aggregates as the components of "I." In his explanation of the five aggregates, for example, he clarifies that the "Buddha declared in unequivocal terms that consciousness depends on matter, sensation, perception and mental formations, and that it cannot exist independently of them."[15] Suffering due to conditioning is thus based upon our own existence. The awareness of our being conditioned is also inevitably conditioned by the context of the subject, although it has some degree of transcendence. So the Buddha also admits he is not completely free from suffering. We are all in the process of being liberated from suffering.[16]

When the Buddha observed actual people, however, he knew that the divisions between castes were arbitrary, without objective basis. For him, actual persons were important, not the typified persons in the Indian caste system. He avoided any abstract discrimination of phenomena, which he regarded as not adequately reflecting the subtle and constantly changing nature of conditioning. The Buddha's view on conditioning did not presuppose determinism or fatalism.

With this attitude, he could negate the efficacy of sacrifices in Brahmanism. Karma meant not the result of one's own past behaviors but the accumulated habitual intentions of the person. He thought that the fundamental intuition of no fixed self and efforts toward improving our habitual thinking and behavior would lessen our suffering. The cultivation of our mind in this dimension was meant toward improving our capacity to deal with the catastrophes facing us, as well as developing our maturity in not causing catastrophes ourselves, which are harmful for us and for others. When one's observation becomes more piercing, one comes to perceive suffering more deeply and to search for its solution more thoroughly. In other words, when one becomes mature, one comes to perceive more profound suffering. This is not a pessimistic development but an advance, since such an intuition is necessary to deal properly with the suffering that life fundamentally entails.

The most serious suffering is caused by conditioning, a concept that might be easily understood in the context of the modern discussions about brainwashing. For example, in the modern world, ideologies such as neoliberalism might foster a comparatively invisible form of suffering, in that they invoke a distorted notion of self.[17] David Loy diagnoses the problem of modern capitalism according to his Buddhist notion of lack.[18] This brainwashing occurring in modern capitalist societies fosters greed for material goods, and utilizes this greed to control people's behavior. The doctrine of No fixed self encourages a more open attitude to the world. People living in this neoliberal society might not realize that they are indoctrinated to believe that their own society is the best possible one, or that they need to possess a particular product, in spite of the fact that they are often being used by a system which ultimately results in other people's gains as well as their own oppression. This is therefore an example of suffering directly caused by human agents.

THE FRUSTRATING SITUATION

The Buddha's proposition of suffering as the first noble truth was due to his unique view on the nature of the world and his vision toward overcoming this suffering. The Buddha's frustration was due to his own absolutist decision to reach the absolute state of happiness while the other contemporary teachers showed relative satisfaction with conditional happiness. The Buddha, however, could not give up his own ideal. His own republic was collapsing, being surrounded by strong kingdoms. There were even some teachers proclaiming that there is no meaning in our life on earth. The Buddha could not be satisfied with ordinary solutions proposing compromised answers. As a prince, he deliberately chose to live the most stringent life on the road as a mendicant, without any hope of reaching his destination. In spite of this, he was a man of unyielding mind. Perceiving the process of causal progress neither in an exaggerated nor in a diminished way, but in a proper way, the Buddha avoided both optimism and pessimism, choosing realism.

The four noble truths are significant for the proper recognition of suffering. In fact, the eightfold path as the fourth noble truth is as important as the practice for the profound awakening to suffering as the first noble truth.[19] Wilfred Cantwell Smith's emphasis on Dharma as the truth about right living is significant in this context:

> Though Nirvana was a distant reality, indescribable, not profitable of discussion, yet the Buddha saw and preached another absolute reality immediately available to every man. This is the moral law. The Buddha taught that in the universal flux, one thing is firm. In the chaos of events, one pattern is permanent. In the ebb and flow of human life, one form is absolute, is supreme, is reliable, is effective for salvation. Ideas come and go; religious institutions rise and fall; the gods themselves have their histories; men's and women's goals are frustrated, and anyway are themselves historical; all human strivings, whether to construct something on earth, or through piety or asceticism to try to escape from or to dominate earthly ambitions, are doomed sooner or later to pass away. Yet through it all one thing is certain, stable, firm, enduring—and is always immediately to hand. That is Dharma: the truth about right living.[20]

In this context, Kalama Sutta, famous as the charter for free inquiry, is also noteworthy as the prerequisite for the recognition of truth. This Sutta proposes the rational and empirical criteria for rejection and acceptance of certain truth claims.

> It is proper for you, Kalamas, to doubt, to be uncertain; uncertainty has arisen in you about what is doubtful. Come, Kalamas. Do not go upon what has been acquired by repeated hearing; nor upon tradition; nor upon rumor; nor upon

what is in a scripture; nor upon surmise; nor upon an axiom; nor upon specious reasoning; nor upon a bias towards a notion that has been pondered over; nor upon another's seeming ability; nor upon the consideration, "The monk is our teacher." Kalamas, when you yourselves know: "These things are bad; these things are blamable; these things are censured by the wise; undertaken and observed, these things lead to harm and ill," abandon them.[21]

These criteria for rejection reveal the Buddha's thoroughly critical attitude in appraising truth claims. Conversely, the criteria for acceptance of certain truth claims should be based upon one's own knowledge that they lead to happiness. "Kalamas, when you yourselves know: 'These things are good; these things are not blamable; these things are praised by the wise; undertaken and observed, these things lead to benefit and happiness,' enter on and abide in them."[22]

This attitude reveals the Buddha's view that we should face the difficulties of life in a square way. Problems should be tackled with honesty if they are to be solved. This attitude of honest observation became the basis of the Buddha's lifelong quest for complete happiness.

CONCLUDING REMARKS

The Buddha's focus upon suffering in the ways described above might be viewed as limiting Buddhism's efforts to practically solve problems within the world, leaving Buddhists only in the domain of spiritual pursuits. However, in facing the peril of an overwhelming catastrophe, the Buddha's choice was actually rational rather than reckless. Turning to the subjective dimension of the catastrophe, the Buddha reached a decisive insight, leading into his formulation of Buddhism's first noble truth—the essential nature of suffering. This subjective turn of the Buddha shed light not only on the suffering of a human being as a sentient subject, but also on the possibility of the improvement of the human mind as an agent. This choice should not be underestimated. Mavis Fenn says as following in defense of the Buddha's efforts:

> Although the Buddha did not directly engage in social activism, his teachings confirmed that personal transformation in the Buddhist sense could not be separated from the transformation of society. The monks and nuns who joined the Sangha in search of personal enlightenment did not practice solely for their own sake. Whether teaching the dharma, observing the precepts, or sitting in meditation, they, too, were working to create the conditions for all beings to attain liberation.[23]

Understanding the human mind, seeking happiness and avoiding unhappiness, is a simple yet straightforward way toward our understanding of both ourselves and the larger universe. It also provides guidance for optimal living within a world full of catastrophes. This is true especially in our present age, in which humankind is actually the major cause of many catastrophes, which might be ascribed to greed, antagonism, and stupidity, for example, ecological disaster and rampant poverty in spite of technological advances. Living in the midst of these self-caused catastrophes, many of which are only growing in seriousness, perhaps it is time for us to revisit in earnest the Buddha's universal truths.

NOTES

1. Mavis Fenn, "Buddhism: Historical Setting," in *The Wiley-Blackwell Companion to Religion and Social Justice*, ed. Michael D. Palmer and Stanley M. Burgess (Oxford: Blackwell Publishing, 2012), 17.
2. Ibid., 17–19.
3. Ibid., 17.
4. Ibid., 19.
5. "Cula-Malunkyovada Sutta: The Shorter Instructions to Malunkya" MN 63, trans. Thanissaro Bhikkhu. Access to Insight Legacy Edition, November 30, 2013, accessed September 17, 2016, http://www.accesstoinsight.org/tipitaka/mn/mn.063.than.html. Here, the Buddha kept a distance from the metaphysical positions that "'The cosmos is eternal,' 'The cosmos is not eternal,' 'The cosmos is finite,' 'The cosmos is infinite,' 'The soul & the body are the same,' 'The soul is one thing and the body another,' 'After death a Tathagata exists,' 'After death a Tathagata does not exist,' 'After death a Tathagata both exists and does not exist,' 'After death a Tathagata neither exists nor does not exist.'"
6. *The Play in Full: Lalitavistara*, trans. Dharmachakra Translation Committee (2013), 149, http://read.84000.co/translation/UT22084-046-001.html.
7. For a full account of their historicity and influence on the Buddha, refer to Alexander Wynne, *The Origin of Buddhist Meditation* (New York: Routledge, 2007).
8. Steven Emmanuel, "Buddhism: Contemporary Expressions," in *The Wiley-Blackwell Companion to Religion and Social Justice*, ed. Michael D. Palmer and Stanley M. Burgess (Oxford: Blackwell, 2012), 33.
9. Wilfred Cantwell Smith, *Faith and Belief: The Difference between Them* (Princeton, NJ: Princeton University Press, 1998), 24–28.
10. Bhikku Bodhi, *The Noble Eightfold Path: The Way to the End of Suffering* (Kandy, SL: Buddhist Publication Society, 1999).
11. Walpola Rahula, *What the Buddha Taught* (London: Gordon Fraser, 1978), 16–28.
12. Ibid., 19.
13. Ibid., 20.

14. Ibid.

15. Ibid., 25. As for the recent discussions on related subjects, refer to *Self, No Self: Perspectives from Analytical, Phenomenological, and Indian Traditions*, ed. Mark Siderits, Evan Thompson, and Dan Zahavi (Oxford: Oxford University Press, 2011).

16. The repeated appearance of the demon Mara as a tempter in the Buddha's life might evidence the fact that the Buddha was not fully free from the bondage of suffering.

17. George Monbiot, "Books: Neoliberalism—The Ideology at the Root of All Our Problems," *Guardian*, April 15, 2016, https://www.theguardian.com/books/2016/apr/15/neoliberalism-ideology-problem-george-monbiot. Here, he argues that "Financial meltdown, environmental disaster and even the rise of Donald Trump—neoliberalism has played its part in them all."

18. David R. Loy, *A Buddhist History of the West: Studies in Lack* (New York: State University of New York Press, 2002).

19. Bodhi, *Noble Eightfold Path*, v–vi.

20. Smith, *Faith and Belief*, 26.

21. "Kalama Sutta: The Buddha's Charter of Free Inquiry," trans. Soma Thera. Access to Insight, Legacy Edition, November 30, 2013, http://www.accesstoinsight.org/lib/authors/soma/wheel008.html.

22. Ibid.

23. Fenn, "Buddhism: Historical Setting," 33.

BIBLIOGRAPHY

Bodhi, Bhikku. *The Noble Eightfold Path: The Way to the End of Suffering*. Kandy, SL: Buddhist Publication Society, 1999.

"Cula-Malunkyovada Sutta: The Shorter Instructions to Malunkya," MN 63. Translated from the Pali by Thanissaro Bhikkhu. Access to Insight Legacy Edition, November 30, 2013. Accessed September 17, 2016. http://www.accesstoinsight.org/tipitaka/mn/mn.063.than.html.

Emmanuel, Steven. "Buddhism: Contemporary Expressions." In *The Wiley-Blackwell Companion to Religion and Social Justice*, edited by Michael D. Palmer and Stanley M. Burgess, 30–45. Oxford: Blackwell, 2012.

Fenn, Mavis. "Buddhism: Historical Setting." In *The Wiley-Blackwell Companion to Religion and Social Justice*, edited by Michael D. Palmer and Stanley M. Burgess, 17–29. Oxford: Blackwell, 2012.

"Kalama Sutta: The Buddha's Charter of Free Inquiry." Translated from the Pali by Soma Thera. Access to Insight Legacy Edition, November 30, 2013. Accessed September 17, 2016. http://www.accesstoinsight.org/lib/authors/soma/wheel008.html.

Loy, David R. *A Buddhist History of the West: Studies in Lack*. New York: State University of New York Press, 2002.

Monbiot, George. "Books: Neoliberalism – The Ideology at the Root of All Our Problems." *Guardian*, April 15, 2016. Accessed September 17, 2016. https://www.theguardian.com/books/2016/apr/15/neoliberalism-ideology-problem-george-monbiot.

Rahula, Walpola. *What the Buddha Taught*. London: Gordon Fraser, 1978.

Siderits, Mark, Evan Thompson, and Dan Zahavi. *Self, No Self: Perspectives from Analytical, Phenomenological, & Indian Traditions*. Oxford: Oxford University Press, 2011.

Smith, Wilfred Cantwell. *Faith and Belief: The Difference between Them*. Princeton, NJ: Princeton University Press, 1998.

The Play in Full: Lalitavistara. Translated by the Dharmachakra Translation Committee, 2013. http://read.84000.co/translation/UT22084-046-001.html.

Wynne, Alexander. *The Origin of Buddhist Meditation*. New York: Routledge, 2007.

Chapter 2

The Missing God

Voices of Despair and Empathy in the Book of Lamentations

Sarah Katerina Corrigan

The *Book of Lamentations* was written specifically in response to the period of crisis or catastrophe experienced in the Babylonian occupation of Jerusalem and the Judean kingdom (597–537 BCE). In 598 BCE, Babylon enacted its first successful assault on the city of Jerusalem and placed King Zedekiah on the Judean throne—a "puppet king" over whom the Babylonians appeared to exercise full control.[1] Ten years later, Zedekiah rebelled against Babylonian authority, and thereby prompted a second invasion. This second assault on the city in 587 BCE brought about a definitive end to the biblical and beloved Jerusalem and the Davidic dynasty: the city, the cultural embodiment of God's promise to Israel, was destroyed, and more specifically, the temple, a site of God's promised presence, was also demolished.[2] The invasion of 587 BCE lasted two years, during which time Jerusalem suffered famine and overwhelming physical, mental, and spiritual devastation—the destruction of the urban promise combined with the deportation of thousands of preeminent Israelite citizens resulted in the utter loss of all the "symbols and props which held life together."[3] It has been argued that the date of the invasion assumed a "metaphorical" dimension in the biblical world; 587 BCE is suspended between the end of an old Israelite world, whose customs and traditions now had to be relinquished, and the dawning of a new era, a future that the Israelites would have never chosen for themselves—one in which all that was "treasured" by the Israelites is cruelly dismantled in the experience Babylonian exile.[4]

Lamentations thus gives voice to the unsettling task of coming to terms with an unfamiliar dystopian world in the aftermath of devastation. The very existence of the Book provides a foundation for the genre of "literature of survival"[5]—testaments to strength and perseverance, on the one hand, and witnesses of immeasurable loss on the social, individual and psychic levels, on the other. *Lamentations'* trifold effect—as "artistic jewel," "theological enigma," and "courageous act of survival"[6]—elucidates for the Biblical reader the catastrophic moment that cannot be undone,[7] the moment in which the beloved past can no longer be remembered without a sense of suffering and betrayal: the narrative identity of the Israelites as a "chosen" people of God has seemingly been destroyed along with the fall of the second kingdom. The singularity of *Lamentations* lies in its questioning not only the character of its own community in the aftermath of the fall of Jerusalem, but also the character and identity of the once-trusted Godhead. It is not only an experience of "narrative wreckage," to borrow Arthur Frank's phrase,[8] but a testament to a "wreckage of identity" on multiple levels. While the larger Biblical narrative of the Israelites' relationship to God has now been called into question in light of the perceived betrayal, humiliation and destruction of Daughter Zion at the hand of the Lord, the community's own "relationship with God" has also been cast into chaos.[9] In this article, we will examine three specific lenses in Lamentations 1 and 2 through which we may better understand the "identity wreckage" that characterizes this event and this literary text—first, the seemingly irreparable rupture between the communal and the divine; second, the destruction of the Israelite identity as God's people; and, finally, the effect of the silent Israelite God in the face of unspeakable sorrow and tragedy. The effect of God's palpable silence in this crisis enacts a rather surprising effect upon the characters of the text, insofar as they are then prompted to voice their own confused understanding of this disaster from multiple perspectives, and, through this process, they become spokespeople for the absent voice in the text.

Indeed, the Book of Lamentations itself is "God-abandoned"[10] and reflects feelings of despair and isolation that people may experience in moments of crisis or catastrophe. The "missing voice" of the divine emerges as the primary subject of the book's poetry—the speakers of *Lamentations* all agree that "God must respond to them in their suffering," and yet "God never speaks."[11] Even amidst Daughter Zion's repeated pleas that God "see" (*ra'ah*) and "pay attention" (*nabat*) to her fallen and abused state, God does not respond.[12] In "vehemence and desperation," Daughter Zion interrupts the narrator's speech and cries out to her maker: "Look (*ra'ah*) and pay attention (*nabat*), for I have become worthless!"[13] O'Connor notes that perhaps "hidden in her plea" is a claim upon God's previous affection or devotion to her, from a past time when he did see and did pay attention to her.[14] Alas, there is no "speech for God."[15] God does not defend himself, and the effect of this silence is erratic; it results sometimes in rage, at other times in tears, sometimes, though admittedly rarely, even in hope,[16] but in all cases, God's missing voice crazes the Book's speakers and elicits unpredictable responses from them as they continue to beg for and, in fact, demand answers from what appears to be a silent, implacable abyss.

What is perhaps most significant in the speakers' response to God's non-response is that they turn, instead, to other human beings for some kind of answer. Indeed, in the second half of the poem in Lamentations 1, Daughter Zion, frustrated and hurt by God's "missing" voice in her grief, addresses "passersby" instead:

Is it nothing to you who pass by on the way? Pay attention and look! Is
    there any pain like my pain, which was severely dealt upon me,
Which the Lord inflicted on the day of his fierce anger?
From on high he sent fire, into my bones it came down.
He spread a net for my feet; he turned me back.
He left me devastated, faint all day long.

Lamentations 1:12–13[17]

Daughter Zion redirects her fierce speech intended for divine ears to those "who pass by on the way," wondering if it is "nothing to [them]" at all, or if they can understand her plight.[18] She abruptly demands that these passersby, in light of God's absence, "pay attention and look," and invites them to use their own moral judgment to discern the duress and injustice of her predicament: "Is there any pain like my pain?"[19] She continues to describe to these passersby a lengthy record of the Lord's transgressions against her: "he sent fire into my bones, [. . .] spread a net for my feet [. . .], left me devastated, [. . .] made my strength fail, [. . . gave . . .] me into their hands, [. . .] made flight of all my mighty men in my midst."[20] From her perspective at this point in the passage, the Lord is guilty and deserves judgment: "As in a winepress, the Lord had trodden virgin Daughter Judah."[21] Moreover, since he will not answer for his injustices, Daughter Zion turns to innocent observers—these passersby—for some kind of verdict. She is addressing them, in fact, as though they were a jury, present as witnesses to judge her victimhood and God's transgressions against her and her people.[22]

While she thus attempts to put God on trial, Daughter Zion begins to call into question her certainty of God's own fault in this matter and her guiltlessness in the fall of Judah. Her address to those "who pass by" remains very brief, and only a few verses pass before she redirects her address to the Lord, crying out yet again with renewed and untired sorrow: "See, O Lord, how distressed I am; my stomach churns, my heart is wrung within me, because I have been very rebellious."[23] While she finds God both guilty of deliberate violence, she nevertheless concedes her own fault and describes the "rebellious" role she has played in precipitating this event:

The Lord is in the right for I have rebelled against his word.
Listen, I beg you, all peoples and see my pain.
My virgins and my young men have gone into captivity.

[. . .]

Hear how I am groaning; there is no one to comfort me.
All my enemies have heard of my wickedness; they exalt because you did it.
You brought the day you proclaimed; let them be like me.

Let all their wickedness come before you and deal severely with them
As you have dealt severely with me on account of all my transgressions
For many are my groans and my heart is faint.
Lamentations 1:18, 20, 21

Daughter Zion, therefore, both condemns and defends God; she understands him as both having acted in "fierce anger," while still remaining "in the right," and in this way her understanding of God mirrors her fractured relationship to her own self, whom she both convicts and acquits simultaneously. Whereas before she had proclaimed herself a victim of God's "fierce anger,"[24] she now nuances this with reflective doubt and finds herself guilty: she "rebelled against his word," was "wicked," and "transgressed."[25] In her lament, Daughter Zion vacillates between different recollections through which she tries to make sense of the past, but these recollections contradict each other, signifying the expansion of fractured consciousness within her own speech; indeed, her recollection extends from the reaction to catastrophe, to God's person, and now to Daughter Zion's own relationship to herself. She has lost any unified narrative of herself, and she cries out to others for clarity—"Listen, I beg you, all peoples and see my pain."[26]

The "narrator" in the *Book of Lamentations* experiences similar inner ambivalence in relation to this catastrophe, and his speech is regularly interwoven with that of Daughter Zion's in the first two chapters of the book.[27] This character does not express this multilayered ambivalence toward himself (as Daughter Zion does toward herself), but rather toward the figure of Daughter Zion. In the earliest parts of the work, the narrator describes Daughter Zion and Jerusalem in a manner that at first may appear sympathetic; in the opening two verses of the book, he portrays "the city once great with people" as a "widow" in mourning, with "tears upon her cheeks."[28] However, almost immediately within the second verse of the introductory speech, the narrator describes her in a clearer and darker tone that suggests her past infidelities: "There is no one to comfort her among all her lovers."[29] Generally, in ancient Israel, women, whether fictive or personified, were not permitted to have multiple lovers, and this addition within the text denotes the narrator's more ungenerous view of the "weep[ing] widow." Thus, only six verses further in the text, we encounter the full insult and injury that the narrator believes Jerusalem or Daughter Zion has brought upon herself, her people, and the nation of Israel:

Jerusalem has sinned grievously; therefore, she has become an unclean thing.
All who honored her make light of her, for they see her nakedness.
Indeed, she herself groans and turns away.

Her uncleanness is on her skirts; she did not remember her future.
She has fallen terribly. There is no one to comfort her.
Lord, look at my affliction for the enemy has made himself great.

The foe has spread out his hand upon all her precious things.
For she has seen nations coming into her sanctuary,
Whom you commanded, "They will not go into your assembly."

Lamentations 1:8–10

Throughout the above passage, the reader may witness the disquieting rise of the narrator's fury, which is now directed against Daughter Zion. Indeed, his speech is not what many have called a "funeral dirge"; it is more accurate to say that it emerges, instead, as a devastating judgment upon Daughter Zion herself, who "sits on the knife-edge between death and survival."[30] In the narrator's eyes, Jerusalem has "sinned grievously" and is now irreversibly "unclean"; she has publicly shamed her own nation, since all have "see[n] her nakedness,"[31] and the "foe has spread out his hand on all her precious things."[32]

After what might be considered brief sympathy, therefore, the narrator seems to have become entirely un-ambivalent in his understanding of Daughter Zion—in his eyes, she is guilty and not to be pitied, but it is at the very verse when the narrator utterly condemns Daughter Zion that she interrupts him with her piercing request (outlined above) to "look (*ra'ah*) and pay attention (*nabat*), for [she] ha[s] become worthless!"[33] Clearly skillful as an orator, she suddenly assumes the narrator's perspective into her own lament, and then goes on to redirect her line of argumentation toward her own fractured relationship with her own self and with God—she, like God, is both innocent and guilty. Indeed, immediately following her speech in the next chapter, this palpable ambivalence is transferred to the narrator's own passionate and furious character, as he turns his anger no longer toward Daughter Zion, but toward God himself, declaring that the Lord "in his anger has set Daughter Zion under a cloud!"[34] He goes on to describe the character of the Lord as an unmitigated force of merciless violence and harm:

The Lord determined to lay in ruins the wall of daughter Zion;
He stretched the line, he did not withhold his hand from destroying;
He caused rampart and wall to lament; they languished together.

Her gates have sunk into the ground; he has ruined and broken her bars;
Her king and princes are among the nations; guidance [Torah] is no more,
And her prophets obtain no vision from the Lord.
Lamentations 2: 8–9, adapted from NRSV translation

Here, the narrator boldly asserts that the Lord's actions against Daughter Zion are not only violent and reprehensible, but also *purposefully* destructive: God "determined" or "planned" to "lay in ruins the wall of daughter Zion"[35]; he did not choose mercy and did not "withhold his hand from destroying" but instead caused intentional destruction—both "rampart and wall . . . languish together."[36] Thus, the urban manifestation of covenant between the Lord and Daughter Zion has been "sunk, ruined, and broken" through deliberate divine violence. Perhaps equally significantly, the very basis of Israelite culture and religious practice is now undermined and effectively inaccessible from this point on to survivors—"Torah is no more," and Daughter Zion's prophets no longer have access to "vision[s] from the Lord."[37] In this sense, from the perspectives of the Book's speakers, God has not only effectively destroyed Daughter Zion; he has also abandoned both her and his people, so that the once more permeable membrane between human and divine has now become a closed boundary. Not only is the past glory of Israel lost, but the nation's very religious foundations have been seemingly eradicated.

In the face of this communal loss of Israel's past, the direction of the narrator's speech changes yet again; he now acts to defend Daughter Zion, completely countering the condemnation of his previous introductory speech. Not only does he sympathize with her, he actually assumes her own defense, as though it were his own; just as Daughter Zion in the previous passage describes her own state as victim at the hands of God, the narrator now echoes her sentiment: "The Lord has destroyed without mercy all the dwellings of Jacob; in his wrath he has broken down the strongholds of daughter Judah."[38] Thus, the narrator redirects the anger and fury he once channeled into the figure of Daughter Zion toward God the nonrespondent. He even goes so far as to intimate that God is the actual enemy of Israel:

The Lord has become like an enemy;
he has destroyed Israel.
He has destroyed all its palaces,
laid in ruins its strongholds,
and multiplied/increased in daughter Judah
mourning and lamentation
Lamentations 2:5

Since God has humiliated Israel so entirely in the "face of the enemy,"[39] the God who "burned" and "consumed" and "destroyed all [Israel's] palaces" is the God "without mercy," who acts only "in . . . wrath."[40] Indeed, the word "multiplied" (*rabah*) is the same word employed in God's command to human beings in Genesis 1:28—"be fruitful and multiply," only now God has not permitted Daughter Judah to multiply in number; he has actually destroyed her numbers, multiplying in her only "mourning and lamentation."[41] Thus, in this sense, the narrator, himself perhaps a dawning exegete, has not only assumed the loss that Daughter Zion so keenly feels, but he has, additionally, elucidated the precise manner in which God has betrayed his promise to his people. Once the very foundations of the covenant have been called into question, God's role in history is called into judgment, and this time it is not Daughter Zion who is met with God's silence, but the narrator himself.

According to O'Connor, "because God never speaks, the book honors voices of pain."[42] While the book honors the overwhelming loss for which no untroubled answer may be given, the poetic function of God's silence also generates agency and complexity in the characters that experience this devastation. In portraying the permeating ambivalence that these characters express toward the site of the traumatic event itself—namely, Israel or Daughter Zion, and also toward the God who permitted it to happen—, *Lamentations*, I have argued, also honors the power of human companionship that can emerge from fractured consciousness. Daughter Zion, who cries out to God in need and despair, understands at first only her own defense, and then she ultimately tries to understand it from the potential perspective of God, conceding, without any actual need to do so, that she must answer, too, for the disaster, even though she is a victim in the traumatic experience. Similarly, in the narrator's trajectory from condemnation of Daughter Zion to her ultimate defense, the narrator exemplifies the power of human empathy to extend from one person's own solipsistic understanding of loss to encompass and share in the narrative of another. In this way, God's silence brings characters to move beyond a single viewpoint or perspective—and thus meditate upon a situation from multiple points of view; in wondering aloud and uttering each individual's different and numerous perspectives concerning the traumatic event, the characters externalize the dialogue with the divine that they hoped they would be granted.

In this way *Lamentations* expresses the anguish of a community who has no intermediary—not only is God silent, but there is also no prophet available to theologize and make sense from catastrophe, as in other biblical books written during the exilic period.[43] In more modern crises of unspeakable magnitude that befall an entire people—after the Lisbon Earthquake, the Holocaust, 9/11, artists and scholars pose similar questions about the problem of evil and God's role in human suffering.[44] Each of these dates assumes the kind of metaphorical quality that Brueggemann originally attributes to

587 BCE, separating an unreachable past from a terror-striking present and future.[45] The process of theodicy then is often prompted by the experience of communal catastrophe, but *Lamentations* allows us to see that questions of theodicy—where exactly God stands in the face of unspeakable loss—are not modern reactions to devastation, but perennial biblical and existential inquiries into the nature of evil and its relation to the human being. Indeed, the reaction of a community to despair and crisis and the absence of God emerges as a timeless phenomenon, and the ranges of response to such communal catastrophe are vast: on the one hand, God's silence in the moment of crisis magnifies the despair and futility of the victim who calls out in vain for an answer, and, on the other hand, God's missing voice emerges as a kind of challenge to the individual and community, an attempt, to quote Abraham Joshua Heschel, "to raise man to a higher level of existence."[46] In a Book that represents various individual perspectives in a moment of communal calamity, *Lamentations* reveals that any potential for "higher level of existence," if such a designation may even apply in the aftermath of 587 BCE, is not limited to the individual's experience alone, but extends to the relationships within a community overwhelmed by grief.

The verbal form of the Hebrew noun for crisis (*misber* משבר) means "to fracture" (*seber* שבר), and this more active sense of the word distinctly characterizes the aftermath of crisis: it is a living fracture, a break, and, thus, an ambivalence. This ambivalence is expressed in the *Book of Lamentations*, in which the members of a destroyed community are forced to look to each other for the comfort they had hoped to hear from God. The people themselves, in this sense, become a surrogate for God, and this new moment of shared crisis is both the beginning of empathy and a re-formation of fractured consciousness. The biblical motif of the city personified as woman comes to its peak, perhaps, in this text, since the many warnings and prophecies about the kingdom's disloyalty and infidelity have been fulfilled, and yet there is no visible or satisfied deity in the catastrophe's aftermath.[47] Lamentation emerges as a language of wound and fracture, but this critical encounter with God's absence has the potential to activate human agency, even in an embryonic form, and provides a space for empathy—on the part of the narrator, who assumes Daughter Zion's perspective, and on the part of Daughter Zion herself, who attempts to discern the limits of God's justice, and, perhaps, even on the parts of millennia of this text's readers. The language of lament thus signifies the pain of unwilling transformation through destruction, the emergence of the new, however undesired and alien, and the birth of empathy toward and among the survivors now living fractured lives—between old and new worlds, the past and the present, and the many characters crying out to hear the divine voice from whom no response is directly given—unless, of course, one considers human lament to be part of divine speech.

NOTES

1. Kathleen O'Connor, *Lamentations and the Tears of the World* (Maryknoll, NY: Orbis Books, 2002), 6.
2. Walter Brueggemann, *Hopeful Imagination: Prophetic Voices in Exile* (Philadelphia: Fortress, 1986), 3.
3. Ibid., 1.
4. Ibid., 7.
5. Tod Linafelt, *Surviving Lamentations* (Chicago and London: The University of Chicago Press, 2000), 18–20.
6. O'Connor, *Lamentations and the Tears of the World*, 7.
7. O'Connor argues in *Lamentations and the Tears of the World*, 13, that the text's acrostic and alphabetic structures are interwoven with the question of chaos in *Lamentations*; they may be understood as an attempt to "give order and shape to suffering that is inherently chaotic, formless, and out of control."
8. Arthur W. Frank, *The Wounded Storyteller: Body, Illness, and Ethics* (Chicago: University of Chicago Press, 2013), 62.
9. O'Connor, *Lamentations and the Tears of the World*, 7.
10. Ibid., 15.
11. Ibid.
12. Ibid., 24.
13. Ibid.; *The HarperCollins Study Bible: Fully Revised and Updated*, ed. Harold W. Attridge (New York: HarperCollins, 2006), Lamentations 1:11c.
14. Ibid.
15. Ibid., 15; *The HarperCollins Study Bible*, Lamentations 1:11.
16. Ibid.; The "strongman" in Lamentations 3, 57.
17. The translation of the primary text will is an amalgam of my own translations and *The HarperCollins Study Bible*.
18. *The HarperCollins Study Bible*, Lamentations 1:12.
19. Ibid.
20. Ibid., 1:13–15.
21. Ibid., 1:15.
22. For more on "judges and courts of law" in ancient Israel, see Roland De Vaux, *Ancient Israel: Its Life and Instructions* (Grand Rapids and Livonia, MI: Eerdmans and Doves, 1997), 152–53.
23. *The HarperCollins Study Bible*, Lamentations 1:20.
24. Ibid., 1:12.
25. Ibid., 1:18–21.
26. Ibid., 1:18.
27. O'Connor terms this character the "narrator" in her work *Lamentations and the Tears of the World*, 18.
28. *The HarperCollins Study Bible*, Lamentations 1:1–2.
29. Ibid., 1:2.
30. O'Connor, *Lamentations and the Tears of the World*, 19–20.
31. *The HarperCollins Study Bible*, Lamentations 1:8.

32. Ibid., 1:10.
33. O'Connor, *Lamentations and the Tears of the World*, 24; Lamentations 1:11.
34. *The HarperCollins Study Bible*, Lamentations 2:1.
35. Ibid., 2:8.
36. Ibid.
37. Ibid., 2:9.
38. Ibid., 2:2.
39. Ibid., 2:3.
40. Ibid., 2:2.
41. Ibid., 2:5.
42. O'Connor, *Lamentations and the Tears of the World*, 15.
43. Although *Lamentations* has often been attributed to Jeremiah, there is still much uncertainty about the Book's authorship (O'Connor, 7).
44. For more on theodicy after the Lisbon earthquake, see Edgar S. Brightman, "The Lisbon Earthquake: A Study in Religious Valuation," *The American Journal of Theology* 23, no. 4 (1919): 500–18; for responses to Holocaust, see Aaron Zeitlin, *Poems of the Holocaust and Poems of Faith* (Lincoln, NE: iUniverse Inc., 2007); additionally, see Edward Rothstein, "Defining Evil in the Wake of 9/11," *New York Times*, October 5, 2002, for a journalistic inquiry into the modern meaning of theodicy post-9/11.
45. Brueggemann, *Hopeful Imagination*, 7.
46. Abraham Joshua Heschel, *God in Search of Man: A Philosophy of Judaism* (New York: Farrar, Straus, and Giroux, 1955), 376.
47. For more on the "feminization of cities" in Biblical theology, see Renita J. Weems, *Battered Love: Marriage, Sex, and Violence in the Hebrew Prophets* (Minneapolis: Fortress, 1995), 44–45.

BIBLIOGRAPHY

Albright, William F. "A Brief History of Judah from the Days of Josiah to Alexander the Great." *The Biblical Archaeologist* 9, no. 1 (1946): 1–16.

Brightman, Edgar S. "The Lisbon Earthquake: A Study in Religious Valuation." *The American Journal of Theology* 23, no. 4 (1919): 500–18.

Brueggemann, Walter. *Hopeful Imagination: Prophetic Voices in Exile*. Philadelphia: Fortress, 1986.

De Vaux, Roland. *Ancient Israel: Its Life and Institutions*. Grand Rapids and Livonia, MI: Eerdmans and Doves, 1997.

Frank, Arthur W. *The Wounded Storyteller: Body, Illness, and Ethics*. Chicago: University of Chicago, 2013.

Held, Shai. *Abraham Joshua Heschel: The Call of Transcendence*. Bloomington, IN: Indiana University Press, 2013.

Heschel, Abraham Joshua. *God in Search of Man: A Philosophy of Judaism*. New York: Farrar, Straus, and Giroux, 1955.

Linafelt, Tod. *Surviving Lamentations: Catastrophe, Lament, and Protest in the Afterlife of a Biblical Book.* Chicago and London: The University of Chicago Press, 2000.

O'Connor, Kathleen M. *Lamentations and the Tears of the World.* Maryknoll, NY: Orbis Books, 2002.

Meeks, Wayne A. Jouette M. Bassler, Werner E. Lemke, Susan Niditch, and Eilieen M. Schuller. *The HarperCollins Study Bible Fully Revised and Updated.* Edited by Harold W. Attridge. New York: HarperCollins, 2006.

Weems, Renita J. *Battered Love: Marriage, Sex, and Violence in the Hebrew Prophets.* Minneapolis: Fortress, 1995.

Westernmann, Claus. *Lamentations: Issues and Interpretation.* Minneapolis: Fortress, 1994.

Zeitlin, Aaron. *Poems of the Holocaust and Poems of Faith.* Lincoln, NE: iUniverse Inc., 2007.

Chapter 3

Patterns of Post-Catastrophic Thought in Ancient China

The Growth of Philosophy After the Warring States Period

Kwon Jong Yoo

INTRODUCTION

This chapter will focus on the Warring States subsequent to the Spring and Autumn Periods. A flowering of Chinese philosophies began to blossom during this period, among them Confucianism, Taoism, Mohism, and Legalism.

The Warring States Period was a time of widespread violence and disorder. The fall of numerous states involved major political and economic shifts, as well as the collapse of a traditional community spirit maintained for centuries by the clan code system. The breakup of the old system, with the resulting confusion and great loss of life, led to a period of deep and wide-ranging upheaval, which entailed large-scale wars and massacres. The number of states that existed in the early Spring and Autumn Period during the Zhou Dynasty was 170,[1] but according to Hsu, sixty-five states had disappeared after 662 BC.[2] In the end, the Warring States Period left only seven powerful states and several weaker ones.

The number of wars fought among the seven powerful states during the Warring States Period was, according to Hsu, over 460.[3] The frequency of wars in this period was numerically lower than in the Spring and Autumn Periods, but their scale was enlarged.[4] Additionally, there were downward drifts of ruling power from sovereign to senior officers, and from senior officers to vassals. State authority was compromised by the private ownership of political power. The poor all over China suffered and died from starvation. Corpses littered the streets, and grains rotted in the warehouses of the royal palace.[5]

This period saw the simultaneous disintegration of numerous components of the ancient social systems established since the founding of the Zhou Dynasty in the eleventh century BC. Fundamental social and political structures such as leadership, ruling codes, modes of production, social hierarchy, diplomacy and education all underwent radical changes because of endless interstate warfare. The society was trapped in a vicious circle.

Some degree of disorder was inevitable due to the replacement of the previous civilization. The Spring and Autumn Periods were accompanied by the transition from the Bronze to the Iron Age. Regional and chronological differences in the appropriation of the new iron technologies brought about power imbalances among sovereign states. This transition overlapped with the gradual debilitation of the Zhou Dynasty's imperial authority, occurring since the beginning of the Spring and Autumn Periods. Struggles for a new Emperor and for regional supremacy among sovereign states were fierce.

The traditional clan code and feudal system were losing their grip and the Zhou Dynasty's hierarchical structure collapsed as changes in state formations occurred as well. In the Zhou Dynasty and the Spring and Autumn Periods, most sovereign states had constructed walled towns. In the Warring States Period, however, they changed to the system of counties and prefectures—a new form of a more autocratic centralized government. With these new state formations, rulers tightened their grip not only on state officials but also on the common people, thus increasing their own tax revenues and shoring up economic and military power. The rulers competed with each other through these means of governance and control. In addition, through the use of iron tools, animal labor, land reclamation, and the dissemination and extension of paddy field agriculture, many states successfully increased agricultural productivity.[6]

The common people fell prey to these competing powers. This new autocratic leadership repressed the people through close surveillance, and forced them to serve the state in a number of exploitative capacities. To strengthen their military power, many states also introduced a mandatory conscription system. The common people were thus mobilized not only to perform forced labor, but also to fight numerous wars, great and small. Many were forced to sacrifice their lives in state conflicts that were actually closer to "massacres" than to wars.[7]

Those with good sense living during this time surely experienced the situation as apocalyptic. Witnessing the people increasingly brutalized in their everyday lives and killed in seemingly endless wars, thoughtful individuals could not help but become alarmed. It was during this time that intellectuals from diverse backgrounds began to establish their own philosophical traditions, with the aim of discovering possible solutions to this scene of apocalyptic chaos. These philosophies provided new paradigms of understanding that helped encourage order and stability in Chinese society. The process of political disintegration and reintegration took almost 550 years—from the beginning of the Spring and Autumn Period (770 BC~403 BC) to the end of the Warring States Period (403 BC~221 BC)— allowing sufficient time for such philosophies to mature and find adherents among thoughtful people looking to make sense out of a disintegrating social order.

We will first consider two influential schools of that time, Legalism and Mohism. Legalism provided the Qin sovereign with a framework of impartial, strict law enforcement, through which Qin was able to seize sovereign authority, conquer the other states and establish a unified empire with considerable accumulated wealth and military power.[8] Philosophers of the school did not believe in improving society inwardly through faith in human nature, and they denied the value of intrinsic morality and virtue as the basis for overcoming social chaos.[9] They trusted only in the objective, external management of law. This system emphasized reward and punishment as means of social control. The Qin state adopted these practical ideas and rapidly became prosperous and powerful, soon succeeding in the subjugation of all other states.

Mohism offered another solution. The father of Mohism, Mozi, studied Confucianism but later opposed it—he believed the Confucian proprieties were too complicated, funeral ceremonies were too magnificent, the mourning period (three years) too long, and that these ultimately damaged human lives and property.[10] His solution involved a more active, direct approach to practical problems. He was said to visit many states, trying to prevent wars between sovereigns. His philosophy counted more than ten principles, such as general love without discrimination, denial of destiny, opposition to aggression, veneration of wise men, standardization of righteousness and its advantages, obedience to Heaven's will and respect of God's reason, frugality in daily life and especially in funerals, denial of enjoyment of music, and so on.[11] Mohist practice selectively applied these principles to fit the specific needs of the state or society. Mozi said,

> "If a state is suffering from poverty, let it know frugality in daily use, especially in funerals. If a state is inclined to luxury with enjoyment of music and indulgence in drinking, let it know denial of enjoyment of music and denial of destiny. If a state tends to be lustful and biased to easily ignore civility, let it know obedience to the Heaven's will and respect of god's reason. If a state disdains, insults, deprecates, and violates other states, then let it know general love without discrimination and opposition to aggression."[12]

Mozi and his followers ran counter to Legalism: they held a humanistic yet practical view that encouraged a strong will and strenuous efforts to work for social salvation.

Legalism and Mohism aimed at instant relief, in contrast to Confucianism or Taoism. Nevertheless, Legalism and Mohism ceased to exist in the history of Chinese philosophy after the fall of the Qin Empire. Instead, Confucianism and Taoism, philosophies that had been relatively impractical without aiming at instant relief, would now gain ascendance.

WHY CONFUCIANISM AND TAOISM AROSE

Even though Legalism had been effective in ceasing the chaos of the time and building up a strong, rich country, its coercive reign could not be long maintained. As the Daze Village Uprising revealed, the punitive reign resulted in revolts from the lowest class.[13] This repressiveness is the reason why the Qin Empire died young. Hence Chinese society during the Warring States had not really escaped from the vicious circle of disorder and destruction. Legalism did not end the circle but merely represented its last stage.

The deepest insights into the roots of discord came from Confucianism and Taoism. For these schools, the problem in Chinese society lay not in the absence of political power but rather in the absence of a morally proper attitude, which alone could produce true authority or leadership. Unfortunately, like so many throughout history, many sovereigns of this time were dazzled by worldly desires, political power and riches. They found it difficult to accept the emphasis on inner truth articulated by Confucianism and Taoism.

The new Han Dynasty had to be careful selecting its ruling ideology, and there were serious reflections on the failure of Qin by the Han Kings. When Dong Zhong Shu (董仲舒) recommended Confucianism and the 7th King Wudi (武帝) of the Han Dynasty accepted it, Dong said the King would uphold the people's morality by his own edifying example and have them restrain desires and passions through institutions.[14] They knew that stabilizing the political situation and establishing a long-lasting dynasty would be impossible with a merely coercive approach to ruling. Why was Taoism not chosen? Taoism also developed a solution to the problem of social disorder, yet it held a small country with a small number of people as the ideal, an ideal also dependent on a Sage as Leader, one having neither selfish desires nor egocentric tendencies. This philosophy required a leader to abandon many worldly things necessary to lead his people, and thus was considered radical and unrealistic by many.[15]

DEVELOPMENT OF CONFUCIANISM

Even though the two philosophies shared fundamental commonalities regarding the emphasis on moral leadership, they were based on remarkable differences, which came from each founder's attitude about human nature and the cosmos as a whole.

Confucius visited Laozi, who used to be Chief Librarian in the Royal Library of Zhou Kingdom, to learn about its institutions and rites.[16] Confucius held a conservative attitude toward honoring the cultural heritage established since the early Zhou Dynasty. His conservatism was firmly based on "the proprieties"—a long-established, traditional set of rites or rituals. His innovation was to connect morality with these proprieties. This constituted his solution to the disintegration of Chinese society. His political solution focused on the cultivation of a morally exemplary ruler who would look after his people as his children. Accordingly, Confucianism compared the relationship between ruler and his people to the father-son relationship. This is why Confucianism emphasized the importance of filial piety, which worked to connect morality with the proprieties.[17] Reinforcing traditional values in terms of filial piety, ritual, and so on, helped reinforce and solidify the social order by emphasizing stability, family and a connection with the past.

The social progress taught by Confucius was based not on a ruler's coercion but on a mutual attunement between the ruler and the people, especially the ruler's virtuous practice. He said,

> "Lead the people with governmental measures and regulate them with law and punishment and they will avoid wrong-doing but will have no sense of honor and shame. Lead them with virtue and regulate them with the rules of propriety (li), and they will have a sense of shame and moreover, set themselves right."[18]

What this idea aimed at was ultimately a social revolution, conducted by cultivating virtue in each person's mind. Confucius' solution thus encouraged social change based on change of individual consciousness.

The Confucian School, established in the Spring and Autumn Periods, continued during the Warring States Period. Confucian scholars shared a strong belief in humanism. All problems are caused by human beings, and the solutions can be accomplished by correcting human beings. In this sense, Confucianism developed with the goal of elevating human dignity in the midst of a disordered society.

Since its adoption by the Han Dynasty as its ruling ideology, Confucianism was the dominant philosophy of China until modern times. Unfortunately, due to the human propensity for greed and the lust for power, many rulers in later times became removed from the original intent of Confucianism.

In these cases, the Confucian paradigm functioned merely as a deceptively pleasant philosophy that masked the ruler's corruption. Yet we must remember that any system based on ideals may sometimes be betrayed, as leaders lamentably cannot always live up to the moral code expected of them.

DEVELOPMENT OF TAOISM

While Confucius was concerned with the proper place of ritual, Taoism was originally linked to officers in charge of historical record. These officers, in recording history with its many falls, fortunes and misfortunes, successes and failures, developed a more holistic "big-picture" view of the reality of human affairs.[19] Their more expansive perspective on the situation led to a conclusion that the existing chaos was an inevitable consequence of provincialism and prejudice. This perspective led them to rise above the ways of society and develop a more radical solution.

Laozi founded Taoism and Zhuangzi developed it, even though there may have been a considerable chronological gap between the two. Zhuangzi was a lower-class officer, but maintained a wide-reaching view on the world and human affairs. Zhuangzi chose Laozi's Taoism by self-study, and developed Taoism with no special line linked to Laozi. Taoists at that time did not formally constitute a school, nor did they develop collective works, as did Confucians; rather they concealed themselves from the world but acted with self-prudence.

What are the values of Taoism? For them the meaning of life is not limited to an individual but involves the life of the entire universe.[20] Their common concern was in keeping life sound; however, their disordered times were seen as running counter to the sound life. Their philosophy was therefore directed toward recovery of the wholeness of the cosmos. Life could be lived more perfectly by stripping away the veneer of civilization, which they considered unnatural. They regarded all the goods of civilization as evil and recommended people remain aloof from them. A return to nature, or a recovery of our original, natural way of life assures the highest quality of human existence.

Laozi may be the philosopher who first emphasized the concept of nature as the core idea of philosophy. The concept in Taoism means not only "Mother Nature" but also a situation free from any outside interference. "Nature" sets aside all artificial things, even ethics, morality, virtue, ritual— indeed all forms of knowledge emphasized by Confucianism. The Taoist starts with recognition of the Tao and ends with the realization of the Tao. The Tao literally means "The Way," the manner of nature. Every person or thing exists according to the way of Nature by autonomously leading its own life or existence. Yet most people cannot understand or practice the Tao because they prefer civilized living, through which they become blind to the way of Nature.[21] Laozi advocated leaving civilization and returning to Nature; however, it is not easy to leave civilization once one has become used to it. Therefore, Taoists advocated the embodiment of the Tao through the deconstruction of the civilized way of life.

What is the essence of the Tao? How to recognize the Tao? How to practice the Tao? Laozi did not give any clear definition. He suggested that giving a definition might be impossible through human language.[22] The Tao is neither an object to be known nor to be defined linguistically. He stressed not learning but doing, living in accordance with the Tao. To learn means to accumulate knowledge daily and adapt oneself to civilization. That was the Confucian way of self-cultivation. But to live the Tao means to throw away what one has accumulated in his/her civilized life and to thus embody Nature.[23]

This understanding of Tao and virtue is different from that found in Confucianism. For Confucian thinkers, the person who embodied the Tao and the virtues has achieved the noblest character by the practice of ethics and the proprieties in the human world. But Taoist concepts are realized only by embodiment of the Tao, which exists beyond human civilization.

Concerning how to embody the Tao, Laozi insisted one had to be as pure as a newborn baby uncontaminated by human civilization. Laozi's approach to the Tao was "negative" in that it placed emphasis on noninterference in other's activity. Laozi recognized the limitations of linguistic expression. Propositional knowledge organized through linguistic definition couldn't constitute the truth about the Tao.

Zhuangzi shared this viewpoint and developed a Taoist conception of knowledge with definite criteria. He divided knowledge into two kinds; knowledge attained by those with a limited view, and true knowledge attained only by the person who has secured a perfect understanding of the Tao with a purified mind.[24] He compared a person who had the narrow view of reality to a big frog in a small pond, and emphasized escape from this narrow view through unity with the Tao.[25] He also emphasized the role of the mind in the realization of the Tao. The Tao is the origin of all things in the world, and virtue is the origin of human being. But virtue is contaminated by the physical body and imprisoned by desires in the world.[26] In order to recover virtue, he offered a method to make the mind as bright and clear as a stainless mirror or a still lake.[27] His method involves three different activities: The first is to wash all passions from the mind. The second is to concentrate the distributed activities of the mind. The third is to forget the self, the society, nature, and so on, and this starts by forgetting rituals and even moral virtues.[28] Zhuangzi actually regarded benevolence and righteousness as contaminating the mind through civilization's negative influences. The pure mind does not wear any cloth of moral virtue. Therefore, asceticism is encouraged to remove these impurities and reveal the original simple mind. These three steps result in brightness of the mind that can light all the things as the sun does.[29] Similarly Laozi described such brightness as a miraculous mirror.[30]

Taoist doctrine was applied by the rulers of the early Han dynasty—from the time of the 1st King until the 7th King approved Confucianism as the official ruling ideology. Taoism provided these rulers with a number of helpful skills and guiding principles. The doctrine of inactivity thus promoted the minimizing of state activity and interference, and helped provide a break for the people from both long-term warfare and the severe oppression of the Legalism prevalent during the Qin Dynasty. But while Taoism was effectively applied to some realistic political concerns, it proved difficult to completely purify society and human nature according to Taoism's somewhat passive and otherworldly ideals.

FEATURES OF CHINESE THINKING

The philosophical history of China is not simple, but Confucianism and Taoism are the basic places to begin the discussion. Confucianism and Taoism both recognized that the war-torn Chinese society of their time was disordered and divided, and both sought an authentic solution. While the Legalists and Mohists carried out their solutions for instant effects, Confucians and Taoists explored deeper underlying themes, hitherto neglected. These themes were the nature of the world and the human mind. Each of their solutions has been divided into different, competing schools of thought. Nevertheless, both philosophies offered a unique approach to solving human problems. They looked directly into human nature itself. This is different from other approaches that ruled through external or objective factors, for example, the law, designed for management and control. These two philosophies focused not on the establishment of complicated theoretical structures as we find in, for example, Western metaphysics, but rather upon forming a sound, balanced character in every individual. They placed more value on cultivation of a self or character. Therefore, their highest attention fixed neither on the establishment of objective knowledge as an absolute reality, nor on logic and rationality as the primary means to produce such knowledge, but rather how to achieve ideal character by the internal embodiment of virtue. Only in this way can a society truly progress from a condition of moral disorder to a state of prosperity and health.

FINAL QUESTIONS: CHINESE PHILOSOPHIES AND CONTEMPORARY GLOBAL CATASTROPHES

The philosophies of Confucianism and Taoism grew out of catastrophe, but how they could possibly help us solve some of the crises of our contemporary world? We now face catastrophes on a global scale such as environmental degradation and the threat of nuclear conflict. Although the Tao, the path to truth, still exists, can we still see it in our busy, technology-saturated postmodern world? Can we access it? Or have we become blinded by the bright lights of short term pleasures, distracted by the accumulation of material things and the quest for social status, power and influence?

These ancient Chinese philosophies focus on the control of desires to reach levels of moderation (Confucianism) or reverting the mind to its original, purified state (Taoism). It is certainly difficult to follow the teachings of these traditional philosophies, to control our desires or to recover the mind's original purity, especially while living in complex Capitalist societies where people compete furiously to acquire ever more wealth and power. However, this tension has always and everywhere existed. It has always been hard to live up to philosophy's ideals, given the fact that we live in the material world. It is ultimately one's own personal decision that leads him/her to search for a wise and meaningful life. And it is up to us, individually and collectively, to decide if we want to maintain the global ecological system by following the wise teachings of the ancients or if, instead, we let ourselves succumb to endless worries about gratifying personal desires, even if we end up destroying the harmony of the entire global system in the process.

NOTES

1. Institute for Studies of Asian History, "Gangjwa Joongguksa I: Godae-munmyeong-gwa Jegukui Seonglip" (Chinese History I: Ancient Civilization and Establishment of Empire), Lecture, ed. Seoul National University (Paju, SK: Jisiksaneopsa, 2011).

2. Cho-yun Hsu, *Ancient China in Transition: An Analysis of Social Mobilities, 722~222 BC* (Palo Alto, CA: Stanford University Press, 1965), 58. Quoted from Institute for Studies of Asian History, "Gangjwa Joongguksa I," 105–06.

3. Ibid., 63–64. Quoted from Youn Daeshik, "Adjustment of War and Moral in Zhanguo ce" [Intrigues], *Korean Political Science Review* 48, no. 1 (2014): 94.

4. Ibid., 58. Quoted from Institute for Studies of Asian History, "Gangjwa Joongguksa I," 106.

5. Gangsoo Lee, *Jungguk Godae Cheolhakui Ihae* [Understanding of Chinese Ancient Philosophy] (Paju, SK: Jisiksaneopsa, 1999), 15.

6. Shin Sunggon and Yun Hyeyoung, *Han-guk-in-eul Wi-han Jung-guk*-sa [Chinese History for Korean Readers] (Paju: Seohaemunjip, 2011), 48–51.

7. Ibid., 51–57.

8. Gangsoo Lee, *Jungguk Godae*, 258.

9. A. C. Graham, *Disputers of the Tao: Philosophical Argument in Ancient China* (La Salle, IL: Open Court, 1989), 278.

10. Lee Gangsoo, *Jungguk Godae*, 155.

11. Ibid., 155–57.

12. Ibid.

13. Shin Sunggon and Yun Hyeyoung, *Han-guk-in-eul Wi-han Jung-guk-sa*, 75–79.

14. Refer to Ban Gu, "Dong-Zhong-Shu-Chuan" [Biography of Dong-Zhong-Shu], in *History of Han Dynasty, vol. 56 no. 26 Hanshu* (Seoul: Gyeong-in-mun-hwa-sa, 1975).

15. Huanglaozhixue had been in prevalent state before Wudi adopted Confucianism as the ruling ideology.

16. It should be kept in mind, however, that there is considerable debate as to the authenticity of the claim that Confucius met Laozi, and indeed as to whether or not many legendary figures in ancient religious and philosophical writings even ever really existed. Therefore how much of this account is apocryphal is a legitimate question. Thanks to an anonymous referee for this point.

17. James Legge, trans., "Chapter 17" in *The Chinese Classics, Vol. 1: Confucian Analects* (Taipei, ROC: Wenshizhechubanshi, 1972).

18. Wing-Tsit Chan, trans., *A Source Book in Chinese Philosophy* (Princeton, NJ: Princeton University Press, 1963), 22.

19. Lee Gangsoo, *Jungguk Godae*, 127.

20. Lee Gangsoo, *Noja-wa-Jangja: Muwi-wa-Soyo-ui-Cheolhak* [Laozi and Zhuangzi: Philosophy of Non Doing and Rambling] (Seoul: Gil, 1997), 22–33.

21. Lee Gangsoo, *Noja-wa-Jangja*, 47–55 and *Jungguk Godae*, 139–40.

22. James Legge, trans., "Chapter 25" in *The Text of Taoism: The Toa Te Ching—The Writings of Chuang-Tzu—The Thai-Shang*, 1st ed. (New York: The Julian Press, 1959).

23. Lee Gangsoo, *Nojawajangja*, 47–55.

24. Lee Gangsoo, *Jungguk Godae*, 140–42.

25. Ibid., 136–37.

26. Ibid., 136–40.

27. James Legge, trans., "The Writings of Chuang Tzu, Chapter 5, Teh Kung Fu or the Seal of Virtue Complete," in *The Text of Taoism: The Tao Te Ching—The Writings of Chuang-Tzu—The Thai-Shang*, 1st ed. (New York: The Julian Press, 1959).

28. Lee Gangsoo, *Jungguk Godae*, 140–42.

29. Ibid.

30. Ibid.

BIBLIOGRAPHY

Chan, Wing-Tsit. *A Source Book in Chinese Philosophy*. (Princeton, NJ: Princeton University Press, 1963).

Daeshik, Youn. "Adjustment of War and Moral in Zhanguo ce" [Intrigues]. *Korean Political Science Review* 48, no. 1 (2014).

Hsu, Cho-Yun. *Ancient China in Transition: An Analysis of Social Mobilities, 722~222 B.C.* Palo Alto, CA: Stanford University Press, 1965.

Graham, A.C. *Disputers of the Tao: Philosophical Argument in Ancient China.* La Salle, IL: Open Court, 1989.

Gu, Ban. "Dong-Zhong-Shu-Chuan" [Biography of Dong-Zhong-Shu]. In *History of Han Dynasty.* 100 vols. Seoul: Gyeong-in-mun-hwa-sa, 1975.

Institute for Studies of Asian History. "Gangjwa Joongguksa I: Godae-munmyeong-gwa Jegukui Seonglip" [Chinese History I: Ancient Civilization and Establishment of Empire]. Lecture. Edited by Seoul National University. Paju, SK: Jisiksaneopsa, 2011.

Lee, Gangsoo. *Jungguk Godae Cheolhakui Ihae* [Understanding of Chinese Ancient Philosophy]. Paju, SK: Jisiksaneopsa, 1999.

Lee, Gangsoo. *Noja-wa-Jangja:Muwi-wa-Soyo-ui-Cheolhak* [Laozi and Zhuangzi: Philosophy of Non Doing and Rambling]. Seoul: Gil, 1997.

Legge, James, translator. *The Chinese Classics.* 2 vols. Taipei, ROC: Wenshizhechubanshi, 1972.

Legge, James, translator. "The Writings of Chuang Tzu, Chapter 5, Teh Kung Fu or the Seal of Virtue Complete." In *The Text of Taoism The Toa Te Ching – The Writings of Chuang-Tzu – The Thai-Shang.* First Edition. New York: The Julian Press, 1959.

Sunggon, S., and Y. Hyeyoung. *Chinese History for Korean Readers.* Paju, SK: Seohaemunjip, 2011.

Chapter 4

Athens in Ruins

Plato and the Aftermath of the Peloponnesian War

John Ross

This chapter will discuss how the catastrophe of Athens during the Peloponnesian War was in large part the tragedy of betrayed ideals. Key works by thinkers like Thucydides and Plato illustrate how the aftermath of the war revealed both an emergent moral anomie within Athenian society as well as a new ethos of brutality, transforming the very soul of the great city of Athens earlier extolled by Pericles. Catastrophes cause people to act blindly and out of raw emotion in the face of darkness and desperation, challenging and even betraying the ideals and values they otherwise hold. While catastrophes may often bring out the finest aspects of human nature, as people sometimes turn toward each other in desperate times, at the same time they can often reveal the ephemeral nature of our loftiest values.

In 404 BCE Athens and its once magnificent Empire lay in ruins. The long walls that fortified the city were torn down, and the Athenian democracy was replaced by a Spartan oligarchy known as The Thirty Tyrants. The Thirty ruthlessly purged the city of its leading democrats, killing them and confiscating their property. Athens' defeat in the Peloponnesian War was a huge tragedy for a city that had ruled the Aegean for fifty years. The loss of life, property, power, and prestige was staggering. Certainly the "Golden Age of Athens" came to an end, but worse was the erosion of the soul of Athens during the war. At the start of the war with Sparta, Athens' leading citizen Pericles (d. 429), as the architect of the city's democratic imperialism, pictured his state as founded on moral excellence and therefore a model for the rest of the world.[1] However, during the long progress of the war the Athenian Assembly was guilty not only of atrocities but also military blunders that ultimately led to Athens' defeat. For Plato the last straw was the judicial murder of his mentor Socrates in the aftermath of the war. Plato tried to devise a political constitution that would correct the faults of the democracy and produce a moral citizenry.

In his famous *Funeral Oration* delivered at the end of the war's first year, recreated by Thucydides in his *History of the Peloponnesian War*, Pericles described the Athenian Empire and it's democracy in the most glowing terms, painting it as the Promised Land of Greece. "Our Constitution is called a democracy because power is in the hands not of a minority but of the whole people. . . . everyone is equal before the law . . . what counts is not membership of a particular class, but the actual ability which the man possesses."[2]

Unlike their regimented militaristic enemy, they were a free people; Athens was open to the world. In addition to every imaginable luxury, Athenians enjoyed the best of the arts and culture.

> And here is another point. When our work is over, we are in a position to enjoy all kinds of recreation for our spirits. There are various kinds of contests and sacrifices throughout the year; in our own homes we find beauty and good taste . . . the greatness of our city brings it about that all the good things from all over the world flow into us.[3]

Athenians valued intelligence and wisdom, which was the source of their courage and success. "Others are brave out of ignorance; and, when they stop to think, they begin to fear. But the man who can most truly be accounted brave is he who best knows the meaning of what is sweet in life and what is terrible, and then goes out undeterred to meet what is to come."[4]

According to Pericles, Athenians were justly proud of their glory, but they would never shame a fellow citizen who had fallen on hard times. Athenians would lend a helping hand and support one another. "We make friends by doing good to others, not by receiving good from them. . . . When we do kindnesses to others, we do not do them out of any calculations of profit or loss: we do them without afterthought, relying on our free liberality. Taking everything together then, I declare that our city is an education to Greece."[5]

Citizens of Athens were generous, kind and benevolent—magnanimous in victory and accepting in (very rare) defeat.

Thucydides insinuates that had Pericles survived he had the talent and energy to turn his picture of Athens into a reality.[6] Unfortunately, Pericles died in the plague that ravaged Athens during the war's first year, leaving less talented, more hawkish factions in control of the city. Pericles had envisioned a defensive war of attrition that avoided attempts at expanding the Empire and a suicidal direct confrontation with Sparta on land. In this way the more bellicose among the Athenians could be satisfied, without sustaining too many casualties. After a short time, both sides would grow weary and welcome a return to the status quo.[7]

But with the death of Pericles his strategy for the war unraveled, as did his portrait of the benevolent, wise Athenian. Thucydides starkly reveals the horrors of war that manifest themselves as the conflict grinds on. The hand-to-hand combat characteristic of Greek warfare in this period was bad enough, but the worst sort of violence occurred between factions in contested cities. No other bond—family, friendship, common decency, or religion—supplanted factional loyalty. The Athenian Assembly dealt ruthlessly with cities that tried to revolt during the war. One such city, Mytilene, saw their revolution crushed by Athens, and Thucydides records the debate in the Assembly as to the appropriate punishment. In response to the bellicose oratory of Cleon, the new leader of the hawkish faction, the Assembly votes to kill all the male inhabitants of Mytilene and sell the women and children as slaves. The only objection Thucydides records is that extermination and slavery might be too severe to be effective, as future revolutionaries might conclude they have nothing to lose—thus the punishment lacked the appropriate deterrent effect. Pericles claimed Athenian characteristics of kindness, benevolence, and mercy, were all notably absent at the debate.[8]

Fortunately for Mytilene the next day the Assembly agrees that killing only the ringleaders of the revolt would be a more effective deterrent, so the rest of the populace is spared. Another city—Melos—was not so lucky. Melos tried to remain neutral in the war but Athens threatened to destroy them if they would not voluntarily join the Empire. The Melians refused and Athens made good on its threat—the men were exterminated and everyone else was sold into slavery. Melos cannot be excused as "collateral damage," and difficult to characterize as anything other than genocide.[9]

History would reveal that the decisive battle in the war with Sparta had occurred well before 404—in 413 outside the city of Syracuse in Sicily. In his *History* Thucydides explains that while a peace treaty with Sparta was in effect, Athens decided to launch a huge armada with the intent of conquering Syracuse—a Spartan ally. Athenian forces would eventually total 200 ships and over 10,000 soldiers at a huge cost—many millions of dollars in today's currency. Syracuse responded by appealing to Sparta for help—a plea Sparta was all too willing to answer since Syracuse was a major food supplier to Sparta. Sparta sent 1,000 hoplites to aid in Syracuse's defense. This response might seem insanely small and ineffectual until we recall that 300 Spartans nearly beat the entire Persian army at Thermopylae in 479 BCE. In fact, it was Athens that was hopelessly out of its depths in Sicily, and they chose the only sensible strategy in the circumstances: run away. Like everything else in this disastrous enterprise the retreat did not go well. In the end the entire force was either captured or killed, the leaders of the expedition were executed, and the armada was sunk. The few survivors of the defeat were held in a quarry on the outskirts of Syracuse, which still looks harsh and depressing. Most of the prisoners died of exposure; a few escaped, straggling back to Athens to tell the tale.

Thucydides makes few value judgments, but it is clear from the text that bad leadership doomed the mission from the start. The flamboyant Alcibiades argued for the invasion citing its huge profit potential, while spinning a tall tale of Sicilian welcome and support. But many correctly thought the enterprise was foolish since it violated the treaty with Sparta and had dubious chances of success given Athens' lack of familiarity with conditions on the ground. The eventual leader of the expedition, Nicias, had actually tried to squash the idea by suggesting that only an invasion force twice the size of the one proposed by Alcibiades could possibly succeed, thinking the Assembly would never go for it. However, Nicias' oratory proved to be so enticing that they agreed to fund the huge armada and put him in charge. Everyone, including Nicias, was lukewarm when it came to assessing his skills as a commander, but all agreed he was lucky. Of course it would not be called luck if it didn't eventually run out.[10]

Thucydides wants us to note a central flaw with democracy in action. Athens was an outlier when it adopted this innovative form of government in 508 BC. Being a relatively unimportant city at the democracy's inception, few took notice of the novelty. However most of the poleis had moved away from any kind of autocracy years before and had adopted some form of citizen participation in their constitutions. The Athenian version pushed the idea of citizen's participation in government to its logical extreme: the citizenry *was* the government. Since they were numerically superior, the lower classes held sway in Athens—not the landed gentry. Every decision was made by a simple majority in the Assembly, and every decision could be just as easily undone.

This last idea was unnerving to some because it struck at the heart of the Greek moral sensibility up to that time. *Dikaiosune* is sometimes translated as "justice," but it might be better understood as meaning acting morally or "doing the right thing." Of course this could be variously interpreted as the will of the gods, Fate, or the Logos—the eternal rationality of the universe. But however the word was interpreted, a core aspect of the concept was that it is beyond human likes and dislikes and certainly beyond human agreement. But Athens adopted conventional morality as a foundation for politics, thus embodying Protagoras' (c. 450 BC) dictum that "man is the measure of all things."[11]

The idea that we could control our fate had been brewing since Thales (c.600) had shown, according to the story, that reason and experiment could predict events such solar eclipses previously thought the result of divine intervention. It was believed that the gods would punish humans for moral transgressions by unbalancing nature, and once we returned to this viewpoint the balance of nature would be restored.

Thales most likely did not consider himself a theological or moral rebel, but his idea does sever the connection between the gods and nature. Implicit in Thales' thought is the suggestion that nature is governed by certain (discoverable) laws, and that we can learn how to rationally comprehend nature. But if the gods are not controlling nature to punish our transgressions, then why follow the rules? Athens' answer, following Protagoras' reasoning, is that we follow the rules because we made them—the body of citizens agreed to them.

Moral relativism was new and could be seen as problematic, until Pericles found a way of emphasizing its strengths and value. As noted above, in his *Funeral Oration* Pericles argued that democracy is the source of a new standard of excellence or virtue. Homeric virtue or arête was embodied in a figure like Achilles: wealthy, powerful, influential, valiant, natural leader, and incredibly successful. However, this excellence, though admirable and worthy of emulation was seen as largely the gift of the gods. Ordinary persons can set their sights on the life of Achilles, but can never attain it without divine assistance. In the democracy, according to Pericles, the ordinary person can be heroic and have the best of everything. Athenians are free to do anything they like. If you can get your fellow citizen's support you can become anything and achieve all of your earthly desires: fame, fortune and power. Democracy was the key to excellence in life and the Empire was proof of that. Athens went from a marginal polis to ruler of the Aegean thanks to democracy, and its citizens benefited handsomely. A standard of living that was previously restricted to a privileged few was now open to everyone. Of course the connection between democracy, virtue, and Empire might have been largely rhetorical flourish. There were certainly dissenters, and even Pericles would admit that the Empire was in reality a tyranny for its member states. But the idea had tremendous appeal, particularly for those who valued self-determination in politics above all else.

Socrates was a dissenting personality who was not convinced of the benefits of democratic virtue—neither did he ascribe to the Homeric variety. Socrates' actual teaching is a matter of academic dispute, but for the sake of expediency we may choose Plato's early dialogues as a fair representation of Socrates' ideas on virtue. When Socrates found an individual who claimed expert knowledge on a particular virtue such as courage, piety, or justice he would quiz that person on the extent of their knowledge of the subject. In the course of the conversation Socrates would offer counterexamples and point out contradictions that followed from the alleged experts' ideas. At the end of the conversation, often no positive conclusion had been reached, and all concerned—reader included—were left still wondering about the nature of the virtue under consideration.

But the exchange was not pointless. In Plato's *Apology* Socrates explains that his goal is wisdom and to attain wisdom you must start out by realizing your ignorance and along the way must admit that that you have not attained your goal. The goal is supremely difficult and embodies a lifelong pursuit. You are constantly improving but you are never done.[12]

This stance on arête or excellence was radical. It was not about success as the Greeks traditionally perceived it—no mention of money, fame, or power or anything most people would relate to the good life. Socrates focus was on ideas and putting them into practice. Hence we can regard his approach as spiritual or psychological—the intent was the improvement of the mind and ultimately the character of the individual.

Socrates' innovation was not universally appreciated in his lifetime. In *The Clouds* Aristophanes satirizes Socrates as a typical sophist of his day who runs a "thinking shop," teaching students to twist the arguments of their opponents to the detriment of all concerned. According to the *Apology*[13] Socrates believed that this caricature had stuck in the mind of Athenians and was partly responsible for his being prosecuted in 399 BC during the aftermath of the successful democratic counterrevolution. It did not help that some of Socrates' students were members of The Thirty.

The trial of Socrates likely reflects the vindictiveness of Athens after the loss of the Peloponnesian War and exposes a moral conflict within their society. By most accounts, Socrates had been a solid Athenian citizen most of his life. As a friend of both Plato's and Pericles' families he was acquainted with some of the Aristocracy. Although not a young man at the time, Socrates was a soldier at the Battle of Potidaea at the beginning of the war and handled himself well, even saving the life of Pericles' nephew Alcibiades. We should also note that Socrates fought in hoplite armor. Since the soldier had to provide his own dear in Athens and it was expensive this fact would indicate that Socrates or at least his family once had been well off and now had fallen on hard times. Many in Athens blamed the moral relativism of the Sophists for the demagoguery and bad decisions that cost Athens the war, and Socrates feared this association.[14] However, in the *Apology* and many other dialogues Plato makes it clear (and Aristotle also agrees) that neither Sophistry nor Science interested Socrates. Socrates was simply an easy target for a scapegoat—the Athenians desperately wanted to blame someone, but really the Athenians had to look no further than themselves. They abandoned Homeric virtue but failed to fully embrace Pericles' vision of a new kind of democratic virtue in which freedom and equality produce wisdom joined with courage and benevolence. Neither did Socratic virtue fare very well; dialectic was not applied in this case for the acquisition of moral virtue but for revenge and political standing.

Plato held a different view of Socrates' mission. The son of an aristocratic family, Plato initially desired a political career, but experience in the world of corrupt Athenian politics convinced him otherwise. He turned his attention to poetry, eventually showing some of his works to Socrates who was a frequent visitor. Socrates' criticisms were so pointed that Plato burned his books of poetry and decided to study philosophy.

If the notion that the forms as separate entities marks a definite turn toward Plato's own thought and away from merely expounding the ideas of Socrates, then the deeper we get into *Republic* the closer we are to Platonic thinking. Plato's *Republic* marks a turning point in his career. While politics and the political situation are never far from his mind in the early dialogues, *Republic* is a sustained effort at discussing the ideal political association. *Republic* in part is Plato's response to the two most catastrophic occurrences in his life: the death of Socrates and the defeat of Athens at the hands of Sparta. Both events are intertwined and both have the same causes in Plato's mind—the democracy and its deficiencies.

Plato perhaps considered the ideal state as outline in *Republic* as an antidote to the arbitrary nature of the democracy that he held responsible for so much tragedy. In the beginning of the dialogue, a discussion ensues on the nature of "justice." In the first part of the dialogue, various definitions of justice are offered and analyzed critically. The most powerful argument was initially offered by Thrasymachus, a noted sophist of the time. Thrasymachus raised the issue of moral relativism, and this forms a central challenge of the entire dialogue. In response to this challenge, Socrates slowly and methodically argues for a realm of eternal, unchanging truths that undergird not only the good society, but reality itself.

Thrasymachus' dialogue with Socrates is, at least for the purposes of this volume on catastrophe and philosophy, the most interesting in the dialogue. On one level it is constitutes a radical version of ethical relativism, because by this view, morality depends only on whoever is in power at the time. Whatever the powerful decide is right becomes the law of the land. This will of course vary with whoever is in power at the time; thus there exists no other objective criterion of morality above and beyond this. Socrates spends much of the rest of the dialogue attempting to argue for a version of an eternal and objective sense of the good in an attempt to meet this admittedly difficult challenge.

There occurs an aporetic moment toward the end of many of the Platonic dialogues, in which the various interlocutors, in the wake of Socrates' intense questioning of their arguments and assumptions, are not sure exactly what to believe anymore.[15] After this aporetic moment, Socrates attempts to reorient the discussion in such a way as provide a more satisfactory philosophical resolution. But in the wake of Athens' devastating military defeat at the hands of Sparta, Athenians collectively faced a thoroughgoing aporia of their own with regard to their culture's basic moral orientation, as a number of venerable Athenian value systems suddenly became no longer believable. The aforementioned Periclean optimism no longer corresponded to the "facts on the ground." Moreover, otherworldly, abstract virtues—like those advocated through complicated arguments by thinkers like Socrates—also failed to convince.

We thus see how this catastrophic military defeat basically brought forth a moral collapse, as Pericles' lofty ideals and rosy picture of Athenian values quickly devolved into a coarser, nihilistic, new "will to power" ethos. Thrasymachus' speech in *Republic,* Book I—in which he famously argues that the real definition of justice is what is in the interests of the stronger party—is a prime example of this new perspective. Thrasymachus advocated a simpler picture of *realpolitik* that illustrated actual human behavior in dark times—the naked "will to power" against the nihilistic backdrop of a total ethical void. In the absence of any objective right or wrong, morality is now defined merely as whichever code or system of laws has been established by brute force. Essentially, morality comes down to power. And since this "power-acquired" moral code can capriciously change with whoever occupies a position of authority at the time, we see the spectre of relativism in Thrasymachus' argument as well.

If one is completely honest about human nature, one must admit there is a degree of truth to Thrasymachus' characterization of morality. Plato's characterization of Thrasymachus in the dialogue is that of a brusque, boorish individual. Thrasymachus' abrasive personality reflects the rough and tumble environment of the port of Piraeus where the dialogue occurs, and he definitely seems angry with Socrates, who despite his many protestations about his ultimate ignorance, often appears somewhat smug and elitist. But nevertheless, Thrasymachus actually has a legitimate point that needs to be addressed. His characterization of human affairs corresponds to the things many people truly believe, the ways people actually act and the ways actual states function much of the time, especially in desperate conditions. This is why many of the arguments put forth by Thrasymachus and other interlocutors in the early part of *The Republic* (especially the *Ring of Gyges* story in which it is argued that "injustice pays better than justice") are in reality formidable challenges to Socrates, who in turn is now compelled to more vigorously defend an objective realm of moral truth in the face of this new reality.[16]

Moreover, it has been argued that Thrasymachus' speech reveals the catastrophe of the Peloponnesian War for Athenian democracy. Thrasymachus' emphasis on power being the sole criterion of morality, combined with similar themes in other works of this time (cf. Thucydides' "The Melian Dialogue"), reveals the morally corrupting effects (and the inevitable and tragic coarsening of the fabric of society) that war inevitably brings. Both texts stressed "a new ruthlessness, with a newly anarchic employment of power, and a new disrespect for . . . tradition."[17] Essentially Thrasymachus argues that might makes right—that the terms of "doing right" are set by the strongest according to their interests. This line of thinking can also be seen in evidence in the Athenian Assembly during the Peloponnesian War. Thus the famous chapters in Thucydides such as the Melian Dialogue reflect all too well how the war constituted a catastrophe for Athens and indeed the entire ancient world. The war was a catastrophe not only because of the physical destruction and loss of life it entailed, but also in large part because of what it did to the Athenians psychologically. These brutal episodes show how war often results in a coarsening and hardening of moral outlook, not only in the individual warriors involved but also in an entire culture. These exemplifications of psychological fallout and spiritual damage thus illustrate war's true cost. We see similar patterns earlier in Greek history, with regard to the mistreatment of Hector's body by Achilles (and its cruel display in front of Priam, Hecuba and Andromache) in Homer's *Iliad*. Such themes are illustrated in Simone Weil's *The Iliad or the Poem of Force*.[18]

Similar patterns continue today. The humiliation of Iraqi prisoners by American guards at Abu Ghraib prison serves as a current example of how war can bring out cruelty and unnecessary ruthlessness in its participants. Dehumanizing the enemy has been well documented as a sociological phenomenon and it has allowed for and rationalized ethically unacceptable behavior in many cases, including large-scale atrocities and genocides. While conduct during wartime often involves the suspension of ethical norms as part of its very nature, it sometimes also normalizes and rationalizes reprehensible conduct by people who otherwise do and/or should know better.

Plato likely considered his ideal state as the antidote to the arbitrary nature of the democracy that he held responsible for much tragedy and injustice. Motivated also in part by the execution of his teacher Socrates, Plato spent the rest of his life arguing for the objective nature of "the good" and some "conduct of affairs that might eliminate the confusion and gross error that he saw around him."[19] Many thinkers (cf. Karl Popper[20]) have argued that Plato's ideal state, upon examination, turns out not to be so ideal after all, that is was actually protofascist, while others (e.g., Aristotle, Machiavelli) argued that since ideal states cannot be enacted anyway, we should instead focus our energies on practical matters of the state in the here and now. We cannot go into these well-trodden arguments in detail here.

Antidemocratic thought has existed through the ages. Since democracy has taken many forms, we cannot speak of Democracy in monolithic terms. The Athenian democracy excluded women, slaves and the foreign-born, so there were not actually all that many people in Athens who could participate in it.

Other issues have been raised regarding democracy generally. Should the will of the people decide elections and other important matters, or are the common people just too ignorant, therefore needing wiser minds to lead them? Plato asked whether people are too easily swayed by rhetoric and public opinion that they can lose their critical thinking skills and descend into mob psychology (see *Republic* 492c).[21] This seems relevant today, in our age of sound bytes, televised conventions, tweets and social media, where carefully crafted images and superficial appeals to emotion hold more sway in the political arena than reasoned argument. Are some individuals simply better fit to govern than others, as thinkers like Nietzsche have argued? Who is to decide who should rule and who not, and exactly what would be the relevant criteria? The answers to these questions are not obvious.

Through the centuries many political alternatives to democracy have been enacted. But they have proven to be neither better forms of government, nor intrinsically less prone to capriciousness, cruelty, corruption or any other form of injustice caused by basic flaws in human nature. This is why many of the problems in Athenian democracy debated in Plato's dialogues—skepticism regarding absolute moral values, abuses of power and authority, looming threats of tyranny and the abuses of oligarchy—as well as the larger question raised by Thucydides of human nature in light of catastrophe—are still pressing around the world today, present in all forms of government, and perhaps even in starker terms.

NOTES

1. Cf. Donald Kagan, *Pericles of Athens and the Birth of Democracy* (London: Secker & Warburg, 1990).
2. Pericles, in Thucydides, *History of the Peloponnesian War*, trans. Rex Warner (New York: Penguin, 1972), II:37.
3. Ibid., II:38.
4. Ibid., II:40.
5. Ibid., II:40–41.
6. Ibid., II:65.
7. Cf. Donald Kagan, *The Peloponnesian War* (New York: Penguin, 2003), 97–100.
8. Pericles, in Thucydides, *History*, III 36ff.
9. Ibid., V 84ff.
10. Ibid., VI 8ff.
11. Cf. Thomas R. Martin, *Ancient Greece: From Prehistoric to Hellenistic Times* (New Haven, CT: Yale University Press, 2013), 141–46.
12. Cf. Thomas C. Brickhouse and Nicholas D. Smith, *Plato's Socrates* (Oxford: Oxford University Press, 1994).
13. Plato, "Apology," in *The Last Days of Socrates*, trans. H. Tredennick and H. Tarrant, Intro and notes by H. Tarrant (New York: Penguin, 2003), 19 c–d.

14. Cf. James Colaiaco, *Socrates against Athens: Philosophy on Trial* (New York: Routledge, 2001), 13–54.

15. For a thorough and many-sided exploration of this interesting concept, see George Karamanolis and Vasilis Politis, eds., *The Aporetic Tradition in Ancient Philosophy* (Cambridge, UK: Cambridge University Press, 2018).

16. For some interesting explorations of Thrasymachus and his worldview, see Curtis N. Johnson, *Socrates and the Immoralists* (Lanham, MD: Lexington Books, 2007) and also the classic analysis by C. E. M. Joad, *Thrasymachus and the Future of Morals* (London: Kegan Paul, 1930).

17. Rex Warner, *The Greek Philosophers* (New York: Signet, 1958). Another interesting text in this regard is Simone Weil, *The Iliad or The Poem of Force* (Wallingford, PA: Pendle Hill, 1981).

18. See also Warner, *The Greek Philosophers*.

19. Ibid.

20. Karl Popper, *The Open Society and its Enemies, Vol. 1: The Spell of Plato* (Princeton, NJ: Princeton University Press, 1971).

21. Plato, *Republic*, trans. A. Bloom (New York: Basic Books, 1968).

BIBLIOGRAPHY

Brickhouse, Thomas C. and Nicholas D. Smith. *Plato's Socrates*. Oxford: Oxford University Press, 1994.

Colaiaco, James. *Socrates against Athens: Philosophy on Trial*. New York: Routledge, 2001.

Joad, C.E.M. *Thrasymachus and the Future of Morals*. London: Kegan Paul, 1930.

Johnson, Curtis N. *Socrates and the Immoralists*. Lanham, MD: Lexington Books, 2007.

Kagan, Donald. *Pericles of Athens and the Birth of Democracy*. London: Secker & Warburg 1990.

Kagan, Donald. *The Peloponnesian War*. New York: Penguin, 2003.

Karamanolis, George and Vasilis Politis, editors. *The Aporetic Tradition in Ancient Philosophy*. Cambridge, UK: Cambridge University Press, 2018.

Martin, Thomas R. *Ancient Greece: From Prehistoric to Hellenistic Times*. New Haven, CT: Yale University Press, 2013.

Popper, Karl. *The Open Society and Its Enemies*. Princeton, NJ: Princeton University Press, 1971.

Plato. "Apology." In *The Last Days of Socrates*. Translated by H. Tredennick and H. Tarrant. Introduction and notes by H. Tarrant. New York: Penguin, 2003.

Plato. *Republic*. Translated by A. Bloom. New York: Basic Books, 1968.

Thucydides. *History of the Peloponnesian War*. Translated by Rex Warner. New York: Penguin, 1972.

Warner, Rex. *The Greek Philosophers*. New York: Signet, 1958.

Weil, Simone. *The Iliad or The Poem of Force*. Wallingford, PA: Pendle Hill, 1981.

Part II

THE MIDDLE AGES/ RENAISSANCE

Preface

The Middle Ages and Renaissance

This section will focus on a number of philosophical reactions to catastrophe during the Middle Ages and the Renaissance. It will, among other things, feature work addressing St. Augustine's *City of God*, written in the aftermath of the 410 sack of Rome by the Goths. St. Augustine lived during a complicated, violent and confusing time and place, North Africa under Roman rule in the very early Middle Ages, following the slow decline and disintegration of the ancient world. The Pagan world was collapsing and a new religious value system—Christianity—was just beginning to spread throughout the Roman world. Soon Christianity would spread across Pagan Europe and consolidate itself politically and theologically to become the dominant power throughout the Middle Ages and beyond. Existing value systems of the Pagan world, for example, Stoicism and Epicureanism, which originated in ancient Greece, offered philosophies of resignation to the war-weary and spiritually exhausted citizens of the Roman world, though Christianity gradually superseded these systems, as it reflected a more compelling and comprehensive narrative of salvation and hope.

Throughout their vying for dominance, Pagans and Christians continuously blamed each other for the calamities occurring during the long Roman collapse. Augustine's *City of God* was a sweeping work of encyclopedic learning, philosophic argument and Christian eschatology, influenced heavily by Pagan philosophy such as the Platonic doctrine of Forms. *City of God* defended Christianity against the charge the Christianity extolled weak values such as humility, forgiveness and otherworldliness, which rendered the Romans powerless to fend off the Barbarian invasions.

Augustine's text also raises another interesting issue—the decadence of the Romans during this crisis and the relation between decadence, nihilism and catstrophe.[1]

The fall into decadent behavior constitutes a recurring theme of societies in crisis. Augustine's railing against the Romans' decadent ways reflects the tendency towards distraction in the face of catastrophe. Perhaps this decadence reflected disillusionment with the newly touted values of Christianity, insofar as modesty and humility didn't offer much protection at the time against the Barbarians at the gates. This decadence also reflected a widespread sense of cynicism, almost nihilism. Unbridled sexuality, hedonism and obscene behavior in the face of a collapsing world reflected a rejection of the otherworldly values of Christianity (which emphasize delayed gratification as this world is merely preparation for the next, cf. Augustine) in favor of short-term indulgence in the face of uncertainty and hopelessness.

We see similar patterns in the civilizational trauma caused later on in the medieval period by the Black Death with all its horrific devastation, and the ensuing loosening of sexual morality described in Boccacio's *Decameron*. Yet because in the Middle Ages, religion was such a powerful force (religion often being inextricably linked with politics), we see both how people turned towards religious belief for comfort to try make sense out of the mass death all around and also how crises served to move thoughtful people to challenge religious orthodoxy. Even if such behavior patterns described by Boccaccio did not actually unfold this way, the issue being raised so fundamentally in this text belies its thematic nature.

This theme will appear later in the interwar period of the 20th century. Decadence in the midst of catastrophe has often been met by attempts by philosophers and religious authorities to draw the population back to a focus on eternal verities instead. Consider the fiery sermons of Isaiah and Jeremiah in Biblical times, or the words of Stoics like Seneca and Marcus who, during the Roman decline, called the population away from the distractions of Rome's "bread and circuses" back to a consideration of life's simple truths. Heidegger's emphasis on "authenticity," written at the height of Weimar decadence and despair, could be similarly interpreted.

We will also look at the Renaissance period in this section. The search for political stability at this time was so strong that it produced some paradoxical phenomena. Machiavelli is often condemned for advocating immoral behavior, yet many don't realize how this advice was proffered in the service of providing for a unified government in a chaotic age of Italian warring city-states and recurring invasions of Italy by foreign powers like France and Spain. The search for political stability often has lent itself to appeals for a unified government; unfortunately throughout history this need for stability has been so strong that it has at times led to brutal dictatorship (e.g., Weimar Germany). To use a contemporary case, it seems as if the Iraqi people at times preferred the stability of Saddam Hussein, in spite of his brutality, to the chaos that followed his removal. Such interesting paradoxes of human nature and political behavior will be explored in this chapter.

NOTE

1. See David Weir, *Decadence: A Very Short Introduction* (Oxford: Oxford University Press, 2018).

BIBLIOGRAPHY

Augustine. *City of God.* New York: Image/Doubleday, 1958. 62–63.
Boccaccio, Giovanni. *Decameron: Norton Critical Edition.* Edited and translated by Mark Musa and Peter Bondanella. New York: Norton, 1977.
Weir, David. *Decadence: A Very Short Introduction.* Oxford: Oxford University Press, 2018.

Chapter 5

Augustine's Anti-Catastrophe

Steven Cresap

INTRODUCTION

A paradigm of philosophical foundation-building is that foundations follow from older foundations, after a period of widespread uncertainty. A serious upheaval—such as a large-scale natural disaster, an economic or climactic crisis, a loss in a global war—produces a personally felt state of anomie, both philosophical and religious, at least among the informed elite. This state of discomfort leads to intellectualized doubt and anomie, then to certainty and the possibility of a new foundation, with its attendant mass movement.

What to call such an upheaval? Three commonly used descriptors reveal usually ignored differences in meaning, if considered by their etymological roots: "tragedy" ("goat-song"), "disaster" ("evil star"), and "catastrophe" ("turning"). If we take their roots seriously, tragedy should probably be used as Aristotle suggested, only for singularly striking negative events concerning individuals of some notoriety. Disaster indicates an event affecting many individuals, but still singular in time and space. Catastrophe is vague enough to suggest a widespread and long-term upheaval, affecting more than one area of culture. The paradigm for cultural change that we are considering has to do mainly with the latter concept, although individual tragedies and disasters have often served, in the popular imagination, to symbolize cultural catastrophes.

We also must consider the variety of viewpoints on events included in catastrophes, from those in the general population who survive direct experience with them to nonparticipants who witness their unfolding, to those who witness or are informed about it but have a special attitude toward such events: the attitude of aesthetes, of enthusiasts for awful spectacles like Longinus and Nero, and the modern critical school of the sublime (the beauty of terror).[1] This chapter will necessarily concentrate on one point of view: that of one of the most influential Church fathers, St. Augustine, Bishop of Hippo. This chapter will explore Augustine's "City of God" to see if and how this classic work can be understood in accordance with the catastrophe / anomic / new foundation paradigm. It is a text explicitly responding to the sack of Rome by the Goths and Huns under Alaric in 410 C.E., and it is a text that became foundational in Christian theology. But what, exactly, is the connection between these two contexts?

CONTEXTS

In his *A History of Civilizations* Fernand Braudel remarks about Saint Augustine,

> For him, faith came first: but he nevertheless declared *"Credo ut intelligam"*—"I believe in order to understand." He also said *"Si fallor, sum"*—"If I am mistaken, I exist"—and *"Si dubiat, vivit"*—"if he doubts, he is alive." It would be misleading to see in these remarks a very distant anticipation of Descartes's *"Cogito ergo sum"*: but they clearly have affinities with it.[2]

What affinities could there be between the fifth-century churchman and the 17th-century philosopher? Braudel sees an affinity not in Augustine's theology but in the fact that he "gave Western Christianity some of its color and its ability to adapt and debate—if only by insisting on the vital need to embrace the one faith in full awareness, after deep personal reflection, and with the will to act accordingly." Systematic doubt, such an important element in Descartes' new foundation in epistemology, seems with Augustine to have been mainly philosophical "coloring," an old rhetorical style meant to reinforce a much older foundation, the certainty of faith.

In his *Confessions* (c. 397) Augustine says of reading Cicero's *Hortensius (45 B.C.E.)* that "the only thing that pleased me in Cicero's book was his advice not simply to admire one or another of the schools of philosophy, but to love wisdom itself, whatever it might be." As Susan Jacoby points out, what wisdom meant to Augustine was Biblical-based faith in the supernatural, which was a lesson that Cicero surely did not intend.[3] It is important to keep in mind Braudel's description of the long-term geographical, social, psychological, and economic causes of change and decay in the underlying structures of a civilization: "all profound forces, barely recognized at first, especially by contemporaries, to whom they always seem perfectly natural, to be taken wholly for granted if they are thought about at all."[4] Ancients were quite well informed about the transience of their communities and cultures through stories transmitted in various ways and recorded by mythmakers both poetic (e.g. Hesiod's Ages) and philosophical (e.g., Plato's Atlantis).

It is difficult to believe that the Empire's city-dwellers, at least, would leap to Lot's daughters' assumption after the destruction of their cities: that the human race had ended except for them and their father (Genesis 19:36). As Gibbon puts it, "the more learned and judicious contemporaries were forced to confess that infant Rome had formerly received more essential injury from the Gauls [the Senones, in 390 BCE] than she had now sustained from the Goths."[5] Augustine pointed out the same thing, of course with a different intent. Generally speaking, the event in 410 seems to have been a bit of a let down, at least for the nonparticipants.

For Augustine, the sack of Rome was neither unprecedented nor particularly catastrophic, which is why his reaction was neither a revelation of new truth nor a conversion. For him, what had happened was a miraculous gift from God, which offered Augustine an opportunity to justify the ways of Providence. To those who blamed the sack of Rome on Rome's embrace of Christianity and its principles of forgiveness, love and humility, Augustine instead pointed to the long-standing decadence of Rome as the real cause. He could thus console his fellow believers by reminding them that Rome, after all, was not yet the City of God. That City as he envisioned it was that sort of culminating, enduring regime that philosophers of history have labeled, variously, as "Caesarism" (Spengler), the "Universal Church" (Toynbee), and "Byzantinism" (Hoffer).

COUNTERCONVERSION

The point of reviewing these reactions, both pagan and Christian, is that, with few exceptions, dealing with the fall of the imperial city was not a matter of catastrophe leading to doubt, and certainly not among the leading interpreters of the event. Doubt, after all, if it is to rise to the level of aporia, which alone can lead to significant ideological change, must be felt on an existential level, or be part of a cultural movement, such as the Salons of the 18th century, the armchair skepticism of Berkeley and Hume, Existentialism or the postmodernist orthodoxies of our own time.

> A state of skepticism and suspense may amuse a few inquisitive minds. But the practice of superstition is so congenial to the multitude that, if they are forcibly awakened, they still regret the loss of their pleasing vision. . . . the fall of any system of mythology will most probably be succeeded by the introduction of some other mode of superstition.[6]

At the time of Rome's fall there was an amazing, unprecedented variety of ideologies on offer—mystically minded Neoplatonists, reactionary Pagans, quasi-Christian barbarians, Gnostics, Manicheans, followers of Mythra and a multiplicity of Christian sects, plus competing religio-philosophical schools such as Stoicism, Indian-influenced Pyhrronism, neo-Platonism, and so on. The movement of peoples from the Middle East and Eurasia had brought the entire menu of self-abnegation, apotheosis, immortality, supernature, theurgy, and sin that we recognize in the 5th-century commentaries. It was syncretism gone wild: Orphism, Mithraism, ritual prostitution, sacred stones, castration and other self-mutilation, cults of Osiris and Sarapis, Bacchus, astrology, Italian gods, Levantine gods, and so on.[7] It was an age when it was possible to confuse Christ with Adonis and both with Orpheus, to try out various rituals as seemed appropriate, and to aspire to transcendence.

We might conclude that this multiplicity of ideologies is evidence of a widespread anomie at the time, which had to color Augustine's reaction to the event of 410, until we reflect that all of these sects were up and coming during the period of the Antonines centuries earlier, arguably the apex of the Empire. Gibbon described the period between the death of the Emperor Domitian to the accession of Commodus (roughly 96 to 180 CE) as a golden age, in which the human race was the most happy and prosperous. The emperors Nerva, Trajan, Hadrian, and the Antonines "delighted in the image of liberty" and tried honorably to restore the Republic.[8] Of course this was partially a rhetorical device, to provide the lynchpin for the decline thesis, and other thinkers painted a dourer picture of the economic and social conditions during that time. For example, Bertrand Russell described the age of the Antonines as militarily and spiritually "tired," and perhaps Stoicism flourished during this time because it itself spoke to an internal malaise and a sense of resignation in a time of brutal warfare and spiritual disintegration.[9] This may also explain how such resignation philosophies were soon replaced by Christianity, insofar as Christianity offered a more comprehensive, compelling and uplifting vision of human redemption. But it is important to realize that this was the period when all the major contending parties of philosophical and religious thought, rational and magical, were busy cementing their belief systems and institutions.

Even neo-Platonism, which laid the metaphysical foundation for Augustine's celestial City, went through a variety of accommodations with the requirements of earthly life, in its traditional role laid down by Socrates and Plato, as philosophical therapy. Permanence was not only an escape from change, but an intellectual stimulus for producing worldly change—as in ecclesiastical institution-building and the elaboration of a universal theology, worldly emanations of the Idea of the Good.

The dislocation of witnessing evidence for the falsehood of one's native beliefs is rarely a matter of simply giving up the quest for certainty. However temporarily clouded by personal and/or social disorientation, certainty is often not diluted by a disastrous situation but on the contrary empowered by it. For most ancients involved in the important questions of loyalty and the future, their reactions typically were not to lose faith in their traditions, whether pagan or Christian or philosophical, but rather to more deeply entrench oneself in one's belief system, to "double down" and provide an explanation consistent with the particular orthodoxy of their schools.

This reaction should be considered *counterconversion*, not in the sense in which James used it, to refer to the loss of faith, but rather what we would call today an extreme form of confirmation bias: a state of denial in which people do not doubt their beliefs even though the situation clearly warrants it. Counterconversion results from the attitude Gibbon called "inflexible zeal" and in tracing its development among Christians—a main cause of its success—he points to its origin with the Jews: "Under the pressure of every calamity, . . . and in contradiction to every known principle of the human mind, that singular people seems to have yielded a stronger and more ready assent to the traditions of their remote ancestors than to the evidence of their own senses.[10]

Counterconversion is characteristic of many persuasions, religious and ideological. If we approve of the beleaguered belief system in question, we consider their adherents in times of crisis as heroic, steadfast, for example, post-Holocaust Jews, Native Americans, Tibetan Buddhists, anti-colonialists, and so on. But if we do not accept their belief system, we consider them as impossibly stubborn bitter-enders: unreconstructed Southerners, post-World War I Imperialists, post-World War II Nazis both paleo- and neo-, Japanese Emperor-worshippers after the Emperor's de-apotheosis, post-Soviet Stalinists, and so on. Given the surprisingly large numbers of anti-converts in each of these cases, it is unlikely that generalizations can be made as readily as with conversion, which is relatively rare.

After 410 Roman pagans demonstrated counterconversion by reverting to the old worry that the presence of Christians was offensive to the Gods. If the city suffered, it was because the Gods were angry—specifically at monotheists who, because of their preference for one sky God, as opposed to several mountain Gods, seemed to be atheists. This is exactly the fear that fueled the Roman persecutions of Christians centuries earlier. Similarly, Augustine's theological interpretation of that event and history as a whole was a counterconversion, insofar as it consoled fellow Christians not by revealing a new truth but by codifying the entire tradition of Christian apocalyptic thinking that had developed centuries before.

Even the specifics of Augustine's millennialism—including the idea of a holy city in the future, the New Jerusalem—had been elaborated by Church fathers well before Constantine's official Christianization of the Empire.

Augustine's conversion to Christianity a decade and a half before the sack of Rome was itself a reversion to an original state of certitude, temporarily clouded by personal and social division. The trouble is that both kinds of division are not wholly available to the sufferer's consciousness, and have to be reconstructed. The social setting of Augustine's mystical experience in the garden was not especially troubling at that particular time. Augustine was part of an upwardly mobile middle-class family living in a city in North Africa that had existed prosperously for three centuries. There were the usual dislocations of multiculturalism: mixed marriages, some political instability, new opportunities in education and business, and, most important for Augustine, the fact that Christianity was official and ascendant.

Hence we witness a proliferation of psychological explanations for Augustine's conversion. Yet mainstream psychological explanations, whether behaviorist, psychoanalytical or existential, inevitably come off as deflating. This is because they are all forms of reductionism, breaking down complex phenomena into their constituent parts. But recall that paradigmatic reductionism was a product of the Enlightenment, which itself was a break from a much older, and often strictly foundational, tradition, what might be called "methological agglomeration." Instead of reducing complex phenomena to simple parts, agglomerators try to comprehend complex phenomena by adding extraneous parts. Lot's daughters did this in assuming the destruction of their city extended to the entire world, and this belief brought negative results. This is a staple of religious doctrine and magical thinking, as well as conspiracy theories across the political spectrum. We all know the dangers, to science and civility, posed by this method. So the deflating effect of psychological explanations might actually be an epistemological tonic, especially in times of upheaval and rapid social change (such as our own), with all their accompanying uncertainty and paranoia.

William James describes his conversion as the uniting of a "divided self." It had a "dynamogenetic quality" that enabled him "to make irruption efficaciously into life and quell the lower tendencies forever."[11] It is the sort of mind cure that James, the pragmatist, had to tolerate, even at the risk of being sometimes surprisingly soft on superstition. But he does manage to suggest the therapeutic effects of the vow of chastity and other purifying and integrating elements in Augustine's postconversion psyche.

Nock says Augustine's conversion after hearing a voice in a garden say "tolle lege" ("take it up [a passage from Paul] and read") embodied "a certainty which he had almost but not quite reached: it was like a long convalescence at the end of which it is sometimes some casual circumstance which at last enables a man to realize that he is well." The conversion experience rested on "the permanence of an early impression and of the religious atmosphere with which his mother had invested his childhood. . . . Christianity is throughout presupposed and present in the subject's subconsciousness."[12]

Freudians have extensively analyzed the fact that Augustine's mother, Monica, was a Christian and his father, Patricius, was a pagan. Jacoby uncovers the roots of Augustine's emotional turmoil in a reverse Oedipus complex: his perception, as a child, "of one parent [his mother] as the representative of just, timeless moral values and the other [his father] as the emblem of worldly striving."[13] But Jacoby's main interest is in the practical value for Augustine of conversion to the state religion: personal purity potentiated by acceptance in a financially and politically powerful church. The aging, post 410 Augustine, high in the hierarchy of an established church, betrays no sense of panic, personal dislocation or, indeed, serious doubt.

OUT OF THIS WORLD

In his screed against fanaticism, *The True Believer*, Eric Hoffer makes a provocative comment on times of trouble:

> The tangibility of a pleasant and secure existence is such that it makes other realities, however imminent, seem vague and visionary. Thus it happens that when the times become unhinged, it is the practical people who are caught unaware and are made to look like visionaries who cling to things that do not exist.[14]

This could certainly describe of the pagans in Rome trying to make sense of their city's downfall. When we try to understand the inner workings of ancient civilizations, we must remember that we are dealing with a spirit world. The difference between the pagan mountain Gods and the Christian sky God shrinks in comparison to the similarity of aspiration, to purity, to holiness, to a Godlike stature, found in most forms of worship. It seems as though the primary concern of nearly all religious and philosophical persuasions at the time was to find a way to escape this physical world.

With Augustine prognostication turns into prophecy: instead of angry local Gods he ingeniously presents a parallel history, that of the City of man and that of the City of God, whose progress was not always evident in the actual history of the Church (the extent to which Augustine identified the City of God with the Catholic Church is a matter of some dispute). In this scheme pagan prognostication and propitiation had to be replaced by prayer, which had little to do with civic salvation in comparison with the hope of individual salvation, and which was no longer based on ritual but rather on a complicated theory, a theologically framed apocalyptic philosophy of history.

Augustine's most effective innovation was the way he detailed the dual pattern he detected in history: the cyclical stasis of the earthly city, with no end and no improvement in sight; and the linear and, in a sense, progressive pattern of the City of God, headed for a millennium of prosperity after the Second Coming of Christ, culminating in the eternal salvation of the faithful. The advantage of this distinction is that Christians could expect not only individual salvation, but the salvation of the whole Christian community.

This dual pattern did have a cost. Because the metaphysical status of the Heavenly City was more supernatural than that of local pagan deities, a true Christian's participation in the city of man had to be touched by considerable ambivalence.

> Thus the things necessary for this mortal life are used by both kinds of men and families alike, but each has its own peculiar and widely different aim in using them. The earthly city, which does not live by faith, seeks an earthly peace. . . . The heavenly city, or rather the part of it which sojourns on earth and lives by faith, makes use of this peace only because it must, until this mortal condition which necessitates it shall pass away.[15]

Although both pagans and Christians, as human beings, share the same need for order and civic concord, as citizens of the earthly city, Christians, because of their faith in the future, were pilgrims, captives, and strangers in the world of politics and war. No wonder Augustine could point to the upside of Rome's partial destruction: Christians miraculously saved, church treasures preserved by the barbarians, and so on.

> In its pilgrim state the heavenly city possesses this peace by faith; and by this faith it lives righteously when it refers to the attainment of that peace every good action toward God and man; for the life of the city is a social life.[16]

Augustine even suggests that the actual experience of physical suffering is different for members of each community. The deeper consolation was that Christians do not even experience catastrophes the way pagans do.

> Though good and bad men suffer alike, we must not suppose that there is no difference between the men themselves, because there is no difference in what they both suffer. . . . For as the same fire causes gold to glow brightly and chaff to smoke . . . the same violence of affliction proves, purges, clarifies the good, but damns, ruins, exterminates the wicked.[17]

This amazing psychological transformation is a striking instance of what Hoffer calls "the depreciation of the present." In all mass movements, whether religious, social or nationalist, there is an "inevitable shift of emphasis once the movement starts rolling":

> The present—the original objective—is shoved off the stage and its place taken by posterity—the future. More still: the present is driven back as if it were an unclean thing and lumped with the detested past. The battle line is now drawn between things that are and have been, and the things that are not yet.[18]

Hoffer also notes that "not only does a mass movement depict the present as mean and miserable—it deliberately makes it so. It fashions a pattern of individual existence that is dour, hard, repressive and dull."[19] Or as Gibbon put it, Augustine "boldly sounded the dark abyss of grace, predestination, free-will, and original sin."[20] Just as Gibbon remarked of the decline and fall of the Roman Empire—"instead of inquiring *why* the Roman Empire was destroyed, we should rather be surprised that it had subsisted so long"[21]—the real surprise of the ascendancy of the Church was perhaps that it was so incomplete. In delineating the different histories of the two cities, Augustine avoided a strict theocracy. The dynamic, ever-changing balance of power between Emperor and Pope, state and church, the secular and the sacred, would run through the history of Christianity for more than a millennium. It is ironic that in order to unite what James called his "divided self," Augustine had to accept that the entirety of human history, and human nature, were themselves inevitably and irreconcilably divided.

NOTES

1. See Steven Cresap, "Sublime Politics," *Clio* 19, no. 2 (1990): 111–25.
2. Fernand Braudel, *A History of Civilizations*, trans. Richard Mayne (New York: Penguin, 1993), 335.
3. Susan Jacoby, *Strange Gods: A Secular History of Conversion* (New York: Pantheon, 2016), 3.
4. Braudel, *A History of Civilizations*, 28.
5. Edward Gibbon, *The Decline and Fall of the Roman Empire*, ed. D. M. Low (New York: Harcourt, 1960), 456.
6. Ibid., 456.
7. Arthur D. Nock, *Conversion: The Old and New Religion from Alexander the Great to Augustine of Hippo* (Baltimore: Johns Hopkins University Press, 1998), 36.
8. Gibbon, *The Decline and Fall*, 1.
9. Bertrand Russell, *A History of Western Philosophy* (New York: Simon & Schuster, 1945), 262.

10. Gibbon, *The Decline and Fall*, 145.
11. William James, *The Varieties of Religious Experience* (New York: Penguin, 1968), 145.
12. Nock, *Conversion: The Old and New Religion*, 265–66.
13. Jacoby, *Strange Gods*, 7.
14. Eric Hoffer, *The True Believer: Thoughts on the Nature of Mass Movements* (New York: Harper, 2002), 69–73.
15. Augustine, *City of God*, chapter 17. www.ccel.org/ccel/schaff/npnf102.iv.XIX.17.html.
16. Ibid.
17. Ibid., chapter 8.
18. Hoffer, *The True Believer*, 69.
19. Ibid.
20. Gibbon, *The Decline and Fall*, 476.
21. Ibid., 525.

BIBLIOGRAPHY

Augustine. *City of God*, in Nicene and Post-Nicene Fathers: First Series, Vol. II. Translated by Marcus Dods. Edited by Philip Schaff. Edinburgh: T&T Clark, 1886 and Grand Rapids, MI: Eerdmans, 1994. *Christian Classics and Ethereal Library*, www.ccel.org/ccel.

Braudel, Fernand. *A History of Civilizations*. Translated by Richard Mayne. New York: Penguin, 1993.

Cresap, Steven. "Sublime Politics." *Clio* 19, no. 2 (1990): 111–25.

Gibbon, Edward. *The Decline and Fall of the Roman Empire*. Edited by D. M. Low. New York: Harcourt, 1960.

Hoffer, Eric. *The True Believer: Thoughts on the Nature of Mass Movements*. New York: Harper, 2002.

Jacoby, Susan. *Strange Gods: A Secular History of Conversion*. New York: Pantheon, 2016.

James, William. *The Varieties of Religious Experience*. New York: Penguin, 1968.

Nock, Arthur D. *Conversion: The Old and the New in Religion from Alexander the Great to Augustine of Hippo*. Baltimore: Johns Hopkins University Press, 1998.

Russell, Bertrand. *A History of Western Philosophy*. New York: Simon & Schuster, 1945.

Chapter 6

Civilizational Trauma and Value Nihilism in Boccaccio's *Decameron*[*]

David J. Rosner

INTRODUCTION: CIVILIZATIONAL TRAUMA AND VALUES CRISES[1]

In the introduction to their edited volume *The Cultural Life of Catastrophes and Crises*, Carsten Meiner and Kristen Veel discuss catastrophes and crises as "disruptions of order."[2] They argue that "through consequences of varying severity, catastrophes and crises change and subvert what we have become accustomed to as the normal state of things, thereby exposing what was previously taken for granted."[3] Yet their book explores not merely the particular catastrophic events themselves, but in the "multi-layered and complex interlinkage between actual events and the cultural processing of these events,"[4] that is, how they "understood in terms of their cultural life . . . how they are interpreted once they occur, and what kinds of cultural representation they subsequently engender."[5] This chapter traces what happens to a civilization's fundamental values during times of catastrophe and specifically how such values are affected by collective psychic trauma. The specific case under consideration here is the Black Death plague, which ravaged Europe starting from around 1348. The chapter examines how some themes in Boccaccio's *Decameron*, perhaps the most influential literary production created in reaction to the plague, can also be considered one of the West's earliest chronicles of a moral/epistemological crisis, and how certain themes in the work, understood as a reaction to the Black Death, can even be seen to reveal

---

[*] An earlier version of this article was published in *Comparative Civilizations Review* 73 (2015); the revised paper appears here with kind permission from the Journal Editor.

elements of trends toward what we now call value nihilism (at least according to Nietzsche's definition of the term).

This chapter will also address the more general question of how crises and catastrophes are to be properly studied, as part of the "methodology" of civilizational studies. I will extend into some new territory the studies of scholars such as Pitirim Sorokin, Joseph Gibaldi and others who have previously read *Decameron* in terms of the theme of civilizational disintegration. I will similarly follow the theoretical lead of Meiner and Veel above insofar as, for this chapter, the crucial moment to examine is not necessarily the external catastrophic event itself, but rather the internal "void of ethics" (cf. Patrizia McBride) that this event has left in its wake. I will also investigate further the implications this "void of ethics" has had upon those of us living in the postmodern West today.

THE ABANDONMENT OF VALUES IN DESPERATE TIMES

According to the *Brown University Decameron Web*, in 1334 an epidemic which would eventually kill 2/3 of China's inhabitants struck the northeastern Chinese province of Hopei, claiming up to 90% of the population . . . carried along trade routes, the "Black Death," as it soon would be called, began to work its way west. . . . In 1346 the plague came to Kaffa, a Genoese cathedral city . . . plague ridden ships from Kaffa brought the disease to Italy. Some cities lost almost all their inhabitants. In Venice at least ¾ died. In Pisa 7/10 of the inhabitants died, and many families were completely destroyed. . . . Estimates of the dead vary greatly . . . throughout Italy, at least ½ the population died.[6]

Boccaccio describes the physical symptoms and progression of the disease in the first chapter of *Decameron*: First there would be the appearance of certain swellings in the groin or armpit, which then would begin to spread, soon appearing at random all over the body. Later on, the symptoms changed, and many people began to find dark blotches on their arms, thighs, and other parts of the body. . . . At this point, this was a certain sign that the person would die."[7]

The question for this inquiry is how did this affect medieval civilization on a spiritual plane, in terms of its basic values? Part of the experience of trauma here was the unique sense of hopelessness spreading through Christendom, due to the fact that no matter whom one was or what actions one took (or didn't take), nothing proved effective to stop the plague's deadly progress. Boccaccio thus writes: "against this pestilence no human wisdom or foresight was any avail."[8] Whether priest or layman, Christian or Jew, rich or poor, man or woman, all fell victim. Neither prayer nor medicine worked. Some desperately beseeched God, seeking penance through self-flagellation or participation in novenas, while others (perhaps equally desperately) attempted to "carpe diem," trying to find a modicum of pleasure wherever possible. But it didn't really matter what the people did, as the plague progressed relentlessly and indiscriminately across Europe. While the mass death wrought by the plague was horrific enough, the accompanying realization of futility must only have exacerbated the collective trauma experienced in Europe at this time.

This sense of despair led to a widespread breakdown of morals. Boccaccio writes that in the face of mass death (and with the hysteria, hopelessness and social disorder attendant upon the recognition that nobody, including the medical establishment and the clergy, could do anything to stop the plague's progress) "the revered authority of the laws, both divine and human, had fallen and almost completely disappeared."[9]

How, more specifically, was this moral breakdown made manifest? For one thing, we see that civilization's most basic family ties and relations were abandoned out of sheer panic and fear for self-preservation. Boccaccio writes "brother abandoned brother, uncle abandoned nephew, sister left brother, and very often wife abandoned husband . . . even worse, almost unbelievable, fathers and mothers neglected to tend and care for their own children, as if they were not their own."[10]

Moreover, in their desperation to quickly rid themselves of diseased corpses, the most sacred rituals in Christianity concerning death and funerals were also suddenly abandoned. People died alone in the streets and were then simply thrown into mass graves:

> The city was full of corpses. Things had reached such a point that the people who died were cared for as we care for goats today . . . so many corpses would arrive in front of a church every day and at every hour . . . when all the graves were full, huge trenches were dug in all of the cemeteries of the churches and into the new arrivals were dumped by the hundreds, and they were packed in there with dirt, one on top of another . . . until the trench was filled.[11]

SEXUAL (IM)MORALITY IN *DECAMERON*: CRISIS OR CATHARSIS?

In what other ways did mass trauma in medieval Christian Europe lead to the questioning of the most basic values of Christianity and of Christendom itself? *Decameron* is interesting in large part because of its specific focus on the loosening of sexual morality. Hence Nancy Reale in "Boccaccio's *Decameron*: A Fictional Account of Grappling with Chaos," writes:

> *Decameron* is a recording of a deep crisis in Italian life in the largest sense and simultaneously Boccaccio's personal crisis of faith. The text repeatedly and courageously questions received assumptions about religion and social organization and offers views of *trecento* Italy that are diverse, often destabilized and destabilizing, and sometimes devoid of an overarching religions faith that would otherwise have been assumed.[12]

We know that medieval Europe was a civilization saturated in religion and dominated by Christianity; religious explanations were offered and accepted without question in response to almost all events in life. Themes of salvation and sin were read into all aspects of human behavior and punishment, and the fear of eternal hellfire was on almost everyone's mind consistently (this obsession explains the one of origins of the indulgence controversy initiated by Luther, et al.). Thus the devastation of the Black Death was commonly explained as God's punishment for human wrongdoing and transgression. Yet the destabilization described above is in many ways the central theme of *Decameron*. This destabilization becomes apparent also when Boccaccio's fictional account focuses upon (through the various tales told by the young people in the "brigata") the loosening of Christian sexual morality as a consequence of the plagues' devastation.

While *Decameron* is a fictional account of Late Medieval Europe's reaction to catastrophe, it is also crucial to note that works of art often act as mirrors, reflecting preexisting cultural patterns and tendencies (albeit sometimes lying just under the surface). Such works of art are not simply created "ex nihilo," completely without context. And the loosening of sexual morality has often been viewed as a basic feature or symptom of societies in breakdown.[13] The civilizationalist Pitirim Sorokin discussed the tendency for civilizations to become increasingly "sensate" as part of the process of gradual disintegration. So one might ask, with medieval Christendom in mind: Did the Black Death trigger, at least as reflected in *Decameron*, the fading of medieval Christendom's more "ideational" culture (in which life's fundamental frame of reference was religion and its transcendent God) and thereby herald the dawning of a more "sensate" culture, now focusing on forbidden sex and decadence?[14]

Decameron is famous for its tales of seduction, including those involving clergy, especially nuns. While perhaps the author was going for some "shock value" here, as background it should be noted that sex among clergy was not completely unknown at this time, and contrary to the modern stereotype that men desire sex more than females, during the Middle Ages women were viewed as more lustful than men. Thus *Decameron* has many instances of women overcome by lust, women with insatiable desires, women needing younger lovers because their older husbands can no longer satisfy them sexually, etc.[15] According to R. Hastings,[16] there is also in *Decameron* a new implicit value system being put forth by Boccaccio, which was certainly "not the general morality of his time," arguing that morality is "based on nature."[17] Hence attention is drawn to the quote by the character Dioneo (on the Tenth Story of the Second Day): "I shall show the . . . foolishness of those who, overestimating their natural powers . . . attempt to mold people in their own image, thus flying in the face of nature." According to Hastings, he then goes on to tell of an old man who cannot sexually satisfy his young wife, a recurrent theme in the *Decameron* . . . according to this . . . interpretation of the laws of nature, a young woman needs to be sexually satisfied and the old man, by failing to do so, quite justly loses her.[18]

We thus see in *Decameron* many instances where Christian morality seems to be conveniently discarded when it is found inconvenient and in conflict with more "natural" sexual desires. For example, one nun confesses to another her lust for a young man (in the story of the "deaf-mute" gardener) and the question is then asked "don't you know that we have promised our virginity to God?" This question is met with the interestingly pragmatic and somewhat jaded rationalization from the other nun: "how many promises do we make him every day which we can't keep?"[19] This example clearly reflects a break with the established Christian morality which dominated Europe during the Middle Ages. Moreover, no one could ever confuse the above emphasis on "nature" with any sort of natural law theology (e.g., that put forth by St. Thomas Aquinas) justifying Christian morality either.

What are we to make of this sudden and clear deviation from traditional Christian sexual morality in *Decameron*, a morality so dominant in medieval Europe, a culture long dominated by the values of religion? Is this apparent disintegration of traditional values in the text an almost nihilistic rejection of Christian morality? First, it should be noted that instances of premarital sex and adultery were much more common during the Middle Ages than many have supposed, and that despite very strong religious and cultural prohibitions, the temptations of the flesh were no less powerful then than they are now.[20] Moreover, even if "nature" is now touted by Boccaccio as a new moral value, this is not, strictly speaking, nihilism (defined as the absence of values altogether) but rather it is just the substitution of new (perhaps more permissive) values for old values. Or could the above serve merely as an extreme and desperate example of "carpe diem," indeed a rationalization for sexual license? After all, when bodies litter the streets at every turn, when the smell of death is everywhere, when your relatives and friends have all died horrible deaths in front of your very eyes, when your own chances of survival are slim to none, when none of the doctors have any idea what to do, when the priests themselves are all either dead or have abandoned their sick parishioners, perhaps only honest way to view the situation is to take the position that nothing makes any sense, there is no cosmic justice, nothing matters anymore, so why not take pleasure in this life while one still can? Tendencies toward decadent sexuality are further detailed by David Herlihy, who writes how "plague mortalities reminded survivors of their own fragile grasp on life, and prompted some of them to spend their remaining hours in revelry."[21] People seemed to desire a temporary victory over death,[22] however illusory, and Herlihy describes how people sacrilegiously danced, played trivial games or committed "unseemly acts" in cemeteries, "over the graves of the dead. Prostitutes solicited in cemeteries, and "fornicators and adulterers trysted among the graves."[23]

Given the context of total catastrophe and existential hopelessness, the impetus toward short-term pleasure must have been strong. This is especially interesting given the belief of most religions (including Christianity, cf. Saint Augustine) that this life is merely preparation for the much more important life to come, thus justifying delaying gratification in the present. We have seen how the element of hopelessness was evident in light of the impotence of both science (medicine) and religion (prayer) to stem the tide of death. How did this affect the prevailing value system?

Christoph Jedan writes:

> Boccaccio notes that . . . in this situation, religion proved ineffective: it did not prevent the outbreak, it did not protect the faithful and it could not prevent the complete disintegration of social structure." Boccaccio notes the widespread disillusion with religion e.g., by referring repeatedly to the inefficacy of prayer and devotion"[24]

> Regarding the widespread licentiousness (especially in the descriptions of the behavior of nuns) described in the tales told by the brigata, "religious values and religious experience . . . are depicted as a façade, concealing a uniform human nature in which desires that are repressed or denied by Christianity are the motivating force.[25]

Some critics might argue here that I've looked at this through too dark a lens and fundamentally misunderstood Boccaccio's point. By this view, *Decameron* is not nihilistic in any sort of serious philosophical sense, but is actually a more playful work that refreshingly pokes fun at the seriousness of medieval religious fundamentalism (e.g., Dante, etc.). *Decameron* takes a fresh look at human beings as they really are (often lustful, light-hearted, imperfect and pleasure seeking) rather than as they haughty, humorless, pious, and cerebral creatures that medieval Christianity seemingly would've liked them to be. Hence the tales told during the brigata, tales of infidelity, lust and adultery, are retold by Boccaccio in a light and almost playful manner. Like the Florentine Renaissance thinkers soon to come (e.g., Machiavelli) Boccaccio has a more human-centered, realistic and "this-worldly" approach to life, and has to some degree tried to leave behind the sterile, theocratic worldview of the recent past. This is the view, for example, of Francesco De Sanctis.[26] Moreover, according to De Sanctis, the emphasis on sensuality, almost ridiculing medieval piety[27] was already present and established in the Italian spirit (many think Italy always took it's religion with a few grains of realism and salt anyway, as opposed to the more dour Northern variants of Christianity). De Sanctis writes: "the book seemed to respond to something in people's souls which had been wanting to come out for a long time . . . "[28] it was, he says, "a time of transition." Yet, on the other hand, and admitting the truths in this incisive analysis, we must remember also that the Decameron was written against the backdrop of the Black Death, the horrors of which Boccaccio himself vividly describes in the Proem. Perhaps going through the horrors of the plague functioned as a catharsis for the Italian people—ironically not as part of a pattern of moral disintegration, but instead as part of the progress from crisis to renewal. Yet *Decameron* was nevertheless still a reaction to an epic crisis, and in such times of crisis, value systems are questioned and often rejected.

Reactions to catastrophe are complicated and many-faceted. Of course we know that most citizens of medieval Europe retained their religious beliefs in the wake of the plague and many might even have increased in the intensity of their religious belief, as which often happens during desperate times. Herlihy thus describes in detail "flamboyant movements of penance" such as the flagellants who "stripped to the waist and whipped themselves with knotted cords,"[29] scourging themselves in expiation for their own sins and those of society."[30] Religious explanation was still the overarching conceptual framework of the time, the basic prism or conceptual framework through which all human experience was inevitably filtered. And these religious impulses were similarly taken to extremes in these desperate times. On the other hand, Boccaccio's text, while certainly illustrating his own personal crisis of faith, perhaps also reflected a repressed undercurrent of a more radical sort of doubt beginning to simmer under the surface of medieval Christendom itself during this horrific time.

Works such as *Decameron* are not conceived or written in a vacuum, but often reflect larger crises on the civilizational level. Interestingly, Pitirim Sorokin uses *Decameron* as evidence of the complexity of the phenomenon of civilizational disintegration (that of medieval Christendom). Sorokin observed that often during this process there occurs a splitting between ideational and sensate tendencies.

He writes:

> the soul of the society in the transition will be split into the *Carpe Diem* on the one hand and on the other into ideational indifference and negative attitude towards all the sensory pleasures. Society itself will be increasingly divided into open, perfectly cynical sinners with their "eat, drink, and love, for tomorrow is uncertain" and into the ascetics and saints who will flee the sensory world into a kind of new refuge . . . such a split has uniformly occurred in small and great transitions and especially in the period of the great transitions from one culture to another. Boccaccio's *Decameron* with its hedonistic company, and the medieval flagellants, mystics and ascetics are the concrete examples of such a split in the transition of the fourteenth century.[31]

This "splitting" thus illustrates the complexity of the reactions to the Black Death (and catastrophes generally) and all likelihood the matter was complicated: so much so that all of these patterns in the realm of psychology and morality were perhaps occurring simultaneously.

APORIA IN THE LATER MIDDLE AGES

What does all this mean? The widespread, indiscriminate death caused by the plague called into question the most basic assumptions of Christian Europe and left it in a state of widespread spiritual aporia. Robert Gottfried writes: "People were traumatized. They lost faith in their own abilities, in the old values, and if not in God then in the traditional ways in which He had been propitiated. Europe was plunged in a moral crisis. The old order was collapsing and the new one was not yet in place."[32]

At the heart of the moral crisis was also a crisis of understanding and explanation—an epistemological crisis. What is an epistemological crisis? Alasdair MacIntyre describes this as "a problem about the rational induction of inferences from premises . . . to conclusions . . . that would enable us to make reasonably reliable predictions."[33] What one "took to be evidence pointing unambiguously in some one direction now turns out to have been equally susceptible of rival interpretations"[34] MacIntyre continues:

> it is not only that an individual may rely on the schemata which have hitherto informed all his interpretations . . . and find that he has been led into . . . error . . . so that for the first time the schemata are put in question . . . but the individual may come to recognize the possibility of systematically different possibilities of interpretation, or the existence of alternative . . . schemata which yield mutually incompatible accounts of what is going on.[35]

Or, perhaps more to the point of this premodern situation (as opposed to the "postmodern" one MacIntyre describes) the epistemological crisis was even more dire. The dominant religious interpretation (in which there exists a coherent moral order or overarching cosmic justice) had been called into question by the indiscriminate nature of the plague, yet there were no other rival explanations to confront, no larger set of alternative explanations among from which to choose. Moreover, there were no coherent or convincing scientific explanations at the time. One couldn't even find another alternative explanation, so there was basically no coherent understanding or explanation of the event at all.

THE SPECTRE OF COSMIC DISORDER

Perhaps in its starkest form, catastrophes like the Black Death raised (and still raise) the prospect of the complete lack of a cosmic order and any moral justice in the universe. This theme goes back much further than medieval times; it paradoxically goes back to the *Bible* itself. Consider the following quote from the Book of Job, as Job, by all accounts a righteous and religions man, loses inexplicably everything he has in the blink of an eye. In the midst of his inexplicable suffering, Job laments of God: "It is all one. He destroys wicked and blameless alike."[36]

This astonishing exclamation by Job helps us understand how it must have felt to experience not merely the wholesale nature of death through the plague but its indiscriminate nature as well. In fact, the quote suggests the entire cosmic order or system of divine justice that religion is built upon either has been somehow overthrown, or perhaps it never really existed in the first place. Perhaps the universe is simply amoral, and things just happen as they must, regardless of any human concerns, any discernible patterns of human behavior or any considerations of morality whatsoever.[37] Let's look at this more closely and how this is played out in the case of the Black Plague, specifically with regard to the indiscriminate nature of the plague's destruction.

One illustration of this indiscriminateness is that there apparently were higher rates of mortality among the clergy than among the general population, especially in England.[38] Clergy generally were among those who ministered to the sick and dying, so this might make sense, yet it on the other hand revealed to many the fundamental impotence of the clergy and the church in the face of this crisis. Moreover, in a great many cases, priests actually abandoned their sick flocks to save themselves. Although priests generally would have been thought to exist on a higher spiritual plane than the average citizen (though perhaps there has always been some cynicism on this score), the abandonment of their flocks by many clergymen caused many citizens to further question the moral integrity of the clergy, and the anger of the masses began to simmer.[39] Gottfried writes: "Many parish priests fled, leaving no one to offer services, deliver last rites and comfort the sick. Flight might have been intellectually explicable, but it was morally inexcusable."[40]

Pitirim Sorokin, in *Man and Society in Calamity*, devotes a chapter to how calamities affect the spiritual life of society. He cites A.M. Campbell's *The Black Death and Men of Learning* to furnish examples of how the demoralization of clergy was decried by a number of chroniclers during this time, for example, John of Reading's lament that many mendicant priests have "become unduly rich through confessions" and were now "seeking after earthly and carnal things," or the Archbishop of Canterbury's charge that the priests "now desire voluptuous pleasures to such an extent that souls are neglected and churches and chapels are empty."[41] This priestly abandonment of their flocks and general bad behavior paved the way for further skepticism of the masses toward the clergy itself, as phenomenon which in turn helped the eventual cause of Wycliff, Luther, and the Reformation. This is relevant further as the Reformation helped usher in, according to Hermann Broch, "the dissolution of values" characteristic of modernity, which it seems to me we still face today in postmodernity. Broch writes:

> In the Renaissance, that criminal and rebellious age, the unified Christian worldview was broken in two halves, one Catholic and one Protestant. With the falling asunder of the medieval organon, a process of dissolution destined to go on for five centuries was inaugurated and the seeds of the modern world were planted.[42]

In this sense, the Black Plague contributed to the Reformation, the decline of religious authority, and the general erosion of the values of medieval civilization as it had traditionally been known.

David Herlihy also discusses another important aspect of the widespread perception of cosmic disorder—how it impacted fundamental debates in late medieval philosophy. Herlihy notes how St. Thomas Aquinas' thought, perhaps the dominant philosophical system of this time, "argued that the universe possessed an underlying order, and that the human intellect could achieve at least a partial understanding of its structure."[43] Yet Herlihy reports how Aquinas' late medieval critics, the nominalists, "claimed that he was wrong on both counts."[44] According to this nominalist perspective, "the human intellect had not the power to penetrate the metaphysical structures of the universe. It could do no more than observe events as they flowed."[45] Again, of course, this viewpoint did not entail the wholesale rejection of religious belief, as the nominalists (like the other major schools of medieval European thought) were always thoroughgoing theists. Yet the nominalists still had to reconcile their religious beliefs with "the experience of plague—unpredictable in its appearance and ... unknowable in its origins, yet destructive in its impact."[46] Herlihy describes how the conception of God put forth by these late medieval critics of Aquinas involved an interesting view of divine omnipotence. This divine omnipotence "meant in the last analysis that there could be no fixed order. God could change what He wanted when He wanted. The nominalists looked on a universe dominated by arbitrary motions," and thus their criticism of Aquinas were "consonant with the disordered experience of late medieval life."[47]

BOCCACCIO'S LESSONS FOR MODERNITY

It might be interesting to now view in more depth this state of affairs from a more modern philosophical lens. The larger questions here are these: what happens to a civilization when it's most basic assumptions and values are ripped asunder? What were the symptoms of the values crisis engendered by the Black Death, and how did this crisis help usher in the eventual disintegration of "Christendom" and its world picture? And how did this values crisis reveal the problem of nihilism, perhaps the most important moral question facing humanity today?

Is *Decameron* in some important sense a nihilistic work? After all, Boccaccio's depiction of the Black Death with its indiscriminate destruction, chronicled the dissolution of a number of basic Christian values. Or is it rather (to paraphrase Patrizia McBride writing on modernity specifically through the writings of Robert Musil) that such crises with their revealing of the indiscriminate, relentless nature of death and suffering "merely provide the conditions" through we can somehow see that a coherent moral order "never really existed in the first place?"[48] And if the latter option is true, how can we deal with this? Nietzsche, the first thinker of modernity to deal comprehensive with the problem of nihilism, argues the problem of nihilism arises when "the problem of why receives no answer."[49] The questioner (in this case the survivor of catastrophe) experiences only a deafening cosmic silence. But Nietzsche seems somewhat unclear on some other key points here. He suggests at one point that nihilism arises when values devalue themselves and no longer hold.[50] But elsewhere he suggests that the problem is that human beings seek "meaning in events that is simply not in them,"[51] and then attempt to fabricate this meaning "solely out of psychological needs."[52] But exactly what are these psychological needs?

This is a complicated question, but basically we need the events in our lives *to make sense* in order to survive psychologically and spiritually in this world.[53] It is a basic human need to make sense of things. An unintelligible world is for many an unlivable one.

But what happens when events don't make sense, and we have no scientific, psychological, religious, or philosophical tools at our disposal to help us make sense out of the events? Survivors are then left bereft in the aftermath of catastrophe—without a guiding set of coherent and consistent principles or values, they are then at a loss to properly explain the events, integrate them, predict future events, and/or put the entire situation into a larger context. Long-standing values and cultural assumptions have proven themselves ineffective, but they have not yet been replaced with new ones. A spiritual void or aporia is thus what is revealed during moments of moral crisis, and as this aporia becomes more widespread and more pervasive in the collective consciousness of a civilization, it increasingly becomes a relevant factor in the process of this civilization's gradual disintegration—until which time a new moral paradigm is somehow eventually put in its place.

The lessons of *Decameron* are important for us to learn because the human need for a coherent guiding value system is still the central philosophical question of our postmodern age. After all, we currently are living at the dawn of the 21st century. What lessons can we apply from the devastation of the Black Death, an event that occurred in such a completely different time and place than our own today? Is it even possible to make intelligible comparative judgments, given the considerable foreignness of the world picture of medieval Christendom as compared with our own, postmodern era? I believe that human nature, if there is such a thing, probably doesn't change dramatically over different times and places. Given certain similar conditions, human beings feel (as they always have and always will) emotions like jealousy, lust, hopelessness, and joy, and they will act and react to stimuli and situations in similar, often predictable ways. Thus, I believe some important applications apply.

First, we are beginning to see the rise and spread of another plague or epidemic—the Ebola outbreak—which may be revisiting many of the issues we have already discussed above. A recent (May 9, 2015) *New York Times* article "Liberia Conquers Ebola, but Faces a Crisis of Faith" highlights some of these similar themes. The article describes how congregants of a Liberian church ceremoniously laid hands on an ailing parishioner, and soon thereafter, "the disease tore through the church, killing eight members, or about a tenth of the congregation."[54] The article reports that many of these otherwise religious people began to have "doubts in their minds about God" in large part because "Ebola's apparent randomness . . . took a toll. Scientists believe that some people have a greater resistance to Ebola, or even immunity. But to church members, the deaths of some, though not others, challenged their faith."[55]

Herlihy discusses similar reactions to the AIDS virus:

Many persons today do not believe what the experts relate about AIDS and its modes of transmission. They still want infected children taken from schools and contacts with the sick severely limited. We seem to witness here too a crisis of confidence in expert opinion, much like the one that occurred in the Middle Ages.[56]

Of course, some panic in the face of widespread epidemic will perhaps always be a part of human nature, as most of us fear death, and are still terrified by the fact that all the expertise and technology we currently possess simply cannot completely protect us and our loved ones in many such cases.[57]

Moreover, on the moral level, we who live in the postmodern West are actually experiencing a "void of ethics" right now. We still have yet to intellectually and spiritually process the catastrophic events of the 20th century—perhaps history's bloodiest century ever. After the horrors of the 20th century, what enduring value system can we now ascribe to in the postmodern West? We may have advanced technology today, but can this technology, or science generally, ever explain which values we should believe in, and why, in an age which featured two brutal world wars and culminated in Auschwitz—a scene of mass death almost incomprehensible in its scale and scope? Further, much postmodern philosophy has offered us nothing beyond various forms of skepticism and relativism.

Mark T. Mitchell writes:

> modernity has reached a dead end. The optimism in which the modern world was conceived and nurtured has been replaced by a thoroughgoing skepticism that denies the possibility of making meaningful truth claims, especially as those claims bear on morality and religion . . . From a certain vantage this situation might appear a stable solution to the . . . bloodletting that moral and religious truth claims spawned. Yet on another level such a position is simply intolerable, for it is inhuman. It is not possible to deny for long the very things for which human souls most yearn. If these sorts of claims are denied . . . they will invariably assert themselves in perverted and often violent ways.[58]

Perhaps the rise of (increasingly violent) religious fundamentalism we now are witnessing worldwide is an attempt by some to fill this void of truth and meaning. But it also seems that in many cases (ISIS, etc.), the fundamentalist cure may be worse than the disease. We in the West have actually been down this path many times before—consider also the bloody cycles of Reformation and Counterreformation, the wars of religion, mass killings of "heretics," witch burnings, and so on, that characterized the early modern period on the European continent, in light not only of the Protestant Reformation but also of the scientific revolution and other major upheavals of thought. During this time, the poet John Donne famously wrote of the anomie and spiritual dislocation experienced so acutely by thoughtful people when "a new philosophy calls all into doubt." This spiritual dilemma thus reveals to us another important pattern in history—that with regards to the question of values in times of crisis, the more things change, the more they remain the same.

NOTES

1. An earlier version of this chapter was published in *Comparative Civilizations Review* 73 (2015); the revised paper appears here with kind permission from the Journal Editor.

2. Carsten Meiner and Kristen Veel, eds., "Introduction," in *The Cultural Life of Catastrophes and Crises* (Berlin: DeGruyter, 2012).

3. Ibid.

4. Ibid. See also Elizabeth Kovach, "Locating the Quotidian in Catastrophes and Crises," review of Meiner and Veel, *Op. cit.*, in KULT_Online. *Review Journal for the Study of Culture* 38 (2014).

5. Ibid.

6. See Brown University Decameron web: www.brown.edu/Departments/Italian_Studies/dweb/plague/origins/spread.php.

7. See Giovanni Boccaccio, *Decameron*, 4. I will refer throughout to *The Decameron: Norton Critical Edition*, Mark Musa and Peter Bondanella, ed. and trans. (New York: Norton, 1977).

8. Ibid., 3.

9. Boccaccio, *Decameron* (Musa & Bondanella), 5. Readings of *Decameron* in terms of civilizational disintegration can be found (though with slightly different emphases) in some other sources, most notably Joseph Gibaldi, "The Decameron Cornice and the Responses to the Disintegration of Civilization," *Kentucky Romance Quarterly* 24 no. 3 (1977). Gibaldi's paper reads *Decameron* through the lens of Arnold Toynbee's *A Study of History*, and thereby illustrates Toynbee's importance to the study of catastrophe generally, and *Decameron* specifically, through Toynbee's argument that civilizations break down not so much because of external conditions but rather because of resulting tendencies toward internal spiritual dissolution. The impact of catastrophe on Toynbee's own life and work is also itself the subject of a later chapter by David Wilkinson in the present book.

10. Boccaccio, *Decameron* (Musa & Bondanella), 5.

11. Ibid., 8.

12. See Nancy Reale, "Boccaccio's *Decameron*: A Fictional Account of Grappling with Chaos," www.nyu.edu/projects/mediamosaic/literature/BoccaccioDecameron 7.

13. John Reilly, "The World after Modernity," *Comparative Civilizations Review* 49, no. 49 (2003): 120.

14. See Pitirim Sorokin, *The Crisis of Our Age* (Oxford: One World Publishing, 1992, original book published 1941). See also Pitirim Sorokin, *Man and Society in Calamity* (New York: Dutton, 1942). Regarding the connection of "sensate" cultures

and nihilism, see Palmer Talbutt, *Rough Dialectics: Sorokin's Philosophy of Value* (Leiden, NL: Brill/Rodopi, 1998).

15. Brown Decameron web: www.brown.edu/Departments/Italian_Studies/dweb/society/sexual-desire.php.

16. R. Hastings, *Nature and Reason in the Decameron* (Manchester: Manchester University Press, 1975), as found in "Nature and Morality" on the Brown University Decameron web: www.brown.edu/Departments?Italian_Studies/dweb/themes_motifs/amore/nature.php.

17. Ibid.

18. Ibid.

19. Boccaccio, *Decameron* (Musa & Bondanella), 66.

20. Brown University Decameron web: www.brown.edu/Departments?Italian_Studies/dweb/society/sex/fornication-adultery.php.

21. David Herlihy, *The Black Death and the Transformation of the West*, ed. S. Kohn, Jr. (Cambridge, MA: Harvard University Press, 1997), 64.

22. Ibid.

23. Ibid. Herlihy cites as the source for this: Jacques Chiffoleau, "La Compabilite de l'au-dela: Les Hommes, La Mort et la Religion dans la Region d'Avignon a la fin du Moyen Age" (Rome: Ecole Francaise, 1980).

24. Christoph Jedan, "Overcoming the Divide between Religious and Secular Values," Introductory Essay in *Constellations of Value: European Perspectives on the Intersection of Religion, Politics and Society*, ed. C. Jedan (Munich: Verlag, 2013), 5.

25. Ibid.

26. See Francesco De Sanctis, "Boccaccio and the Human Comedy," in *The Decameron: Norton Critical Edition*, ed. and trans. Mark Musa and Peter Bondanella (New York: Norton, 1977).

27. Ibid., 216.

28. Ibid., 217.

29. Herlihy, *Black Death*, 68.

30. Ibid., 67.

31. Sorokin, *Crisis of Our Age*, 301–02.

32. Robert S. Gottfried, *The Black Death: Natural and Human Disaster in Medieval Europe* (New York: Free Press, 1983), 103.

33. Alasdair MacIntyre, "Epistemological Crises, Dramatic Narrative and the Philosophy of Science," in *Why Narrative? Readings in Narrative Theology*, ed. Stanley Hauerwas and L. Gregory Jones (Eugene, OR: Wipf & Stock, 1997), 138.

34. MacIntyre, "Epistemological Crises…," 139.

35. Ibid.

36. *Oxford Study Bible*, Job 9–22.

37. See David J. Rosner, "Self-Deception and Cosmic Disorder in the Biblical Book of Job," *Cosmos & History* 11, no. 1 (2015): 285–98.

38. Gottfried, *The Black Death*, 62.

39. This anger was also taken out elsewhere. The Jews of Europe, traditional scapegoats of Christendom, were predictably accused of poisoning the wells and spreading the plague, and were often massacred en masse throughout this time.

40. Gottfried, *The Black Death*, 84.

41. A. M. Campbell, *The Black Death and Men of Learning* (New York: Columbia University Press, 1931), as cited in Sorokin, *Man and Society*, 175.

42. Hermann Broch, "The Dissolution of Values," in *The Sleepwalkers* (London: Quartet, 1986), 480.

43. Herlihy, *Black Death*, 72.

44. Ibid.

45. Ibid.

46. Ibid., 72–73.

47. Ibid., 73.

48. See Patrizia McBride, *The Void of Ethics* (Evanston, IL: Northwestern University Press, 2006), 12.

49. Friedrich Nietzsche, *Will to Power*, trans. Walter Kaufmann and R. J. Hollingdale, ed. Walter Kaufmann (New York: Vintage/Random House, 1968), 9.

50. Ibid.

51. Ibid., 12.

52. Ibid., 13.

53. See also Peter Berger, *The Sacred Canopy* (New York: Image/Doubleday, 1967).

54. Norimitsu Onishi, "Liberia Conquers Ebola but Faces a Crisis of Faith," *New York Times*, May 9, 2015.

55. Ibid.

56. Herlihy, *Black Death*, 69.

57. Certainly our own age, even with its advanced science and technology, remains vulnerable to scenes of disaster and catastrophe. In fact, a horrific disaster of another sort (a massive earthquake) recently ravaged the country of Nepal, with the death count exceeding 6200 people. Scientists apparently had been expecting a massive earthquake in this s part of the world for some time. But given the current limits of seismological science, they simply could not predict exactly when such an event would occur, and thus authorities could not realistically order mass preemptive evacuations. Moreover, because such events are caused by shifts of tectonic plates deep inside the Earth, there apparently really wasn't much anyone could've done about it anyway, short of simply abandoning their country (an ancient and fabled land with a rich spiritual heritage) permanently. Living in such an area is more or less a gamble, one which 5000 people (and countless other wounded and traumatized survivors) simply lost. Exactly how the Nepalese people attempt to process the horror of the event remains to be seen.

58. Mark T. Mitchell, "Polanyi, MacIntyre and the Role of Tradition," *Humanitas* xix, no. 1–2 (2006). www.nhinet.org/mitchell19-1.pdf.

BIBLIOGRAPHY

Berger, Peter. *The Sacred Canopy*. New York: Image/Doubleday, 1967.

Boccaccio, Giovanni. *Decameron: Norton Critical Edition.* Edited and translated by Mark Musa and Peter Bondanella. New York: Norton, 1977.

Broch, Hermann. *The Sleepwalkers.* London: Quartet, 1986.

Brown Univ. Decameron web: www.brown.edu/Departments/Italian_Studies/dweb/index.php.

De Sanctis, Francesco. "Boccaccio and the Human Comedy." In *The Decameron*, edited and translated by Mark Musa & Peter Bondanella. New York: Norton, 1977.

Gibaldi, Joseph. "The Decameron Cornice and the Responses to the Disintegration of Civilization." *Kentucky Romance Quarterly* 24, no. 3 (1977).

Gottfried, Robert. *The Black Death: Natural and Human Disaster in Medieval Europe.* New York: Free Press, 1983.

Hastings, R. *Nature and Reason in the Decameron.* Manchester: Manchester University Press, 1975.

Herlihy, David. *The Black Death and the Transformation of the West.* Cambridge, MA: Harvard University Press, 1997.

Jedan, Christoph, editor. *Constellations of Value: European Perspectives on the Intersection of Religion, Politics and Society.* Berlin: Verlag, 2013.

Kovatch, Elizabeth. "Locating the Quotidian in Catastrophes and Crises." Review of Meiner & Veel, *The Cultural Life of Catastrophes and Crises.* KULT–online. *Review Journal for the Study of Culture* 38 (2014).

MacIntyre, Alistair. "Epistemological Crises, Dramatic Narrative and the Philosophy of Science." In *Why Narrative? Readings in Narrative Theology*, edited by S. Hauerwas and L. G. Jones. Eugene OR: Wipf and Stock, 1997.

McBride, Patrizia. *The Void of Ethics.* Evanston, IL: Northwestern University Press, 2006.

Meiner, Carsten and Kristin Veel, editors. *The Cultural Life of Catastrophes and Crises.* Berlin: DeGruyter, 2012.

Mitchell, Mark T. "Polanyi, MacIntyre and the Role of Tradition." *Humanitas* xix, no. 1–2 (2006). www.nhinet.org/mitchell19-1.pdf.

Nietzsche, Friedrich. *Will to Power.* Translated by Walter Kaufmann and R. J. Hollingdale. Edited by Walter Kaufmann. New York: Vintage/Random House, 1968.

Onishi, Norimitsu. "Liberia Conquers Ebola, but Faces a Crisis of Faith." *New York Times*, May 9, 2015.

Oxford Study Bible. Oxford: Oxford University Press, 1992.

Reale, Nancy. "Boccaccio's *Decameron*: A Fictional Account of Grappling with Chaos." www.nyu.edu/projects/mediamosaic/literature/BoccaccioDecameron.

Reilly, John. "The World after Modernity." *Comparative Civilizations Review* 49, no. 49 (2003): 120–31.

Rosner, David J. "Self-Deception and Cosmic Disorder in the Biblical Book of Job." *Cosmos and History* 11, no. 1 (2015): 285–98.

Sorokin, Pitirim. *The Crisis of Our Age.* Oxford: One World Publishing, 1992. Original book published 1941.

Sorokin, Pitirim. *Man and Society in Calamity.* New York: Dutton, 1942.

Talbutt, Palmer. *Rough Dialectics: Sorokin's Philosophy of Value.* Leiden, NL: Brill/Rodopi, 1998.

Chapter 7

The Search for Stability in Chaotic Times

Niccolo Machiavelli

Diana Prokofyeva

This chapter explores Machiavelli's writings in the context of the volatile historical environment of the 15th- to 16th-century Europe. Considering history as a dialectical process, we will consider some contemporary analogies and comparisons to these chaotic times.

Italy during this period was the epicenter of the Renaissance and was the most culturally developed country in Europe. But the political situation in Italy at the time was violent and uncertain. Machiavelli lived during the wars of conquest between the Italian city-states. These city-states were in constant conflict with each other, leaving Italy hopelessly fragmented. Many of the rulers were selfishly pursuing material enrichment while others pursued territorial domination. In such an environment, no negotiations about Italian unity could realistically amount to anything. The spirit of competition, conflict, and private interests stood above national health and prosperity. Italy as a nation was badly weakened by these internal struggles and its lands then became of special interest for foreign countries such as France and Spain. As a result, Italy was invaded by these foreign powers on numerous occasions, and even during moments of respite, the threat of invasion from these foreign powers was ever looming like a dark cloud.

If we postulate two main goals of the state and the government in particular, they would be first the safety and security of citizens through foreign policy, and second, the possibility for citizens to realize their economic and human potential. Without the first component, it is practically impossible to bring to life the second one. At the same time, meaningful national development is impossible without the internal social processes of generational succession, economic health, and business continuity.

The lack of continuity and stability at this time resulted in the actual absence of a united Italian State; this constituted a state of a catastrophe—a state in danger of disappearance. We may apply here Arnold J. Toynbee's conception of "challenge and response," a problematic situation to be resolved.[1] Not only did internal strife constitute an existential threat to Italy, but the possibility of foreign military invasion was also an external threat. Fertile lands with a mild climate and people with a rich and original culture—all these were attractive to foreign rulers ready to become occupiers. The constant fighting among Italian city-states made them easy targets for invasions by foreign countries such as France and Spain. What could be more catastrophic for the country than to jeopardize its further existence?

If a society continuously engaged in such political distractions and protracted internal wars, it would soon cease to develop as a nation and as a unique culture. Being a patriot as well as a theoretician, Machiavelli saw the danger of the loss of the Italian territories. Under these circumstances, his writings emphasized the absolute necessity of strong control under a persevering ruler. Such a leader should not be interested in satisfying personal interests and obtaining pleasures. Rather the ruler should be focused on the interest of the State, and the best qualities to provide this characteristic are personal vanity and bravery. Accordingly, Machiavelli's *The Prince* is fundamentally involved in politics, which he considered the primary means of avoiding the existential catastrophe of losing the country and its identity. Thus, Machiavelli doesn't differentiate between political ambitions and personal motivations. They should complement one another in achieving the goal of political power. Reflecting on this, Machiavelli came to the conclusion that honorable behavior is useless here. Besides ambition, struggling for power supposes bravery, strength, and a dose of cunning and egoism. This is why Machiavelli, in his search for stability as a stronghold of Italian state, advocates such radical means to achieve it.

Political instability constitutes a catastrophic state of affairs on a number of levels and it is worth discussing them here. First, on the micro level, there is the considerable psychological toll taken on individuals living in environments of political or economic instability. People living under such conditions may likely experience heightened anxiety, as everyday life becomes increasingly unpredictable and precarious. In such an environment, self-interested behavior may proliferate, as people may feel compelled to take what they can now for themselves, because, even more than usual, no one knows what tomorrow will bring. Instability strengthens the instinct of self-preservation, which frightened people will necessarily pursue, if necessary without regard for conventional morality or social norms. Note how these environmental factors can be seen as relevant to Machiavelli's more general characterization of human nature. His negative view of human nature certainly has some universal truth to it and this is partly why *The Prince* is a classic. Yet Machiavelli also paints human nature with a very broad brush—not everyone is selfish and fickle, and even people who are, are not this way all the time. So, while Machiavelli's characterization of human nature contains aspects of universality, it was also likely influenced by the profound and frightening volatility of his own particular environment, and reveals the effects such instability can have on human psychology and behavior. Second, on a macro level, Machiavelli knew that political instability constitutes a catastrophe for the state generally, as it quickly can become an existential threat to the state's basic economic and cultural future. If people are constantly preoccupied with problems of survival under violent and unpredictable war conditions, and find themselves primarily concerned with defending their territories from foreign invasions, they won't have the time or energy to pursue their normal activities. During peacetime, citizens are busy with daily work, and they work not only for their own survival and good, but also toward the growing power and glory of their nation, even without their realizing it. If such production and normal functioning ceases, the healthy development of the state stops as well. It will not be able to grow in terms of economy and culture. It would not be able to move forward and fulfill its potential in any meaningful sense. And more severe wars may actually push a society backward in its development, destroying its economic reserves as well as its cultural heritage. Machiavelli knew that a strong state that could ensure the safety of its citizens was necessary. People would respect and fear its sovereign, who would be able to keep the state stable and prosperous. There would be no attempts by foreign powers to invade his territory, and the country will be able to develop and increase its material and spiritual wealth.

Machiavelli is one of Europe's most misunderstood thinkers. Although many have traditionally considered him an immoral thinker who presumed the worst in human nature and advocated ruthlessness in politics, he was actually an Italian patriot because he took this longer view. Machiavelli was looking for a bulwark, something solid and indestructible in his volatile, turbulent times. This bulwark should specify the path like a lighthouse in a stormy sea. When everything around is changing rapidly, with nothing solid to rely on, it is necessary to find steady support in order to understand exactly how to proceed. A powerful independent state became this stronghold, and it was up to the ruler to set the right course for its continuous strengthening and growth. In this sense Machiavelli is an effective example of a thinker whose main goal was the search for stability in times of upheaval and rapid change.

Machiavelli was born in 1469 in Florence, where he grew up and received a solid education, including knowledge of the classics of Latin and Italian literature. In his letter of March 9, 1498, to the Florentine ambassador in Rome, Ricciardo Becchi, we read that he had been interested in politics since his youth. During that period he had already started to analyze the changes that were in process around him and began to draw his own conclusions.[2]

Machiavelli's beginning as a political thinker also took place in a period of competition of two old dynasties—Medici and Pazzi. The Medici family was one of the most powerful families in European history. From early childhood Lorenzo de'Medici was groomed for a political career. He was talented, colorful, and decisive—driven by the goals of holding the reins of government. He also had the support of the citizens and nobility of Milan and Florence. But society was not homogeneous regarding its political views. There were thus occasional anti-Medicean conspiracies, so it was increasingly important for Medici to attract the backing of citizens and hold it.

John Najemi discusses two sociopolitical reasons for these conspiracies, which had their roots in the Volterra massacre and the Pazzi conspiracy. The first reason was that Lorenzo de' Medici sought to elevate his own family and concentrate power in their hands only. He could not stand any competition. The second was that in bringing some individuals and families closer to the Medici, he inevitably pushed away others.[3] Such problems in Volterra were also connected with economic issues. There was monopolistic control over the markets by the Medici and their allies. Lorenzo harshly reacted to threats to his authority. All outbreaks of violence were immediately met with greater levels of violence.

Machiavelli was also the contemporary of "the Pazzi conspiracy" of April 26, 1478. The Italian clan of Pazzi was older than the Medici. These two ancient powerful families were struggling for influence in various Italian cities, and at the papal court. It was a competition between two political forces that may be considered political elites. This brought further instability into the Italian social reality. The economic situation was also problematic. Power struggles are often accompanied by economic instability and turbulence. Capital was concentrated in the hands of the Pazzi family and Pope Sextus IV. Lorenzo de Medici made a number of political moves to benefit himself, to the detriment of the Pazzi. This gave the Pazzi the impetus to act against the Medici. The opinion of the city's population was divided—there was some dissatisfaction with the regime because Lorenzo de Medici was considered a harsh ruler who ignored the values of the old Republican liberty. The representatives of the Pazzi planned a conspiracy against the head of the Florentine republic, Lorenzo de'Medici, and his brother Giuliano de'Medici. Pazzi declared Lorenzo a tyrant and demanded the restoration of the Florentine republic's former liberties. The conspirators believed Francesco Pazzi would take the place of Lorenzo the Magnificent. Another conspirator was Pope Sextus IV's nephew, Girolamo Riario.[4] Pazzi wasn't alone in this initiative to overthrow the Medici. The plot was supported by large banking houses, and also by Pope Sextus IV, who supported his relatives and promoted them to high Church positions.[5] Machiavelli suggested the cause of the conspiracy was that property was taken from Pazzi by orders of the Medici. Everything happened quickly, accompanied by unimaginable acts of violence—behavior often used as an instrument of influence in troubled political circumstances. But the conspiracy failed, and despite the fact that Giuliano was killed, Lorenzo escaped. With the other unsuccessful conspirators—it was necessary to track them down and punish them. As Machiavelli would later write in "The Prince," the city's citizens did not support the conspirators. It is easier for people to be on the side of winners—those who stay alive. People feel sympathy for the victims of a conspiracy and hostility toward the conspirators. As long as the regime was not onerous for the people, they did not feel sufficient hatred for Lorenzo to raise a rebellion and maintain the Pazzi. Victory was on the side of those who acted quickly and decisively. Lorenzo's forceful reaction was absolutely necessary in this critical situation. It was a bright example of strengthening his influence and power in order to procure stability. The whole affair made a huge impression on Machiavelli.

All the conflicts and contradictions of Machiavelli's time were described in his *History of Florence*. Machiavelli analyzed the bitter struggle for land and power between the influential Italian families, and its role in the existing political turbulence and uncertainty. The institution of the family had always been the most respected in Italy (this is what is usually meant by "traditional" or "conservative values"), and the competitive spirit among families became a fierce struggle for influence and wealth. The Church also possessed considerable influence, and since Rome was the center of papal authority, it could be considered another political elite. Rome had not only religious authority; it also possessed much land and wealth, and was not going to cease its efforts to preserve and increase them. The illusion of the Church existing only within the religious sphere gradually started to reveal itself. The Pope could make his own army with the purpose of increasing wealth and conquering more territories. Many of the Renaissance popes were notoriously corrupt, with large sums of money and luxurious hunting villas at their disposal, many of them secretly fathered illegitimate children, etc. Machiavelli saw that clergymen often acted in their own secular interests; thus his attitude toward the Church was critical. Power and authority interested the Churchmen no less than secular leaders. Having been able to acquire some lands due to the strengthening of his secular power, the Pope (Julius II), however, failed to hold them and lead Italy to prosperity. In general, Machiavelli was not against religion. But he recognized it as a subtle and effective tool of social control. Since people don't always know what is (and is not) in their own interest, Machiavelli argued that rulers could use religion to explain and consolidate certain laws—then the laws would be unquestioningly accepted by the people because of the perceived gravitas of religious edicts. In addition, the Church gives people absolute moral norms on which they rely. No matter whether they are driven by the desire for piety or by fear of punishment (whether earthly or in the afterlife), more pious, humble citizens are the result. Watching the actions of the Church of Rome, Machiavelli notes that Italy as a nation failed to become whole in part due to them. The Roman Church was not strong enough for the centralization of power, but was not willing to give up its acquisition of territories and material ambition.

Despite such political instability, the economic situation in Italy was more prosperous than in other lands. Northern Italy was the place where the first capitalist model of relations was born. And of course, the economic recovery contributed to the general cultural upsurge as well. This economic development supported the spread of ideas and arts patronage, resulting in an unsurpassed flowering of creativity and innovation. It thus encouraged the general trend toward humanism and the glorification of man as a creature with great potential.

Machiavelli's theory of statecraft was unique. We will not find in Machiavelli any romantic idealized speeches that extol the glory of humanity. There is no model of an ideal state to create a blueprint for a perfect society, as in More's *Utopia* or Plato's *Republic*. He considered such utopian works useless and impossible to implement. He actually believed them to be harmful because they give false hope. Idealists often do not last long in this world because their ideals simply do not correspond to the harsh reality of human nature: "How we live is so different from how we ought to live that he who studies what ought to be done rather than what is done will learn the way to his downfall rather than to his preservation."[6]

Society will never be able to achieve the ideal static condition. There is no sense in focusing attention on what will never happen, such as we see in the ideal states conceived by thinkers such as Plato and Thomas More. In fact, the violent fate of Thomas More, who died in the Tower of London as a martyr for his Catholic beliefs, underscores the truth of Machiavelli's words.

Machiavelli's aim was to show the reality of the situation in Italy, to analyze it with clear vision and to indicate what must be done. Instead of ethereal dreams of universal happiness and ideal political systems, Machiavelli provides an analysis of historical events and its consequences, an analysis of his contemporary situation, and a realistic account of human nature. He considered it is better to concentrate on the fact that the state needs to become stronger here and now.

To write meaningfully about Renaissance Florence, it was important for Machiavelli to study history and learn from it. As a statesman, diplomat, and scholar of classical history, Machiavelli had an abundance of data at his command, which he used to develop his political theory. He admired ancient Rome and its history, and always kept it in mind while formulating his doctrines.

But although Machiavelli studied history as a natural process, he knew that the essence of our world has always remained unchanged—there always has been good and evil, right and wrong. In Machiavelli's view, human beings act according to "human nature." Human nature doesn't change from place to place or from time to time. Human nature was dominated by the instinct of self-preservation, but at the same time there exists some greed, envy, and so on. By no means does Machiavelli justify or admire such things, rather the opposite. He just acknowledges the obvious fact. He writes: "Of mankind we may say in general they are fickle, hypocritical, and greedy of gain."[7]

Many were shocked at this stark, unflattering portrayal. But Machiavelli does not neglect positive human qualities such as courage, intelligence, and valor. To his mind good and evil are present in every human being from birth. And they usually go together. He merely affirms that positive qualities are manifested much more rarely than negative ones.

The desire to possess neighboring lands or wealth leads to strife and wars. For example, some states become stronger and more powerful, and some become slack. A strong state will give people political stability and the opportunity to live and to work without having to constantly fight for their very survival and worry about outside attacks. Laws should provide security and order. Hence Machiavelli's idea of laws: "All those who have written upon civil institutions demonstrate (and history is full of examples to support them) that whoever desires to found a state and give it laws, must start with assuming that all men are bad and ever ready to display their vicious nature, whenever they may find occasion for it. If their evil disposition remains concealed for a time, it must be attributed to some unknown reason; and we must assume that it lacked occasion to show itself; but time, which has been said to be the father of all truth, does not fail to bring it to light".[8] Sometimes traditions and customs are sufficient to compel citizens to act in a civilized way, but at other times it is necessary to enact laws to restrain people. However, this does not necessarily deny citizen's freedoms, which can be used to protect their own property and dignity. If citizens are thus assured, secure, and satisfied in this manner, then they will not rebel against the governor.

We can draw an interesting parallel between these aspirations and the situation in modern states, where the main political goals are achieving internal strength and stability, while exerting a growing international influence. Most of the modern president's speeches and actions are targeted toward generating citizen's patriotism and overall positive popular sentiment. We may consider this an extension of Machiavelli's instructions. We are actually now faced with a situation in which the political alienation and powerlessness of citizens has degenerated into a phenomenon of a cult of personality or political fetishism, and in which all content has been replaced by form. Some representatives of power seem to be charismatic and confident, but in reality this is mostly public relations. For Machiavelli, appearance is more important than reality if it helps establish a unified state.

What exactly is the relation between an actual political figure and his/her appearance/image? Machiavelli famously wrote: "Everyone sees what you appear to be, few experience what you really are."[9] This issue, while always relevant to politics, has become even more important today in our image-based, technology-driven culture. Perhap political figures often don't wield real power anymore, but exist, like the image of the Wizard of Oz projected on the screen in the Emerald City, as the creation of "the man behind the curtain." According to the postmodernist thinker Jean Baudrillard, contemporary society has become saturated with screen-based images, sound-bytes, tweets, and so on, to the degree that we have all but forgotten about the original reality that preceded them. "Signs of the real have substituted and replaced the real"[10] as "reality itself has begun merely to imitate the image or appearance, which now precedes and determines the real world."[11]

A number of phenomena manifest themselves here. First, people can't effectively tell the difference between appearance and reality. Moreover, they often prefer image to reality because it lulls them into a false sense of security. Further, appearance and reality have blurred into each other. Ultimately, what is currently happening is that the image has actually replaced the reality in all relevant respects so that the reality by this time has simply faded into oblivion. This emphasis on appearance versus reality has become even more pronounced today than it was during Machiavelli's time.

Because of the primacy of appearance over reality, especially in the political arena, Machiavelli puts the sovereign's personality into the forefront. This no-nonsense politician is like a competent theater director, who can direct the play he needs, using appropriate manipulations. The sovereign must conduct policy by thinking several moves ahead. Of course, the governor cannot do everything alone. It is important to put a team together correctly. The sovereign himself chooses his close associates. The people in his circle must be completely loyal to him. Policy thus must resemble a clear, well-thought-out game of chess. The sovereign must be able to assess situations astutely. This means that in one time period, according to the circumstances, it might be better to operate openly and boldly, while in other circumstances to be more secretive and careful. Recognizing the existence of fate and circumstances, Machiavelli appeals to the leader to analyze these shrewdly and act in the most profitable way. It is simply a matter of pure pragmatics—not "what should be," but rather a matter of "what works," given the particular circumstances. However, he is not advocating any sort of manipulative behavior for its own sake—the goal is a larger one—to lay a blueprint specifying how to achieve and retain power for the overarching goal of securing a powerful unified Italy.

Machiavelli's political philosophy was conceived as a science. He was not interested in discussing a utopian project or an ideal State, but rather a state based on practical and realistic principles. In these respects his image of an ideal sovereign was copied from the example of Cesare Borgia. For Machiavelli, he was the model of intelligence, shrewdness, and bravery, the greatest politician of his time. Machiavelli gives many examples of his actions based on qualities that led to positive results—the all-important perspective of securing and keeping political power in turbulent times. Machiavelli was the ambassador of the Florentine Republic and in that capacity he spent much time with Borgia at Imola. He was instructed to negotiate with Cesare, who was a commander leading a large military force. There he entered into polemics with Valentino (by which name Cesare Borgia was also known). In addition, he listened, watched, and drew his conclusions.

Machiavelli has often been criticized for advocating immorality, duplicity, and so on, in the political arena. In this connection, the following passage is often referenced:

> Any man who tries to be good all the time is bound to come to ruin among the great number who are not good. Hence a prince who wants to keep his authority must learn how not to be good, and use that knowledge, or refrain from using it, as necessity requires.[12]

Machiavelli's advice was actually neither "moral" nor "immoral" but rather "amoral"—it was simply pragmatic "means to ends" reasoning. But he believed the ends were noble and therefore justified the means. The ends did not involve the holding of power for its own sake or for self-aggrandizement, but rather for the sake of a powerful unified Italy. Without a strong country, the chaos that Machiavelli saw all around him would be perpetuated indefinitely.

It was Borgia who wanted to unite the scattered Italian lands and rule over them. Machiavelli praises the political foresight of Cesare Borgia. He perceives Valentino's cruelty as a benefit, since with such cruelty he was able to subjugate and bring order to the Romagna. Cruelty instills fear, especially if it is the cruelty of a ruler. With harsh measures and reprisals, he shows what he is capable of in cases of disobedience and betrayal. To inspire fear without inspiring hatred is a difficult balancing act, but it is the art of an effective sovereign, who depends only on himself.[13] As an example, consider the public execution of Valentino's companion and the governor of Romagna—Ramiro de Lorca.[14] De Lorca was caught acting with undue cruelty toward his subjects and stealing grain for his population and the army. Borgia also suspected him of conspiring with his enemies. When the governor was arrested and thrown into a fortress, all those who considered themselves unjustly offended by de Lorca were allowed to submit complaints about him. As a result, after the trial the governor's head was planted on a spear and installed in the market square next to his body. It was a demonstrative punishment for a person who failed Borgia's trust. This was a lesson for his enemies and his supporters alike. In fact, the citizens were happy with this punishment of their Governor. For Machiavelli, hatred and contempt may be caused by an encroachment on the property or honor of citizens, and thus the sovereign should definitely avoid these methods. If he complies with these rules, his own vices may go unnoticed. Moreover, the image of the sovereign should be pleasing to ordinary people. Machiavelli believes that people are often captives of deception and self-deception. Since appearances are more important than reality in the world of politics, the sovereign should take care to maintain this deception as needed.

The Prince was written as a handbook of advice for Lorenzo de Medici—a practical treatise on statecraft. The proper image of the sovereign is the one that is respected (and to some degree feared) by both subjects and enemies. At the time Machiavelli was in disfavor for alleged involvement in a plot against the Medici and was exiled from Florence. This exile was a very bitter pill for him to swallow. Nevertheless, he hoped to return to politics and to approach the ruler for a position. He openly addressed Lorenzo the Magnificent with the fact that he could become an outstanding leader for Italy. This could happen if he would listen to the advice given in the treatise, and if he would take for his examples the brightest commanders of the past. In *The Prince* we read of the art of government in different political and social conditions, and those that can interfere with the ruler's ability to seize power and build a strong state. According to Machiavelli, theory and practice are dialectically interconnected.

Writers have argued that Machiavelli justifies and even glorifies humanity's lowest instincts and intentions. But we need to remember the serious political instability characterizing the Italian lands at that time. Machiavelli was attempting to provide a blueprint for a resourceful leader to unify Italy and to prevent invasions by foreign powers. A strong ruler should know not only how to win political power but also how to maintain it when it is under threat. To do this he should be calculating and distrustful if necessary, because he may face acts of treason and disloyalty, mostly from those closest to him. It is thus important for "the ruler to be as cunning as a fox to escape traps and enemies and to be as brave as a lion to earn respect."[15] The Prince need not conform to the hopes and aspirations of the people. It is not necessary for him to always fulfill his promises. The main objective is to project an image that corresponds with people's hopes. The purpose of the Sovereign is to guarantee a strong state. Thus, during war and other desperate times it is acceptable to implement and stratagems considered reprehensible in everyday life if they help him reach this end.

In no case does Machiavelli justify these vices in and of themselves. He is not indifferent to or unaware of the concepts of "good" and "evil." However, real life is far from its idealized image. We have to face human frailties and imperfections as they are, in their various manifestations. Theory is tested for validity only in practice.

According to Machiavelli, a person who lives only by the rules of goodness and morality is doomed to death, because most people around him are living under the influence of vices, passions, and selfish ambitions.[16] Realizing that the political stage is a completely different sphere, Machiavelli offers some allowances to the people acting within it. Both vices and virtues are more visible in powerful people; they are more obviously public than in others. But human nature itself does not change, and The Prince must know it's fundamental laws. People are never satisfied with what they have. A person may be happy with something for a short while, but then gets accustomed to it and no longer feels satisfied. Something else now becomes the object of his desire. People are short-sighted and are not used to thinking several moves ahead. People do not think about the consequences of their actions, do not learn from life's examples or even heed simple conventional wisdom.

Since the governor's main purpose is to retain power, he should understand which flaws prevent him from doing so and remove them. Moreover, there are vices that could help retain power and ensure his safety. In the end "vices" and "virtues" don't really matter in and of themselves—the only relevant issue for Machiavelli's vision of statecraft is which tactics will help the prince keep power and maintain stability.

Power assumes great responsibility, and Machiavelli is well aware of it. But if a leader takes responsibility and assumes power for the sake of strengthening the state and the people, it is permissible to achieve this by duplicitous ends if necessary. Consider, for example, the concept of honor. The sovereign can break his word if keeping it turns out contrary to his own interests. If the sovereign cannot do this as a matter of moral principle, someone might overtake him.

Machiavelli also defines cruelty as an ugly means of establishing and maintaining power. Its only justification might be personal safety and self-defense. The Emperor may decide to use it when he sees that nothing else will work except savage reprisal against his enemies. But such cruelty should not be excessive, or go beyond what is necessary to achieve the limited goals it needs to accomplish. It should not be used at all when the royal power is out of danger. The Sovereign should not be cruel to his subjects simply to keep them in a state of fear. Sooner or later, a ruler's cruelty will try the patience of his subjects, and he will be hated and soon overthrown.

The most revolutionary aspect of *The Prince* lies not in what is discussed, but in what is ignored. Machiavelli divides morality and politics, but this division is not his invention. In his view, he just states the facts and draws moral lessons from them. Before Machiavelli, all political theoreticians concentrated on the aim of the state. Power was considered merely as a means of attaining justice, welfare, or freedom. But Machiavelli separates this power from any discussion of morality. The state is now an autonomous system of values, and it is independent from other sources.

Machiavelli discusses how people behave in actuality, not how they should behave. We may consider his work as a reflection of the harsh realities of political life. Machiavelli believed that his political philosophy was the cold, hard truth. Machiavelli searched for the "strong-arm" that could finally unite the disparate lands of Italy and protect the nation from foreign threats. For this reason, his works should be perceived in the context of the catastrophic and volatile time in which they were created. But this is not all. The pronouncements that seem harsh to us now were necessary for political survival in early 16th-century Italy. And if we look closely, we may see that they are just as necessary for political survival today, all across the world, here and now.

NOTES

1. Arnold J. Toynbee, *A Study of History* (Moscow: Progress, 1991), 140–41.

2. Niccolo Machiavelli, *The Letters of Machiavelli*, accessed December 19, 2017, http://drevlit.ru/texts/m/makkiavelli_10pisem.php#11.

3. John M. Najemi, *History of Florence, 1200–1575* (Sussex, UK: Wiley, 2006), 347–48.

4. Christopher Hibbert describes the plot against the Medici in his book *The Rise and Fall of the House of Medici* (New York: Penguin, 1980).

5. Jan Wierusz Kowalski, *The Pope and the Papacy* (Moscow: Izdat. Political Literature. 1991) accessed December 19, 2017, http://bookre.org/reader?file=131929.

6. Niccolo Machiavelli, *The Prince*, in *Historical and Political Writings* (Moscow: NF. "Pushkin's Library," LLC "Publishing House AST," 2004), 101.

7. Machiavelli, *The Prince*, 104.

8. Machiavelli, *Discourses on the First Decade of Titus Livy*, in *Historical and Political Writings* (Moscow: NF. "Pushkin's Library," LLC "Publishing House AST," 2004), 148–49.

9. Machiavelli, *The Prince*, 108.

10. Jean Baudrillard, *Simulation and Simulacra* (Ann Arbor, MI: University of Michigan Press, 1994).

11. Dino Felluga, "Models on Baudrillard. On Simulation," in *Introductory Guide to Critical Theory*, www.purdue.edu/guidetotheory/postmodernism/modules/baudrillardsimulation.html.

12. Machiavelli, *The Prince*, 101.

13. Machiavelli, *The Prince*, 106.
14. See Rafael Sabatini, *The Life of Cesare Borgia* (Moscow: AST, Poligrafizdat, 2010), 384.
15. Machiavelli, *The Prince*, 107, 115.
16. Machiavelli, *The Prince*, 101.

BIBLIOGRAPHY

Avtorkhanov, Abdurakhman. *Stalin and the Soviet Communist Party: A Study in the Technology of Power*, 3rd ed. Frankfurt/Main: Possev-Verlag, 1983.

Baudrillard, Jean. *Simulation and Simulacra*. Ann Arbor, MI: University of Michigan Press, 1994.

Felluga, Dino. "Modules on Baudrillard. On Simulation." In *Introductory Guide to Critical Theory*. www.purdue.edu/guidetotheory/postmodernism/modules/baudrillardsimulation.html).

Hibbert, Christopher. *The Rise and Fall of the House of Medici*. New York: Penguin, 1980.

Hobbes, Thomas. *Writings*. Vol. 2. Moscow: Mysl, 1991.

Kowalski, Jan Wierusz. *The Pope and the Papacy*. Moscow: Izdat political literature, 1991. http://bookre.org/reader?file=131929.

Machiavelli, Niccolo. *Discourses on the First Decade of Titus Livy* in *Historical and Political Writings*. Moscow: NF. "Pushkin's Library," LLC "Publishing House AST," 2004.

Machiavelli, Niccolo. *On the Way to Deal with the Rebel Subjects of the Valdichiana*. In *Historical and Political Writings*. Moscow: NF. "Pushkin's Library," LLC "Publishing House AST," 2004.

Machiavelli, Niccolo. *The Prince* in *Historical and Political Writings*. Moscow: NF "Pushkin's Library," LLC "Publishing House AST," 2004.

Machiavelli, Niccolo. The Letters of Machiavelli. http://drevlit.ru/texts/m/makkiavelli_10pisem.php#11.

Najemi, John M. *History of Florence, 1200–1575*. Sussex, UK: Wiley, 2006.

Toynbee, Arnold J. *A Study of History*. Moscow: Progress, 1991.

Sabatini, Rafael. *The Life of Cesare Borgia*. Moscow: AST, Poligrafizdat, 2010.

Part III

MODERNITY I: EARLY MODERN PERIOD

Preface

Modernity I

Although early modernity is often hailed as age of scientific discovery, the new age of reason, and so on, these descriptions don't do justice to the rampant hysteria, violence, and cosmic insecurity of the time, exemplified in the turbulent years of the Wars of Religion, witch burnings, charges of heresy, and so on.

Discussed in this chapter are the scientific revolution and its implications. While these intellectual developments hailed the beginnings of modernity and forms of scientific progress, they also prompted expressions of widespread intellectual and spiritual anomie, and thus for many people these developments were themselves experienced as catastrophes. John Donne's proclamation that a "new philosophy calls all into doubt" illustrated the wide-ranging epistemological upheaval caused by the scientific revolution that colored the theoretical background for the inquiries of thinkers like Descartes. Catastrophes need not always explicitly involve natural disasters or wars through which everyday existence is suddenly thrown into disarray—but they can also occur on a more intellectual plane and still result in widespread spiritual dislocation, causing collective, far-reaching value shifts within an entire civilization.

This section contains papers exploring theodicy as a response to the problem of evil, discussed previously but now pushed further in Voltaire's *Candide*, which mercilessly ridiculed the supposed rationality/optimism of Leibniz (aka Dr. Pangloss)—that this, after all, is the "best of all possible worlds." How did the devastation of the Lisbon Earthquake provide the backdrop for *Candide?*

One way of dealing with natural evils—catastrophes like earthquakes and plagues—is to try to accept the very real possibility that the physical world is basically amoral. Events such as floods, earthquakes, and so on, proceed of necessity according to the laws of nature, with no apparent regard for humanity or human conceptions of justice, injustice, proportionality, and the like. Although we experience them as catastrophes from our human standpoint, from the strictly scientific perspective, they are merely natural events (e.g., tectonic shifts) occurring out of necessity given the laws of nature; we have no choice but to impose our moral and emotional categories upon them as these events are experienced by us. In reality, they are neither good nor bad, or perhaps they are "beyond good and evil." Earlier in this book, in the essay on Boccaccio, reference was made to Nietzsche's discussion of the genesis of nihilism in *Will to Power*. Nietzsche suggests it arises out of the disappointment felt when we discover that despite the human tendency to seek a transcendent meaning in all events, this transcendent meaning is simply not to be found in them.[1] He writes further that this need to provide a transcendental explanation has been "fabricated solely from psychological needs."[2] Thus, natural disasters like the Black Death, discussed in the last chapter, and the Lisbon Earthquake discussed in this one, highlight the disturbing possibility that despite our desires for an overarching narrative of meaning, transcendence, and human exceptionalism, we may very well inhabit an amoral and indifferent universe. Whether we have the inner strength to stare down this ultimately amoral universe is another question, but it certainly is not a task for the weak of spirit.[3]

NOTES

1. Friedrich Nietzsche, *Will to Power*, ed. W. Kauffmann, trans. W. Kauffmann & R. J. Hollingdale (NY: Vintage/Random House, 1968), 9.
2. Ibid.
3. See also Brian Leiter, "The Truth Is Terrible," *Journal of Nietzsche Studies* (Fall 2018 forthcoming). Available at SSRN: https://ssrn.com/abstract=2099162 or http://dx.doi.org/10.2139/ssrn.2099162.

BIBLIOGRAPHY

Nietzsche, Friedrich. *Will to Power*. Edited by Walter Kauffmann, translated by Walter Kauffmann & R. J. Hollingdale. New York: Vintage/Random House, 1968.
Leiter, Brian. "The Truth is Terrible," *Journal of Nietzsche Studies* (Fall 2018, forthcoming). Available at: https://ssrn.com/abstract=2099162 or http://dx.doi.org/10.2139/ssrn.2099162.

Chapter 8

Three Catastrophes and One Philosopher

Atrocious Wars and the Political Ideas of Thomas Hobbes

David Wilkinson

Thomas Hobbes (1588–1679) is one of the greats of political philosophy. Hobbes was acquainted with, and his political thought influenced by, three great political catastrophes: the Peloponnesian War of 431–404 BC, the Thirty Years' War of 1618–1648, and the English Civil Wars of 1642–1651. He examined the Peloponnesian War as a translator of its history, the Thirty Years' War as a translator of political correspondence, and the English Civil Wars as twice a political refugee. While most of his work and reputation as a political philosopher is derived from his relentless defense of authority against sedition and rebellion, Hobbes was also well acquainted with and mindful of state failure.

In the years 1640–1668, Hobbes produced four highly original political writings, which we shall cite respectively as *Elements, Citizen, Leviathan,* and *Behemoth.* However, Hobbes' first major work was his 1628/29 translation of Thucydides' *History of the Peloponnesian War*.[1]

HOBBES AND THE PELOPONNESIAN WAR

The Peloponnesian War pitted democratic Athens and its allied states, its subject peoples and colonies, and its ideological confederates in torn states against the Peloponnesian League of oligarchic states led by Sparta, Corinth, and Thebes, with Syracuse, Persia, oligarchic parties, and rebellious Athenian subjects eventually associated. The war ultimately proved catastrophic for Athens, which was disarmed, stripped of empire, and subjugated to Sparta and Spartan appointees. Sparta replaced Athens as the strongest power of Hellas (Greece), and, beguiled by victory, sought to dominate, only to be toppled in its turn from that place in 371 BC. Thucydides wrote of the origins of the war and of its events only to 411 BC.

In the Peloponnesian War, Athens came near to suffering extirpation, the destruction of the city and enslavement of its population. Though Athens survived, it never regained its previous preeminence in wealth and power. Other Greek cities were even less fortunate, and Thucydides attends to their misfortunes; his history shuttles among strategic debates, major battles and major atrocities.[2] Some such atrocities were inflicted by conquerors upon Hestiaea, Aegina and Potidaea (their populations expelled, Th. 1.114, 2.27, 2.70), Plataea, Scione, and Melos (the men killed, women enslaved, Th. 3.68, 5. 32, 5. 116), Torone (the men held for ransom, women and children enslaved, Th. 5.3), Mycalessus (general massacre, Th. 7.29), and Iasus (the population enslaved and sold, Th. 8.28)

Other polities suffered outrages self-inflicted in civil strife: Corcyra (Th 3.69–85, 4.46–48), Argos (Th. 2.94), and Samos (Th. 8.21). And not only cities suffered atrocities: "At the commencement of the war, all . . . the traders of the Athenians and their allies . . . whom the Lacedaemonians captured at sea when they caught their vessels off the coast of Peloponnesus . . . were treated by them as enemies and indiscriminately slaughtered, whether they were allies of the Athenians or neutrals."[3]

Thucydides' view of the war is summarized in Th. 1.23: "But as for this war, it both lasted long and the harm it did to Greece was such as the like in the like space had never been seen before. For neither had there ever been so many cities expugned and made desolate, what by the barbarians and what by the Greeks warring on one another (and some cities there were that when they were taken changed their inhabitants), nor so much banishing and slaughter, some by the war some by sedition, as was in this."[4]

What might be learned from reflecting upon such a disaster? Hobbes' introductory material for his *Thucydides* tells us what he thought he learned. And the frontispiece of the *Thucydides* has a lesson as well. In his lectures on *Word and Image in the Philosophy of Thomas Hobbes*, Quentin Skinner[5] has very usefully drawn attention to the emergence in Renaissance book-production "of the iconographical Frontispiece in which the argument of the book was foreshadowed and summarised in visual terms," and pointed out that the frontispieces to Hobbes' major works contain iconographic cues toward their chief political ideas.

The 1629, 1634, and 1676 frontispieces of Hobbes' *Thucydides* contrast the chief opponents in the Peloponnesian War, Spartans to the left, Athenians to the right. Sparta is pictured with the label *Endoxotate Lakedaimōn*, "most glorious Lacedaemon." Athens is *"Hellados Hellas Athinai,"* "Athens, the Hellas of Hellas" (attributed to Thucydides in *The Greek Anthology* 7.45), most reminiscent of Thucydides' Pericles styling

Athens "the school of Hellas" (Th. 2.41.1). These epithets are highly honorific and equally complimentary, in ironic contrast to the inglorious examples Thucydides' text would show that these glorious teachers had set (figure 8.1).

Figure 8.1 Frontispiece for Hobbes' Translation of Thucydides, 1676.

The governance of Sparta is indicated by a panel showing *hoi aristoi*, "the best," or rather Sparta's oligarchy of ephors conversing at a table and presided over by a (co-)king sporting crown and scepter. The governance of Athens is represented by a panel showing an orator speaking down to *hoi polloi*, "the many," and prefigures the critique of democracy both in Thucydides' text and in Hobbes' commentary ("In it the weaknesses and eventual failures of the Athenian democrats, together with those of their city state, were made clear").[6]

In the frontispiece, Sparta is personified by its co-King Archidamus II (r. c. 467–427 BC), Athens by the orator Pericles (c. 495–429 BC). Archidamus and Pericles were portrayed by Thucydides as alike in their inclination toward limiting the aims and actions of their states in the war. After their deaths, however, they were replaced by adventurous, dynamic and thrusting leaders—Cleon and Alcibiades for Athens, Brasidas and Lysander for Sparta—disposed to seek the unlimited objective of total victory through the unlimited means of what was called in World War I in German-occupied Belgium *Schreckligkeit*—"terror" or "frightfulness." Their gifts to Hellas were ethnic cleansings, androcides, enslavements, massacres, impoverishment and fearful memories. Thus the Hobbesian iconography celebrates moderation in the persons of the (failed) moderates of both sides.

Hobbes' view of Thucydides is further expressed in his Epistle Dedicatory to Sir William Cavendish, and a note "To the Readers,"[7] Thucydides is recommended to Cavendish "for his writings, as having in them profitable instruction for noblemen, and such as may come to have the managing of great and weighty actions" (v), and to the "readers" as being the best performer of "the principal and proper work of history," which is "to enable men, by the knowledge of actions past, to bear themselves prudently in the present and providently toward the future" (vii).

Hobbes' opinion on the comparative merits of various forms of government is developed, via Thucydides, in his prefatory essay "Of the life and history of Thucydides,"[8] where he judges approvingly that Thucydides "least of all liked the democracy" of Athens on account of its inconstancy and its appetite for desperate, dangerous and ruinous resolutions. He disliked the government of "the few," as especially prone to ambition and sedition. A mixture of "*the few* and *the many*" was better than either alone (xvii). But "he best approved of the regal government" (xvi–xvii).

The two forms of "regal" government in Athens in Thucydides' era, when Athens' hereditary kingship had long since receded into myth, were both of them atypical, and needed explanation. The earlier monarchy was that of the "tyrant" Peisistratus (r. c. 546–527 BC), and the early (non-tyrannous) rule (527–514 BC) of his son and chief successor Hippias. Of them Thucydides says "to say the truth, these tyrants held virtue and wisdom in great account for a long time, and taking of the Athenians but a twentieth part of their revenues [i.e. rents], adorned the city, managed their wars, and administered their religion worthily."[9] Indeed, Peisistratid rule is praised also by Aristotle ("more constitutional than tyrannical"),[10] and Herodotus ("Pisistratus ruled the Athenians, disturbing in no way the order of offices nor changing the laws, but governing the city according to its established constitution and arranging all things fairly and well").[11]

The second "regal" period Hobbes sees in Athens was the domination of Pericles over the Athenian democracy, as expressed in Thucydides' encomium: "For as long as he was in authority in the city in time of peace, he governed the same with moderation and was a faithful watchman of it; and in his time it was at the greatest. And after the war was on foot, it is manifest that he therein also foresaw what it could do. He lived after the war began two years and six months. And his foresight in the war was best known after his death. For he told them that if they would be quiet and look to their navy, and during this war seek no further dominion nor hazard the city itself, they should then have the upper hand. But they did contrary in all. . . . [Pericles] being a man of great power both for his dignity and wisdom, and for bribes manifestly the most incorrupt, he freely controlled the multitude and was not so much led by them as he led them. Because, having gotten his power by no evil arts, he would not humour them in his speeches but out of his authority durst anger them with contradiction. Therefore, whensoever he saw them out of season insolently bold, he would with his orations put them into a fear; and again, when they were afraid without reason, he would likewise erect their spirits and embolden them. It was in name a state democratical, but in fact a government of the principal man."[12]

Hobbes sums up these cases of "regal government" at Athens: Thucydides "more . . . commendeth" the government of Athens "both when Peisistratus reigned (saving that it was an usurped power), and when in the beginning of this war it was democratical in name but in effect monarchical under Pericles."[13]

I believe that there is a strong case to be made for the proposition that in the process of translating Thucydides, Hobbes became a Thucydidean disciple. For example, the topic of human nature and the political consequences of that human nature was to become a constant theme in Hobbes' work, and I believe that, given Hobbes' unstinting praise for Thucydides, that we are well justified in taking the judgments voiced by Thucydides upon human nature in general and treating them as Hobbes' opinions as well. Thucydides (1.22.4) offered "the plain truth about past events and those that at some future time, in accordance with human nature, will recur in similar or comparable ways"[14]:

Thucydides' judicial voice is strongest in his commentary upon the civil war in Corcyra, and I accordingly quote it here in Hobbes' version. (Th. 3.82–86)

"For afterwards all Greece, as a man may say, was in commotion; and quarrels arose everywhere. Now in time of peace they could have had no pretence nor would have been so forward to call them in; but being war and confederates to be had for either party, both to hurt their enemies and strengthen themselves, such as desired alteration easily got them to come in. And many and heinous things happened in the cities through this sedition [i.e. that 'between the patrons of the commons, that sought to bring in the Athenians, and the few, that desired to bring in the Lacedaemonians'] which though they have been before and shall be ever as long as human nature is the same, yet they are more calm and of different kinds according to the several conjunctures. For in peace and prosperity as well cities as private men are better minded because they be not plunged into necessity of doing anything against their will. But war, taking away the affluence of daily necessaries, is a most violent master and conformeth most men's passions to the present occasion. . . . The cause of all this is desire of rule out of avarice and ambition, and the zeal of contention from those two proceeding. For such as were of authority in the cities, both of the one and the other faction, preferring under decent titles, one, the political equality of the multitude, the other, the moderate aristocracy, though in words they seemed to be servants of the public, they made it in effect but the prize of their contention; and striving by whatsoever means to overcome both ventured on most horrible outrages and prosecuted their revenges still farther without any regard of justice or the public good, but limiting them, each faction, by their own appetite, and stood ready, whether by unjust sentence or with their own hands, when they should get power, to satisfy their present spite. . . . The neutrals of the city were destroyed by both factions, partly because they would not side with them and partly for envy that they should so escape. . . . And the common course of life being at that time confounded in the city, the nature of man, which is wont even against law to do evil, gotten now above the law, showed itself with delight to be too weak for passion, too strong for justice, and enemy to all superiority."

A reader of Thucydides cannot escape the sense that he was chronicling a needless and avertable disaster brought on by human character when that was left unleashed rather than checked by political leaders and institutions. And I think it is fair to say that the Hellenic catastrophe, as viewed through the words of Thucydides and the Thucydidean discipleship of Hobbes, affected Hobbes' political philosophy in several ways. Democracies and oligarchies are untrustworthy as forms of government. The leadership of One is to be preferred, even if that leadership is usurped and on that account "tyrannous" or demagogic and populist, provided only that the goals and behavior of the One are modest and moderate, preferring justice and the public good to the power and profit of their faction. But in war, and even more in civil war, such leadership is not to be expected. And Hobbes translated Thucydides during a great and "similar or comparable" war.

HOBBES AND THE THIRTY YEARS' WAR

Hobbes' translation of Thucydides is dated 1628–1629. The Thirty Years' War in Europe is dated 1618–1648. By the time Hobbes' *Thucydides* was published, that war had already involved the Holy Roman Empire, Spain, Hungary, Croatia, the Netherlands, German protestant states, Denmark, Stuart England and Scotland, Transylvania, the Ottoman Empire, Poland, France, and French Huguenots; Russia, Poland-Lithuania, and the Cossacks would later be drawn in.

Hobbes was well acquainted with the politics and violence of European affairs during the Thirty Years' War and the brutality of the war itself. Between 1615 and 1628, he translated more than seventy diplomatic papers from the continent for two English aristocratic patrons, both named William Cavendish, one now known as second earl of Devonshire[15] and the other as first Duke of Newcastle.[16]

There were certainly gains and losses in power from the Thirty Years War—Spain and the Empire were hurt, the Papacy was humiliated, France and Sweden rose, the Netherlands and Portugal were freed. Governments could more confidently establish their sectarian religions and persecute their own religious nonconformists (or not) to their hearts' content with no expectation of foreign obstruction.

But the war was generally thought loathsome. Estimates of the war death toll (from violence, disease, and famine) vary widely, around a median of 7.5 million. The worst devastation was to be visited upon Germany in a civil war within the Holy Roman Empire. In 1628/9 the worst (such as the sack of Magdeburg, May 1631) was yet to come, but by 1628/9 a comparison to the ruinous Peloponnesian War would already have been apt. The Thirty Years' War occasioned the first known anti-war art, the etchings of Jacques Callot (1592–1635), "The Miseries and Misfortunes of War," published in 1633. Figure 8.2 shows three of Callot's commemorative images: the pillaging of a house, the looting of a monastery, and the looting and burning of a village. Rabb[17] cites Callot, and also Rubens, whose 1639 *The Horrors of War* was expressly intended to represent "unfortunate Europe, who, for so many years now, has suffered plunder, outrage and misery."[18]

Figure 8.2 Plates 5, 7, and 17 from Jacques Callot, *Les Miseres et les Mal-heurs de la Guerre*, Paris, 1633.

HOBBES' ELEMENTS OF LAW

And in 1640, during the Franco-Swedish phase of the Thirty Years' War, before the English Civil War proper, but during the earliest part of the Wars of the Three Kingdoms, there circulated in manuscript Hobbes' *The Elements of Law, Natural and Politic,* in two parts, *Human Nature* and *De Corpore Politico*, "concerning men as a body politic."[19] The *Elements* mainly contains themes of the political obligations of those who are ruled, themes later expounded upon, tinkered with, and tempered in *De Cive* and *Leviathan*. The horrors of the Peloponnesian War and the Thirty Years' War provide the catastrophic background of violence and existential insecurity against which Hobbes' teachings must be seen. Men fear untimely, unnecessary, premature, violent death, inflicted upon them by other men, and they have reason for their fear, because they have passions that lead them to injure others. But every man desires self-preservation, and they ought to, and generally do, so value their self-preservation as to give up the pursuit of those passions that lead them to inflict and suffer violence. Peace is the sine qua non for self-preservation. Reason requires the subjection of a people to some common and absolute sovereign power, which it is their duty to obey. The state exists to prevent its people from incontinently murdering one another. Peace, not freedom, political rights, religious liberty, is the great political value and objective, attained by absolute obedience to a sovereign power.

While most of Hobbes' writing, and most Hobbesian argumentation, has to do with the absoluteness of monarchy and the near-unlimited obligation of the ruled to obey their rulers, we shall continue to focus more upon the obligations of the rulers to the ruled—"the duty of him or them that have the sovereign power."[20] For the law over sovereigns Hobbes quotes Cicero: "*Salus populi suprema lex*—"The welfare of the people shall be the supreme law."[21] The general law for sovereigns is that: "they procure, to the uttermost of their endeavor, the good of the people." This good includes the establishing of such doctrines and rules as they believe to be the true way to "eternal good." The sovereign would accordingly establish for the people of its whatever religion it judged true. But as to the temporal good of people, "it consisteth in four points: 1. Multitude. 2. Commodity of living. 3. Peace amongst ourselves. 4. Defence against foreign power."[22]

Thus, the ruler's duty requires that the numbers of the people should be increased; they should have no more restraint on their liberty than is needed for the good of the commonwealth; the economy should be so regulated as to increase the wealth of the people. Hobbes takes some pains to set out and prescribe against "causes concurring to sedition," including what would today be described as the "tragedy of the commons," as well as perceptions of unfairness in taxation and abuse of authority, private ambitions, the creation of factions, and the existence of opinions that tend to justify resistance to the public authority. The final necessary duty of the sovereign is the avoidance of unnecessary wars of ambition, vainglory, and petty revenge, while having "money, arms, ships and fortified places ready for defence."[23]

It hardly need be said that neither the deeds of the rulers of Hellas in the Peloponnesian War, nor those of the greats of Germany during the Thirty Years' War, could be cited as evidence of their performance of those sovereignly duties. Foreign adventures, invasions and disasters, bloody faction, devastation, and depopulation were their contribution to the "good of the people." Their acts rather were of that class that "tend to the hurt of the people in general" and so "be breaches of the law of nature, and of the divine law," surely deserving "the pain of eternal death."[24]

HOBBES AND THE ENGLISH CIVIL WAR

The English Civil War is usually dated 1642–1651, but may also be seen as a part of the British Civil Wars, or the Wars of the Three Kingdoms (England, Scotland, Ireland), 1639–1653. In these wars, Royalists for King Charles I Stuart (r. 1625–1649) fought partisans of the Long Parliament (sat 1640–1649 and again 1660). Further, Scottish Presbyterians fought successive English rulers in religious and ethnic power struggles; and Irish Catholics fought Irish, English, and Scottish Protestants for land, for Catholic religious liberty, and for Irish territorial autonomy. In this complex of wars, perhaps 200,000 soldiers and civilians perished of violence, famine, and disease.

Hobbes was very personally affected by the Wars of the Three Kingdoms, but primarily by the English Civil Wars. At the outset a friend and associate of Stuart Royalists, Hobbes defended monarchy and autocracy. *Elements* 1.19.7 counseled subjects to obedience, and justified their commanders' use of power to "by the terror thereof" produce unity and concord in the body politic. The Long Parliament increasingly disliked friends of monarchy and autocracy. Charles I, who was infirm in their defense, permitted his chief civil counselor, Thomas Wentworth, Earl of Strafford, to fall into the hands of his Parliamentary enemies; Strafford was arrested in 1640 and executed in 1641. Charles' chief religious counselor, William Laud, Archbishop of Canterbury, was arrested in 1641 and executed in 1645. In 1640, soon after Strafford's arrest, and fearing Parliamentarist disapproval of *Elements,* Hobbes decamped to Paris[25] where he published *De Cive* ("The Citizen," Latin text circulated 1641, published 1642) intended to be the third part of a trilogy, *The Elements of Philosophy.* As it chanced, the other parts were published later, as *De Corpore* ("The Body," in fact on logic, on first principles of philosophy narrowly construed, on mathematics, and on physics, published 1655) and *De Homine* ("Man," actually on perceptual psychology and optics, published 1658).

De Cive itself has three parts, "Liberty," "Dominion," and "Religion," in the Latin "Sub titulo Libertatis . . . Imperii . . . Religionis"). As Skinner

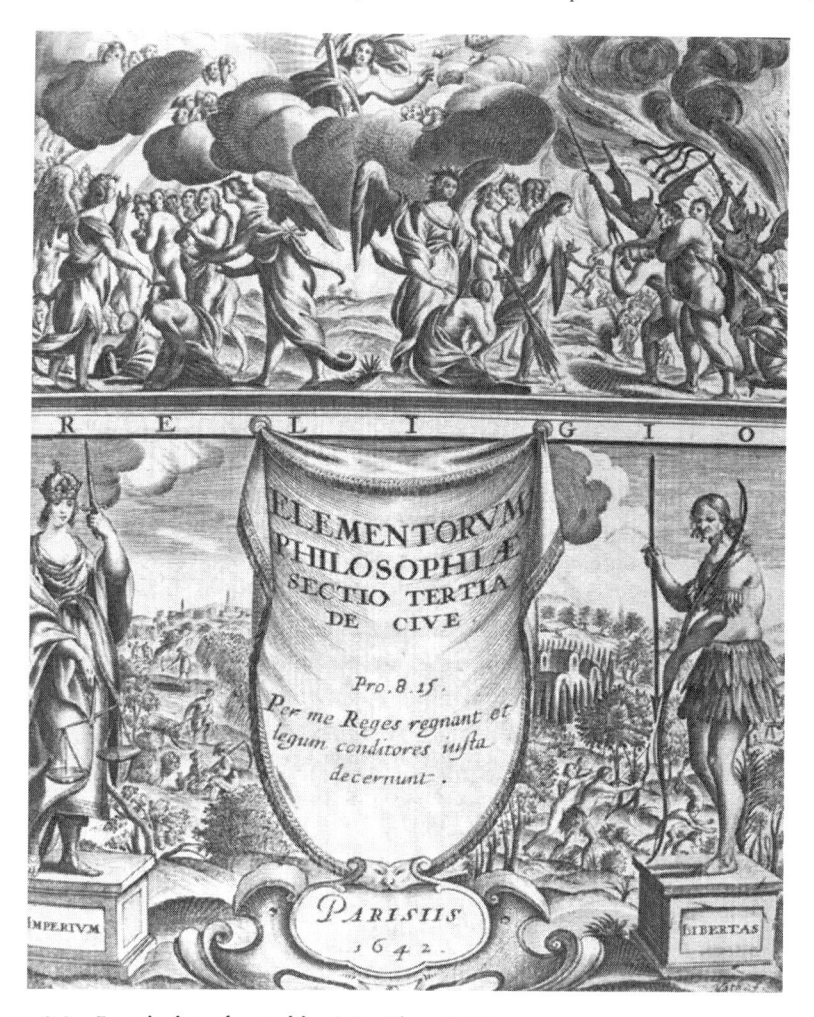

Figure 8.3 Frontispiece for Hobbes' *De Cive*, 1642.

argues, the imagery of the frontispiece sums up the entire argument. Per Skinner, "Hobbes first attempted to offer a visual summary of his political theory in the Frontispiece to *De Cive*, the earliest published version of his political theory, which appeared in a Latin edition in Paris 1642. An elaborate Frontispiece shows the whole of human life being lived out under *Religio*, and illustrates what Hobbes takes to be the fundamental dilemma in politics: whether to insist on liberty or submit to sovereign power. The way of life surrounding the figure marked *Libertas* is shown to be uncertain and uncivilised, whereas peace and prosperity are shown to accompany the figure of *Imperium*."[26] On the right stands an ugly, grimacing, ill-dressed "Libertas" armed with bow and spear, behind whom men hunt men: the "state of nature." On the left is the civil realm, guarded by calm, well-garbed "Imperium" who holds the scales of judgment and the sword of punishment; behind her are peaceful grainfields yielding a bounteous harvest.

The pictured world of "Imperium" was not matched by the reality of the Three Kingdoms in the late years of Charles I's rule. In the Wars of the Three Kingdoms, as in the Peloponnesian War and the Thirty Years' War, there were massacres as well as battles. Ireland was the principal seat of such reciprocal massacres. Massacres of Catholics and Protestants, whether civilians or prisoners of war, were noted especially in Ulster in 1641–1643[27]; and Cromwell's conquest of Ireland for the Commonwealth in 1649–51 (with guerrilla war to 1653), accompanied by plague and famine, was noted for massacres at Drogheda and Wexford (September–October 1649). We may see in Hobbes' acquaintance with the three catastrophes here recounted the basis for his language[28] decrying "the miseries and horrible calamities that accompany a civil war, or that dissolute condition of masterless men without subjection to laws and a coercive power to tie their hands from rapine and revenge . . ." and for his obsessive recapitulation of the overwhelming importance of peacekeeping to the legitimacy of government.

THE HOBBESIAN DUTIES OF THE SOVEREIGN AND THE CAREER OF CHARLES I

The English translation of *De Cive* (Hobbes, 1949) was published in 1651, just before *Leviathan,* and after the unhappy ending of the political career of King Charles I. (We shall cite that translation hereafter as *The Citizen*, though it was published as *Philosophicall rudiments concerning government and society*.) Chapter XIII of *The Citizen* is "Concerning the Duties of Them who Bear Rule." As in the *Elements*, for rulers the law supreme is the safety of the people, the common benefit: for "dominions were constituted for peace's sake, and peace was sought after for safety's sake."[29] "Safety" however means "the welfare of the most part," "happiness," to "live delightfully." Rulers are obliged, so far as laws can effect it, "to furnish their subjects abundantly, not only with the good things belonging to life, but also with those that advance to delectation."

The benefits of subjects respecting this life only may be distributed into four kinds. 1. That they be defended against foreign enemies. 2. That peace be preserved at home. 3. That they be enriched as much as may consist with public security. 4. That they enjoy a harmless liberty. For supreme commanders can confer no more to their civil happiness than that being preserved from foreign and civil wars, they may quietly enjoy that wealth which they have purchased by their own industry.[30]

Defense requires spies, standing armaments, military budgets, and pre-emptive "lessening of the power of foreigners whom they suspect."[31] Sound doctrines should be taught in public schools; tax burdens should match benefits received. Obedient subjects should be cherished, the factious restrained, and factions dissolved. Punishments should be clearly defined by law or practice, and judges themselves subjected to judgment. As regards "perverse doctrines," Hobbes says[32]: "It is . . . the duty of those who have the chief authority, to root those out of the minds of men, not by commanding, but by teaching; not by the terror of penalties, but by the perspicuity of reasons. The laws whereby this evil may be withstood are not to be made against the persons, erring, but against the errors themselves. . . . I therefore conceive it to be the duty of supreme officers to cause the true elements of civil doctrine to be written, and to command them to be taught in all the colleges of their several dominions."

Quentin Skinner has perspicaciously pointed out (2002a: 303) that Hobbes' three major works on civil science were all published "for the first time in England and for the first time in English" at almost the same time, and after the death of Charles I: the political section of *Elements* appeared in May of 1650, *The Citizen* in March 1651, and *Leviathan* in April or May of that year. And as in *Elements* and *The Citizen*, so in *Leviathan* (Lev. 30) the "office" of the sovereign is "the procuration of the safety of the people," and not merely "a bare preservation, but also all other contentments of life, which every man by lawful industry, without danger or hurt to the Commonwealth, shall acquire to himself." Further to this, in Chapter 17 of *Leviathan*, we read of the purpose of a Commonwealth, which is " to defend [men] from the invasion of foreigners, and the injuries of one another, and thereby to secure them in such sort as that by their own industry and by the fruits of the earth they may nourish themselves and live contentedly."

Hobbes strikes the theme again and again. Lev. 17: "the common peace and safety"; "our peace and defence"; "peace at home, and mutual aid against their enemies abroad"; "peace and common defence." Lev. 18, the same, elaborated: "the preserving of peace and security, by prevention of discord at home, and hostility from abroad; and when peace and security are lost, for the recovery of the same."

Few if any rulers of European states involved in the Thirty Years' War could be said to have fulfilled these criteria. And King Charles I of England? Let us review the history of the Wars of the Three Kingdoms from the perspective of a Hobbesian critic, a critic now not of the ruled but of the rulers, focusing upon their management of "perverse doctrines" and doctrinaires, and upon the preservation of the subjects from foreign and civil wars.

Charles' reign began in 1625. That year he launched a naval expedition against Spain, which was defeated. In 1627 he sent a naval expedition against France, which was defeated. Lacking funds, he made a loser's peace with France (Treaty of Suza, 1629) and Spain (Treaty of Madrid, 1630). Charles then turned his attention to making and enforcing radical changes in the religion and politics of England and Scotland. By the time *De Cive* was written, John Bastwick, Henry Burton, and William Prynne had (1638) had their ears cropped, been fined, and sentenced to perpetual imprisonment imprisoned for life for denouncing bishops and episcopacy. In 1639 Charles had attempted to use force against Scotland so as to enforce episcopacy and his preferred religious doctrine upon the unwilling Scots; he failed (First Bishops' War, 1639). He tried again and was defeated again (Second Bishops' War, 1640); the Scots invaded England to extort an indemnity and a subsidy. When Charles convened an English Parliament to raise funds, he failed, and got instead demands to limit his power and punish his ministers. There followed a Catholic revolt in Ireland (Irish Confederate Wars, 1641–1653) which Charles could not subdue. Next began a war between Charles and his English Royalist followers on one side and Parliament and its own army on the other (First English Civil War, 1642–1646); Charles was defeated and imprisoned, escaped, and was recaptured. Charles, in custody, nonetheless managed to rouse Royalist rebellions (Second English Civil War, 1648–1649), and an invasion of England by the Scots, now on the King's side (1648–1649); Charles' forces were defeated. Charles I, having accumulated a record of perseverance in failed warfare and governance that would be difficult to match in the history of fiasco, was put to death by the Parliamentarians (1649).

We may reasonably see the concept of the duty of the sovereign laid down in *Elements, The Citizen,* and *Leviathan* as constituting a test against which to measure real rulers, and Charles I in particular. Let us look more closely at the failures of rulers per *Leviathan*, which expressly cites among them "negligence or unskillfulness of governors and teachers." There can be dissolution by the sovereign's error: "if he transfer the militia, he retains the judicature in vain, for want of execution of the laws; or if he grant away the power of raising money, the militia is in vain; or if he give away the government of doctrines, men will be frighted into rebellion with the fear of spirits."[33] Further in chapter 18, Hobbes comments directly on the English Civil Wars:

"If there had not first been an opinion received of the greatest part of England that these powers were divided between the King and the Lords and the House of Commons, the people had never been divided and fallen into this Civil War; first between those that disagreed in politics, and after between the dissenters about the liberty of religion, which have so instructed men in this point of sovereign right that there be few now in England that do not see that these rights are inseparable, and will be so generally acknowledged at the next return of peace; and so continue, till their miseries are forgotten, and no longer, except the vulgar be better taught than they have hitherto been."

HOBBES AND THE AFTERMATH OF THE ENGLISH CIVIL WARS

Many vicissitudes accompanied and followed the downfall of the King. A military coup of December 1648 (Pride's Purge) expelled the majority of members of Parliament in order to create a "Rump Parliament" with a revised majority ready to execute Charles. That done, the Rump proceeded in March to abolish "the office of King" for England and Ireland, more or less casually and incidentally abolished the House of Lords, and in May 1649 declared England a "Commonwealth and Free State" to be governed by the Rump Parliament itself.[34] The self-created Commonwealth was greeted by a third "English Civil War," or rather an Anglo-Scottish War, between the Rump and the Scots, who had continued royalist, now on behalf of Charles I's son and successor Charles II (1649–1651). The Commonwealth was victorious. As a final act, the Irish rebels (and other Royalists) were crushed in Ireland by 1653. The "Wars of the Three Kingdoms" ended, having together left hundreds of thousands dead of violence, famine, and disease, Ireland devastated, and Ireland and Scotland reduced de facto to occupied provinces of England. The domestic peace, which it is the Hobbesian duty of the rulers to provide, and which had been forfeited under Charles I, had at last been established. Let us accordingly inspect that doctrine and that work.

Again Skinner's analysis (2012) of the frontispiece is in point. We recall that the Frontispiece to the 1642 Parisian Latin edition of *De Cive* showed the overarching realm of religion, where a divinity presides over the judgment of humans by angels, some receiving comfort, some given over to demons for chastisement. That supreme religious realm has evanesced in the iconography of the *Leviathan* (see figure 8.4), where a different order emerges. We see a peaceable kingdom, a city with its countryside, watched over by a giant whose body comprises a multitude of tiny humans, all gazing up to the head of the giant. That crowned giant holds the sword of temporal power in its right hand; and in its left hand, as a bishop would hold it, the giant a crozier, the insigne of a prelate, a governor of a church, and a cannon, on the right that of ecclesiastical power with a cathedral and a bishop's mitre.

Skinner (2012) provides an extensive commentary on the Leviathan frontispiece. Political power trumps religion. Authority comes not from the heavens but from the multitude who comprise that power and who at the same time look up to it. There is no longer offered a choice—Athens or Sparta, Imperium or Libertas, natural freedom or civil dominion; there is only

122   David Wilkinson

Figure 8.4 Frontispiece for Hobbes' *Leviathan*, 1651.

dominion. Under the united civil and ecclesiastical power is the peace of a city and countryside, sunlit, unfortified.

The "pillars" to left and right below Skinner interprets as the dangers to dominion, rather than its occasions and venues. On the left is the lower echelon of civil power, with castle, and beneath it a noble's coronet. In lower levels are the troubles these powers can make, says Skinner. On the left are a cannon, weapons arranged as a trophy implying a battle, and the battle itself. On the right is a thunderbolt—the Papal "thunderbolt of excommunication" (Lev. 42). Beneath it are the weapons of clerical disputations, the logical weapons of scholasticism—horns marked "dilemma," a trident labeled "syllogism," and three two-pronged forks—spiritual-temporal (Lev. 29), direct-indirect (two kinds of power—Lev. 42), and real-intentional (in Aristotelian-Anselmian-Thomistic doctrine, a contrast between what exists in reality and what exists only in the mind, immaterial, incorporeal—Lev. 5, 12, 34). Below the tools of doctrinal disputation is a disputation itself, with opposing clerics to right and left, a judge to the rear and a jury to the front. Skinner perceives a rebel church making up its own ecclesiastical laws—here represented by the princes of the Roman Catholic Church in conclave.

Regardless of the proper interpretation of the "pillars," it is clear that Commonwealth is pictured by Hobbes as having authority over the church, which is to say, over religion. And in fact the Rump Parliament of 1649–1653 exercised such authority, dethroning bishops, retaining the established Church of England but as a Calvinistic Presbyterian state church, and tolerating "independents."

HOBBES AND THE ENGAGEMENT CONTROVERSY

The Rump Parliament also practiced a very Hobbesian social contractarianism. In February 1649 the Rump demanded that an "Engagement" to "adhere" to "this present Parliament" be subscribed to by the members of the Council of State, a large executive body that the Rump had created nine days before. In October 1649 the Engagement was extended by the Rump Parliament to itself, to officers of army and navy, their soldiers and sailors, to judges and lawyers, to municipal counselors, to members of the university community, to ministers admitted to benefices, and to pensioners—virtually the entire literate population."[35] Then on January 2, 1650, the Rump went farther, and commanded all men over the age of 18 to take the "Engagement," in the following form: "I do declare and promise that I will be true and faithful to the Commonwealth of England as it is now established without a king or House of Lords."[36] The courts of law were to refuse justice to all men who had subscribed to the engagement; they could neither sue nor defend themselves.[37]

The Engagement Act was intended to further the unity of the country, which it did not.

The Engagement was controversial and was not universally taken.[38] The Presbyterian clergy preached against it,[39] meetings were held within the parliamentary party to address those who "scrupled," the Parliament's Lord general Thomas Fairfax declined the engagement, and the test became neglected by 1651. The denial of justice to nonsubscribers was repealed by Cromwell's handpicked "Barebones Parliament" in November 1653[40] and in January 1654 the now Lord Protector Cromwell rescinded the Engagement itself.[41]

One rationale for the Engagement was "to the end that those which receive benefit and protection from this present government may give assurance of their living quietly and peaceably under the same, and that they will neither directly nor indirectly contrive or practise any thing to the disturbance thereof."[42] Thus the Engagement was a proposed contract of obedience which offered protection and sought peace. The offering of the Engagement is a thoroughly Hobbesian act. As Martinich notes, Hobbes' idea that what makes an apparent government into a legitimate one are two things:

"(1) the power to protect people and (2) the consent of the people protected to have that power be its government."[43]

As noted above, Skinner[44] sees significance in the near-simultaneous English publication of the political section of *Elements* in May of 1650, of *The Citizen* in March 1651, and of *Leviathan* in April or May 1651. This was the era of the Rump Parliament and the Engagement controversy, and Hobbes engaged in the Engagement controversy by propounding a political theory that justified those defeated in the civil wars taking the Engagement to the victors. As Skinner contends, Leviathan is indeed "the greatest of the numerous tracts in favor of 'engagement'."[45]

What has become of Hobbes' Stuartian Royalism? *Leviathan* 21 contains a clear doctrine regarding the termination of a subject's contract to submit to the sovereign. "The obligation of subjects to the sovereign is understood to last as long, and no longer, than the power lasteth by which he is able to protect them. For the right men have by nature to protect themselves, when none else can protect them, can by no covenant be relinquished." Charles I had of course lost that power in Scotland by 1639, in Ireland by 1641, and in England no later than by 1642.

And in his "Review and Conclusion" to *Leviathan* Hobbes provides an argument for the legitimacy of taking the Engagement: expressly citing the civil wars, he declares "the point of time wherein a man becomes subject to a conqueror is that point wherein, having liberty to submit to him, he consenteth, either by express words or by other sufficient sign, to be his subject. When it is that a man hath the liberty to submit, I have shown before in the end of the twenty-first Chapter; namely, that for him that hath no obligation to his former sovereign but that of an ordinary subject, it is then when the means of his life is within the guards and garrisons of the enemy; for it is then that he hath no longer protection from him, but is protected by the adverse party for his contribution."

Hobbes may or may not himself have taken the Engagement. He certainly did report himself to the authorities and submit to them.[46] And Noel Malcolm sees the evolution of Hobbes' views in the Leviathan from the stance of a loyal royalist hostile to the rebels to a realist adjusting to the need to obey a new regime,[47] and notes (33) that in *Leviathan*, unlike the *Elements* and *The Citizen*, Hobbes speaks of the acquisition of sovereign power by conquest (see Lev. 20).

HOBBES AND THE PROTECTORATE

Beginning with the Second Civil War of 1648–1649, there were many lesser political disorders in England. A second military coup, of April 20, 1653, led by the Rump's own Lord General Oliver Cromwell, conqueror of Scotland and Ireland, forcibly dissolved the Rump. Cromwell (as Lord General) and his "Council of Officers" of the Army issued a declaration upon the dissolution of the Parliament April 22, 1653,[48] declaring that Ireland and Scotland were "reduced to a great degree of peace, and England to perfect quiet." This coup paved the way for Cromwell to undertake a five-year term as "Lord Protector of the Commonwealth of England, Scotland and Ireland."

At the extreme of change, in say 1656, the Three Kingdoms had become a single "Commonwealth of England, Scotland and Ireland," in fact a military dictatorship under the Lord Protector Oliver, who ruled England through 11 military districts under the Major-Generals of the "New Model Army," whilst Ireland and Scotland, having been violently subjugated, had each a single Major-General to govern them. Peace of the Commonwealth was thus maintained by a very "visible power to keep them in awe, and tie them by fear of punishment to the performance of their covenants" (Lev. 17).

The Rump had undertaken the First Anglo-Dutch War (1652–1654), a seesaw naval war. Cromwell having expelled the Rump made peace with the Netherlands, so doing more of the Hobbesian governmental duty by adding peace abroad to peace at home. The further duties of prosperity and population growth, however, were not established; for 1630–1670 there was minimal population growth, and in general that period "was one of chronic dearth."[49]

There were other severe imperfections in the protectorate, from a Hobbesian point of view. The doctrine of a mixed state, denounced by Hobbes (Lev. 29), "what is it to divide the power of a Commonwealth, but to dissolve it") was reinstated. The Protectorate called two Parliaments; in the first, 1654–1655, none of the Protector's 84 bills was passed; in the second, the power to tax, which from a Hobbesian perspective should have been absolute in the hands of the Protector, having been left in the hands of Parliament, the rule of the Protectorate through the Major-Generals was undermined by the Parliament's refusal to raise the taxes needed to support the Army. Further, in the case of Naylor the Quaker demonstrator, the Parliament claimed for itself the right of judicature that had belonged to the old House of Lords. All this was clean contrary to Hobbes' assertion (Lev. 30) that "it is the office of the sovereign to maintain [the essential rights of sovereignty] entire, and consequently against his duty, first, to transfer to another or to lay from himself any of them," viz. when he "acknowledgeth himself subject to the civil laws, and renounceth the power of supreme judicature . . . or of levying money and soldiers when and as much as in his own conscience he shall judge necessary."

Nonetheless, peace, the Hobbesian essence, was established in the Protectorate, and in 1656, during the Protectorate, Hobbes, defending his *Leviathan*, gave himself congratulations, on the ground that his doctrine "hath framed the minds of a thousand gentlemen to a conscientious obedience to present government, which otherwise would have wavered in that point."[50]

HOBBES, THE RESTORATION, AND BEHEMOTH

Cromwell died in office in 1658, and after more vagaries and two more military coups, by Generals John Lambert and George Monck respectively, Charles II was called to the throne and the Commonwealth dissolved. "Constitutionally, it was as if the last nineteen years had never happened."[51] Separate English, Irish and Scottish Kingdoms and Parliaments were re-established. However, the English "Cavalier Parliament" of 1661–1679 was overwhelmingly Royalist, unlike its predecessor the Long Parliament of 1640–1660, which was republican, so the constitutional arguments of the past were not at once renewed. The (Episcopal) Church of Ireland, representing a small fraction of the population, was reinstated and privileged as national church, but religious persecution of Catholic and Presbyterian dissidents in Ireland was largely nominal, and most contention revolved around war-related land claims of Catholics and Protestant. However, under the royalist "Drunken Parliament" of Scotland, bishops were reinstated and the Presbyterian majority persecuted, laying up troubles for the future.

Still, peace at home continued. Indeed, warfare in Europe after 1648 became "milder," "more civilized," less bloody, and less ruinous to civil society. Rabb largely attributes the "more settled and relaxed" society from c.1670 to a revulsion against the brutality of the Thirty Years' War.[52]

The last work of Hobbes we shall consider here is his *Behemoth: the History of the Causes of the Civil Wars of England and of the Counsels and*

Artifices by which they were carried on from the year 1640 to the year 1662. *Behemoth* was composed c. 1666–1669,[53] well after the Restoration of King Charles II. *Behemoth* consists of four dialogues between a witness to the wars "A," and a student of the wars, "B." In the first dialogue A declares that Charles was sovereign of England "by right of a descent continued above 600 years" (107), of Scotland for longer, of Ireland since Henry II, presumably since the Henrician conquest of Ireland in the 1170s. B then asks how King Charles I could possibly have been overthrown, there having been trained soldiers enough for an army of 60,000, with ammunition and forts.

A then proceeds to develop a catalogue of regime failures under Charles I. Overall, as Martinich says, "*Behemoth* is in effect a case study of what Hobbes in *Leviathan* had claimed would go wrong with a government if his principles were not followed. . . . To his sorrow and to the sorrow of the nation, Charles I was too accommodating to Parliament, allowed the universities to teach doctrines that subverted his authority, and acted too moderately when factions challenged first his policies and later his very legitimacy."[54] But again there is no explicit scolding for Charles, as there is for all the seditious factions: writing between the lines remains necessary under the Restoration.

England's Restoration government honored Hobbes, but it was non-Hobbesian. The king did acquire the vital Hobbesian monopoly for force, by *The King's Sole Right over the Militia Act* of 1661—but this was an Act of Parliament! The Restoration state was clearly a mixed one, with an elected Parliament organizing religion (Clarendon Code), impeaching ministers, controlling taxation. Yet domestic peace was essentially maintained.

VICISSITUDES OF SOVEREIGNTY IN ENGLAND

Although, toward the end of the fourth dialogue of *Behemoth*, there is a summary of the fourteen "shiftings of the Supreme Authority" (376) in England from King Charles I to King Charles II, as among two Protectors, four Parliaments, two juntas—with two intervals where no "Supreme Authority" was found—regrettably Hobbes never undertook a full narrative of the vicissitudes of English sovereignty. If Hobbes had been freed from the need to write between the lines, he would doubtless have expanded upon his rueful account in *Leviathan* (29) of the crippling concessions of power from William the Conqueror to the Church and from William Rufus to the Barons, with the consequent church-state struggle between Thomas Becket and Henry II, and the baronage-monarch struggle under King John.

We may speculate upon what a liberated Hobbes might have said concerning the residence of sovereignty in England from William I through Richard III, given the political struggles of those four centuries—in the earlier civil wars of England—the succession war between William II Rufus and Robert Curthose (1088–1091), the Anarchy of 1135–1154, the First Barons' War against King John (1215–1217), the Second Barons' War against Henry III (1264–1267),the Third Barons' War against Edward II (1321–1322), and the Wars of the Roses (1455–1487). Sovereignty must have been disputed, or have migrated, or have evaporated, just as in the 1640–1660 period of the *Behemoth*.

But civil wars are not then only abridgements of Hobbesian sovereignty. Not simply the enduring presence of the Lords Spiritual privileged by William the Conqueror, the Lords Temporal privileged by William Rufus, and the Commons, separated from the Lords in 1341, but also the monarchical deference and mixed-statism implied by these powers being called upon to approve royal proposals for taxation, suggests that there may never have been a genuinely Hobbesian sovereign of England. Perhaps Hobbes might have extended his approval of the Tudor monarchs, the fiscally talented Henry VII, and the severely autocratic Henry VIII (*Behemoth* 181–182) to find them sovereign. On the other hand, *Behemoth*'s assertion (107) that in 1640 Charles I held the Sovereignty can hardly stand, given that from his accession in 1625 onward Charles had to beg money from a series of Parliaments that gave him instead recriminations and demands.

If there were rarely or never a true Hobbesian sovereign in England, most or all of its history could no doubt have been sorted and classified into the categories of state failure developed in chapter 29 of *Leviathan*, "Of Those Things That Weaken or Tend to the Dissolution of a Commonwealth."

In *Elements, The Citizen,* and *Leviathan,* Hobbes avoids any direct criticism of Charles I; but what is implicit is sufficiently devastating. But why indirection? Likely both a personal fear of persecution and a genuinely aporetic philosophical impasse.

Leo Strauss lists Hobbes among twenty-one heterodox philosophers who thought independently, suffered persecution, and "wrote between the lines"; and he cites Hobbes in particular as one among "modern" who looked forward to an enlightened future, and "concealed their views only far enough to protect themselves as well as possible from persecution."[55] Hobbes fled from England to France in 1640 to escape the fate of Bishop Roger Manwaring, who "preach'd his doctrine" of obedience to the king, and was imprisoned and ruined by Parliament.[56] He fled from France to England in 1651 in fear of "Roman clerics whose teachings he had successfully attacked"[57] and/or to escape the fate of Anthony Ascham, who likewise preached Hobbesian obedience to the Commonwealth, and was assassinated in 1650 by Royalists.[58] And early in the Restoration, 1666–1668, some of the bishops in the Cavalier Parliament proposed to have him burnt as a heretic, but Hobbes was the ex-tutor of Charles II, had free access to His Majesty, and survived nicely.[59]

Given such perils, for the enlightenment of the future political theorists, it would have served no purpose to berate explicitly a deceased king, himself beyond enlightenment or reform; let the readers learn to read between the lines!

But there was more than fear of persecution to constrain Hobbes' writing during the reign of Charles I; there was genuine philosophical aporia. Charles I's inability to maintain or to restore order in his three kingdoms was problematic for Hobbes' peace-focused political philosophy in that it created a perplexing contradiction between fundamental Hobbesian principles. Hobbes' perplexity can be summarized in two sentences.

1. Rulers who fail to keep the peace should be criticized and set straight, in the interests of restoring the peace.
2. But rulers must not be criticized, as this is seditious and tends to promote rebellion and undermine peace.

So Charles I while reigning was somewhat problematic for Hobbes, in that Hobbes thought his King's blunders must but must not be criticized. (Cromwell once in power, on the other hand, was not problematic for Hobbes, since Cromwell had imposed peace by effective force, and so needed no criticism, only obedience.)

Hobbes' kept rule 2, but only for present rulers, but waived it for past rulers, as the latter are invulnerable to sedition. Thus to enlighten (and covertly criticize) Charles I, it was acceptable to (overtly) criticize William the Conqueror and William Rufus, who were beyond harm. And later, to enlighten and instruct Charles II, it became acceptable to (delicately) criticize Charles I postmortem, in a way that would earlier have been (for Hobbes) intolerably seditious.

HOBBES AND CATASTROPHE, PAST AND PRESENT

In his life, Thomas Hobbes reflected upon one past war catastrophe, observed another at a distance, and twice fled a third. Roused by catastrophes, he wrote against catastrophe, in favor of peace, autocracy, good government and obedient submission.

In today's world, we can reflect upon many past catastrophes, observe many others at a distance, and some of us have fled the same. We know of catastrophes in our past of a scale perhaps beyond Hobbes' imagining—totalitarian genocide and nuclear war. Ongoing failed-state and civil war catastrophes we have, in plenty and in prospect.

As to the future, a Second Nuclear War catastrophe is actively threatened daily, and the capability of initiating it increases. There may come large-scale social migrations consequent on climate change and inundations. We may round out this list by mentioning natural catastrophes (plagues, volcanic eruptions, asteroid impacts) that could scale well up from present experience and lead to social breakdown and mass flight and invasion by survivors.

Then have we, who seem to know far more of catastrophe than did Hobbes, anything to learn from Hobbes in our relation to our catastrophes? A conversation may be possible.

In *The Citizen*, Hobbes asserts that "the state of commonwealths considered in themselves, is natural, that is to say, hostile. Neither if they cease from fighting, is it therefore to be called peace, but rather a breathing time."[60] And in *Leviathan* 13, he says "in all times, kings, and persons of sovereign authority, because of their independency, are in continual jealousies, and in the state and posture of gladiators; having their weapons pointing, and their eyes fixed on one another; that is their forts, garrisons, and guns upon the frontiers of their kingdoms; and continual spies upon their neighbours; which is a posture of war." And in Lev. 21: "in states and Commonwealths not dependent on one another, every Commonwealth, not every man, has an absolute liberty to do what it shall judge, that is to say, what that man or assembly that representeth it shall judge, most conducing to their benefit. But withal, they live in the condition of a perpetual war, and upon the confines of battle, with their frontiers armed, and cannons planted against their neighbours round about."

Hobbes did not propose a social contract among states. His generalized foreign policy was defensive and *status quo*: sovereigns must protect their subjects from foreign invasion, and might make temporary leagues for that purpose. Today, however, I imagine that Hobbes would be willing at least to consider whether the global scale of our most dangerous potential catastrophes makes Hobbesianly rational a contract amongst sovereigns to abjure their several sovereignties.

As to the means, we may consult again Hobbes to the Savilians: "the settlement of sovereign power without any army, must proceed from teaching"[61] and indeed from teaching in the universities. I can imagine a resurrected Hobbes seeking to frame the minds of two hundred-odd jealous armed states to gain the same value of assured peace through the surrender of their independence and through "conscientious obedience" to a government of their creation. An autocracy, of course. Perhaps to be commended to China, as consistent with the "China Dream," for benevolent implementation, "When China Rules the World"?[62] But on the catastrophes proper to China, and to universal states, one must turn to Arnold Toynbee—see *infra*!

ACKNOWLEDGMENTS

The splendid work of the Tufts University Perseus Digital Library, editor-in-chief Gregory R. Crane, and the inspiring Hobbes teaching of Herbert A. Deane of Columbia and Judith N. Shklar of Harvard are gratefully acknowledged by the author.

NOTES

1. See Thucydides, *The History of the Grecian Wars*, trans. Thomas Hobbes, in *The English Works of Thomas Hobbes of Malmesbury*, ed. William Molesworth (Aalen: Scientia Verlag, 1966).
2. See Helen H. Law, "Atrocities in Greek Warfare," *The Classical Journal* 15, no. 3 (December 1919): 132–47.
3. Thucydides, *Peloponnesian War*, trans. B. Jowett (Oxford: Clarendon Press, 1881), 2.67.
4. Thomas Hobbes, *The English Works of Thomas Hobbes of Malmesbury*, ed. William Molesworth (Aalen: Scientia Verlag, 1966), 26.
5. See Quentin Skinner, "Word and Image in the Philosophy of Thomas Hobbes," Résumé of seminar at the University of Geneva, Institute for the History of the Reformation, May 7, 2012, https://www.unige.ch/ihr/fr/archives/seminaires2011-12/resumeskinner/; "Word and Image in the Philosophy of Thomas Hobbes," lecture at the Warburg Institute, November 21, 2012, YouTube video, 56:30, accessed August 23, 2016, https://www.youtube.com/watch?v=uVnhKMEhlN0.
6. Hobbes, 1994b, "The Prose Life," 246.
7. Hobbes, 1966b, "The Epistle Dedicatory" and 1966c, "To the Readers."
8. Hobbes, 1966d, "Of the Life and History of Thucydides."
9. Thucydides, *Peloponnesian War*, trans. Hobbes, 6.54.5; cf. Jowett trans., in which the Peisistratid rule was not until very late violent, nor "unpopular or oppressive to the many; in fact no tyrants ever displayed greater merit or capacity than these."
10. Aristotle, *Athenian Constitution, Aristotle in 23 Volumes*, vol. 20, trans. H. Rackman (Cambridge, MA: Harvard University Press; London: William Heinemann Ltd., 1952), 14.3; cf. 16.2–17.1, 18.1.
11. Herodotus, *Histories*, trans. A. D. Godley (Cambridge, MA: Harvard University Press, 1920), 1.59.6.
12. Thucydides, *Peloponnesian War*, trans. Hobbes, 2.65.
13. Hobbes, 1966d, xvii.
14. Thucydides, *The Peloponnesian War*, trans. Steven Lattimore (Indianapolis, IN: Hackett Publishing, 1998); Hobbes' version is "the truth of things done and which (according to the condition of humanity) may be done again, or at least their like."
15. A. P. Martinich, *Hobbes: A Biography* (Cambridge, UK: Cambridge University Press, 1999), 38–39.

16. See Noel Malcolm, *Reason of State, Propaganda and the Thirty Years War: An Unknown Translation by Thomas Hobbes* (New York: Oxford University Press, 2007).

17. Theodore K. Rabb, *The Struggle for Stability in Early Modern Europe* (New York: Oxford University Press, 1975), 128–45.

18. See Peter Paul Rubens, *The Letters of Peter Paul Rubens*, trans. and ed. Ruth Saunders Magurn (Cambridge, MA: Harvard University Press, 1955), 409.

19. Hobbes, *The Elements of Law, Natural and Politic*, ed. and prefaced Ferdinand Tönnies, new introduction M. M. Goldsmith (London: Frank Cass, 1969); Hobbes, "The Prose Life," 245–53.

20. Hobbes, *Elements of Law*, 2.9.1.

21. Marcus Tullius Cicero, *Traite Des Lois* [Laws] = *M. Tullii Ciceronis De Legibus: Texte Et Trad.*, ed. and trans. Georges de Plinval (Paris: Société d'édition Les Belles Lettres, 1959), 3.8.

22. Hobbes, *Elements of Law*, 2.9.3.

23. Ibid., 2.9.1–9.

24. Ibid., 2.9.1.

25. Ibid., 1994b, 247; see also Martinich, *Hobbes: A Biography*, 122–23, 161–62, 309.

26. Skinner, "Word and Image," 2012.

27. Richard Bellings, in Sir J. T. Gilbert, *A Contemporary History of Affairs in Ireland, from 1641 to 1652* (Dublin: Irish archaeological and Celtic society, 1879–80), 14–15.

28. See Thomas Hobbes, *Leviathan*, ed. Noel Malcolm, in *Clarendon Edition of the Works of Thomas Hobbes*, vols. 3–5 (Oxford: Clarendon Press, 2012), 18.

29. Hobbes, *The Citizen*, 2.13.2.

30. Thomas Hobbes, *De Cive: Or, The Citizen. Edited with an Introduction by Sterling P. Lamprecht* (New York: Appleton-Century-Crofts, 1949), 2.13.6.

31. Ibid., 2.13.8.

32. Ibid., 2.13.10.

33. Hobbes, *Leviathan*, 18.

34. See Samuel Rawson Gardiner, *Constitutional Documents of the Puritan Revolution, 1625–1660*, 3rd rev. ed. (Oxford: Clarendon Press, 1906), 381–88.

35. Quentin Skinner, 2002b, "Introduction: Hobbes' Life in Philosophy," 19; see Samuel Rawson Gardiner, *History of the Commonwealth and Protectorate, 1649–1660* [i.e.1656], vol. 1 (London: Longmans, Green & Co., 1894–1901), 196–97.

36. Gardiner, *Constitutional Documents*, 391; *Acts and Ordinances*, 325–29.

37. Gardiner, *History*, vol. 1, 5–8, 215–16; *Behemoth* 356; Heath 1663: 651.

38. Blair Worden, *The Rump Parliament, 1648–1653*, 1–82, 219–20, 225–32.

39. Gardiner 1894–1901, v. I: 275.

40. Gardiner 1894–1901, v. II: 261–62; *Acts and Ordinances*, 774–75; Heath 651.

41. Gardiner 1894–1901, v. II: 316; *Acts and Ordinances*, 830–31.

42. B. Worden, *The Rump Parliament, 1648–1653* (Cambridge, UK: Cambridge University Press, 1974), 227.

43. Martinich, 224.

44. 2002a, 303.
45. Skinner 2002b, 21.
46. Hobbes 1994c, 260; Malcolm 2012, 100.
47. 2012: 24, 65–82.
48. Gardiner, 1906, 400–04.
49. Kari F. Helleiner, "The Population of Europe from the Black Death to the Eve of the Vital Revolution," in *The Cambridge Economic History of Europe from the Decline of the Roman Empire, Vol. 4: The Economy of Expanding Europe in the Sixteenth and Seventeenth Centuries*, ed. E. E. Rich and C. H. Wilson (Cambridge, UK: Cambridge University Press, 1967), 1–95, 53.
50. Thomas Hobbes, "Six Lessons to the Savilian Professors of Mathematics," 336.
51. Tim Harris, *Restoration: Charles II and His Kingdoms, 1660–1685* (London: Allen Lane, 2005), 47.
52. Rabb, *Struggle for Stability*, 3–4, 76–78, 116–45.
53. See Paul Seaward, "General Introduction" in Thomas Hobbes, *Behemoth, or The Long Parliament*, ed. P. Seaward in *Clarendon Edition of the Works of Thomas Hobbes*, vol. 10 (Oxford: Oxford University Press, 2010), 6–10.
54. Martinich, 323.
55. Leo Strauss, "Persecution and the Art of Writing" (Glencoe, IL: The Free Press, 1952), 33–34.
56. John Aubrey, "The Brief Life: An Abstract of Aubrey's Notes," 235–36; Thomas Seccomb, "Roger Manwaring," in *Dictionary of National Biography*, vol. 36 (London: Smith, Elder & Co., 1893), 235–36.
57. Hobbes, 1994b, 249.
58. Hobbes, 1994c, 260; Martinich, 209–10, 222.
59. Aubrey, 236–37; Martinich, 320–22.
60. Hobbes, *De Cive*, 2.13.7.
61. Hobbes, 1966e, "Six Lessons," 335.
62. See Angang Hu, *China 2030* (Heidelberg: Springer 2014); Martin Jacques, *When China Rules the World: The End of the Western World and the Birth of a New Global Order* (New York: Penguin, 2009); Minhfu Liu, *The China Dream: Great Power Thinking and Strategic Posture in the Post-American Era* (Beijing: CN Times, 2015).

BIBLIOGRAPHY

Acts and Ordinances of the Interregnum, 1642–1660. Originally published by His Majesty's Stationery Office, London, 1911.

Aristotle. *Athenian Constitution. Aristotle in 23 Volumes*, Vol. 20. Translated by H. Rackham. Cambridge, MA: Harvard University Press; London: William Heinemann Ltd., 1952.

Aubrey, John. "The Brief Life: An Abstract of Aubrey's Notes." 231–245 in Hobbes, 1994.

Aylmer, Gerald E. *The Interregnum: The Quest for Settlement, 1646–1660.* London: Macmillan, 1972.

[Bellings, Richard.] In Sir J. T. Gilbert. *A contemporary history of affairs in Ireland, from 1641 to 1652.* 3 vols. Dublin: Irish archaeological and Celtic society, 1879–80.

Burgess, Glenn. "Usurpation, Obligation and Obedience in the Thought of the Engagement Controversy." *The Historical Journal* 29, no. 3 (Sept. 1986): 515–36. Accessed August 30, 2016. doi:10.1017/S0018246X00018896.

Cicero, Marcus Tullius. *Traité Des Lois* [Laws] = *M. Tullii Ciceronis De Legibus: Texte Et Trad.* Edited and translated by Georges de Plinval. Paris: Société d'édition Les Belles Lettres, 1959.

Gardiner, Samuel Rawson. *History of the Commonwealth & Protectorate, 1649–1660* [i.e.1656]. 3 vols. London: Longmans, Green, 1894–1901.

Gardiner, Samuel Rawson, editor. *Constitutional Documents of the Puritan Revolution, 1625–1660.* 3rd Edition, revised. Oxford: Clarendon Press, 1906.

Goldsmith, M. M. "New Introduction." v–xxi in Hobbes, 1969.

Harris, Tim. *Restoration: Charles II and His Kingdoms 1660–1685.* London: Allen Lane, 2005.

Heath, James. *A brief chronicle of the late intestine war in the three kingdoms of England, Scotland and Ireland, with the intervening affairs of treaties, and other occurences relating thereunto as also the several usurpations, foreign wars, differences and interests depending upon it: composed and ended by the happy restitution of our Sacred Soveraign King Charls the Second: with all memorable affairs since his time: in four parts, as the government and its usurpations altered, from the year of our Lord 1637 to this present year 1663 / faithfully collected and compiled by James Heath. The Second Impression greatly enlarged.* London: Printed by J.B. for W. Lee, 1663. Accessed August 30, 2016 through Early English Books Online, http://eebo.chadwyck.com/.

Helleiner, Kari F. "The Population of Europe from the Black Death to the Eve of the Vital Revolution." In *The Cambridge Economic History of Europe from the Decline of the Roman Empire Volume 4. The Economy of Expanding Europe in the Sixteenth and Seventeenth Centuries,* 1–95. Edited by E. E. Rich and C. H. Wilson. Cambridge, UK: Cambridge University Press, 1967. doi: 10.1017/CHOL9780521045070.

Herodotus. *Histories.* Translated by A. D. Godley. Cambridge, Mass.: Harvard University Press, 1920.

Hobbes, Thomas. *De Cive: Or, The Citizen.* Edited with an Introduction by Sterling P. Lamprecht. New York: Appleton-Century-Crofts, 1949.

———. *The English Works of Thomas Hobbes of Malmesbury.* 11 vols. Edited by William Molesworth. [London: J. Bohn, 1839–1845.] Reprint, Aalen: Scientia Verlag, 1966.

———. "The Epistle Dedicatory." iii–vi in Hobbes 1966, Vol. VIII.

———. "To the Readers." vii–xi in Hobbes 1966, Vol. VIII.

———. "Of the Life and History of Thucydides." xiii–xxxii in Hobbes 1966a, Vol. VIII.

———. "Six Lessons to the Savilian Professors of Mathematics." 181–356 in Hobbes 1966, Vol. VII.

———. *The Elements of Law, Natural and Politic.* Edited and Prefaced by Ferdinand Tönnies. New Introduction by M. M. Goldsmith. 2nd Edition. London: Frank Cass, 1969.

———. *The Elements of Law, Natural and Politic: Part I, Human Nature, Part II, De Corpore Politico; with Three Lives.* Edited by J. C. A. Gaskin. Oxford: Oxford University Press, 1994.

———. "The Prose Life." 245–253 in Hobbes 1994.

———. "The Verse Life." 254–264 in Hobbes 1994.

———. *Behemoth, or The Long Parliament.* Edited by P. Seaward in *Clarendon Edition of the Works of Thomas Hobbes,* vol. 10. Oxford: Oxford University Press, 2010.

———. *Leviathan.* Edited by Noel Malcolm. 3 Vols. *Clarendon Edition of the Works of Thomas Hobbes,* vols. 3–5. Oxford: Clarendon Press, 2012.

Hu, Angang. *China 2030.* Heidelberg: Springer, 2014.

Jacques, Martin. *When China Rules the World: The End of the Western World and the Birth of a New Global Order.* New York: Penguin, 2009.

Law, Helen H. "Atrocities in Greek Warfare." *The Classical Journal* 15, no. 3 (December 1919): 132–47. Accessed 8/30/2016.

Liu, Mingfu. *The China Dream: Great Power Thinking & Strategic Posture in the Post-American Era.* Beijing: CN Times, 2015.

Locke, John. *Two Tracts on Government.* Edited by P. Abrams. London: Cambridge University Press, 1967.

Malcolm, Noel. *Reason of State, Propaganda, and the Thirty Years' War: An Unknown Translation by Thomas Hobbes.* New York: Oxford University Press, 2007.

Malcolm, Noel. *Editorial Introduction.* Vol. 1 of Hobbes, 2012.

Martinich, A. P. *Hobbes: A Biography.* Cambridge, UK: Cambridge University Press, 1999.

Rabb, Theodore K. *The Struggle for Stability in Early Modern Europe.* New York: Oxford University Press, 1975.

Rubens, Peter Paul. *The Letters of Peter Paul Rubens.* Translated and Edited by Ruth Saunders Magurn. Cambridge, MA: Harvard University Press, 1955.

Seaward, Paul. "General Introduction." 1–70 in Hobbes, *Behemoth.*

Seccomb, Thomas. "Roger Manwaring." *Dictionary of National Biography,* vol. 36. London: Smith, Elder & Co., 1893.

Skinner, Quentin. "Conquest and consent: Thomas Hobbes and the engagement controversy." 79–98 in *The Interregnum: The Quest for Settlement, 1646–1660.* Edited by G. E. Aylmer. London: Macmillan, 1972.

———. "Conquest and consent: Hobbes and the engagement controversy." 287–307 in Skinner, *Visions.* 2002.

———. "Introduction: Hobbes' life in philosophy." 1–37 in Skinner, *Visions.* 2002.

———. *Visions of Politics: Hobbes and Civil Science, Vol. 3.* Cambridge, UK: Cambridge University Press, 2002.

Skinner, Quentin. "Word and Image in the Philosophy of Thomas Hobbes." Résumé of a research seminar held in the University of Geneva, Institute for the History of the Reformation, May 7, 2012. Accessed 8/19/2016. https://www.unige.ch/ihr/fr/archives/seminaires2011-12/resumeskinner/.

———. "Word and Image in the Philosophy of Thomas Hobbes." Lecture delivered at the Warburg Institute, November 21, 2012. YouTube video 56:30. Published on Feb 10, 2013. Accessed August 23, 2016. https://www.youtube.com/watch?v=uVnhKMEhlN0.

———. "Hobbes and the Iconography of the State." Lecture delivered at University College Dublin in 2015. Published on Jan 4, 2016. Accessed August 23, 2016. https://www.youtube.com/watch?v=IOeEN_s_blE.

Strauss, Leo. "Persecution and the Art of Writing." In *Persecution and the Art of Writing*, 22–37. Glencoe, IL: The Free Press, 1952.

The Greek Anthology. Translated by W. R. Paton. Vol. II, Book 7, Chapter 45. London: William Heinemann Ltd, 1917.

Thucydides. *Thucydides Translated into English to Which Is Prefixed an Essay on Inscriptions and a Note on the Geography of Thucydides by Benjamin Jowett*. Translated by B. Jowett. Oxford: Clarendon Press, 1881.

———. *The History of the Grecian Wars*. Translated by Thomas Hobbes. In *The English Works of Thomas Hobbes of Malmesbury*, Vol. VIII–IX. Edited by William Molesworth. [London: J. Bohn, 1839–1845] Reprint, Aalen: Scientia Verlag, 1966.

———. *The Peloponnesian War*. Translated by Steven Lattimore. Indianapolis, IN: Hackett Publishing, 1998.

Underdown, David. "Settlement in the Counties 1653–1658." In Aylmer, *The Interregnum*, 165–182.

Woolrych, Austin. "Last Quests for a Settlement 1657–1660." In Aylmer, *The Interregnum*, 183–204.

Worden, Blair. *The Rump Parliament, 1648–1653*. Cambridge, UK: Cambridge University Press, 1974.

Chapter 9

"A New Philosophy Calls All into Doubt"

The Epistemological Crises of Early Modernity (and why they matter now)

David J. Rosner and Steven Cresap

This chapter explores the similarities between the wars of religion of early modern Europe and those occurring today, primarily between Islam and the West. It will explore how these wars of religion arose in the context of civilizational upheavals. Psychological mechanisms involved in religious belief and doubt will then be analyzed and applied to these cases. Connections will also be explored with the concept of epistemic humility.

WARS OF RELIGION IN EARLY MODERNITY

In early modern Europe, many people were killed, often burned at stake, over charges of "heresy." Michael Shenefelt writes:

> "In 1586, a decade before Rene Descartes was born, the Archbishop of Trier ordered some one hundred twenty alleged witches burned to death for interfering with the weather. Another sixty three were burned at the stake in Bavaria a few years later for having caused hail, thunderstorms, and a plague among cattle." . . . None of this was improbable for the period. People all over Europe believed themselves possessed by devils, demons and fiends. And many people concluded that the only way to escape these wicked spirits was to execute their neighbors. Executing neighbors was nothing new. For more than half a century. . . . Christians throughout Europe had been killing one another in a vast struggle over whose version of Christianity was theologically correct. . . . Europe was still staggering through the last phases of the Wars of Religion,

during which many ridiculous claims of spiritual certainty produced much bloodshed . . . modern epistemology was born at a moment of particular pain and paranoia in the development of modern Europe.[1]

Why was this time characterized by such mass hysteria, anxiety and violence? One of the most oft quoted lessons of the Scientific Revolution is that the shift from geocentric astronomy to the heliocentric model brought to the fore the unsettling realization that man is not the center of universe, as was previously believed. The Earth is now to be considered one planet among many in a vast, possibly infinite universe. Pascal thus famously said "The eternal silence of these infinite spaces fills me with dread."[2]

Galileo's nemesis Cardinal Bellarmine thought the Copernican universe was just a local illusion, as if given to us out of God's generosity to help with navigation. The larger picture of the universe still involved crystalline spheres and heaven above. Therefore, not everyone was scared of the "infinite spaces." Moreover, most of the people, who were illiterate, paid little attention to this debate. Modern science was not an explanatory framework for most people – just as it is not today for many Americans. What is the degree to which such paradigm shifts in the world of ideas actually impact the lives and worldviews of the vast majority of people? Are these paradigm shifts only relevant to a civilizations' "intelligentsia" or do such ideas "seep" gradually into the general consciousness? Religious fundamentalism in the United States has grown and spread after the 1960s and 1970s cultural revolutions as a result of the aporias generated as a result of these movements. But who among the fundamentalists actually views it that way? Early modern thinkers such as Francis Bacon and Descartes, who both practiced forms of systematic doubt, were well aware that confusion could be had not only in academic controversies but also in popular beliefs and prejudices, such as the magical thinking normal for the time.

COSMIC ORDER VS INCOHERENCE IN "THE NEW PHILOSOPHY"

The "new philosophy" (discoveries in astronomy pointing to a heliocentric conception of the universe) challenged the existing medieval framework and was met by no small amount of fear and anxiety, as the very coherence of the world's most long-standing assumptions was now called into question. What is interesting is how in this case, it was "the new philosophy" itself that was experienced as the catastrophe of the time for many educated European Christian believers. Science and philosophy were not separated into disciplines as they are now; science was considered "natural philosophy." The "new philosophy called all in doubt" insofar as it dramatically challenged fundamental, long-standing Church doctrines, and thus constituted a large part of the unfolding process of the gradual dissolution of European ecclesiastical authority. Hence John Donne's famous passage:

And new philosophy calls all in doubt
The element of fire is quite put out
The sun is lost and the earth and no man's wit
Can well direct him where to look for it
And freely men confess that this world's spent
When in the planets and the firmament
The seek so many new; they see that this
Is crumbled out again to his atomies
Tis all in pieces, all coherence gone.[3]

According to E. Tillyard, "The world-picture which the middle ages inherited was that of an ordered universe arranged in a fixed system of hierarchies but modified by man's sin and hope of his redemption. Everything had to be included and everything had to be made to fit and to connect."[4]

Tillyard argues that this conception was also characteristic of the Elizabethan period as well. He also writes "the conception of order is so taken for granted, so much a part of the collective mind of the people, that it is hardly mentioned except in explicitly didactic passages."[5] Tillyard quotes Shakespeare's *MacBeth, Troilus and Cressida* and so on, as examples of this general world picture—as these are in part cautionary tales illustrating that when the natural order is challenged, even in the political realm, only conflict, death and evil can ensue.

Further complications were provided by the Protestant Reformation, which caused fissures in the perceptions of infallibility and moral authority of Catholic Church, and a schism within European Christianity. A number of writers and theorists believed this also to constitute another crack in the heretofore impregnable wall of Christian Europe. These two developments reveal how early modernity was fundamentally characterized by anomie and deep aporia, both moral and epistemological. How to make sense of the world when one's most basic explanatory framework has been so radically questioned?

CERTAINTY AND FANATICISM

It would be instructive to also consider here the work of Descartes, and his place in the history of philosophy. Descartes' quest for certainty seems unintelligible and excessive to many contemporary students in introductory philosophy classes. But when some context is provided, it becomes clear that this was no pathology—it was an attempt to ascertain what could be known for certain in a world in which suddenly the most basic assumptions were now shown to be uncertain and everything previously believed seemed suddenly open to question.

Descartes writes:

> The Meditation of yesterday has filled my mind with so many doubts that it is no longer in my power to forget them. And yet I do not see how I shall be able to resolve them; and as though I had suddenly fallen into very deep water, I am so taken unawares that I can neither put my feet firmly down on the bottom nor swim to keep myself on the surface. . . . I shall continue always in this path until I have encountered something which is certain, or at least, if I can do nothing else, until I have learned with certainty that there is nothing certain in the world.[6]

This "Cartesian anxiety" has been effectively described by Richard Bernstein:

> It is the quest for some fixed point, some stable rock upon which we can secure our lives against the vicissitudes that constantly threaten us. The specter that hovers in the background . . . is not just radical epistemological skepticism but the dread of madness and chaos where nothing is fixed, where we can neither touch bottom nor support ourselves on the surface. With a chilling clarity Descartes leads us . . . to a grand and deductive "Either/Or." Either there is some support for our being, a fixed foundation for our knowledge, or we cannot escape the forces of darkness . . . and . . . chaos.[7]

Of course, the urge for certainly was to some degree already a feature of European culture. The Scholastic perspective on learning was based on extreme reliance on authority, often the authority of the ancients or the Bible. Exact, correct answers, apodictic certainty by means of sacred text and Aristotelian logic, were the goals of argumentation. Yet what happens when these authorities (and their sources of information) are challenged?

Descartes' obsessive doubting in the *Meditations*, and Bacon's dismissal of our most basic ways of thinking and feeling in his "Idols of the Mind," reveal their firm sense of certainty in the face of doubt. The role of actual theological and cosmological disputes is relatively slight in their arguments. They are critical of the ordinary sources of knowledge and consolation among not only the learned but also the population at large: they dismiss astrology as well as the academic disciplines, common prejudices as well as theories. Michael Shenefelt writes that "philosophy . . . was in many ways a search for reasonableness. . . . What made Descartes most interesting . . . was not merely his belief in the reality of reasonableness. Rather it was his equally firm conviction that the societies of his own time were profoundly unreasonable. And this further conviction also deeply affected his conception of what philosophy ought to be."[8]

We see such tendencies in Bacon also. In *The Novum Organum* ("Idols of the Tribe"), Bacon questions the basic religious impulse, the desire for safety and hope in the face of disaster. In the context of identifying what we know as "confirmation bias"— our understanding always supports an adopted opinion even in the face of better evidence to the contrary—he strikes at what is perhaps the fundamental religious impulse, the consoling notion that God will protect us. He describes the reaction of an unnamed person to being shown a picture about a natural disaster, a shipwreck, in which the survivors were depicted as having "paid their vows." When asked whether he did not now acknowledge the power of the gods, the spectator has a remarkably subversive reply. "Aye, but where are they painted that were drowned after their vows?" "And such is the way of all superstition, whether in astrology, dreams, omens, divine judgments, or the life; wherein men, having a delight in such vanities, mark the events where they are fulfilled, but where they fail, though his happen much oftener, neglect and pass them by."[9]

So what we find is a veiled but bold denial of one of our most existential religious impulses, the need to find meaning in catastrophe. Bacon, like Descartes, seems to have had a remarkable intellectual and emotional courage, a firmness of belief that rivals the convictions of the believers. But in spite of this, and in spite of what later philosophers may have made of them, the early modern scientists, even those like Descartes and Bacon who were embedded in war and politics, never became fanatics, and in fact, resisting the temper of the times, embarked upon a search for the foundations of rationality in an otherwise irrational world.[10]

What else can be said regarding the fanaticism so widespread at this time? People at this time believed strongly in the claims and assumptions of their religious teachings. Or did they? Perhaps they secretly had their doubts. We often feel the need to convince other people that we are right and they are wrong, about religion, politics, sports, or anything else. We want other people to agree with us, to see the world the way we do. We get upset if people disagree with our views. But why do we act this way? Perhaps we all sometimes need to *convince ourselves* of the certainty of our beliefs. Consider further how deep this need must have been in the face of the pervasive ground-level uncertainty engendered in early modern Europe by both the Scientific Revolution and the Protestant Reformation.

CONTEMPORARY WARS OF RELIGION: ISLAMIC FUNDAMENTALISM VS THE (POST-)MODERN WEST

These considerations can be applied to wars of religion today. The Islamic fundamentalist movement grew out of the political and cultural void left in the Middle East following the collapse of the Ottoman Empire in the early 20th century. Islamic fundamentalism was/is a conservative reaction to the breakdown of a long-standing political and cultural framework, as well as an expression of anger at the Western powers for the cultural imperialism involved in the Ottoman collapse.[11] Roger Griffin writes regarding Robert Lifton: "It is the anomie experienced by all rapidly secularizing societies that has moved movements such as . . . al Qaeda . . . mobilized by the belief that moral regeneration can only be brought about by acts of cathartic terrorism directed towards mainstream society . . . such surgical violence aims to purge the corruption of a decadent modernity. . . . Acts of violence committed in order to the protect an ancient religious culture thus stem from a modern permutation of an ultra conservative and reactionary response to the terror of anomie."[12]

Here we have a difficulty separating religious motives from the secular. At the root of the distinction are the elements of "regeneration," "catharsis," "purging," and so on, which are not typical secular values.[13]

If we can speak of wars of religion as distinct from other kinds of war, we note that modern, supposedly secular wars have been more destructive than any wars of the early modern period. We also mark a distinction among motives and the psychology of survival. Instead of engaging in hostilities to defend one's territory or extend one's reach for economic or political reasons, religious warriors seem motivated by a transcendent vision of spiritual exaltation (which does not necessarily rule out the baser stimuli). What is behind this apparent difference in motive and psychology of survival? Historically, it appears that fanaticism and religiously motivated violence become widespread in times of upheaval. Such upheavals reveal an anomie related to the questioning of the dominant faith or ideology, with the social effect of an increase in conversions and the gaining or losing of faith.

Over the last few years we have witnessed the rise and spread of the newest and most lethal offshoot of Islamic radicalism—ISIS—featuring beheadings of prisoners videotaped and broadcast online, burnings of prisoners in cages, etc. We have seen also the destruction of priceless (pre-Islamic) antiquities from the Assyrian empire, in the ancient cities of Nimrod, Palmyra, etc.

THOUGHTS ON THE PSYCHOLOGY OF RELIGIOUS BELIEF AND UNBELIEF

We will now consider the psychology of religious (and other) beliefs, and the role of "the anxiety of uncertainty" in this process. We will then look at the implications of this.

There are interesting features of fundamentalist religious conversions. Mathjis Pelkmans has written extensively on the phenomenon of doubt. According to Pelkmans, "often very religious people seem so certain of and unwavering in their beliefs." But this certainty may be more apparent than real. He explains: "Religious and secular conviction can have powerful effects, but their foundations are often surprisingly fragile. In fact, the firmer the endorsement of ideas, the weaker the basis of these notions may be. Recent converts are often particularly fervent in acting out their convictions, precisely because of their greater (and momentary) ability to suspend lingering doubt. And intense ideological movements can only retain their fervor by actively denying ambiguity."[14]

Similarly, Julie McBrien writes: "perhaps we have been too busy erasing doubt. . . . We tend to downplay or erase the role indecision and uncertainty plays in our own daily lives, minimizing it in our own (self) representations in order to avoid being seen as weak, indecisive, or easily persuaded."[15] McBrien discusses "our desire for certainty—a world without doubt." "Although such assurances of certainly are no more than a chimera, our collective (and individual) craving for them is not. . . . Generally speaking, we don't like doubt and we are constantly trying to elude it.[16]

Why are our religious convictions often more fragile than they may appear? We first and foremost believe what our senses tell us, and it often doesn't appear to us as if things happen in this world according to traditional religious conceptions of divine justice. And talk of the afterlife involves going beyond what we have any experience of. In her review of Pelkman's book, *Ethnographies of Doubt*, Alice Bloch writes of the complexities surrounding these features of religious belief:

> Pelkmans . . . posits that doubt and belief should be seen as "co-constitutive parts," and that "instead of being the opposite of belief, doubt is often implicated in it." "In the chapter by Giulia Liberatore's study of newly practicing Somali Muslims in London, we meet Maryam, whose lifestyle has changed since she began "'practicing' Islam more seriously" in recent years. Grappling with thoughts on the nature of "paradise," she admits, "I'm freaked out paradise will have restrictions . . . I know I shouldn't be saying this but I've given up so much stuff here and I just want to make sure it's all worth something."[17]

Religious lives require restrictions and sacrifices in this world but from the viewpoint of our everyday experience, no one really knows what form "the world to come" takes or even whether it exists. This may be one occasion for doubt, though there are other possible occasions as well.

Similar themes are discussed by Anne-Sophie Lamine in her paper "'I doubt; Therefore I am': Facing Uncertainty and Belief in the Making,"[18] which begins with a quote from Hannah Arendt: Human affairs are characterized by "isolated islands of certainty in an ocean of uncertainty."[19] Lamine writes: "religion has often been considered an affective response to the existential crisis of uncertainty . . . through providing supposedly infallibly true answers to natural an existential questions. But religious 'belief' does not necessarily isolate people from uncertainty and doubt . . . belief is often complex and messy, with people's beliefs regularly subject to oscillation and periods of doubt."[20] Lamine discusses different modalities of doubt, yet makes room for the sorts of cases discussed in this paper, those on the extreme end of the spectrum where "people strive to reduce or to avoid doubt while searching for pure religion, which often results in the rigidification of religious identities and beliefs."[21]

Lamine also explains the oscillation between belief and doubt citing George Simmel, who "paid attention to the internal contradictions of the individual which he calls 'contradictions of spiritual life' or 'opposing and incompatible forces at work within the soul.'"[22] Lamine discusses the implications of Simmel's insights regarding fundamentalist religion (though she notes that they may apply also to other extremes of belief, for example, rigid atheism or even political beliefs): "One response when coping with this tension may be the development of uncompromising beliefs . . . this rigidification is characterized by the total assent to a system of propositions, leaving no room for the transformation of normative positions."[23]

These discussions all implicate a tendency among fundamentalist believers to "double down" on the side of belief when confronted with naturally occurring doubt, as a means of eradicating any unsettling ambiguity or uncertainty. As the modern world is so fundamentally characterized by uncertainty, the need here is for religious belief to be absolute and uncompromised to counter this uncertainty and thus provide psychological relief. Any cracks in the wall of absolutism must therefore be quickly dismissed, repressed, or overcompensated for in the other, extreme direction.

Consider also that in our postmodern, secular age, religion is no longer the only explanation for life and its complications, no longer the filter through which all events are processed. We now have scientific explanations, and a host of other non-theistic ethical systems through which we can attempt to make sense of our world. Religion is now relegated to one option among many in a crowded marketplace of ideas and explanations.

Hence Charles Taylor writes:

> We live in a condition where we cannot but be aware that there are a number of different construals, views which intelligent, reasonably undeluded people, of good will, can and do disagree on. We cannot help looking over our shoulder from time to time, looking sideways, living our faith also in a condition of doubt and uncertainty.[24]

This holds true in the world of Islamic fundamentalism as much as any other world. "Jihadi John," the ominous masked executioner in the ISIS beheading videos later assassinated by U.S. airstrikes, grew up in cosmopolitan London, UK, attended University, and was exposed to secular Western life. The perpetrators of the 9/11 attacks were similarly exposed to Western culture. But they found it threatening. Perhaps they were among the alienated—never fully assimilated or accepted into European culture. Or their worldviews were threatened by modernity itself, where the absolutist beliefs of their fathers now had to confront various forms of radical relativism and skepticism.

Arie Kruglanski, John Jost, et al., in their article "Political Conservatism as Motivated Social Cognition," have conducted empirical research on religious fundamentalists and others on the far right of the political spectrum. They have researched how this worldview has been shown in a variety of contexts to reflect unease with ambiguity, a need for "closure" when situations are left unresolved, as well as discomfort with incomplete or tentative answers.[25] Given these findings, an attraction to moral absolutism would presumably be strong among such individuals. We would also not be surprised to find negative attitudes toward "modernity" among some within this population today, as "modernity" has essentially involved the systematic challenging of existing explanatory frameworks on a number of fronts and has therefore embraced uncertainty, doubt and other forms of relativism as constitutive of reality. However, two caveats are in order here. First, there is a substantial difference between run-of-the-mill political/economic conservatives and fundamentalist religious fanatics, as the belief spectrum here is wide. Second, absolutistic perspectives are often exemplified by extreme leftists and atheists as well. Ideological "purists" of all political stripes maintain increasingly rigid and uncompromising belief systems when confronted with serious challenges and doubts.

Let us now consider a number of key questions regarding belief and unbelief. How many religions have there been throughout human history? Hundreds? Thousands? How many are still extant now? How could only one of these really be correct and all the others false? How could anyone possibly know this? What exactly would be the criterion for such knowledge? Prophets like Moses, Jesus, and so on would likely be considered crazy in these postmodern times if they claimed God spoke to them. With regard to truth claims in religion, it seems we may *believe* x but we don't really *know* it. Definitions of these terms are complicated and have been much debated in contemporary epistemology; we cannot rehearse the arguments here. The bottom line, as many have argued, is that claims to religious knowledge are based on "faith," rather than reason.

Yet if one is indeed secure in this faith, why would one need to persecute and even kill people who believe otherwise about one's religion (i.e., internecine Shia vs Sunni conflicts, or Protestant versus Catholic violence)? What explains the need felt by so many believers to persecute and kill those who practice another religion, or who don't believe in any religion at all? Consider again the recent destruction by ISIS of antiquities in Iraq and Syria that predated Islam (similar atrocities were also committed by the Taliban against Buddha statues in Bamiyan, Afghanistan). Why the need of these radical Islamic believers to destroy all physical reminders of pre-existing religion?

One answer could be that it is a form of magical thinking in a tribal context: the presence of unbelievers in your territory causes God to bring catastrophes onto your tribe. Romans thought the Olympian gods would punish them if they did not persecute the Christians. It's an evolutionary, autonomic, and often irrational behavior among humans: to defend one's own tribe and traditions. In times of insecurity, anxiety can easily turn into rage and intolerance against others.

Another answer lies in what could only be called basic cosmic insecurity. ISIS justified this destruction of ancient pre-Islamic ruins by claiming it was destroying idols (and thus idolatry), like Abraham (Ibrahim) did in his father's house. Yet erasing all traces of pre-Islamic religion perhaps reveals more about the fundamentalists' insecurity than anything else, as they may be trying to convince themselves of the primacy of their religious belief in an uncertain modern world where there are now multiple explanations for so many phenomena, including the origins of the universe, as well as competing truth claims with supporting "revelations." Ultimately the faith of many of these religious believers is thin and fragile because of a basic admission they have not the courage to make—that no mortal human being in this world really knows with certainty the ways of God (if indeed there is such a truth at all).

Some have argued that the wars of religion, then and now, were not really ever about religion at all—that they are/were about political or economic power, with religion serving as the pretext for struggles over power, land, and money. This might explain some of the picture, but it is reductionist. For why was religion specifically chosen as the vehicle for these conflicts? That is to say, why could people not just admit they are fighting over land, money or power? Why try to disguise it at all? Perhaps theological formulations are like hypocrisy: the homage vice pays to virtue. But religion has never been completely eradicated from the human world picture. Jesus and the early Christians were not really motivated by struggles for power and money. The young Saudis who crashed their planes into the World Trade Center were not dirt-poor. Many of the young people traveling to Syria to train for ISIS come from affluent European countries. Religion has traditionally furnished the human race's most comprehensive explanation for the meaning of life. This is why people have fought over it. Science, on the other hand, was never meant to answer value questions such as life's meaning, the meaning of right and wrong, how to live, etc. One of the reasons there are no wars of science is that science does not offer the existential security and promise of personal redemption that religious faiths do. The spirituality of science has to do with curiosity, and redemption comes in the form of pursuing the life of the mind. As for connecting with something larger than ourselves, scientists do this through observing the universe and participating in the progress of science as a universal community. None of this reaches the soothing level of complete belief in an afterlife or a commitment to a crusade to bring on the end times.

EPISTEMIC HUMILITY IN APORETIC TIMES

Lately there has appeared in philosophy a renewed interest in the concept of epistemological humility. What is it and why it is needed now? For one thing, a sincere acceptance of basic human aporia is long overdue. If one is honest, one would have to admit that no one really knows why we are here on this planet, how we got here, what death will bring—what it all means. Most of us don't even know how we are going to pay this month's electric bill, let alone if there is God in heaven, and if so, what God's nature is, God's relation to mankind, which religion (if any) is "right," and so on. This idea in fact goes back to ancient times; consider the following fragment from the pre-Socratic Greek philosopher Xenophanes:

> "And of course the clear and certain truth no man has seen, nor will there be anyone who knows about the Gods and what I say about all things. For even if, in the best case, one happened to speak just of what has been brought to pass, still he himself would not know. But opinion is allotted to all."[26]

Given the profound limits of human knowledge, it seems the height of arrogance for anyone to assert that he/she "knows" the answer to these questions. And what about going so far as killing those who disagree with our religious beliefs? Given that none of us really know the answers to life's most difficult existential questions, this can be explained as cosmic insecurity so far-reaching that it can only be alleviated through "reaction-formation," functioning as a cathartic purge.

Theorists have argued that extremist religious fundamentalism involves a number of premises. One is the claim to "absolute truth."[27] Another is a form of Manicheanism, a perspective in which the world is divided into forces of good versus evil. This dichotomy can only be resolved through a coming apocalyptic battle between these forces, a battle constituting a "purification" of the world. This is often enacted in terms of blood sacrifice (in the form of holy war or—what we have seen so much of lately—acts of "terror" against the perceived forces of evil).[28] Yet how can these believers, given the vast multiplicity of religions and all the other belief (and unbelief) systems, be certain that it is in fact *their* belief system that constitutes the one "absolute truth," while all the others are false? And what could even count as evidence for this, besides logically circular appeals to the relevant scriptures? Moreover, regarding Manicheanism, how can these believers be sure that it is in fact *they* who are on the right side of the equation? This is where epistemic humility becomes relevant. These people cannot know these things at all, and neither can anyone else. Certainty regarding metaphysical realities is simply not available to any of us as mortal human beings.

In light of our fundamental ignorance about life's most basic questions, rather than fighting each other over whose version of religion and life is correct, we should try harder to have more compassion for others and their (our shared) existential predicament, as we are all finite human beings in the same epistemic boat. This sort of paradigm shift—toward epistemic humility and compassion for our finite brethren—a mutual recognition and admission of our universal ignorance—might help reduce the amount of strife in the world. But there may be darker aspects of human nature that are stronger—innate propensities toward conflict and strife—that would prevent this from ever happening on a global scale. Perhaps some policy related proscriptions would therefore have to be formally put into place by a supra-national entity in the interests of rationality and the long-term best interests of humanity. The UN serves a similar purpose today. Of course, it has problems and limitations. We can only hope that our rational instinct toward cooperation will prevail and save the human race—both from its propensity toward arrogant baseless exceptionalism, and all the primitive conflicts that inevitably follow in its wake.

NOTES

1. See Michael Shenefelt, "Philosophy as the Search for Reasonableness," in *Many Faces of Wisdom*, ed. Phil Washburn (Upper Saddle River, NJ: Prentice-Hall, 2003), 126.

2. Blaise Pascal, *Pensees* (1660), trans. Krailsheimer (New York: Penguin, 1995).

3. John Donne, "The Anatomy of the World," in *The Complete Poetry and Selected Prose of John Donne and The Complete Poetry of William Blake*, intro by R. S. Hiller (New York: Modern Library, 1946), 165.

4. Eustace Tillyard, *The Elizabethan World Picture* (New York: Vintage, 1959), 6.

5. Ibid., 9.

6. Rene Descartes, *Discourse on Method* and *Meditations*, trans. F. E. Sutcliffe (Baltimore, MD: Penguin), 102, as quoted in Ami Harbin, *Disorientation and Moral Life* (Oxford: Oxford University Press, 2016), 65.

7. Richard Bernstein, *Beyond Objectivism and Relativism* (Philadelphia: University of Pennsylvania Press, 1983), 18.

8. Shenefelt, "Philosophy as the Search," 127–28.

9. Francis Bacon, *The New Organon*, ed. L. Jardine and M. Silverthorne (Cambridge, UK: Cambridge University Press, 2000); Aphorisms, Book One, paragraph 46.

10. Cf. Shenefelt, "Philosophy as the Search."

11. Toby Huff, "Before and After Nine-Eleven: A Civilizational Clash," *Comparative Civilizations Review* 60, no. 60 (Spring 2009): 49–78.

12. See Roger Griffin, *Modernism and Fascism* (London: Palgrave, 2007), 347. Griffin develops these ideas further in his book *Terrorist's Creed: Fanatical Violence and the Human Need for Meaning* (London: Palgrave, 2012).

13. Note however, that some theorists see the transcendent pleasures of fighting to involve such elements: See also Ernst Junger, *On Danger* and J. Glenn Gray, "The Enduring Appeals of Battle." Also see Weber and Freud.

14. Mathis Pelkmans, "Outline for an Ethnography of Doubt," in *Ethnographies of Doubt: Faith and Uncertainty in Contemporary Societies*, ed. Mathis Pelkmans (London: IB Tauris, 2013).

15. Julie McBrien, "Afterword—In the Aftermath of Doubt," in *Ethnographies of Doubt*, 252.

16. Ibid.

17. Alice Bloch, "Book Review: Ethnographies of Doubt," *The Humanist* (August 2014). See https://newhumanist.org.uk/articles/4728/book-review-ethnographies-of-doubt-by-ed-mathijs-pelkmans.

18. Anne-Sophie Lamine, "'I Doubt; Therefore I Am': Facing Uncertainty and Belief in the Making," in *Religion in Times of Crisis*, ed. G. Ganiel, H. Winkel, and C. Monnot (Leiden, NL: Brill, 2014). This is vol. 24 in the series *Religion and the Social Order*.

19. From Hannah Arendt, *The Human Condition*. See Lamine, 72.

20. Lamine, 73.

21. Ibid. Lamine also cites K. Pargament, *The Psychology of Religion and Coping* (New York: Guilford Press, 1977).

22. Lamine, 75. The original cite is to George Simmel, *Essays on Religion* (New Haven: Yale University Press, 1997).

23. Lamine also cites here W. Stahl, "One Dimensional Rage: The Social Epistemology of the New Atheism and Fundamentalism," in *Religion and the New Atheism: A Critical Appraisal*, ed. A. Amarasingam (Leiden, NL: Brill, 2010).

24. Charles Taylor, *A Secular Age* (Cambridge, MA: Harvard University Press, 2007), 11.

25. See Arie Kruglanski, John T. Jost, Jack Glaser, and Frank J. Sulloway, "Political Conservatism as Motivated Social Cognition," *Psychological Bulletin* (APA) 129 no. 3 (May 2003): 339–75.

26. Xenophanes, frag. B34. See James Lesher, "Xenophanes," in *The Stanford Encyclopedia of Philosophy* ed. E. Zalta (Fall 2014).

27. C. Kimball, *When Religion Turns Evil* (New York: HarperCollins, 2008).
28. See Roger Griffin, *The Terrorist's Creed*, 96ff.

BIBLIOGRAPHY

Bacon, Francis. *The New Organon.* Edited by L. Jardine and M. Silverthorne. Cambridge, UK: Cambridge University Press, 2000.
Bernstein, Richard. *Beyond Objectivism and Relativism.* Philadelphia: University of Pennsylvania Press, 1983.
Bloch, Alice. "Book Review: *Ethnographies of Doubt.*" *New Humanist* (August, 2014).
Descartes, Rene. *Discourse on Method* and *Meditations.* Translated by F.E. Sutcliffe. Baltimore, MD: Penguin, 1968.
Donne, John. "Anatomy of the World." In *The Complete Poetry and Selected Prose of John Donne and The Complete Poetry of William Blake.* Introduction by R.S. Hillyer. New York: Modern Library, 1946.
Griffin, Roger. *Modernism and Fascism.* London: Palgrave, 2007.
Griffin, Roger. *The Terrorist's Creed: Fanatical Violence and the Human Need for Meaning.* London: Palgrave, 2012.
Harbin, Ami. *Disorientation and Moral Life.* Oxford: Oxford University Press, 2016.
Huff, Toby. "After and Before Nine-Eleven: A Civilizational Clash." *Comparative Civilizations Review* 60, no. 60 (Spring 2009): 49–78.
Kimball, Charles. *When Religion Turns Evil.* New York: Harper Collins, 2008.
Kruglanski, Arie, John T. Jost, Jack Glaser, Frank J. Sulloway. "Political Conservatism as Motivated Social Cognition." *Psychological Bulletin* (APA) 129, no. 3 (May 2003): 339–375.
Lamine Sophie. "I Doubt, Therefore I am: Facing Uncertainty and Doubt in the Making," in *Religion in Times of Crisis.* Edited by Ganiel, Winkel, et al. Leiden, NL: Brill, 2014.
Lesher, James. "Xenophanes," in *The Stanford Encyclopedia of Philosophy* (Fall 2014). Edited by E. Zalta. hpps://plato.stanford.edu/archives/fall2014/entries/xenophanes.
McBrien, Julie. "Afterword—In the Aftermath of Doubt." In *Ethnographies of Doubt: Faith and Uncertainty in Contemporary Societies.* Edited by Mathis Pelkmans. London: IB Tauris, 2013.
Pascal, Blaise. *Pensees* [1660]. Translated by A. J. Krailsheimer. New York: Penguin, 1995.
Pelkmans, Mathis. "Outline for an Ethnography of Doubt." In *Ethnographies of Doubt: Faith and Uncertainty in Contemporary Societies.* Edited by M. Pelkmans. London: I.B. Tauris, 2013.
Shenefelt, Michael. "Philosophy as the Search for Reasonableness" in *Many Faces of Wisdom,* edited by Phil Washburn. Upper Saddle River, NJ: Prentice Hall, 2003.
Taylor, Charles. *A Secular Age.* Cambridge, MA: Harvard University Press, 2007.
Tillyard, Eustace M.W. *The Elizabethan World Picture.* New York: Vintage, 1959.

Chapter 10

The Metaphysics of Catastrophe—Voltaire's *Candide*[*]

Carsten Meiner

When Voltaire published *Candide* in 1759, Europe was experiencing enormous political, financial, and ecological problems, and it would not be an understatement to claim that this short philosophical novel was written in the sign of catastrophe.[1] Even if catastrophe should be pluralized, as we know that *Candide* was written against the backdrop of a series of catastrophic events, two of them stand out as major sources for Voltaire. First of all, we have the earthquake in Lisbon in 1755. The fact that this catastrophe caused tsunamis and fires, destroyed large parts of the city and triggered a series of intellectual interventions on the part of enlightenment philosophers such as Pope, Rousseau, and Voltaire is well known. It also engendered new house-building techniques and is sometimes considered to have given birth to modern seismology. In fact, the Marquis de Pombal designed a questionnaire, sent to all the parishes in Portugal, through which the authorities wanted to collect material for what was to be considered an objective description of the causes and consequences of the earthquake. In any event, the earthquake stands out, at least in any history of European literature, as the causa prima of *Candide*. Second, *Candide* was written in the midst of the Seven Years' War, which was not only a conflict between England and France but also between Prussia and Austria, and lasted from 1756 until 1763. The war actually involved all major powers in Europe at the time and took place in North America as well as in Europe between England and France and their changing allies. The conflict ended with the Treaty of Paris, which had as a key result a new equilibration of the European power balance, as France lost many of its possessions, Prussia confirmed its status as a power to be reckoned with and the British Empire was born due to English success in Canada and North America.

---

[*] This paper was reprinted from Carsten Meiner & Kristen Veel, eds., *The Cultural Life of Crises and Catastrophes* (Berlin: DeGruyter, 2012) with kind permission of the publisher.

What is interesting about these two events is not only that they form an easily visible background for *Candide* but also that they furthermore have been compared to two major catastrophes in the 20th century, namely the Holocaust and World War I. The earthquake in Lisbon has been analogized to the Holocaust because it transformed European culture and philosophy fundamentally. Adorno wrote that "the earthquake of Lisbon sufficed to cure Voltaire of the Theodicy of Leibniz"[2] (transforming, as it were, the notions of good and evil, fate, and responsibility). In addition, the German philosopher Werner Hamacher analyzed in a parallel way how the earthquake changed the very vocabulary of European philosophy: "Under the impression exerted by the Lisbon earthquake, which touched the European mind in one [of] its more sensitive epochs, the metaphorics of ground and terror completely lost their apparent innocence; they were no longer figures of speech."[3] Be it in its indubitable Cartesian grounding, the *More Geometrico* of Spinoza or Leibniz's pre-established harmony, rationalist deductive discourse was "traumatized" as a way of thinking and Voltaire had a huge part in formulating the critique of and the alternatives to this a priori way of thinking. Just like one had to ask how poetry was possible after Auschwitz, one had to question or redefine the all-good benevolence of God after Lisbon.[4]

If these analogies have been made between the earthquake in Lisbon and the Holocaust, the Seven Years' War has correspondingly been paralleled to World War I. Both involved most of the European countries in changing alliances, both took place on a vast number of geographical scenes, both resulted in massive human losses (an estimate of more than one million deceased is generally accepted for the Seven Years' War), putting the arbitrary nature of war to show, and both led to important changes in the balance of power in Europe. This global nature of the Seven Years' War led Winston Churchill, for instance, as the first of many to compare it to World War I. Even if these comparisons run the risk of being anachronistic, they serve to render more noticeable the extent and gravity of the catastrophic context in which Voltaire writes. And references to other contemporary catastrophes, for instance to epidemics, the so-called Little Ice Age peaking in the 1740s or religious persecution (the Jesuits were evicted from Portugal in 1759, from France in 1763), would augment and solidify the general image of the Voltairian context as one where crises, catastrophes and dramas seemed to be the rule rather than exceptions. As André Magnan states concerning this catastrophic context:

> 1755–1758 : années troublées, années terribles. Cette vue n'est pas rétrospective : les contemporains en parlèrent ainsi [. . .]. Séismes en série, en France, en Afrique, en Allemagne, après l'épouvantable désastre de Lisbonne (1er novembre 1755). Hostilités, puis guerre ouverte (1756) entre les deux superpuissances

du temps, l'Angleterre et la France : "guerre mondiale" avant la lettre, bientôt étendue à presque toute l'Europe par le jeu des alliances, aux Amériques et aux Indes par ses prolongements coloniaux. Attentats contre des monarques (Paris, janvier 1757 ; Lisbonne, 1758 septembre). Instabilité des trônes, des pouvoirs, des frontières, des rangs : un Ordre menacé."[5]

[1755–1758: troubled and terrible years. That view is not just retrospective because/as the commentators of the time talked about them in that way. A series of earthquakes in France, Africa and Germany after the horrible disaster in Lisbon on the first of Novembre 1755. Hostilities, then open war (1756) between the two superpowers of the day, England and France: "World war" *avant la letter*, soon spread out almost all over Europe, by way of alliances then to America and to the West Indies by way colonisation. Attacks on monarchs (Paris in January 1757, Lisbon in Septembre 1758) and Instability of thrones, powers, borders and classes: a threatened world order]

Magnan stresses that, for a mid-eighteenth-century reader, meeting the first line of *Candide*: "There lived in Westphalia..." corresponds to a modern reader encountering the sentence "There lived in Soweto/in Auschwitz/ in Verdun."[6]

The synthesis operated by Voltaire, in order to subsume and identify all of these problems as well as the contemporary cultural malaise under one heading, was that of the Theodicy, the justification and explanation of the existence of evil in a world created by an omnipotent and all-good God.[7] This problem is central to any monotheism; in Christian theology man was created with a free will and, according to Augustine, Adam could have chosen not to sin. To turn one's back on God equals the entrance of Evil into the world, free will missing, as it were, its target and consequently corrupting itself. Evil becomes the absence or lack of Good, as a *privatio boni*: evil did not as such exist in advance, no Manichaean principle structured man's original choice, but surfaces as man chooses to direct himself toward something lower than God. Challenged by alternative versions (Gnostic, Epicurean, and neo-Platonist ones), Christian anthropology endures as the horizon for theorizing the problem of Evil. With the advent of seventeenth-century rationalism, scientific revolutions and the general faith in the explanatory powers of reason against the exclusive authority of the Scriptures, the causal relation between the existence of evil and original sin grows more and more difficult to maintain. The relation is either radicalized as in its Jansenist versions (Pascal and Port-Royal) or it is put to new tests, for example by Pierre Bayle who sceptically absolves the relation between moral and religion, while Fenelon cultivates a quietist attitude in which meditation dissociates man from evil. But it is Leibniz who, in 1695, forged the concept *theodice* from *theo* (God) and *dike* (justice, law, rule), as a concept meant to coordinate the defence and justification of the universe's imperfect dimensions. In 1709, he writes the text *Essais de Théodicée. Sur la bonté de Dieu, la liberté de l' homme et l'origine du mal*, which asks directly how it is possible for evil events and actions to exist in a world created by a being that is all-knowing, all-powerful and all-good. Leibniz's metaphysical explanation holds that a created world necessarily will be imperfect in contrast to its creator from whom it is separated. Leibniz is thus able to sustain that it is nonetheless the best of all worlds. If God exists, he is also perfect, and if he is perfect, he is necessarily all-powerful, all-good, all-knowing and righteous and he will necessarily have created the least imperfect world of all imperfect worlds. That obvious errors and flaws exist is to be understood in relation to the universe as a whole and its pre-established harmony: just as one cannot criticize even the best watchmaker for using determinate and thus imperfect pieces, which is the very nature of these pieces, for his watches, one cannot criticize God for having created man as a human being because he must necessarily have created man as perfect as possible. Of course, other arguments in favour of the compatibility of the existence of God, and of that of evil, were advanced during Leibniz's time and by himself, indicating that evil is in fact a divine punishment, inscribed in a course of events that we do not understand but whose higher purpose is fundamentally good. Or, that is the argument of Rousseau in the following century, whereby human beings are themselves responsible for most of the catastrophes that happen around the world. In any case, these kinds of conceptions of the cosmological order of the world and man's place therein underpin much of 17th-century-thinking, and it is exactly catastrophes like the earthquake in Lisbon and the Seven Years' War which defy this conception and inform the analysis of evil, the possible alternative explanations thereof and especially the new ways of dealing with this problem that Voltaire more or less implicitly suggests. All of the very real catastrophes that 18th-century-man experiences come to function as, if not refutations, then as empirical question marks to this cosmological order incarnated in the saying that "we live in the best of all possible worlds."

Voltaire deals with the catastrophic context as a context not only in need of reconstruction but also in need of *rethinking*.[8] It is indeed a catastrophe that Lisbon crumbled under earthquakes and tsunamis and that the Jesuits were persecuted, as well as it is a catastrophe that they persevere in their dubious activities elsewhere, and it is a catastrophe that the Spanish and Austrian wars of Succession led only to the Seven Years' War, but the real catastrophe is that metaphysical thinkers, be it Leibniz, Pope or Rousseau, continue to ruminate optimistically about the order of things despite these real-life catastrophes. In France, Voltaire is often considered the thinker of Evil par excellence, as Corneille would be that of Glory, Pascal that of Anguish, Rousseau that of Nature. One of his points about the existence of evil or catastrophes is that the catastrophic quality of any event is indeed inherent in the event itself as a constitutive attribute,[9] but the fact that Voltaire considers the world as immanently evil, is overshadowed by another and even more catastrophic piece of evidence. The real catastrophe, Voltaire maintains, resides in the distorted relation between the optimism of metaphysics and real-life events inasmuch that the former identifies and subsumes on the background of a priori reasoning and thereby ascribes positive qualities to clearly life-negating events in order to morally justify the existence of these events.[10] That kind of metaphysical thinking on catastrophes is the more or less explicit target of Voltaire in *Candide*.

But what does Voltaire do in order to refute the metaphysics of catastrophe? What kind of argument does Voltaire propose to contest this metaphysically apodictic but in his eyes worldneglecting and consequently blind will to optimism? First of all, Voltaire's *modus demonstrandi* distances itself from any deductive reasoning, that is from ways of reasoning going from general premises to conclusions about particular matters. He does not even go into serious discussion on the deductive logic, or lack thereof, of theology, instead limiting himself to a presentation of theological argumentation through the character of Pangloss, so sarcastic that it presents deductive rationalism and real-life catastrophes as virtually incommensurable. Secondly, and most importantly, he presents the reader with a series of catastrophic events from which might be induced a new vision of the anatomy of the catastrophic as well as a way of dealing with this world-inherent, if not world-constitutive, quality. This restructuring of the ways in which we think of the catastrophic is essential to understanding Voltaire's critique of the metaphysics of catastrophe. To capture this restructuring it will be necessary to paraphrase relatively systematically the thirty chapters which constitute *Candide*. The restructuring is in fact formal, and it is only through a survey of the long series of catastrophes in *Candide* that the argument which Voltaire proposes against the metaphysics of catastrophe will come forth as a *formal* piling up of catastrophes. If such a survey tires the reader, there is in fact a point in the very fact that Voltaire tires us with endless repetitions of all kinds of catastrophes.

In the first chapter of the novel the reader learns that Candide was born and raised in a castle in Westphalia, and the narrator informs his readers that Pangloss, Candide's teacher, "proves incontestably that [. . .] in the best of all possible worlds, his lordship's country seat was the most beautiful of all mansions and her ladyship the best of all possible ladyships."[11] Candide is, however, expelled from the very same castle in chapter one, like from the Garden of Eden (and of ignorance), by the Baron (aristocracy analogous to divine power), who cannot accept Candide's sincere affection for his daughter Cunégonde who is physically punished. Evil lives at the core of the best of all worlds in the guise of aristocratic, prejudiced ideas and unjust will to prevent any attempt at the mixing of social classes, and even in the guise of hypocrisy when Pangloss is seen "behind some bushes giving a lesson in experimental physics to her mother's waitingwoman."[12] What should be noted in this context is that Evil exists originally and indubitably in spite of any optimistic argument in favour of the world being logically good. In this first chapter, the contrast between well-intended arguments and manifest evil actions is flagrant, but as the novel evolves the former seems to lose argumentative power and the latter, as the examples of evil pile up, takes over the novel. Every single chapter contains at least one but often many instances or examples of evil which stand in clear contrast to the optimism which had been taught to Candide in the castle and with which he encounters the world.

In chapter 2 the straying Candide is enrolled in the Bulgarian army (commonly identified as a symbol of its Prussian counterpart, which took part in the Seven Years' War) and is punished for having wanted to go for a walk. In chapter 3 he experiences the terrors of warfare and Protestant bigotry and meets his old teacher Pangloss, who, as he learns in chapter 4, is disfigured (by the syphilis contracted in the bushes in chapter one). In the same chapter he learns that Cunégonde has been raped and killed by the Bulgarians, who also destroyed the castle from which Candide was evicted. Pangloss, however, explains by way of an absurd argument that syphilis was the necessary condition for the arrival of chocolate in Europe. The juxtaposition of class struggle, hypocrisy, war, rape, disease and religious fanatics with that kind of confident argument in little more than seven pages demonstrates the unbridgeable discrepancy between speculative optimism and evil as an everyday fact, a discrepancy which is to be continued and widened during the rest of the novel.

In chapter 5 they go by boat to Lisbon but are caught in a storm. The helpful Anabaptist, who had taken care of Candide earlier on and cured Pangloss of his disease, drowns as he tries to help one of the ungrateful sailors aboard. This chapter also includes the earthquake in Lisbon, where 30,000 thousand people die and Pangloss unremittingly argues in favour of the necessity of these catastrophes as "a manifestation of the rightness of things, since if there is a volcano in Lisbon it could not be anywhere else. For it is impossible for things not to be where they are, because everything is for the best."[13]

Chapter 6 takes place in Lisbon, where Candide and Pangloss are kept prisoner and whipped (Pangloss is even hanged) as an act of faith, but they are eventually rescued by an old woman who, in chapter 7, introduces Candide to a woman who turns out to be Cunégonde. The latter tells Candide her terrible story about how she was mutilated by the Bulgarians, stolen and sold and is now shared by two men, the grand inquisitor and the Jew Issachar, both of whom are killed by Candide in the following chapter! The momentary happiness connected to the finding of Cunégonde is quickly replaced by manslaughter committed by the not so candid main character. Cunégonde,

Candide and the old lady go to Cadiz and then to Paraguay because Candide, due to his experience in the Bulgarian army, is appointed head of a military mission whose goal it is to neutralize a group of Jesuits said to have caused an Indian tribe to mutiny against their Spanish king. A short stint of optimism surfaces as they embark on the voyage for the New World but it is instantly interrupted as the old lady tells her story, which largely surpasses that of Cunégonde in misery. Once in Buenos Aires the New World proves to be just as catastrophic as the old one: the governor wants to and succeeds in marrying Cunégonde and Candide has to flee again.

The setting of chapter 14 is at the Jesuit's, who is described as greedy and unjust. Candide, who has brought a servant, Cacambo, along from Cadiz meets Cunégonde's brother, who has become an officer after yet another terrible story and whom Candide kills after a quarrel! Evil, crises and catastrophes are unquestionably everywhere. This causes Candide and Cacambo to run off again, now in Jesuit-costumes. After having killed two monkeys by accident they are captured by an Indian tribe planning to eat them; however, they lodge an appeal to the Indians' reason and are eventually set free. If the New World thus seems to have shown if not a human then at least a sensible face, this is nothing compared to the famous description of the next destination of Candide and Cacambo, the well-ordered and abundantly rich Eldorado. This chapter stands out as an exception from the novel's enumeration of examples of cruelty, misery and catastrophe. Their arrival in Eldorado is astonishing to its inhabitants, as mountains and precipices "shelter from the greed of European nations,"[14] and as it is in any case impossible to escape Eldorado, the Promised Land, this place comes to act as a counterexample of perfect but inaccessible virtues. Once they are helped to leave Eldorado, because Candide misses his beloved Cunégonde, the problems start again—they leave Eldorado with incredible amounts of gold and diamonds on "huge red sheep faster than the finest horses of Andalusia,"[15] but they also lose most of it in only ten lines. They go to Surinam, where they experience the cruelty of the colonies incarnated by a slave lacking both a hand and a foot, "the price of your eating sugar in Europe."[16] Candide reacts with tears to this information and starts having real reservations about and even mistrust toward Pangloss' more and more absurd doctrine asserting that "we live in the best of all worlds" and that "all is good." Candide is robbed of the rest of his diamonds and exposed to the unfairness of a judge: "This behaviour drove Candide to desperation. He had certainly experienced misfortunes a great deal more grievous; but the judge's indifference and the coolness of the captain who had robbed him, affected his spleen and plunged him into the deepest of melancholy."[17] This psychological evolution in Candide, and the transformation of his vision of the order of the world, is paralleled by his wish to hire the saddest man in the country to accompany him back to France.

The choice falls upon Martin, a Manichean whose pessimistic worldview is promptly exemplified by a shipwreck and the drowning of one hundred men. In chapter 21 Candide's understanding of evil has now matured so much as to make it possible for him to ask if Martin thinks that "men have always massacred each other, as they do today, that they have always been false, cozening, faithless, ungrateful, thieving, weak, inconstant, meanspirited, envious, greedy, drunken, miserly, ambitious, bloody, slanderous, debauched, fanatic, hypocritical, and stupid?"[18] The answer to that question is, of course, "Yes."

The rest of the chapters all exemplify some kind of evil, catastrophe or crisis: greedy and incompetent doctors, the need to bribe policemen, public execution, prostitutes, the overthrowing of kings and Cacambo, Cunégonde, the baron and Pangloss all turned into slaves, the latter grotesquely insisting on the wellbeing of the world when Candide asks him "When you had been hanged, dissected, and beaten unmercifully, and while you were rowing at your bench, did you still think that everything in this world is for the best?"[19] They all end up living together in Constantinople and Candide, having promised to marry the now old and wrinkled Cunégonde, does so even though he does not really desire it. The baron opposes himself to the marriage and is, as a parallel to the initial eviction that he himself conducted, expelled from the house. The novel ends with the group meeting an old man who calmly states that the only thing he does is to cultivate his farm: "My children help me to farm it and we find that the work banishes those three great evils, boredom, vice and poverty."[20] This triggers the conclusion to the novel. First, Candide says that the old man seemed to have done much better for himself than the six kings they had been talking to earlier on, and Candide utters the famous line *Il faut cultiver notre jardin*, "We must go and work in the garden," thereby cutting off the necessity for further examples of evil and of speculation on that very matter.

The purpose of this lengthy summary of the novel was to show how Voltaire established an argument against the metaphysics of catastrophe, against the metaphysically apodictic yet blind optimism of Leibniz, Pope, Rousseau and Pangloss. As announced earlier, Voltaire's *modus demonstrandi* consists of a negation of the religious deductions of the abovementioned thinkers by structuring a series of examples of catastrophes. As should be clear from the survey of the novel, every single chapter includes one or several catastrophes, disasters, crises which function as a corrective parallel to the idea of "the best of all worlds" exemplifying again and again the presence of evil, be it man-made or natural. Whenever the metaphysical argument is put forward, Voltaire first seems to grant that "maybe it is true that we live in the best of all worlds," but then points to yet an example of a catastrophe: "We live in the best of all worlds, but look at that slave without hands or at that woman being raped, or that unjust judge!" Moreover, if our summary of the novel may seem unexciting, even wearisome due to its monotony, this is exactly the point Voltaire wants to make—the world is a repetition of all sorts of moral, natural, sexual, military, economic, social and disease-related crises, disasters and catastrophes and the very narrative reiteration of all these incidents forms a series of examples, in other words an induction. Instead of conceiving of the catastrophic by deducing the real catastrophes from a priori apodictic theological patterns of thought, Voltaire establishes a series of concrete examples whose exemplarity is to be evaluated and discussed. This undeniable aspect of the repetition of catastrophes *ad absurdum* is exactly what makes the Voltairian and the metaphysical conceptions of catastrophe incommensurable. If the repetition does not necessarily exclude positive explanations of catastrophes, it nevertheless underlines the insupportable, unforgettable, inhuman and life-distorting aspects of catastrophe. Voltaire's point is that if those aspects continue to be present and to influence our lives, it is the very optimism of the metaphysics of catastrophe which will eventually come under fire. Against the "rationality" of optimism Voltaire mobilizes a quantitative argument: how long can the "truth" of deductive reason resist the incalculable inhumanities of the empirical events, stories and data which keep testifying to the possibility of another and contradictory truth on the existence of evil? The world may be the best of all worlds and we may be convinced by the deductive arguments sustaining that claim, but what if one experiences a catastrophe every day? Every hour? What if everybody experiences a catastrophe every day or every hour? What if history is a series of catastrophes? Then the world may still be the best of all possible worlds, but the argument sustaining that claim is doomed to relative impertinence. The claim would not be untrue but relegated to the domain of either logical irrelevance or moral misconduct, because it is possibly the best of all worlds but still not a very good one, a catastrophic one actually, at least according to Voltaire. In that way *Candide* becomes a catalogue of catastrophes, which never really logically argues with deduction but rather *out-exemplifies* it. In this way Voltaire does not so much rely on a rhetoric of counterexamples but rather on a rhetoric of parallel argumentation. The final scene is exemplary with regard to this strategy, and it is even more eloquent insofar as it is Pangloss who performs this parallel inductive argument:

High estate, said Pangloss, is always dangerous, as every philosopher knows. For Eglon, King of Moab, was assassinated by Ehud, and Absalon was hanged by his hair and stabbed by three spears; King Nehab, the son of Jeroboam, was killed by Baasha; King Elah by Zimri; Joram by Jehu; Athaliah by Jehoiada; and King Jehoiakim, King Jehoiachin, and King Zedekiah all became slaves. You know the miserable fate of Croesus, Astyages, Darius, Dioysios of Syracuse, Pyrrhus, Perseus, Hannibal, Jugurtha, Ariovistus, Caesar, Pompey, Nero, Otho,

Vitellius, Domitian, Richard II of England, Edward III, Henry IV, Richard III, Mary Queen of Scots, Charles I, the three Henrys of France, and the Emperor Henry IV? You know?[21]

This historical and empirical series of examples of evil is contrary to the usual deductive and metaphysical arguments that Pangloss has been putting forward all along. It echoes the inductive mode of arguing that the novel has been establishing throughout the thirty chapters, an argument parting from individual cases of catastrophes, disasters and crisis which together form the basis for a general argument concerning the existence of evil.[22] The novel does this in a very general mode, showing that evil exists everywhere and is created in all kinds of contexts by nature and by man, whereas Pangloss' induction only concerns royal ill fortune independently of geography and historical time. That Pangloss, the former deductive thinker, pronounces this induction is a sign that Candide and Martin can finally go beyond the discussion of the speculative explanations of the existence of catastrophe to formulate what to do to counteract the terrors of the world.

In the context of alternative visions and the negotiation of the obvious omnipresence of Evil, the sentence "Il faut cultiver notre jardin" ("we must go and work in the garden") deserves a detailed analysis.[23] "Il faut" could be translated into "it is necessary" and consequently signals in French an impersonal imperative. The English translation "we must go" does not really represent this impersonal aspect, which happens to be important because the necessity does not come from a metaphysical instance but from a certain world experience: "On the background of what we have witnessed it is necessary to . . ." seems to be the implied meaning of "il faut." This conclusion shows that man reacts to the events and dramas of the world, not to some speculative and abstract reasoning on his place in the world. More precisely, the observation of the world and its catastrophes and, of its "instances of evil," does not require man to speculate and explain but to act: "il faut cultivar." Again, the English translation "go and work" does not capture all of the semantic dimensions of the sentence. "Cultiver" signifies to work in the sense of making things grow, but it also connotes to the transformation of a natural realm into a more *culturally* dignified state of being. "Cultiver" is thus also in opposition to a state of nature, which is of course a very eighteenth century, at least Voltairian, way of conceiving of what man can do to make the world a better place. "Cultiver" then has two meanings in the context of the novel: firstly that the remaining characters will find some sort of peace of mind in concentrating on the work in the garden, instead of travelling around the world discovering its natural state of catastrophe. Secondly, however, "Cultiver" also means to develop, to improve, to process and to bring forth the richness of nature through human intervention, actively and not speculatively to go beyond the state of catastrophe. Finally, "Garden" then signals such an intermediary space between nature and culture, a dynamic space at the same time liable to natural degradation and full of riches to be extracted by man. Finally, the French text says "notre jardin" and not "the garden." Consequently, the text also underlines that the process of cultivation and of peaceful enrichment, as opposed to the destructive nature of the catastrophic world, is a collective one. Both the passive peace and active nature-processing are collective and dependent on the definition of a limited place where and which "we" work. Voltaire had not only been pointing to the sheer existence of catastrophes, but also to their multitude, their repetition and their quantity—in this way creating an inductive principle for his novel, enumerating over and over again examples of concrete evil against the optimistic and naïve deductions of rationalism. The "garden" is a solution because vices are kept at bay due to the collective and ego-negating nature of the work carried out there and because this work is synonymous with a civilizing effort not only controlling nature but also extracting the "best of this world." Instead of rationalist philosophy trying to make the world fit into a pre-established scheme of the order of the world, and instead of travelling the world in search of utopian spaces defying the never-surrendering presence of Evil, Voltaire proposes a pragmatic vision of life on earth whose foundation is a collective and consequently sound metabolism between nature and culture, between man and the world, accepting as a condition of life the dialectics of good and evil rather than seeing it as a problem to solve once and for all.[24] The real catastrophe for Voltaire is not so much the earthquake in Lisbon, the Seven Years' War, rape, diseases and injustice, nor the fact that all of these catastrophes co-exist. The catastrophic aspect of these events is not so much the fact that they shatter and destroy life or that our ideas about the way of the world are destroyed but that these cruel and destructive events do not seem to change anything in the rationalists' conception of the world, and even if they affect their moral and logical ideas about the construction of the world it seems extremely hard to accept and follow through these new ideas about the world, that is to act accordingly. According to Voltaire, man is not only driven but also constituted by a will to err in his thinking about the world. This "man's constitutive errorcapacity" allows him to neglect reflecting upon the world from the world's point of view. Man does not change his way of thinking but keeps thinking and acting in ways which are not in keeping with the basic physical and moral structure of the world, so we therefore inflict damage, harm and injustice upon ourselves and each other. The Voltairian conception of catastrophe in *Candide* is original. Usually, a catastrophe is considered as an eruptive event—exceptional, order-unsettling and profoundly disruptive—whereas Voltaire's vision of the world seems to be constituted by an endless series of catastrophes forming the norm or rule of the world and not the exception to an otherwise positive and good world. One could talk about a catastrophe effect rather than catastrophes, in the sense that all of the many catastrophes in the novel do not have a violent, disruptive or exceptional effect but rather a choking, nausea-like effect on the main characters in the novel: the suffocating effect of catastrophe derives from the repetition of catastrophes, which seems to come before its eruptive and singular nature. Further, catastrophe is ubiquitous, a fact which is suffocating in itself, and realizing that this fact had been veiled, repressed and "theodicized" by centuries of world-disdaining thinking does not make things less dramatic; in fact, that is the real catastrophe.

NOTES

1. This paper was reprinted from Carsten Meiner and Kristen Veel, eds., *The Cultural Life of Catastrophes and Crises* (Berlin: DeGruyter, 2012) with kind permission of the publisher.

2. Theodor Adorno, *Negative Dialectics* (New York: Routledge, 1990), 361.

3. Werner Hamacher, "The Quaking of Presentation," in *Premises: Essays on Philosophy and Literature from Kant to Celan* (Palo Alto, CA: Stanford University Press, 1996), 263.

4. See Thomas Downing Hendrick, *The Lisbon Earthquake* (New York: Lippincott Company, 1957); as well as Lauer and Unger.

5. André Magnan, *Voltaire. Candide ou l'Optimisme* (Paris: PUF, 1987), 16–17.

6. Ibid., 14.

7. See Ian Wade, *Voltaire and Candide. A Study in the Fusion of History, Art, and Philosophy* (Princeton, NJ: Princeton University Press, 1959) in particular, 1–84.

8. For an interpretation of Voltaire's vision of freedom, providence and destiny in all his novels and short-stories, see Chapter III in Jacques van den Heuvel, *Voltaire dans ses contes* (Paris: Armand Colin, 1967).

9. See Jean Goldzink, "La métaphysique du mal," *Europe* 72, no. 781 (1994).

10. See Jean Sareil, *Essai sur Candide* (Genève: Droz, 1967).

11. François Voltaire, *Candide* (Harmondsworth, UK: Penguin, 1973), 20.

12. Ibid.

13. Ibid., 35.

14. Ibid., 79.

15. Ibid., 74.

16. Ibid., 86.

17. Ibid., 89.

18. Ibid., 96.

19. Ibid., 136.

20. Ibid., 143.

21. Ibid.

22. In connection with the notion of repetition it is interesting to study the linguistic aspects of the novel, as done by Pierre Ducretet and Marie Ducretet, *Voltaire*

– *Candide. Etude quantitative* (Toronto and Buffalo: University of Toronto Press, 1974).

23. Of course, much has been said about the garden in Voltaire from both a textual and a biographical point of view. For an original and thorough version of the latter see Geoffrey Murray, *Voltaire's Candide: The Protean Gardener, 1755–1762* (Genève: Studies on Voltaire and the Eighteenth Century, Vol. LXIX, 1970).

24. See Karliss Racevskis, *Modernity's Pretenses. Making Reality Fit Reason from Candide to the Gulag* (New York: State University of New York Press, 1988).

BIBLIOGRAPHY

Adorno, Theodor Wiesengrund. *Negative Dialectics*. New York: Routledge, 1990.
Ducretet, Pierre and Marie Ducretet. *Voltaire—Candide. Etude quantitative*. Toronto and Buffalo: University of Toronto Press, 1974.
Hamacher, Werner. "The Quaking of Presentation" in *Premises: Essays on Philosophy and Literature from Kant to Celan*. Palo Alto, CA: Stanford University Press, Stanford, 1996.
Hendrick, Thomas Downing. *The Lisbon Earthquake*. New York: Lippincott Company, 1957.
Lauer, Gerhard and Thorsten Unger. *Das Erdbeben von Lissabon und der Katastrophendiskurs im 18. Jahrhundert*. Göttingen: Wallstein Verlag, 2008.
Heuvel, Jacques van den. *Voltaire dans ses contes*. Paris: Armand Colin, 1967.
Goldzink, Jean. "La métaphysique du mal." *Europe* 72, no. 781 (1994).
Magnan, André. *Voltaire. Candide ou l'Optimisme*. Paris: PUF, 1987.
Murray, Geoffrey. *Voltaire's Candide: the Protean Gardener 1755–1762*. Genève: Studies on Voltaire and the Eighteenth century, Volume LXIX, 1970.
Racevskis, Karlis. *Modernity's Pretenses. Making Reality Fit Reason from Candide to the Gulag*. New York: State University of New York Press, 1988.
Sareil, Jean. *Essai sur Candide*. Genève: Droz, 1967.
Wade, Ian. *Voltaire and Candide. A Study in the Fusion of History, Art, and Philosophy*. Princeton, NJ: Princeton University Press, 1959.
Wellbery, David. *Positionen der Literaturwissenschaft, Acht Modellen am Beispiel von Kleists "Das Erdbeben in Chili."* München: C. H. Beck, 1993.
Voltaire, François. *Candide or Optimism*. Translated by John Butt. Harmondsworth, UK: Penguin Books, 1973.

Part IV

MODERNITY II: HIGH MODERNITY

Preface
Modernity II

World War I, "The Great War" of 1914–1918, has long been considered the locus classicus for the beginning of the age of catastrophe in the twentieth century, ushering in the period known as "high modernity." Yet Robert Musil offered the fascinating diagnosis that "everything that appeared in and after the war was present before the war."[1] And how could it really have been otherwise? Friedrich Nietzsche proclaimed in the late nineteenth century how "nihilism waits at the door" and warned of a "gloom and eclipse of the sun whose like has probably never yet occurred on Earth."[2] Nietzsche writes contemptuously of philosophy professors and ivory tower academics, those content to live comfortable, status-quo lives, having long ago abandoned their original charge of truth-seeking, especially in dark times when intellectual courage is most needed:

> Now, how does the philosopher view the culture of our time? Very differently, to be sure, from how it is viewed by those professors of philosophy who are so well contented with their new state. When he thinks of the haste and hurry now universal, or the increasing velocity of life, of the cessation of all contemplativeness and simplicity, he almost thinks that what he is seeing are the symptoms of a total extermination and uprooting of culture. The waters of religion are ebbing away and leaving behind swamps or stagnant pools; the nations are again drawing away from one another in the most hostile fashion and long to tear one another to pieces. The sciences, pursued without any restraint and in a spirit of the blindest laissez faire, are shattering and dissolving all firmly held belief; the educated classes and states are being swept along by a hugely contemptible money economy. The world has never been more worldly, never poorer in love and goodness. The educated classes are no longer lighthouses or refuges in the midst of this turmoil of secularization; they themselves grow daily more

restless, thoughtless and loveless. Everything, contemporary art and science included, serves the coming barbarism.[3]

Later, Sigmund Freud, living as a Jew in viciously anti-Semitic interwar Vienna, himself had to flee the Nazi onslaught in 1938. Years before, he had written in various contexts how the and the polite, orderly, repressed civilization of Victorian Europe with its ornate architecture and glittering ballrooms, was but a thin veneer covering the abyss existing just beneath the surface, a veneer "liable at any time to be pierced by the destructive force of the underworld."[4] In fact, the presage of catastrophe, "the coming barbarism" so prescient in the writings of these thinkers, was very soon to be brutally borne out.

Further, many of these thinkers of modernity (Nietzsche, Sartre, Freud, Marx) argued that the long-standing religious ordering of experience (previously discussed here as a means of staving off the specter of amorality and meaninglessness) was no longer believable. For Nietzsche, not only has the Christian God "lost his power over beings and the determination of man" but actually "the entire realm of ideals, norms, principles, ends, and values, which are set above being in order to give it an order, purpose or meaning" has now become untenable. So what could now be the guiding principles for Western civilization? And what if there aren't any guiding principles anymore? Would we be living in what Castoriadis called "A Society Adrift"? Are we now?

The twentieth century featured stunning progress in the sciences, yet perhaps wins the award for history's bloodiest. World War I began in August 1914, with the young men of Europe marching proudly off to war "with plumes and full dress parades" only to confront the brutal conditions of trench warfare. With progress in technology came new weapons such as the machine gun and poison gas, which now allowed for the killing of large numbers of people at once. "Over the four year period of war, the lines moved only slightly, and advances, often costing the lives of thousands of men, were measured in yards. The most costly battle of the war, the Battle of the Somme, lasted four months in 1916 and took the lives of 1,100,000 with no significant change in positions."[5] The futile mass death of World War I ushered in an era of widespread disillusionment and anomie, described by Durkheim as constitutive of modernity itself. There was thus a widespread perception that the old European order (political, cultural, moral) was breaking down. The sense of spiritual dislocation was highlighted in the movements toward abstraction in the art—and toward atonality in the music—of this period.

World War II then brought the Holocaust, inexplicable in its range and brutality, a genocidal catastrophe without precedent, which further questioned the efficacy of human reason and the optimism of the enlightenment.

The Nazi Holocaust constituted a singular catastrophe in the annals of history for a number of reasons. Six million Jews were killed by the Nazis as part of Hitler's "final solution" to the "Jewish question," with millions more non-Jews killed as well. The rich culture of Eastern European Ashkenazi Jewry was effectively destroyed, its destruction the logical conclusion of centuries of pervasive and violent anti-Semitism throughout "Christian" Europe. The Holocaust forces us to confront deep questions about human nature—including how the civilized German nation that gave us the genius of Beethoven, Goethe, Kant and Schelling, could also be responsible for the most comprehensive genocide in recorded history. Consider also that the mass killing in the concentration camps was carried out by the Germans with clockwork precision and maximum efficiency, even while their overall war effort was crumbling.

Hannah Arendt also raised the famous question of "the banality of evil," how those who carried out "the final solution" could shoot children in front of their parents by day and then go home to their own loving families at night, committing atrocities "all in a day's work." The Holocaust thus confronts us even more forcefully with the barbarism lying just beneath the surface of "civilization." What could even constitute a meaningful response to such a deep chasm of moral darkness? Can the horrors experienced in Auschwitz even be expressed adequately or do they merely call up the limits of language? World War II effectively ended with the atomic mushroom clouds of Hiroshima and Nagasaki, bringing not only untold death and destruction, but ushering in the nuclear age with all the attendant fears and anxieties which fueled the Cold War, still with us today.

NOTES

1. Robert Musil, *Tagebucher*, as discussed in Patrizia McBride, *The Void of Ethics: Robert Musil and the Experience of Modernity* (Evanston, IL: Northwestern University Press, 2006).

2. Karl Löwith, Richard Wolin (ed), George Steiner, (trans) *Martin Heidegger and European Nihilism* (New York: Columbia University Press, 1995), 191.

3. Friedrich Nietzsche, "Schopenhauer as Educator," in *Untimely Meditations,* trans. gersimon, © 2000, 2–4 excerpts trans. R. J. Hollingdale (Cambridge, UK: Cambridge University Press, 1984).

4. Stefan Zweig, *The World of Yesterday* (Lincoln: University of Nebraska Press, 1964), 4.

5. Mary Ann Witt, Charlotte Vestal Brown, Roberta Ann Dunbar, Frank Tirro, Ronald G. Witt, et al., *The Humanities: Cultural Roots and Continuities* (New York: Houghton Mifflin, 2001) 376–77.

BIBLIOGRAPHY

Arendt, Hannah. *Eichmann in Jerusalem: A Report on the Banality of Evil.* New York: Viking Press, 1963.
Löwith, Karl. *Martin Heidegger and European Nihilism.* Edited by Richard Wolin. Translated by Gary Steiner. New York: Columbia University Press, 1995.
McBride, Patrizia. *The Void of Ethics: Robert Musil and the Experience of Modernity.* Evanston, IL: Northwestern University Press, 2006.
Nietzsche, Friedrich. *Untimely Meditations.* Section 1 Translation by Gersimon, © 2000. 2–4 excerpts edited by Daniel Breazeale. Translated by R. J. Hollingdale. Cambridge, UK: Cambridge University Press, 1984.
Witt, Mary Ann, Charlotte Vestal Brown, Roberta Ann Dunbar, Frank Tirro, Ronald G. Witt, et al., *The Humanities: Cultural Roots and Continuities.* 10 vols. New York: Houghton Mifflin, 2001.
Zweig, Stefan. *The World of Yesterday.* Lincoln: University of Nebraska Press, 1964.

Chapter 11

Nietzsche and the Catastrophe of 19th-Century Democracy

Phil Washburn

Nietzsche's writings have an intensity and urgency unmatched by other philosophers' writings. "God is dead." "There are no moral facts whatever." "Man is a rope, tied between beast and overman—a rope over an abyss."[1] One reason Nietzsche wrote in such a highly charged style was that he believed Europe was facing a crisis. Like other writers in the late nineteenth century, he believed modern society was changing rapidly, but in the wrong direction. Something needed to be done immediately to alert people to the danger and reverse the trend. He was like the madman in one of his parables who rushes into the marketplace and shouts at people to get their attention.

Beneath the heated rhetoric Nietzsche presented a complex and subtle analysis of the crisis, and a challenging solution to it. In this chapter I would like to propose an interpretation of his analysis and solution. I would not claim that it is the one and only correct interpretation. I don't think Nietzsche intended his works to have only one interpretation. He was an artist as well as a philosopher, which means he produced a set of writings that is fascinatingly ambiguous, multifaceted, and labyrinthine. It is also dynamic, in the sense that new generations see new things in it. Different readers can study his work and interpret it in different ways, as they can with a painting, a play, or a symphony; some interpretations may be better than others, but many can be legitimate. I think Nietzsche intended his readers to find their own interpretations.

I want to examine the hypothesis that Nietzsche was a "moral Darwinist," comparable to the Social Darwinists who were writing at about the same time. I will fill in some of the details about Darwinism below, but the basic idea is that Nietzsche believed there are moralities (sets of values and rules that guide individuals and groups of people), they evolve over time, they compete with each other, and some are more successful than others. I suggest that using this evolutionary framework allows us to understand and connect many of his key ideas, and it gives us a coherent picture of his outlook. This is not to say that Nietzsche would accept this label, because he would not. He explicitly criticized Darwin, and his views about conflicting value systems differ from Darwin's theory of evolution in some ways. Nevertheless, the similarities are there, and the analogy is useful.

Nietzsche's moral Darwinism was his response to a catastrophe. I will begin by describing the catastrophe, as Nietzsche understood it, and then his response.

THE CRISIS FACING EUROPE

Nietzsche reached maturity in the late 1860s, publishing his first book, *The Birth of Tragedy Out of the Spirit of Music*, in 1872. A number of writers in the 1850s and 1860s pointed to what they perceived as a broad problem facing Europe, or rather a collection of problems grouped under the heading of "the triumph of the bourgeoisie," or "the rise of the masses." By the 1860s in much of Europe the middle class had gained political and economic power. The British Reform Bill of 1867 extended voting rights to a much larger percentage of the population than had been allowed to vote before. Increasing industrialization and trade meant living standards for the middle class improved. Even the working class and the urban poor had some leisure and disposable income, leading to mass consumption. The ideals of democracy, equality, and "respectability" were endorsed by most people in Europe.

These overt conditions may not seem to be a catastrophe, but some observers claimed that the catastrophe was in the underlying attitudes of the newly prosperous citizens. For example, in 1859, John Stuart Mill published his book *On Liberty*, in which he decried "the tyranny of the majority." He said the middle class had struggled against kings and nobles for centuries, but now that it had power, it became tyrannical itself. It enforced conformity on the whole society; it imposed its values of security, contentment, and uniformity on everyone. (He took the phrase "tyranny of the majority" from Alexis de Tocqueville's *Democracy in America*, where Tocqueville made the same criticism of American society.) One of Nietzsche's colleagues at the University of Basel, where he taught in the 1870s, saw a similar crisis. Jacob Burckhardt was famous for praising individualism and creativity in his book, *The Civilization of the Renaissance in Italy* (1860). In 1871 he published *Force and Freedom*. Michael Curtis summarizes its warning: "Mediocrity was the real diabolical force in the world. Civilization had to be protected against the masses gaining ascendency in society and uninterested in true liberty. . . .The preservation of culture was important above all, for this was the real expression of man."[2]

Like other writers, Nietzsche saw the triumph of the middle class as a catastrophe. It was a crisis of values. The majority of Europeans had become complacent, satisfied, good-natured, and dull, he said, and they didn't want anything or anyone to upset their comfortable existence. This is a problem because such an outlook discourages artists, innovators, experimenters, and other agents of cultural progress from challenging the status quo.[3] Nietzsche traced the roots of the crisis to the widespread acceptance of Christianity. Christians value compassion, humility, relieving suffering, loving one's neighbor, and preparing for the next life, but Nietzsche said these values contain within themselves the seeds of the destruction of European civilization. How could compassion and humility be destructive? We can understand his analysis of the catastrophe best through a Darwinian perspective.

A DARWINIAN PERSPECTIVE

Charles Darwin's revolutionary book, *The Origin of Species*, was published in 1859. It immediately caused strong disagreements among the educated public because it implied that human beings were not created all at once in their present form (in the image of God). Instead, humans gradually evolved from simpler animals such as the apes, monkeys, and small mammals, whose origins could be traced all the way back through reptiles, fish, and worms to the primordial single-celled organisms. Furthermore, humans' qualities, such as their ability to reason, to create laws, to love, to write poetry, and so on, are really adaptations to the changing environments that allowed them to survive and reproduce, comparable fundamentally to birds' migration, ants' social structure, and deer mating calls.

Darwin's basic theory is elegant and extremely powerful. Based on his extensive and detailed observations of the natural world, he said (a) organisms produce numerous offspring, but (b) not all the offspring can grow to maturity because of limited resources. Therefore, (c) they compete for the resources. In addition, (d) the offspring differ from each other in small ways, which give some offspring advantages over others. Consequently, (e) over time the offspring with advantages produce more offspring of their own, and their advantageous traits spread through the whole population. As this process continues, new species arise.

Some writers, such as the British author Herbert Spencer, applied Darwin's theory to history and societies. It was Spencer who coined the phrase "survival of the fittest." Spencer and other Social Darwinists claimed that societies are like organisms in some ways. Over time they develop increasing specialization and interdependence of parts.[4] They also compete for scarce resources, like fertile land, or trade, or oil. Societies differ in certain ways, and some differences are advantages in the competition. For example, some societies may be more inventive than others, or more aggressive, or more disciplined. The societies with advantages grow and expand. Over time, those advantageous characteristics spread to other societies. The societies with disadvantageous traits shrink and disappear; that is, the inefficient institutions disappear and groups adopt practices that are more like the successful societies.[5]

Nietzsche applied a Darwinian perspective to the contemporary crisis in values. He claimed that if we survey the history of various civilizations around the world, we can see different moralities rise and fall. He was especially interested in the fall of the aristocratic, competitive morality of ancient Greece, exemplified in Homer's epics, and the rise of the Judeo-Christian morality, which gradually prevailed in Europe. The aristocrats' values he called "master morality," and the Christians' values he called "slave morality." Nietzsche's perspective is Darwinian in so far as he wanted to show how the slave morality arose and evolved. He wasn't content to contrast the two moralities; he wanted to explain how they originated and developed over time. He wanted to give a "Genealogy of Morals." Slave morality was a reaction to master morality, and in a sense it was competing with master morality. Moreover, slave morality succeeded in the competition because it satisfied a basic human instinct, as we will see. But it was a catastrophe for humanity as a whole.

Nietzsche used the term "slave morality" because it embodies the values of slaves. Slaves live in fear of powerful masters, and therefore they value safety. They want the masters to be merciful and have pity, and so they value mercy and pity for those who suffer. They feel a close bond to their fellow slaves, because there is safety in numbers, and because of the sharp contrast with the unapproachable masters. Slaves comfort each other. Therefore they value community, cooperation, close ties. Since they live in fear and try to escape the wrath of their masters, they think nothing of dissembling and lying to protect themselves.

The Greek masters, on the other hand, valued strength, courage, self-confidence, and the ambition to prove oneself. They were proud, and had no reason to lie about anything.

According to Darwin, organisms evolve by satisfying basic needs so they can reproduce. Nietzsche proposed that value systems such as slave morality evolve by satisfying instincts. The most basic instinct driving humans is the will to power, that is, the instinct to control and dominate one's environment and express oneself. This is more basic than the will to survive. We want to live, of course, but an even deeper urge is to feel power over the world, to manipulate and change anything or anyone in whatever way we choose. Any trait or behavior that increases one's power will be adopted.

But slaves in the ancient world faced a serious problem. They felt tremendous anger and hatred toward their masters, but they couldn't show it or even admit it because to do so would bring a terrible punishment. Their hatred was thwarted. But the will to power cannot be denied. The slaves therefore turned their anger and hatred back toward themselves. Nietzsche said they learned to suppress and condemn everything vital and alive in themselves—their ego, their pride, their anger, their sexuality, their urge to dominate and express themselves.

The really ingenious stroke was the next step, because it allowed them to satisfy their instinct indirectly. They came to believe that their passions and dreams of violence against the masters were "evil," not just dangerous, but morally wrong. And therefore the masters' ego and urge to dominate were evil and wrong as well. The slaves fervently propagated these new attitudes, and paradoxically they spread. But adopting such a difficult, self-denying, ascetic way of life requires an explanation, because it is so unnatural. Nietzsche's explanation was that holding up slave values as "good," was an exquisite form of revenge on the masters, who became "evil." The slaves created a reversal of values so that what had been admired—strength, pride—became evil and wrong. They found a way to express their will to power after all.[6]

We can call this a Darwinian explanation of the rise of slave morality because of its similarity to Darwin's theory of evolution. But Nietzsche was applying the basic idea of changes resulting from competition to psychology. In the realm of values, the needs that must be satisfied are psychological, not biological. We all have a strong psychological need to assert our will to power and shape an identity. The masters expressed their will to power directly, by controlling slaves, but that option was available to only a few. The slaves found a way to express their will to power, by exerting a tremendous control over their own natural urges, and further, by exacting revenge on the masters by calling their own self-denial "good," and the masters' values "evil." This morality spread among the masses of slaves and defeated the master morality.

SLAVE MORALITY AS CATASTROPHE

What Nietzsche called "slave morality" was similar to the middle class values condemned by other writers in the late nineteenth century. He thought it was a catastrophe. But disparaging democracy and compassion could be seen as merely the complaints of the upper class, who resented the growing power of the masses. Or it could be seen as the sour grapes of misfits—"I can't participate in bourgeois activities, I don't fit in, so that system of values must be worthless." A more serious criticism would explain exactly why equality and the other values are undesirable. Nietzsche articulated a specific, genealogical analysis of the new attitudes, and he developed a more detailed critique of it. He attacked slave morality in three ways. First, he famously said "God is dead."[7] He meant that the belief in God is dead. In an age of Darwin, of giant leaps in physics and chemistry, of knowledge of different cultures, of universal education, it was no longer possible to believe in the traditional image of a personal, omnipotent Father figure watching over us, who handed down absolute rules we must follow. No intelligent person could reconcile such a childish belief with his or her understanding of the world, or with his or her understanding of the ways the mind creates self-serving myths.

But belief in God is the foundation of the slave morality. In its simplest form, it teaches people that they must suppress their natural desires in order to receive a greater reward from God after death. Why are the feeling of superiority and power and pleasure wrong? Because God says so. Slaves have been slaves for so long that they need a master to command them. So they believe in a Divine Master. But if God is dead, there is no reason to accept such a slavish, degrading attitude.

In its more sophisticated form, slave morality might teach people that the absolute rules of kindness, humility, self-sacrifice, and equal rights are simply built into the nature of humanity and society. We grasp them with our innate moral sense, our conscience, without needing to believe in a Divine Master to command us. Or (with Kant) we say that the very nature of morality itself consists of treating everyone as equals and bound by universal rules. But in his second attack, Nietzsche said this is gross hypocrisy and self-deception. He believed his genealogical analysis of the origins of slave morality showed that the slaves were actually asserting their will to power over the masters by undermining the masters' scale of values. Unconsciously, of course. They were also asserting their will to power over their own instincts. The slaves compete among themselves to see who can be the most saintly, the most generous, the most self-abnegating. But it is hypocritical and self-contradictory to condemn pride and power, and at the same time feel proud of the power one has to control one's urges and actions.

The first two criticisms of slave morality attempt to show that it is incoherent. It is inherently unstable and can't last because its foundation is illusory, and it is self-contradictory. Nietzsche's third attack stemmed from his overall Darwinian perspective. Slave morality attempts to deny or stop the evolution of humanity by escaping from life itself. In this way it can degenerate into a kind of nihilism. "Nihilism" comes from the Latin word for nothing, and in the second half of the nineteenth-century "nihilism" meant different things to different groups. For Nietzsche, to say slave morality is nihilistic is to say it is inconsistent with life itself. It is a denial of life. When slaves condemn master morality, they are condemning the body, the passions, competition, and instead longing for an impossible peace, eternal quietude, changeless security. As Nietzsche said in the last paragraph of *On the Genealogy of Morals* (in Walter Kaufmann's translation):

> this hatred of the human, and even more of the animal, and more still of the material, this horror of the senses, of reason itself, this fear of happiness and beauty, this longing to get away from all appearance, change, becoming, death, wishing, from longing itself—all that means—let us dare to grasp it—a will to nothingness, an aversion to life, a rebellion against the most fundamental presuppositions of life, but it is and remains a will! And, to repeat in conclusion what I said at the beginning: man would rather will nothingness than not will.

Willing nothingness is a kind of neurotic contradiction. (It is a will not to will, an attempt to express one's vitality by suppressing one's vitality.) But beyond that, Nietzsche was also saying that slave morality attempts to escape from the process of natural selection. It is a preference for the stillness of death over the struggle of life, and in that sense it is a kind of nihilism.

The slaves' hatred of life leads to another fatal weakness, according to Nietzsche. He said the prevalence of slave morality in the modern world prevented the further evolution of humanity. It was a dead end. If everyone is officially equal and of equal worth, then no one can be better than anyone else. No one is allowed to be superior. But it is only through the appearance of superior beings that a group evolves and improves. Nietzsche put it this way:

> Every elevation of the type "man," has hitherto been the work of an aristocratic society and so it will always be—a society believing in a long scale of gradations of rank and differences of worth among human beings, and requiring slavery in some form or other. Without the pathos of distance, such as grows out of the incarnated difference of classes, . . . that other, more mysterious pathos could not have developed either, that longing for an ever-increasing widening of distance within the soul itself, the formation of ever higher, rarer, more remote, tenser, more comprehensive states, in short, precisely the elevation of the type "man," the continued "self-overcoming of man," to take a moral formula in a supra-moral sense.[8]

Nietzsche was not arguing for a return to slavery, but he was arguing for elitism, that is, a differentiation among types of people based on talent, ambition, sensitivity, will power and other forms of creativity. He claimed that the visible, physical differences among the successful, the average, and the failures in life produce "that other more mysterious pathos" of distance within the mind, the distance between excellence and mediocrity, between striving to improve and settling for being average. It is the distance between what one could become through a supreme effort, and what one is now. Without the external distance and "differences of worth among human beings," people will not develop the internal distance, and will not attempt to improve. Humanity will stagnate. He meant we will stagnate culturally and psychologically.

This criticism of slave morality is Darwinian only in an extended sense. Nietzsche was assuming that the further evolution of humanity ought to occur, and slave morality is harmful in so far as it prevents further evolution. Darwin did not claim that evolutionary change was good or bad; it was simply a fact. The "fittest" that survive are not the best in any moral sense but only those who can produce the most offspring who live to maturity. But for Nietzsche, the possibility of the continued evolution of human nature was an essential condition for any morality. It was necessary in order for humanity to become "better," no matter how one defines "better." If we can conceive of moral progress at all—if we can suppose that humanity has not yet reached absolute perfection—then we must hope that the human race will continue to evolve. But to evolve culturally and psychologically we need innovators, experimenters, creators who expand our imaginations, and eccentrics who provide us with models that challenge the status quo. We will return to these innovators below.

NIHILISM AND NIETZSCHE'S RESPONSE

In comparing slave morality and master morality we come to the most basic question that obsessed Nietzsche in all his works, and has obsessed philosophers since the time of Socrates: how can we decide that one set of values is better than another set of values? Or that one morality is better than another? By what standard can we say one set of standards is better than another? For example, by the standard of maximizing happiness, we can say cooperation and generosity are better moral rules than competition and ambition. Cooperation and generosity (probably) lead to more happiness for everyone than competition and ambition do. But by the standard of producing outstanding individuals such as Leonardo de Vinci and Steve Jobs, we can say competition and ambition are better moral rules than cooperation and generosity. But now how do we decide between the standards of maximizing happiness or producing outstanding individuals? On what basis can we say one of those is a better value than the other? We can call this "the basic value question."[9]

Nietzsche had a complex answer to this question, and I think his answer can be characterized as "moral Darwinism." According to this interpretation, Nietzsche was applying the basic ideas of Darwin's theory of natural selection to the history of value systems and moralities. Values are psychological states. To value something (e.g., honesty) is to have positive feelings about it, to admire it, to desire to possess it or promote it or recommend it to others.

Thus where Darwin was describing competition and survival among organisms, Nietzsche was describing competition and survival among psychological states in an individual. There is an analogy between organisms' struggle to exist in nature and an individual's struggle to exist as an individual. According to Darwin, organisms have a basic drive to survive and produce offspring at the biological level. The more offspring they produce, the more fit they are. Nietzsche's view is analogous. He said humans have a basic drive to survive and produce "offspring" on a psychological level. Every person wants to be himself or herself, over and above continuing to breathe and have a heartbeat. The analogy on the psychological level is expressing one's individuality, creating something of one's own, producing "offspring" in the form of actions, words, policies, influences, solutions, artworks, theories, buildings, or whatever one can produce. Producing psychological and cultural offspring is a form of the will to power.

Being genuinely creative is not easy, just as winning the competition in the natural world is not easy. The values of master morality are not attractive to people immersed in slave morality. Nietzsche said that in order to be creative one must welcome the pain of self-discipline, which is a kind of cruelty against oneself.[10] But these strenuous demands on oneself enable one to survive as a self, not as a biological individual but as a psychological individual, with a unique identity. They are necessary for a person to develop her own mind and personality. The alternative is to imitate others, follow orders, suppress desires, try to be just like everyone else, be popular and approved by the group. It is to be a good democrat, a good socialist, a good utilitarian, a good Christian. On the psychological level, slave morality leads to the extinction of the individual. It is still a form of the will to power, as we saw earlier, but toward the goal of extinguishing the self rather than expanding the self.

In several places Nietzsche presented his notion of the ideal toward which humanity should aspire—the Ubermensch, or "Overman"—but he never described his idea in detail. He mentioned Julius Caesar, Goethe, and Napoleon as examples of "higher types" of people, but he also says in *Thus Spake Zarathustra* that no Overmen have ever existed.[11] Nietzsche could argue that master morality is superior to slave morality because the former allows for the possibility of improvement and the latter does not, even if he did not specify in detail what kind of improvement will occur in the evolution of humankind. This would be a kind of "formal" argument for master morality. Nietzsche could say that the notion of an ideal to aspire to (any ideal) requires hierarchy, and is incompatible with complete equality. This concept of an ideal is one part of Nietzsche's answer to the basic value question.

The other part is his concept of the will to power. He can still affirm in a Darwinian fashion that improvement will be the fulfillment of basic instincts. What makes Nietzsche's examples worthy of admiration is their successful expression of the will to power. But the greatest power is power over oneself. It is the possession of titanic, Dionysian instinctive drives, harnessed and channeled by an equally superhuman, Apollonian ordering principle and self-discipline. As Robert Solomon says "The Ubermensch is he who overcomes himself, he who masters (through sublimation) all of the beastly, destructive, especially self-destructive, drives within himself; the all-too-human passions and fears would lead him to be comfortable and secure rather than creative."[12] Nietzsche believed that creativity had greater moral value than security and comfort. Socrates and Jesus were also examples of higher types of people. Such remarkable, energetic, focused individuals will naturally attract others to themselves, so their psychological power will probably lead to social or political influence as well.

Walter Kaufmann quotes Nietzsche as saying "The problem I thus pose is not what shall succeed mankind in the sequence of living beings (man is an end [Ende]), but what type of man shall be bred, shall be willed, for being higher in value" and "The goal of humanity cannot lie in the end but only in its highest specimens."[13] But who are "its highest specimens," and by what standard are they the highest? In pointing to Napoleon, Goethe, and others as higher types of humanity leading to the Overman, it may appear that Nietzsche is begging the question. However, he would argue that the will to power is a premoral source of all moral values, whether Christian or aristocratic. His examples show what is possible for humanity. They show an alternative, future way of expressing the will to power besides the collectivist, conformist way. They are a kind of "existence proof" that further evolution is possible. They are "higher" in the sense that they inspire more experiments rather than closing the door to any progress.

In positing the further evolution of humanity as a desirable goal, Nietzsche differed from Darwin. Another difference was in his understanding of the impetus of evolution. For Darwin, evolutionary change is a slow, blind process. Random variations gave some individuals advantages over others in the competition for scarce resources. But Nietzsche was thinking of the evolution of values and human feelings. He believed individuals in his time had some degree of choice over the kind of people who would exist in the future. At the level of culture, evolution is Lamarckian rather than Darwinian. Jean Baptiste Lamarck said that animals acquire traits during their lives and pass these on to their offspring. Giraffes, for example, stretch their necks to reach leaves, their necks get longer over the years, and their offspring inherit the parents' longer necks. Lamarck was mistaken about biological evolution. But in the realm of culture and psychology, people can change their values and try, at least, to pass on the changes to later generations. Nietzsche urged his readers to recognize the value of master morality, demand more of themselves, and help prepare the way for the new philosophers and masters of the future.[14]

The analogy between biological evolution and psychological evolution is not perfect, and one can imagine other objections to this interpretation of Nietzsche's views. For example, to say master morality enables the individual to survive as a unique individual (not a herd animal), seems different from saying master morality itself survives, or competes with slave morality. Was Nietzsche saying individuals struggle and compete and survive, or moralities compete and survive?

But these ideas are not really in conflict. Master morality is embodied in individuals. The only way it can exist is in the individuals who hold the values of courage, self-discipline, and so on. Richard Dawkins proposes something similar in his influential book *The Selfish Gene*. According to Dawkins, it is genes that compete and survive, and individual organisms are their carriers, so to speak. Individual organisms are expendable, so long as they fulfill their function of passing on the genes to a new generation.[15] Nietzsche could say the same thing about master morality. The individuals who express it are born and die, but the morality itself lives on and evolves into new forms. The example set by great artists, scientists, explorers, and leaders, who follow a master morality, inspires others to try to become creative individuals as well.

The deep changes occurring in European society in the late 19th century gave rise to another movement that would be critical of Nietzsche's proposals. Earlier I mentioned Nietzsche's claim that slave morality was a kind of nihilism, a will to nothingness, and a denial of life. But it is still a will, he said, and so it confirms his view that the will to power is the basic drive motivating people. But in the 1860s other writers advocated a more radical kind of nihilism. They said nothing is good or evil, nothing is right or wrong, nothing matters. They would deny that they were exerting power over their own instincts. They didn't care about instincts, or virtues, or anything else. They would say they don't have a drive to survive as an individual or to produce offspring. In 1861 Ivan Turgenev published his novel *Fathers and Sons* in which a character takes such a nihilistic point of view. Later in the century some anarchists put this idea into practice, declaring that they would destroy the entire rotten, current society by setting off bombs in public places and assassinating public figures. Radical nihilism is a challenge to Nietzsche's moral Darwinism, since Nietzsche was trying to show that master morality is valuable, whereas the nihilists claimed that nothing has value.

Nietzsche could respond to the radical nihilist by arguing that the position is self-contradictory and ultimately incoherent. When the nihilist says nothing is good or evil, he is also asserting a will, and a value. He is asserting that his own belief is better than the Christians' belief or Nietzsche's belief. If he chooses to believe that nothing has value, it must be because he thinks that statement is true, and that it is better to believe true statements than false ones. If he holds any beliefs at all (e.g., "grass is green"), then he places more value on some things (some beliefs) than others. But he said nothing has value. Thus his position is self-contradictory.

THE APPEAL OF NIETZSCHE'S RESPONSE

If we interpret Nietzsche as a moral Darwinist, then his view was that master morality was more adaptive than slave morality. Master values made their possessors more fit, psychologically, than slave values, in the sense that they could survive as selves and produce offspring—creative expressions—better than followers of slave morality. But the claim about adaptation leads to a possible objection. According to Darwin, if a trait is adaptive, the organisms with that trait (e.g., better camouflage) multiply and the trait spreads through the population. But slave morality has spread through the population. It is more popular than master morality. Nietzsche's starting point was the recognition that Christianity, socialism, democracy, and so on were prevalent in Europe. That was the catastrophe he wanted to reverse. It appears that slave values have been more successful than master values in the Darwinian sense of "success."

But the popularity of slave morality is not a problem for Nietzsche's moral Darwinism because popularity is not a measure of fitness or advantage in a set of values at the psychological level. This is so for two reasons. First, as we noted above, slave values may be widespread, but they are an evolutionary dead end. They prevent the further adaptation of humans to changing circumstances, and the creation of higher, more comprehensive experiences. They prevent the survival of unique selves and their "offspring." They would lead to the extinction of great innovators, transformative artworks, and new dimensions of human possibility. Evolution is a continuous, on-going process. To put this in more positive way, fitness in the realm of culture means producing many ideas, deeds, artworks, discoveries, and projects that inspire others. It means possessing the courage, adventurous spirit, confidence, and "pathos of distance" that allows for creativity and further evolution. This is a sort of fertility or productivity, analogous to producing biological offspring, but it exists only among a few people. Thus fitness in the realm of psychology, culture, and values is forward looking rather than outward looking. It is more a matter of potential for further growth than a matter of popularity.

Nietzsche gave a second reason for rejecting popularity as the measure of the fitness or success of a morality.

> One has to get rid of the bad taste of wanting to be in agreement with many. "Good" is no longer good when your neighbor takes it into his mouth. And how could there exist a "common good"! The expression is a self-contradiction: what

can be common has ever but little value. In the end it must be as it is and has always been: great things are for the great, abysses for the profound, shudders and delicacies for the refined, and, in sum, all rare things for the rare.[16]

He was saying that master morality is superior to slave morality if it appeals to the great, the profound, and the refined individuals. And of course it would, since the great and profound people value striving and excellence, and recognize the gradation of ranks.[17] In this respect Nietzsche's moral Darwinism is different from biological Darwinism. In biology, natural selection leads to the spread of a trait throughout a whole population. The adaptiveness, or excellence, of a trait just consists of its tendency to spread through later generations. But adaptiveness or excellence in human values has to be judged by their role in a person's psychology. Do they make a person an excellent person? The word "excel" comes from the Latin verb meaning to raise up, to elevate, to make prominent. A psychological inclination that makes a person equal to others, or average, or that makes him or her choose comfort and ease over difficulty, cannot make a person excellent, by definition. Nietzsche said the question we should ask in evaluating a morality is not "how many choose it," but "who chooses it?"[18]

Nietzsche did not believe master morality was best for everyone. In one sense this might not be controversial. A diet, or exercise regimen, or occupation, or a set of goals, might be good for some and not good for others, and everyone could agree. But Nietzsche was discussing moralities. We normally think that the basic foundations of morality are the same for everyone, that is, if morality exists at all. But recall that Nietzsche said: "there are no moral facts." In other places he said he was a nihilist. He meant that he understood that what people think of as morality is an illusion. They think it is part of the objective world, but actually it is an expression of their own feelings and desires. He wanted to usher in a new way of thinking about moral values—master morality—which was fearlessly honest, and based on an individual's will to power.

Nietzsche questioned everything, including the nature and value of truth. He believed that science does not give us an objective, true picture of the world, because scientists' observations and interpretations are guided by their values. This is another difference from Darwinism, which is supposed to be objectively true. But then if truth is called into question, the statement that people are driven by a will to power and to express themselves may not be true. Nietzsche believed that all so-called truths depended on one's perspective, or point of view, and what is true from one perspective might not be true from another perspective. For example, in discussing women and their instincts he reminded his readers that he was presenting his truths, not an absolute truth, and he was inviting the readers to consider whether or not his truths could also be their truths.[19]

A further complication in interpreting Nietzsche's point of view is that he was not simply analyzing ideas dispassionately. He was also promoting certain values. The subtitle of *On the Genealogy of Morals* is "A Polemic." When he praised the higher types of people and claimed that master morality was superior to slave morality, he wasn't simply asking for intellectual assent. He was calling for an emotional change in the reader. To come to believe that one value, for example, ambition, is better than another value, for example, humility, is to acquire certain feelings about ambition and humility and to want to act in certain ways. This suggests that his defense of master morality is not an abstract argument, or an objective set of reasons that should persuade any rational person.

These considerations apply to his moral Darwinism. For Nietzsche, it is true that organisms struggle for survival and evolve, and it is true that humans struggle for psychological survival and try to "become who they are," to be themselves. But this is a truth for the great, the profound, the refined, not for everyone. In several places he said he was not writing for a wide audience but only for a select few. Nietzsche's moral Darwinism is about competition and adaptiveness on the level of psychology, of feelings, of finding one's identity and expanding it. The theory will be attractive to some but not others. Some will say "Nietzsche's truth is also my truth"; that is, it helps me find myself, it forces me to examine my inner drives, to channel them, to be more creative, to preserve and express my individuality. Others will not see the value (i.e., truth) of the theory, according to Nietzsche. Does it make sense, then, to say he has made a convincing case for the superiority of master morality, if he expects most people to reject it?

One possibility is to interpret Nietzsche as a "moral psychoanalyst" as well as a moral Darwinist. Nietzsche often said that people of the herd were "sick," and they actually valued their sickness, whereas masters were healthy. His defense of master morality may be more like a diagnosis and prescription for a patient than a rational argument. Specifically, a prescription for a mental patient, a person with a neurosis. Nietzsche's ideas are similar in some ways to Freud's ideas. When a patient came to Freud with a problem, Freud didn't explain to the patient what was causing his problem. Instead, he helped the patient review his past so he could discover how he got into his current predicament, which was painful and preventing him from leading a normal life. (He helped the patient construct a personal genealogy.) Ideally, the patient discovered his past mistake, when he blocked some wish and repressed the memory of it. When he gained that self-understanding, he could deal with the wish consciously and rationally. The neurotic behavior and the frustration ceased. Freud did not "convince" the patient of what he should do. Rather, he helped the patient recognize his own needs and what thwarted them, so the patient became free to be himself. Freud acknowledged his debt to Nietzsche, and we can interpret Nietzsche's defense of master morality and moral Darwinism as similar to Freud's treatment of his patients. Some will understand master values and recognize their superiority to other values, and others will not.

CONCLUSION

A little knowledge of Nietzsche's works is a dangerous thing. He said he would be misunderstood, and he was, disastrously, by the fascists. One can select parts of his works and take them literally. For example, he spoke of strength, and commanders, and war, as desirable things, and one can interpret him to mean physical strength, military commanders, and war between nations. Deeper study of his writing, however, reveals that he meant psychological strength, commanding by personal example, and war among one's own instincts.

But if everything is a matter of interpretations and there is no objective truth, as Nietzsche maintained, could the fascists claim that their interpretation is just as legitimate as others? Nietzsche would say no. Some interpretations are more faithful to experience or a text than others. But the ultimate test of the truth of an interpretation is its promotion of health, vitality, and creativity.[20] An interpretation of Nietzsche in terms of physical struggles among individuals or nations, rather than spiritual struggles among values and moralities, stifles growth and creativity, and is therefore false.

Nietzsche's elitism is disturbing to most people today. His references to the "herd" and "herd animals" are offensive, even as metaphors. What Nietzsche considered a catastrophe most people today would regard as progress. So should Nietzsche's defense of master morality be dismissed as incompatible with our more enlightened, egalitarian attitudes? Perhaps. But it isn't easy to do, because his probing explorations remind us that we must explain why we say democracy and compassion and security are better values than his values. His historical consciousness, and his acute analyses of motivations (including unconscious motivations), explode any claim to "self-evident" truths. The value of Nietzsche's writing is that it forces people to reexamine their assumptions about morality, and it confronts the conventional wisdom as a challenger, or as a competitor. That is exactly as Nietzsche said it should be.

NOTES

1. These quotes are from *Thus Spake Zarathustra* and *Twilight of the Idols*.

2. Michael Curtis, *The Great Political Theories, Vol. 2* (New York: Avon Books, 1981), 185.

3. Ralph Waldo Emerson had expressed similar ideas in 1841 in his essay "Self-Reliance": "These are the voices that we hear in solitude, but they grow faint and inaudible as we enter into the world. Society everywhere is in conspiracy against the manhood of every one of its members. . . . The virtue in most request is conformity. Self-reliance is its aversion. . . . Whoso would be a man, must be a nonconformist. . . . No law can be sacred to me but that of my nature. Good and bad are but names very readily transferable to that or this; the only right is what is after my constitution; the only wrong what is against it."

4. Herbert Spencer, *The Study of Sociology* (London: Henry S. King, 1873), chapter 14, accessed January 10, 2015, http://oll.libertyfund.org/titles/1335.

5. "I preach to you, then, my countrymen, that our country calls not for the life of ease but for the life of strenuous endeavor. The 20th century looms before us big with the fate of many nations. If we stand idly by, if we seek merely swollen, slothful ease and ignoble peace, if we shrink from the hard contests where men must win at hazard of their lives and at the risk of all they hold dear, then the bolder and stronger peoples will pass us by, and will win for themselves the domination of the world. Let us therefore boldly face the life of strife, resolute to do our duty well and manfully; . . . Above all, let us shrink from no strife, moral or physical, within or without the nation, provided we are certain that the strife is justified, for it is only through strife, through hard and dangerous endeavor, that we shall ultimately win the goal of true national greatness." Theodore Roosevelt, "The Strenuous Life," [1899] in Brian Tierney, Donald Kagan, and L. Pearce Williams, eds., *Social Darwinism: Law of Nature, or Justification of Oppression?* 3rd ed. (New York: Random House, 1977), 22–26.

6. Nietzsche explains this evolution in the first essay, "On the Genealogy of Morals," in *Basic Writings of Nietzsche*, ed. and trans. Walter Kaufmann (New York: Modern Library, 1968); and more briefly in *Beyond Good and Evil*, trans. R. J. Hollingdale (London: Penguin, 1990), section 260.

7. Nietzsche mentions the death of God in *Dawn* [1881] and *The Gay Science* [1882] in *Basic Writings*, and makes it a central theme of *Thus Spake Zarathustra* (1883–85).

8. *Beyond Good and Evil*, section 257.

9. Nietzsche poses the question in one form in the Preface of the Genealogy: "under what conditions did man devise these value judgments good and evil? and what value do they themselves possess?" Are the two standards of happiness and excellence really distinct? Does one collapse into the other? The utilitarian who advocates the standard of maximizing happiness would probably argue that promoting individuality is really a form of utilitarianism. Outstanding individuals are valuable only because they increase the majority's happiness in the long run. On the other hand, an elitist might argue that increasing people's security and living standards—happiness—is valuable because that would give more people the opportunity to achieve something really outstanding. How many Mozarts or Einsteins have we missed because of poverty and misery? But utilitarians and elitists would resist the other side's claims, and neither reduction is obviously true.

10. "Almost everything we call "higher culture" is based on the spiritualization and intensification of cruelty—that is my proposition; . . . Here, to be sure, we must put aside the thick-witted psychology of former times which had to teach of cruelty only that it had its origin in the sight of the sufferings of others; there is also an abundant, over-abundant enjoyment of one's own suffering, of making oneself suffer—and wherever man allows himself to be persuaded to self-denial in the religious sense, or to self-mutilation, as among Phoenicians and ascetics, or in general to desensualization, decarnalization, contrition, to Puritanical spasms of repentance . . . he is secretly lured and urged onward by his cruelty, by the dangerous thrills of cruelty directed against himself." *Beyond Good and Evil*, section 229.

11. Michael Tanner says Zarathustra announces that the meaning of the earth is the Uebermensch. "But what we now wait for," Tanner adds, "is some illumination about how the Uebermensch is the meaning of the earth, what steps might be taken to bring about his arrival, and what he will be like when he appears. Unfortunately we get very little information about any of these matters." Roger Scruton, Peter Singer, Christopher Janaway, Michael Tanner, *German Philosophers: Kant, Hegel, Schopenhauer, Nietzsche* (Oxford: Oxford University Press, 1997), 397.

12. Robert C. Solomon, *From Rationalism to Existentialism: The Existentialists and Their Nineteenth-Century Backgrounds* (Lanham, MD: University Press of America, 1972), 134.

13. Walter Kaufmann, *Nietzsche: Philosopher, Psychologist, Antichrist*, 4th ed. (Princeton, NJ: Princeton University Press, 1974), 311–12.

14. Gregory Moore argues that Nietzsche did not believe that organic evolution was driven by competition for scarce resources, with the more fit specimens gradually dominating the gene pool. Instead, like other German scientists and philosophers cited by Moore, he believed living beings had an innate drive to develop, grow, assert themselves, and transform themselves, in other words, gain more power. "Nietzsche and Evolutionary Theory," in *Blackwell Companions to Philosophy: A Companion to Nietzsche*, ed. K. Ansell Pearson (Hoboken, NJ: Wiley, 2007), accessed November 20, 2016. https://ezproxy.library.nyu.edu/login?url=http://search.credoreference.com/content/entry/wileycniet/nietzsche_and_evolutionary_theory/0. For a more detailed discussion of Nietzsche's relation to Darwin, see John Richardson, *Nietzsche's New Darwinism* (Oxford: Oxford University Press, 2004), published February 2006 to Oxford Scholarship Online, who says the following on p. 3: "Most of what Nietzsche says about Darwin and Darwinism is hostile. . . . But I think this pointed animosity is—here as often elsewhere in Nietzsche's campaigns—misleading. He is so eager to distinguish himself, because he knows how much he has taken over from Darwin—how big a part of his own view, this Darwinism looms. I think Nietzsche profits when we notice and expose this shared ground. His position is stronger when we become aware—against his own efforts—of this Darwinian element in it. His views on a range of basic questions turn out to be more credible when we do justice to this element."

15. Richard Dawkins, *The Selfish Gene* (New York: Oxford University Press, 1976).

16. *Beyond Good and Evil*, section 43.

17. Aristotle says something similar about virtue, which is the mean between extremes. The mean is "determined by logos ("reason," "account"), and in the way that the person of practical reason would determine it" (1107a1–2). We can't state a general rule for determining the mean; we depend on people with practical experience. According to Richard Kraut, Aristotle "says that the virtuous person 'sees the truth in each case, being as it were the standard and measure of them' (1113a32–3)." *The Stanford Encyclopedia of Philosophy*, ed. Edward N. Zalta (Summer 2017 ed.). This suggests that we know the mean, or virtue, in a particular situation by listening to virtuous people who can discern it. Nietzsche says we know human excellence by listening to rare, great people who can see it.

18. Here again, it may appear that Nietzsche is begging the question of basic value, that he is simply assuming that ambition is morally better than humility and self-sacrifice, and that individuality is better than conformity. And we know it is better because ambitious, individualistic people say it is. But I think he would say he isn't begging the question, so long as we believe long-term progress is possible. Increasing equality rules out long-term progress, because it rules out experimentation, eccentricity, celebrating difference. We can't be sure what the better people of the future—the Overmen—will be like, he says, but we can be sure that if we try to make everyone equal, there will be no better people of the future. Only refined, rare, great individuals can judge what may lead to progress.

19. "Having just paid myself such a deal of pretty compliments I may perhaps be more readily permitted to utter a few truths about 'woman as such': assuming it is now understood from the outset to how great an extent these are only—my truths." *Beyond Good and Evil*, section 231.

20. "The falseness of a judgment is to us not necessarily an objection to a judgment: it is here that our new language perhaps sounds strangest. The question is to what extent it is life-advancing, life-preserving, species-preserving, perhaps even species breeding; and our fundamental tendency is to assert that the falsest judgments (to which synthetic judgments a priori belong) are the most indispensable to us, . . ." *Beyond Good and Evil*, section 4.

BIBLIOGRAPHY

Curtis, Michael. *The Great Political Theories*. Vol. 2. New York: Avon Books, 1981.

Dawkins, Richard. *The Selfish Gene*. New York: Oxford University Press, 1976.

Kaufmann, Walter. *Nietzsche: Philosopher, Psychologist, Antichrist*. 4th ed. Princeton, NJ: Princeton University Press, 1974.

Kraut, Richard. "Aristotle's Ethics." *The Stanford Encyclopedia of Philosophy*. Edited by Edward N. Zalta. Palo Alto, CA: Stanford University, Summer 2018. https://plato.stanford.edu/archives/sum2018/entries/aristotle-ethics/.

Moore, Gregory. "Nietzsche and Evolutionary Theory." *Blackwell Companions to Philosophy: A Companion to Nietzsche*. Edited by K. Ansell Pearson. Hoboken, NJ: Wiley, 2007. Accessed November 20, 2016. https://ezproxy.library.nyu.ed

u/login?url=http://search.credoreference.com/content/entry/wileycniet/nietzsche_and_evolutionary_theory/0.

Nietzsche, Friedrich. *Basic Writings of Nietzsche*. Edited and translated by Walter Kaufmann. New York: Modern Library, 1968.

———. *Beyond Good and Evil*. Translated by R. J. Hollingdale. London: Penguin, 1990.

Scruton, Roger, Peter Singer, Christopher Janaway, Michael Tanner. *German Philosophers: Kant, Hegel, Schopenhauer, Nietzsche*. Oxford: Oxford University Press, 1997.

Solomon, Robert C. *From Rationalism to Existentialism: The Existentialists and Their Nineteenth-Century Backgrounds*. Lanham, MD: University Press of America, 1972.

Spencer, Herbert. *The Study of Sociology*. London: Henry S. King, 1873. Accessed January 10, 2015. http://oll.libertyfund.org/titles/1335.

Tierney, Brian, Donald Kagan, L. Pearce Williams, editors. *Social Darwinism: Law of Nature, or Justification of Oppression?* 3rd ed. New York: Random House, 1977.

Chapter 12

Ludwig Wittgenstein—Philosophy in the Twilight of the Habsburgs

John Ross

Ludwig Wittgenstein was born in Vienna during the last days of the Habsburg Empire. Since Wittgenstein's biography is intertwined with the fate of Austria, I would like to examine how Austro-Hungary's social and political demise affected Wittgenstein's philosophy. A number of excellent studies have investigated Wittgenstein's connection to his Viennese roots, and it is not my purpose here to analyze this literature. Rather it is remarkable that Wittgenstein spent his formative years at least tangentially connected to many significant thinkers in the midst of the collapse of the Austro-Hungarian Empire. Although they had less effect than they might have hoped, artists and writers that Wittgenstein knew and admired urgently warned of the coming catastrophe and called for change and reform. It is hard to imagine that Wittgenstein was unaffected by this message. Yet Wittgenstein is primarily thought of as a philosopher of language and a logician. That is certainly true, but I would agree with those that argue that his work had a much wider significance, particularly when it comes to the collapse of the Habsburg Empire.

The story of the Habsburgs is an intriguing tale of Eurocentric global politics that is unfortunately sometimes not well understood in Anglo-American circles. In the early eleventh century Count Radbot and his brother Werner the Bishop of Strasbourg built The Habichtsburg—The Castle of the Hawk— a somewhat modest fortification occupying the Tyrol region of what is now Switzerland. By the start of the twelfth century the family adopted the name of the castle as its own thus beginning the Habsburg dynasty. The family was enterprising, successful, and eventually became extraordinarily wealthy and powerful. By the thirteenth century the Hapsburgs ruled Germany and Austria and from 1441 onward the house became synonymous with the Holy Roman Empire. The Habsburg Charles V (1500–1558) was titled Holy Roman Emperor, King of Spain, King of Italy, Archduke of Austria, Lord of the

Netherlands, and Duke of Burgundy. The Spanish conquistadores operated in the New World under his direction, and eventually the reach of the empire extended as far as the Philippines. Charles V was most often referred to simply as "Charles of Europe."[1]

It would be a mistake to assume that the astonishing expanse of Habsburg power was accomplished through conquest—although use of force was not out of the question. Rather the leader of the family acted like a CEO who orchestrated the affairs of the noble families that officially made up the ruling class. Membership in the ruling class was strictly controlled, limited to those families of the purest pedigree. Their estates, business holdings, and marriage relationships were equally controlled. Marriage and business association were the most common tools of Habsburg territorial acquisition.[2]

It would equally be incorrect to think of the Habsburg clan as comprised of boorish businessmen. They were extremely religious and keenly aware of their connection to the Catholic Church—a mutually beneficial arrangement. The Habsburgs were nearly unequalled in their patronage of the arts. Once they firmly established the family in Vienna the city was continually overflowing with the greats in all the arts. Many European notables in painting, music, opera, and architecture flourished in Vienna at one time or other.

Neither science nor industry were neglected. Mach, Hertz, Boltzmann, and eventually Einstein were all successful in Vienna. The Austrian economy under the Habsburgs made great strides during the Industrial Age, and the achievement of great wealth was not restricted to Aristocracy. For example, from middle class beginnings Ludwig Wittgenstein's father Karl became a captain of the steel industry—the Andrew Carnegie of Europe—and grew enormously rich in the process. When the noble title "von" was offered to him he refused. It should be noted the Karl spent lavishly supporting the arts. The "Palais Wittgenstein" as it was known boasted thirteen grand pianos. Klimt painted family portraits. Brahms and Mahler were frequent houseguests, sometimes performing their own works for family gatherings.[3]

The Habsburgs traditionally were politically conservative—hardly surprising for a European Royal House. Empress Maria Therese (1717–1780), although conservative in many respects—particularly with regard to religious toleration—began a process of reforming and modernizing the Empire. Most of the reforms initially focused on upgrading and centralizing what was essentially a feudal regime in order to facilitate taxation and military conscription. However, once it became known that there existed an authority above the landed nobility that was receptive their interests the ordinary person complained loudly regarding being abused by the local aristocracy. Particularly galling was the feudal obligation of the "Robot" which was a certain amount of forced labor owed to the landlord. This service could be 3 days a week and sometimes more during certain periods. Such servitude left the worker little time to cultivate his or her own land resulting not only in a decline in productivity but also a decline in tax revenues. The thus disgruntled farmer or worker hardly welcomed the prospect of military service, often preferring self-inflicted bodily injury to conscription. Maria Therese "negotiated" with the aristocracy to improve the lives of the ordinary citizen by introducing a number of improvements such as the eventual elimination of the Robot, allowing the small farmer access to the market, and offering public education. The process of reform was continued and enhanced by her sons Leopold (1747–1792) and particularly Joseph II (1741–1790). Politically the overall effect was a stronger central government and the positioning of the monarchy as a unifying force in the multiethnic empire.[4]

Ultimately the political left gained power in parliament by aligning itself with the central administration, which they saw as a vehicle for liberalism. Thus the nineteenth century saw the introduction of many liberal reforms such as sweeping away the last vestiges of feudalism, parliamentary reforms, the extension of voting rights, freedom of the press, the closing of Jewish ghettos, the removal of the restrictions on Jews marrying non-Jews, and allowing Jews to enter the University and the professions.

By the mid-nineteenth century Vienna under Habsburg rule probably appeared to many as the idyllic fulfillment of the promise of the Enlightenment. The giants of industry, science and the arts deftly guided the beauty and prosperity of a magnificent Empire on which the sun truly never set. However closer inspection revealed a darker reality—a view often shared by many of the intellectual circles that populated the ubiquitous coffee houses of Vienna. At the dawn of the 20th century there were no shortage of oracles warning that the Austro-Hungarian Empire teetered on the brink of collapse and was threatening to drag the rest of the world down with it. The satirist Karl Kraus (1874–1936) called Vienna a "research lab for world destruction." Unfortunately, Kraus was right. Two of the 20th century's greatest horrors—World War I and Nazi Germany—both emanated from Vienna.[5]

Many of the political problems facing the Austro-Hungarian Empire in the nineteenth century were typical of those facing all of modern Europe and were obvious enough to the general population to spawn the revolutions of 1848: political oppression and corruption, abuses by the aristocracy, the plight of the working class, poverty, lack of housing and medical care for the poor, religious intolerance, the political and social marginalization of women—for starters. However, the Habsburg Empire experienced a unique set of social and political pressures because it was cobbled together from a dizzying array of nationalities with unique languages and cultures that often demanded greater autonomy, often punctuated with threats of riots, protests, and general anarchy. The Habsburg family was not personally immune to the political turmoil. During the reign of Emperor Franz Joseph (1848–1916), his wife the Empress Elisabeth was assassinated by an Italian anarchist in 1898 and of course the assassination of his nephew Ferdinand by a Serbian Nationalist touched off World War I.

The belief in access to the administration was a key to unity in the empire, but this tool could be viewed as an Achilles' heel. The idea that each group had the ability to directly petition the Empire often actually exacerbated racial problems. In addition to the ordinary tug of war we might expect from competing ethnic groups, each new acquisition of territory or the welcoming of refugees from the nearly constant warfare on the empire's borders brought fresh problems of integration. Some groups resented intrusion or the loss of traditional rights and privileges. New groups or traditional minorities often demanded more inclusion and a greater share of political power. Any real or imagined lack of attention on the part of the Empire only served to intensify the shouting, inviting greater retaliation from the opposition. Of course the aristocracy would have welcomed an increase in control over local affairs and so their relationship with the administration was often contentious. The nobility was not above supporting local strife in order to make the point that their direct control was necessary for social order.

In all of this language became a focal point of contention. Naturally many groups saw their language as a principle focus of cultural identity and pushed for its use as an official language within their area. Likewise, a group that held a favored position because of numbers, tradition, or economic influence resented any sharing or abrogation of linguistic rights. A constant refrain was that along with their language, their culture and society was being degraded. Such concerns only served to heighten tensions between ethnic groups.

One of the major social problems within the Empire that cut across every social divide was a persistent anti-Semitism. In the lands ruled by the Habsburg's Jews were officially discriminated against since the Middle Ages. The pattern of discrimination was similar all over Europe, but in the Habsburg domains anti-Semitism could be particularly virulent. After 1867 when the barriers to education and trade were officially lifted, Jews responded by aggressively pursuing those careers that had been denied to them for so long, unless they had been willing to renounce their Jewish heritage and completely assimilate. Science, engineering, industry, medicine, law, social sciences, and journalism all experienced a large influx of Jewish practitioners.[6]

Unfortunately, many of the middle- and lower-class Germans resented this influx and painted it as the ruination of German culture. Jews were lumped in with the other non-German groups in the Empire according to the blossoming ideology of Pan-Germanism which opposed any racial diversity. Pan-Germanism would eventually become a full-blown political movement culminating in the success of the Christian Social Party headed by Karl Lueger who was elected mayor of Vienna in 1897. The Christian Socialist movement attracted a young Adolf Hitler who would eventually take control the party *and transform it into National Socialism.*[7]

This fraying of the society and the political tensions in the Empire received attention from all quarters—particularly from the arts. Numerous artists, writers, and scientists, among them Kraus, Loos, Kokoschka, Schiele, Schnitzler, Musil, Freud, and Schoenberg all attempted to illustrate and address in one way or the other the decay that was festering in the Habsburg domains. All the same, the Empire was set inextricably on an implosion course and much of this work either produced outrage at its presence or fell on deaf ears. It as if many were shouting "fire!" in a crowded theater, but the audience still sat there either annoyed at the interruption or remained, slightly bored, watching the show.

To try to completely understand all the causes, events, and responses surrounding the collapse of the Austro-Hungarian Empire is beyond the scope of the essay. Thus, I would like to concentrate on the philosophical response to the crisis—particularly Wittgenstein's response. Wittgenstein was one of the 20th century's most important philosophers, and one the greatest philosophers associated with Vienna. Wittgenstein was in a unique position to observe the events leading up to the dissolution of the Austro-Hungarian Empire. His only published book—the *Tractatus*—was completed in the trenches during World War I. Wittgenstein smuggled the completed manuscript to Bertrand Russell while he languished in an Italian POW camp. Wittgenstein's family was among the most wealthy, powerful, and influential in Vienna. So it might be reasonable to assume that if he had anything philosophical to say on the collapse of the Empire it would deserve to be heeded.

Yet as a philosopher Wittgenstein was unique. It would be overstating the case to say he was educated as a philosopher. Prior to entering the university, we know that he read Schopenhauer and thereby likely gained a good insight into Kant's ideas. At school he received a rigorous classical education that included a thorough instruction in classical Latin; so we can assume he read something of the usual Latin Classics. He read Tolstoy—particularly the short stories, and during the war he read Tolstoy's version of the Gospels. Apparently his family kept him abreast of the cutting edge in Viennese arts and letters. Probably because of his family he became an avid fan of the satirist Karl Kraus, and like many of his educated contemporaries he eagerly awaited each new issue of Kraus' journal *Die Fackel* (The Torch)—he even had it delivered to the makeshift hut he occupied in Norway prior to the start of World War I.[8] In the years prior to his studying at Cambridge, it was Kraus and his circle that included Oscar Kokoschka, Adolph Loos, Peter Altenberg, Georg Trakl, and Arnold Schoenberg that attracted the majority of Wittgenstein's attention when we consider his influences in contemporary Viennese philosophy and culture. Wittgenstein also claimed he was greatly influenced by the psychologist Otto Weininger. After Weininger's suicide in 1903 his work *Sex and Character,* which was highly regarded by Kraus, attained cult status in Vienna. After the war, Wittgenstein was the principle architect on a house for his sister, which in its logical approach to design and lack of ornamentation shows the strong influence of the architect Adolph Loos. Although it is not a view universally shared, it has been argued by Janik and Toulmin that the *Tractatus* owes a great deal to the views espoused by Kraus and his compatriots.[9]

Of course, Wittgenstein has been connected to the "Vienna Circle" that gathered around Moritz Schlick. However, this connection was made after World War I and the publication of the *Tractatus.* Wittgenstein had more influence on the positivism that developed out of the Vienna Circle rather than the other way around.[10]

Once we get a feeling for Karl Kraus's work, his influence on the iconoclastic Wittgenstein should come as no surprise. Kraus's *Die Fackel,* a journal dedicated to satirically attacking the corruption in Vienna, particularly in the media, was nearly compulsory reading among Viennese cultural elite. While Kraus tirelessly campaigned for social justice, he ultimately was not content with merely focusing attention on the problem. Rather he wanted to point out what he believed was the cause of corruption, and he wanted show the means for its elimination. Kraus argued that the corrupting influence in society was rooted in the misuse of language, and he argued that the solution to the presence of evil in the society was to be found in the purifying of the German language—in a pure German evil could not be spoken. However, I would argue that for Kraus, this position was more like a matter of faith, seeing himself as a prophet rather than a philosopher. When one of his readers complained that during the war between Japan and China Kraus was focused in his journal on the trivialities of grammar and punctuation his response was extraordinary:

I know it is all pointless when the house is on fire. But I must do this as long as it is possible for, if the people responsible had always taken care that all the commas were in the right place, Shanghai would not be burning.[11]

Kraus's task was to purge language of dissembling nonsense—the mask that lead to falsehood. There was a moral purity that was connected to the proper use of language. "Something I cannot get over: that a whole line can be written by half a man" (Half Truths p. 49). The integrity of language is equal to the integrity of the human being. The purity of language for Kraus was a personal rigorous moral quest.

It might be tempting to see what Kraus was doing in terms of contemporary political correctness. The closer modern analogue might be that Kraus was exposing and rejecting political "spin." Politicians often twist language to make objectionable or corrupt actions seem palatable or even moral. Examples are legion: bribes become "campaign contributions," civilian casualties are "collateral damage," errors in judgment are "unforeseen consequences" etc. In Kraus's day he noted that concentration camps were described in the media as "protective custody."[12]

To equate correct language use with moral correctness may seem absurd. However, it may be clearer if we relate Kraus's idea to Socrates' search for definition. In Plato's formulation of the thoughts of his teacher, Socrates critique becomes about ideas and eventually recognizing eternal truths. But Socrates in the dialogues focuses a lot of his attention on language and the meaning of words. So for example in the beginning of *Republic* Socrates is looking for the *meaning* of "justice" (dikaiosune—literally: doing the right thing). Presumably by clarifying the definition for certain members of his audience they were then able to go on to make the right choices about the right thing to do. Hence the purpose of focusing of the meaning of ethical terms—justice, piety, courage, and so on—was that clarifying the terms would lead to the correct ethical actions. Whatever Socrates actually believed about the relationship between ideas and language is not relevant here. Kraus clearly identified the two—thinking, for Kraus, happens exclusively in language and so mangling language mangles thought and thereby wreaks havoc with morals and culture. Language can be used to hide or evade the truth—to obfuscate and confuse. Language is the weapon of hucksters and con-men, false prophets and charlatans, and of course demagogues and dictators. Through satire Kraus would try to unmask them all. Kraus' quest was ultimately moral.[13] However, we should note that it is rumored that Herman Goering had a complete collection of Die Fackel.

The members of Kraus' circle produced works in their own fields in the same spirit: trying to tear down the obstacles to truth and reality. In his famous essay Loos compares the style of excess ornamentation in the architecture of Vienna to a crime. For Loos Vienna was architecturally a "Potemkin City"—a series of facades that were supposed to exemplify the beauty of the city but were in fact wasteful and served only to hide larger economic and social problems.[14] His buildings were derided for being too stark and functional. Schoenberg, Kokoschka, Trakl, and Schiele all used forms of a direct encounter dissonance to shock the viewer out of a complacency that refused to acknowledge the reality of the decay that was eroding Austrian society.[15]

Wittgenstein in the *Tractatus* was working in the same vein from a philosophical point of view. Wittgenstein was clearly absorbed is the problems of logic and the foundations of logic. But he was just as absorbed as Kraus in the connection between language and ethics. Kraus was imploring his readers to have the character and commitment to purify their use of language. Wittgenstein was saying that in order to be meaningful at all it *must* be so. The only way to view the world correctly is through a logically correct language. Only once we have completed this rigorous exercise can reality and truth appear.

> My propositions serve as elucidations in the following way: anyone who understands me eventually recognizes them as nonsensical when he has used them—as steps—to climb up beyond them. (He must, so to speak, throw away the ladder after he has climbed up it.) He must transcend these propositions, and then he will see the world aright.[16]

Clearly the *Tractatus* is meant as a steppingstone to what Wittgenstein believes is a correct view of the world. As such the work's genesis has much to do with Wittgenstein's influences in prewar Vienna, but its audience is intended to be far wider. Certainly in the above quote Wittgenstein is making an extraordinary claim. To evaluate that claim let's examine the development of the *Tractatus* a little more closely.

Wittgenstein's initial professional pursuit had been in aeronautical engineering with an interest in jet propulsion. At some point while he was a student in Manchester in 1908 Wittgenstein turned his attention from aeronautical engineering to questions of the logical foundations of mathematics. He may have had an interest in the topic previously, but reading Russell's *Principles of Mathematics* published in 1903 seems to have caused him to pursue the topic in earnest. Wittgenstein became familiar with Gottlob Frege's work on the same topic through Russell's discussion in the *Principles* of Frege's *Foundations of Arithmetic*. Sometime in the next two years he planned a book of his own on the topic. He took his proposal for a manuscript on the subject to Gottlob Frege in Jena and eventually Frege sent him back to Russell in Cambridge.[17] Clearly the project Wittgenstein had in mind eventually became the *Tractatus*. In the preface to the *Tractatus* he mentions his debt to Russell and Frege's "great works" as major influences on his thinking. He sent Frege a copy of the book and the two carried on a correspondence, but only Frege's letters to Wittgenstein survive. The *Tractatus* elicited mostly confusion from Frege—particularly when it came to Wittgenstein's statement in his preface that the point of the book was an ethical one. Frege claimed the idea was strange to him.[18]

Wittgenstein's intellectual relationship to Russell was complex, and it is beyond the scope of this essay to sort it out. At Cambridge Wittgenstein became enmeshed in Russell's research into the logical foundation of mathematics and Russell's view on the problems of philosophy—problems that were delineated in the *Principles*: questions of meaning, truth, the reality of mathematical objects, the foundations of number, the concepts of space and its relation to geometry, the idea of motion, and so on. The question of ethics or "metaphysical" issues: God, the Soul, the Ego, and so on, as one might expect in such a treatise, did not come up. These questions are equally as foreign to the interests of the *Principles* as they are to Frege's *Foundations*. However, they occupy the *Tractatus* from remark 6.4 to the end of the book. We certainly could disregard the preface and these passages as some have.

However, I can see no reason for disregarding such a large portion of the text, and to do so would argue that his only philosophical interest and influence was Russell and the foundation of mathematics contrary to Wittgenstein's own statement. Russell's influence is of course undeniable but Wittgenstein also mentions Boltzmann, Schopenhauer, Kraus, Loos, and Weininger—all of whom he knew prior to coming to Cambridge.[19] I would agree with those who would argue that Wittgenstein brought many of the philosophical problems with him to Cambridge from Vienna, and we should take him at his word when he says that the point of the work is an ethical one. As far as an ethical point is concerned I would agree that the *Tractatus* is a most influenced by Kraus: an attempt to uncover the purity of language—an activity that leads one to the truth and a moral life.

The *Tractatus* is a notoriously difficult work, but for our purposes I think it can be best understood if we concentrate on the seven major propositions proposition that function something like chapter headings and form the outline of the book.

1. The world is all that is the case.
2. What is the case—a fact—is the existence of states of affairs.
3. A logical picture of facts is a thought.
4. A thought is a proposition with sense.
5. A proposition is a truth function of elementary propositions.
6. The general form of a truth function is $[p,\xi,N(\xi)]$. This is the general form of a proposition.
7. What we cannot speak about we must pass over in silence.

I would not be so rash to claim that I can present the unarguably correct interpretation of the above propositions, but if there is a generally agreed upon interpretation of the above I think it would be close to the following. Wittgenstein equated the world—everything that exists or the total collection of "facts"—with everything about which we can form meaningful propositions. If you can't form a meaningful proposition about something then there is no question of truth or falsity, existence, or nonexistence—there are no questions at all. If we cannot form a meaningful proposition, Wittgenstein states, thought is not possible. There reason, according to Wittgenstein, is that "facts" result from a connection of "objects." Although "object" is a technical term in Wittgenstein's version of logical atomism, for simplicity's sake if we say the "The book is on the table" we have a relationship between two objects. For Wittgenstein the proposition is meaningful because it expresses a possible relation between two objects and so we have something to actually think about. If I said: "The glorble is flooping" I have something that looks like a sentence, but for Wittgenstein "glorble" and "flooping" do not name objects; so there can be no connection between objects and therefore nothing meaningful is present and no thought is possible. Hence without a connection between objects we have no facts, no meaning, and no thought. We could have the *appearance* of meaning, but in actuality we have only nonsense. The key idea (which Wittgenstein later repudiated) is that words are meaningful only when they name objects, and for a proposition to be meaningful the relationship between the words mirrors a possible relationship of objects. This idea Wittgenstein referred to as the picture theory of language. For a proposition to be true the stated relationship between the objects must actually exist—if the book is on the floor the proposition "the book is on the table" is meaningful but false. The upshot is that the collection of meaningful propositions—those that are about possible combinations of objects—represents all that can be said—all that can be thought about.

It would hardly be surprising if the connection between ethics and the above was unclear at this point. Many early commentators and readers—particularly members of Schlick's Vienna Circle—took the book as a philosophical support for logical positivism. The last statement meant simply that the ethical and metaphysical were relegated to nonsense, and overall only empirical statements are meaningful.

However, this view represents only a cursory reading of the text. Since Wittgenstein explicitly states in the preface that the sense of the book is that what can be said can be said clearly or else we must not say anything at all, then if he merely wanted to say ethics shouldn't be talked about he would have done so. But he says much more. He says that since facts in the world simply occur the statements of value are not in the world, but must transcend the world (TLP 6.41–6.421). Value is something we *add* to the world: "The world of the happy man is different from that of the unhappy man" (TLP 6.43). Any meaning to life is not found in the world—the solution to the riddle of life "in space and time lies outside of space and time." (TLP 6.4312) But again we should note that Wittgenstein does not say that the solution to the riddle of life does not exist. However, he does say that because the question cannot be put into words then neither can the solution. Ethics or value is not a philosophical issue—at least not in the traditional sense. For Wittgenstein, there ought to be no ethical theories endless debated in texts, journals, forums, and so on. Ethics is not a scientific quest.

But is it not a quest at all?—Should we not be moral?—And what ought we to do? Are there no rules? Should we do whatever comes into our heads? Wittgenstein does not say that either. "There are, indeed, things that cannot be put into words. They *make themselves manifest*." (TLP 6.522). In other words, whatever is ethical or unethical must be shown not said.

Wittgenstein is saying ethics is a matter of what we do. Being ethical is a matter of choosing to make what you value manifest—to show what you value, what you believe, and what you find meaningful. Morality is not a question of ascribing to a faith or a theory—but of what you do. In this regard Wittgenstein's idea in the *Tractatus* fits into a Kantian mold—you choose certain moral rules or maxims because they are right in themselves and you follow them only because you chose them. But again Wittgenstein is clearly repudiating his adherence to any ethical school, and just as clearly he is not arguing for any ethical theory.

However, if the above is correct then Wittgenstein is certainly enjoining us to *act* ethically, but, and this is the crux of the matter—exactly how are we supposed to know what the right action is?

Wittgenstein is not going to tell us what we ought to do. But he is going to show us how we are to purge the nonsense form our language and thereby our thoughts. Questions, ideas, theories, and the like that cannot be given meaning must ruthlessly excised—they carry no weight. We cannot hide behind the nonsense, using it to justify or color our actions. Actions must be allowed to speak for themselves. Wittgenstein's ethics in the *Tractatus* amounts to a rigorous, logical pursuit of truth. In many ways, along with Kraus, I think we can describe Wittgenstein's ethical approach as Socratic.

Hopefully the connection to Kraus is evident at this point. Kraus was opposed to the misuse of language that evades reality by glossing over actions and ideas that degrade society—such as using ideas like "glory" and "patriotism" to disguise the horrors of World War I. Kraus' approach was reflexive—responding to the media of his day. Wittgenstein's approach was philosophical—trying to solve all of the problems at once with a unified theory of the relationship between language, logic, thought, and reality.

In the end neither Kraus, his circle, nor Wittgenstein had much success stemming the destructive forces that gripped the Habsburg Empire. The artistic and philosophical insistence on showing society the truth and dissuading those in power form using deception to their advantage had little impact. In Austria, World War I propelled the Empire toward its demise followed closely by the inception of the Third Reich and World War II. Along with many of their compatriots both Kraus and Wittgenstein suffered personally and professionally in that process. Kraus shuttered *Die Fackel* in 1936 after unsuccessfully combating the Nazi rise to power. He withheld publication of his most biting satire of the Nazis for fear reprisals against himself and his friends. Wittgenstein initially left philosophy following his military service, serving as a schoolteacher in a remote Austrian village. He returned to Cambridge in 1929, eventually becoming embroiled in Nazi persecutions because of his Jewish heritage. After the Anschluss Wittgenstein renounced his German citizenship and became a British subject in 1939. His family members in Vienna were labeled as Jews, and, although at the beginning it was inconceivable to them, they were at risk of having their property seized, being arrested, and perhaps ending up in a concentration camp. In order to rescue his family, Wittgenstein helped negotiate paying the Nazis what amounted to a huge bribe.[20]

So why was it that the literature, art, and philosophy in Vienna at the turn of the 20th century did so little to ameliorate the social injustices of the time, avoid the catastrophe of World War I or stem the tide of the Nazis? Why did it fail to accomplish its goal? It is not as if reformers of the 20th century uniformly failed, as evidenced by the successes of Gandhi and Martin Luther King.

I don't think we can blame the earnestness, virtue, talent, or intelligence of the practitioners. If we can speak of their fault at all, I would argue that we can blame the method. Kraus' main weapon was satire, but the reader has to have a certain level of sophistication and be capable of a modicum of personal reflection in order to appreciate satires' personal moral value. Adolph Loos's logical architectural style was intended as a moral counterpoint to the inefficient and wasteful lavishly ornamented buildings that he thought sapped the economic and cultural vitality of Vienna.[21] His work did generate a reaction in the public sphere, but only a level of distaste—when Loos completed a building across the street from the entrance to the Emperor's Palace, Franz Joseph closed the entrance so he would never have to look at the offending edifice. Egon Schiele's pictures of gaunt, disfigured, and abused prostitutes (who were sometimes barely in their teens) did not spur his audience to address the evils of child prostitution. It landed Schiele in Jail for obscenity. Wittgenstein may have valued plain speaking, but the *Tractatus* is anything but. The message perhaps stung a little, but its effect was neutralized by the immune system of the Empire.

It's not that I want to blame the artist or philosopher completely. Loos was correct: the new methods of construction—steel, glass, formed cement—could be put to better use creating modern efficient housing rather than ornamented exteriors, the only purpose of which was allowing the wealthy occupants to masquerade as Renaissance Aristocracy. Rather than a Strauss waltz, Schoenberg's *Pierrot Lunaire* is a more fitting prelude to the "guns of august." I agree with Kraus that one of the great detriments to society is misusing language to enhance corruption. But at the risk of seeming biased in favor of my own interpretation, I would like Wittgenstein to have the last word: morality is a matter of what you do, not what you say.

NOTES

1. Andrew Wheatcroft, *The Habsburgs: Embodying Empire* (London: Penguin Books, 1996), 1–38. See Alan John Percival Taylor, *The Habsburg Monarchy, 1809–1918* (Chicago: University of Chicago Press, 1976).

2. See William M. Johnston, *The Austrian Mind: An Intellectual and Social History, 1848–1928* (Berkeley, CA: University of California Press, 1983), 39–44.

3. Brian McGuiness, *Young Ludwig: Wittgenstein's Life, 1889–1921* (Oxford: Clarendon Press, 2005), 17–23.

4. Pieter M. Judson, *The Habsburg Empire: A New History* (Cambridge, MA: Belknap Press, 2016), 51–102.

5. See Frederic Morton, *A Nervous Splendor: Vienna 1888/1889* (New York: Little, Brown & Co., 1979).

6. Steven Beller, *Vienna and the Jews, 1867–1938: A Cultural History* (Cambridge, UK: Cambridge University Press, 1989), 188–206.

7. Carl E. Schorske, *Fin-De-Siècle Vienna: Politics and Culture* (New York: Vintage Books, 1981), 116–46.

8. Ray Monk, *Ludwig Wittgenstein: The Duty of Genius* (New York: The Free Press, 1990), 106.

9. Allan Janik and Stephen Toulmin, *Wittgenstein's Vienna* (Lanham, MD: Ivan R Dee, 1996), 190–201.

10. See Rudolf Haller, *Questions on Wittgenstein* (Lincoln, NE: University of Nebraska Press, 1988), 1–25.

11. Quoted in Frank Field, *The Last Days of Mankind: Karl Kraus and His Vienna* (New York: St. Martin's Press, 1967), 30.

12. Harry Zohn, ed., *In These Great Times: A Karl Kraus Reader*, trans. Joseph Fabry and Max Knight (Chicago: University of Chicago Press, 1990), 105–14.

13. Jonathan McVity, "The Twist: *Dicta and Contradicta* in Context," in *Dicta and Contradicta*, trans. J. McVity, ed. Karl Kraus (Champaign, IL: University of Illinois Press, 2001), 130–32.

14. Adolf Loos, *Ornament and Crime: Selected Essays* (Riverside, CA: Ariadne Press, 1998), 167–76.

15. See Thomas Harrison, *1910: The Emancipation of Dissonance* (Berkeley, CA: University of California Press, 1996).

16. Ludwig Wittgenstein, *Tractatus Logico-Philosophicus*, trans. C. K. Ogden, intro. B. Russell (Ballingslöv, SE: Chiron Academic Press, 2016), 6.54.

17. See Monk, *Wittgenstein: The Duty of Genius*, 28ff.

18. Gottlob Frege to Ludwig Wittgenstein, September 16, 1919, trans. Burton Dreben and Juliet Floyd, www.bu.edu/philo/files/2011/01/CorrespondenceEnglish.pdf, 41.

19. Ludwig Wittgenstein, *Culture and Value*, trans. Peter Winch (Chicago: University of Chicago Press, 1984), 19.

20. Monk, *Wittgenstein: The Duty of Genius*, 394–400.

21. See Loos, *Ornament and Crime*.

BIBLIOGRAPHY

Beller, Steven. *Vienna and The Jews: 1867-1938: A Cultural History*. Cambridge, UK: Cambridge University Press, 1989.

Field, Frank. *The Last Days of Mankind: Karl Kraus & His Vienna.* New York: St. Martin's Press, 1967.
Frege, Gottlob. Gottlob Frege to Ludwig Wittgenstein, September 16, 1919. Translated by Burton Dreben and Juliet Floyd. www.bu.edu/philo/files/2011/01/CorrespondenceEnglish.pdf.
Haller, Rudolf. *Questions on Wittgenstein.* Lincoln, NE: University of Nebraska Press, 1988.
Harrison, Thomas. *1910: The Emancipation of Dissonance.* Berkeley, CA: University of California Press, 1996.
McVity, Jonathan. "The Twist: *Dicta and Contradicta* in Context." In Karl Kraus, *Dicta and Contradicta.* Translated by Jonathan McVity. Champaign, IL: University of Illinois Press, 2001.
Janik, Allan, and Stephen Toulmin. *Wittgenstein's Vienna.* Lanham, MD: Ivan R Dee, 1996.
Johnston, William M. *The Austrian Mind: An Intellectual and Social History, 1848-1928.* Berkeley, CA: University of California Press, 1983.
Judson, Pieter M. *The Habsburg Empire: A New History.* Cambridge, MA: Belknap Press, 2016.
Loos, Adolf. *Ornament and Crime: Selected Essays.* Riverside, CA: Ariadne Press, 1998.
McGuiness, Brian. *Young Ludwig: Wittgenstein's Life 1889-1921.* Oxford: Clarendon Press, 2005.
Monk, Ray. *Ludwig Wittgenstein: The Duty of Genius.* New York: The Free Press, 1990.
Morton, Frederic. *A Nervous Splendor: Vienna 1888/1889.* New York: Little Brown, 1979.
Schorske, Carl E. *Fin-De-Siècle Vienna: Politics and Culture.* New York: Vintage Books, 1981.
Taylor, Alan John Percival. *The Habsburg Monarchy, 1809-1918.* Chicago: University of Chicago Press, 1976.
Wheatcroft, Andrew. *The Habsburgs: Embodying Empire.* London: Penguin Books, 1996.
Wittgenstein, Ludwig. *Tractatus Logico-Philosophicus.* Translated by C. K. Ogden. Introduction by Bertrand Russell. Ballingslöv, SE: Chiron Academic Press, 2016.
Wittgenstein, Ludwig. *Culture and Value.* Translated by Peter Winch. Chicago: University of Chicago Press, 1984.
Zohn, Henry (Editor). *In These Great Times: A Karl Kraus Reader.* Translated by Joseph Fabry and Max Knight. Chicago: University of Chicago Press, 1990.

Chapter 13

Atonality in Music and the Upheavals of High Modernity

Robert Quist

During the first decades of the twentieth century, music, like the other arts, underwent stylistic changes that were more revolutionary than earlier eras. The most revolutionary change in music centered on harmony or tonality. From 1908 to 1911, the Austrian composer Arnold Schoenberg composed the first works that lacked a tonal center, or, in other words, were atonal. Earlier traditional tonal composers focused on key centers. Composers like Mozart and Beethoven centered their works on a single key. Thus Beethoven's *Eroica* symphony begins and ends in the key of E-flat. Schoenberg's teacher, Gustav Mahler, was the first composer to end a major work in a different key than the one he started. Nevertheless, Mahler, for the most part, used traditional chords and scales. When Schoenberg abandoned the use of a central key and traditional chords and scales, several other composers adopted atonality. Upon hearing the new atonal works, the general public was shocked. Even today, more than 100 years later, listeners struggle to appreciate atonal compositions. To many, atonality was a form of anarchy akin to the Italian Futurists who called for the downfall of traditional institutions. Yet Schoenberg considered himself a traditionalist, following in the footsteps of Wagner and even Brahms. There was, however, a revolutionary component regarding atonality that reflected a sense of catastrophe and apocalypse, which is the focus of this chapter.

From a mythical point of view, atonality contravened the structure of the cosmos. For centuries, tonality was considered a structural force of our world and its orbiting planets. Composers and music theorists since the ancient Greeks endeavored to link their works to the mystical writings of Pythagoras. Plato used Pythagoras's music theory to show the cosmic structure and function.[1] The so-called music of the spheres was reborn with the Renaissance and Baroque musical theorists. Because harmony was divine in nature, it could influence the divine soul of human beings. The sounding together of pitches created consonant or dissonant intervals. Consonant intervals, such as fifths and octaves facilitated stability while dissonant intervals, such as seconds and tritones, created instability. The Renaissance composer Palestrina worked out a system where dissonant harmonies functioned in order to emphasize consonant harmonies at structural points called cadences. Over the centuries, dissonance was used to bring about a resolution to consonant ends. In a sense, Schoenberg discarded consonance and the structural implications that followed. Perhaps unknowingly, Schoenberg was musically destroying the mythical cosmos with his atonal works. Yet he regarded himself much more as a creator than a destroyer.

The harmonic cosmos was a difficult myth for Schoenberg to destroy and recreate. To many theorists, however, Schoenberg was simply an agent in a natural progression. Proponents of Schoenberg claimed that he did not destroy tonality, but rather tonality fell on its own accord. Beethoven composed music with long passages of dissonant music that were more developmental than simply preparing for consonant endings. Wagner and Liszt also emphasized dissonance at least as much as consonance. The last two symphonies of Mahler (9th and 10th) revealed long passages of atonality. It is noteworthy that Mahler composed these works about the same time (1908 and 1910) that Schoenberg embarked on atonality. In his book, *Music in Transition*, Jim Samson devoted most of the chapters to this natural progression to atonality idea. At one point, he claims that there are more similarities between tonal and atonal music than differences.[2] This evolution theory of increasing complex harmony offered strong support for the arrival of atonality. Samson noted, "His rejection of tonality was in no sense a reaction against his nineteenth-century predecessors but was rather a result of his desire to build upon and extend their achievements without falling into facile imitation of them."[3]

The evolution theory had a parallel in German expressionism. The purpose of the movement was not unified by a common aesthetic theory like Impressionism. Rather, the motivation for expressionism was merely a support for free expression. Schoenberg was like these other artists in searching for a larger vocabulary of expression. Even the idea that the arrival of atonality marked a cultural progression, rather than a sudden, radical break appeared to have a parallel in artistic abstraction. The symbolist works of Gauguin, the proto-cubist works of Cézanne, and, especially, the German Expressionist works also showed a movement toward abstraction. Schoenberg was a member of the German Expressionist group in Munich called Der Blaue Reiter (The Blue Rider), which was headed by Wassily Kandinsky. Kandinsky is known as the first artist to abandon representation and paint completely abstract works. Both Kandinsky and Schoenberg influenced each other. It should be noted that Der Blaue Reiter was an apocalyptic title, referring to one of the four horsemen of the Apocalypse. Franz Marc wrote the prospectus of the 1911 almanac, which included, "one stands before the new works as in a dream, and hears the horsemen of the Apocalypse."[4] The Doomsday theme of the group appears to clash against the evolutionary idea. Both atonality and abstraction were shocking departures from the traditional styles, and the end-of-the-world theme reflects an end rather than a natural progression. Clearly, they both must have known that what they were doing was more revolutionary than evolutionary.

The harmonic evolution theory does not explain everything regarding atonality and Schoenberg. Carl Dahlhaus made some important exceptions to this evolution idea:

> Those who speak of historical necessity, of the dictates of the historical moment which Schoenberg obeyed, make the event appear more harmless than it actually was. The suspension of the existing order, the proclamation of the musical state of emergence, was an act of violence. And thus the theories with which Schoenberg attempted to justify the emancipation of the dissonance are characterized by a helplessness which prevents us from taking them at their word as being motives for compositional decisions.[5]

Both Schoenberg and Kandinsky made the conscientious and decisive decisions to abandon two of the most valued traditions. And Dahlhaus, who can be considered a supporter of Schoenberg's music, called the move to atonality an act of violence. Thus, there is an inherent confliction; on one hand Schoenberg is building on the past, on the other he breaks from it. The contradiction, however, resided more in Schoenberg than it did in historians' ability to understand him. Dahlhaus continues, "The fact that anarchical and law-giving tendencies or instincts conflicted in Schoenberg's thinking, forming a complicated configuration which forces one to read him twice if one wishes to understand him, has never been underestimated, and for this reason the phrase, 'conservative revolutionary' seemed appropriate."[6] Thus, Dahlhaus understood that Schoenberg was both a revolutionary and a traditionalist. He was not simply going with the current into atonality, nor was he completely rejecting past styles.

There were also cultural influences that promoted radical changes in art and music. Most of the early modern artistic movements reacted against the modern world, specifically industry and technology. The Post-Impressionists, the Fauves, and the German Expressionists were influenced by primitive cultures as an answer to the growing industrialized world. The idea that tonality had run its course paralleled the idea that the modern world had reached the end of its development from the Enlightenment. Thus the artistic movements shared a need to create something new and different in the wake of the Apocalypse. It, therefore, seems appropriate that both approached their art from a mythical and religious angle.

Schoenberg and Kandinsky described their works and theories with religious terms. Kandinsky's famous book, *On the Spiritual in Art* (1914) examined painting components, especially color, as reflections of the human soul.[7] Likewise, Schoenberg would describe his works and harmony as religious, which went beyond a simple metaphor:[8]

> To understand the very nature of creation one must acknowledge that there was no light before the Lord said: "Let there be Light." And since there was not yet light, the Lord's omniscience embraced a vision of it which only His omnipotence could call forth. We poor human beings, when we refer to one of the better minds among us as a creator, should never forget what a creator is in reality. A creator has a vision of something which has not existed before this vision. And a creator has the power to bring his vision to life, the power to realize it.[9]

Schoenberg considered atonality as a creation or discovery of something that did not exist before. Put in a Biblical and mythical sense, the creation of atonality followed the destructive flood that wiped out tonality. The Old Testament allusions not only reflect Schoenberg's Jewish background, but they show that Schoenberg thought on a cosmic scale with respect to music.

Atonality was also placed both inside and outside nature. The common criticism against atonality was that it did not conform to the "natural" pitches of the overtone series. Dissonance sounded abrasive to audiences as well. Yet Schoenberg considered the triad to be unnatural and that dissonance could be found more in nature: "The simple chords of the earlier harmony do not appear successfully in this environment . . . these simple chords, which are imperfect imitations of nature, seem to us too primitive."[10] Dahlhaus, also, made a strong argument that the overtone series and the harsh label applied to dissonant intervals belong more in myth and our perception than they do in the realities of nature.[11] The ancient Greek modes, presumed to be based on the Pythagorean theorem, had little in common with modern modes and scales. Conventional musical theory owes most of its existence to Jean-Philippe Rameau's theoretical writings than anything in nature or ancient Greek philosophy.

In a certain respect, however, Schoenberg was still working within a mythical context. Although atonal composers avoided respecting key centers and used dissonance to function for a sense of momentum to a final goal, atonal compositions were still based on a traditional scale—the chromatic scale. Schoenberg was aware of this when he rejected the term "atonality" in favor of the term "pan-tonality" to describe his music. He also disliked the use of atonal music to accompany horror films, and, thus be associated with darker emotions. Schoenberg held a great fondness for dissonance and felt that his music "emancipated" dissonance from its traditional role. Yet even dissonant chords and scales could sound triadic. The diminished chord and scale held triads within its structure. He preferred the all-interval tetrachord because it contained all the intervals, but did not sound triadic.

Schoenberg's love of dissonance was shared with the philosopher Nietzsche. In Nietzsche's book *The Birth of Tragedy*, dissonance was celebrated in its connection to tragedy:

> Here it becomes necessary to take a bold running start and leap into a metaphysics of art, by repeating the sentence . . . that existence and the world seem justified only as an aesthetic phenomenon. In this sense, it is precisely the tragic myth that has to convince us that even the ugly and disharmonic are part of an artistic game that then will in the eternal amplitude of its pleasure plays with itself. But this primordial phenomenon of Dionysian art is difficult to grasp, and there is only one direct way to make it intelligible and grasp it immediately: through the wonderful significance of musical dissonance.[12]

Nietzsche's celebration of painful dissonance, however, did not include the abandonment of tonality all together. Since Nietzsche used Wagner's opera *Tristan und Isolde* as an example, and since Nietzsche's own compositions were tonal, we could conclude that he was referring to the more expanded tonality. The tonality of Wagner's opera did emphasize dissonance as noticed in the famous first chord, now called the "Tristan chord," which was a half-diminished chord. Schoenberg called the tonality of Wagner, Mahler, and Wolf, "suspended tonality" and compared it to non-chord tones, like passing tones, or, even suspensions.[13] In his dissertation, Bolland noted that Nietzsche's dissonance corresponded to the idea of the Dionysian.[14] Thus, consonance equated to the Apollonian ideal. Like Mahler, Schoenberg was a follower of Wagner, and his earlier works, such as *Verklärte Nacht* (Transfigured Night, 1889), reflect the orchestral color and chromatic harmony of Wagner, especially *Tristan und Isolde*. Therefore, he would have been aware of Nietzsche's ideas in his early book, even if he had not read it. Wagner is also known for his love of Norse mythology and the Ragnarok legend concerning the end of the world. Götterdämmerung was the title of his last Ring Cycle opera, and the title meaning "the twilight of the gods" was the German translation of Ragnarok. However, despite the title, Wagner's opera had nothing to do with the Ragnarok legends of the Eddas nor even the end of the world. Moreover, Nietzsche was anti-Christian and regarded Christian ideas, like the Apocalypse, as pessimistic nihilism. It was Kandinsky's eschatological ideas and paintings that linked Schoenberg's atonality to catastrophe. Yet

Nietzsche's love of dissonance ran counter to his teacher, Arthur Schopenhauer, who described dissonance as a "beast."[15]

Schoenberg and Kandinsky experienced a shared sense of horror once they entered the German Expressionist phase of their careers. When Schoenberg composed his first atonal pieces, he was undergoing a personal crisis that was started when Mahler left him in Vienna. Although Kandinsky and Schoenberg met in person in 1911 (about four months following Mahler's death), Kandinsky, together with fellow German Expressionist painter Franz Marc, heard Schoenberg's music at the beginning of that year. Kandinsky was so moved by the music, he wrote a letter to Schoenberg claiming, in effect, that they both had a similar vision.[16] Kandinsky stated in his letter: "'Today's' dissonance in painting and music is merely the consonance of 'tomorrow.'"[17] Franz Marc, as well, was influenced by Schoenberg's new music. He expressed amazement that music with no sense of tonality could exist, and then he echoed Kandinsky's idea by stating: "A so-called dissonance is only a more remote consonance."[18] Once Kandinsky started to paint his abstract works, he became overwhelmed by the possibilities: "A terrifying abyss of all kinds of questions, a wealth of responsibilities stretched before me. And most important of all: What is to replace the missing object."[19] Schoenberg's embarking on atonality created another crisis of a similar type to Kandinsky. The almost limitless possibilities of using all twelve tones forced Schoenberg to write smaller works. While Busoni and, especially, Webern felt no need to compose large works, composing large works was important to Schoenberg.

The artistic crises of Schoenberg and Kandinsky may have contributed to the catastrophic subject matter of their ensuing works. Klaus Kropfinger noted catastrophic imagery in Kandinsky's Sketch 1.[20] Others have noted an end-of-the-world theme in Kandinsky's masterpiece, *Composition VII*.[21] While Schoenberg did not base his works on major Biblical catastrophes, his early atonal works are based on murder and insanity. His opera *Erwartung* (Expectation) depicts a delirious woman, stumbling over her dead lover, whom she murdered and repressed the memory of the deed. Schoenberg's early atonal masterpiece *Pierrot Lunaire* (Moonstruck Pierrot) is a collection of songs dealing with the horrific experiences of the Commedia dell'arte's sad clown, Pierrot. The most notorious song is called "Rote Messe" (Red Mass). It describes Pierrot, in a ritual fashion, tearing the heart out of a priest, while performing Mass, and showing the bloody heart to the congregation.

Schoenberg's early atonal compositions and Kandinsky's early abstract paintings gave German expressionism its nightmarish reputation. They also seemed to prefigure the horrors of the impending World War I. *Erwartung* was composed in 1909, *Pierrot* 1912, and *Composition VII* was painted one year before the war broke out. Moreover, the gloomy subjects were different than what they had previously made. Kandinsky's non-abstract paintings were sunny landscapes reflecting the Post-Impressionists. Schoenberg's earlier tonal works, such as *Verklärte Nacht* (Transfigured Night, 1899), were based on more optimistic texts. It could be concluded that atonality and abstraction were used to express horror and catastrophe; but this would be too simple.

Listeners to the first atonal works of Schoenberg regarded his music as a reflection of anarchy. His father was an anarchist, and there were indications that Schoenberg was fascinated with anarchy.[22] Yet, according to Bolland, this was a "mischaracterization." The apocalyptic themes in Kandinsky and Der Blaue Reiter were meant to be the cleansing before paradise and the New Jerusalem.[23]

There is little historical documented evidence that atonality and abstraction were used to express doom and destruction. In fact, the theoretical writings of Wilhelm Worringer expressed the opposite. In his 1906 dissertation, *Abstraktion und Einfühlung* (Abstraction and Empathy), Worringer argued that abstraction becomes more evident in times of crises as a way to remove the artist from the realities of destructive life. Moreover, abstraction is not, Worringer continued, limited to the modern world, but can be seen in primitive cultures. Nature instills dread and horror into primitive cultures. Technology and knowledge have only made the horror of natural forces more palpable. Worringer wrote:

> We might describe this state as an immense spiritual dread of space. . .Not that primitive man sought more urgently for regularity in nature, or experienced regularity in more intensely; just the reverse: it is because he stands so lost and spiritually helpless amidst the things of the external world, because he experiences only obscurity and caprice in the inter-connection and flux of the phenomena of the external world, that the urge is so strong in him to divest the things of the external world of their caprice and obscurity in the world-picture and to impart to them a value of necessity and a value of regularity.[24]

Once Worringer published his dissertation in 1908, it was read and admired by the Expressionists.[25] The connection with Worringer, however, did not explain why many styles of abstraction and almost all styles of atonality were connected to disturbing subjects. If Kandinsky's abstraction was a buffer to the real horrors of external life, then it was a thin buffer. While Marc painted tranquil scenes of nature before the war, his style changed with his *The Fate of the Animals* (1913).

During the earlier years of the 1920s, Schoenberg developed the 12-tone method. This method uses all twelve tones of the chromatic scale in what are called rows or sets. It made writing atonal pieces easier, since once the row is selected, the composer does not have to consider other tones. The 12-tone pieces function much like the scales and keys that pre-atonal composers used. It was an idea that was influential. Most all of Schoenberg's pupils adopted this technique, and it expanded to other aspects, such as rhythm and dynamics with the postwar composers. Yet the atonality in Schoenberg's works sounded just as shocking to spectators. Part of this was due to Schoenberg deliberately avoiding symmetrical sets.

The German Marxist philosopher Theodor Adorno proposed a reason why atonality seemed deliberately shocking. Tonality had become an ideological tool that worked for the ideas of the upper class. Whether it was in the hymns of the church or the anthems of the nations, tonality helped the masses remain loyal to the state. Atonality not only eschewed a traditional component, it seemed unpatriotic and irreverent.

Yet even atonality could be suspected of containing upper-class ideology. After World War II, Adorno wrote that it was barbaric "to write lyric poetry after Auschwitz."[26] The statement suggested that making art to be a vehicle for romantic escapism and popular appeal does more to worsen global violent trends. He became infamous for attacking jazz and Jean Sibelius—the Finnish nationalist composer.

While Adorno's statement was written well after Schoenberg embarked on atonality, it revealed part of Schoenberg's atonal motivation. One could argue that Schoenberg's switch from Wagnerian chromaticism to atonal expressionism was, in some part, a rejection of late Romantic trends. The switch happened during the bloody first decade of the twentieth century. The world was becoming more violent than it had ever been. Great Britain had invented the modern concentration camp in 1900 in Africa during the Boer War, which killed approximately 28,000 women and children. Germany adopted Britain's concentration camp idea in South-West Africa five years later, which quickly turned into extermination camps. Germans oppressed Polish children in their own county by flogging them if they did not speak German. In Russia, Tsarist forces oppressed Jews and the working poor until a full-scale revolution broke out in 1905. Russia had also lost over 120,000 men in a war with Japan. Thus, the switch to atonality and abstraction could be seen as appropriate for the times.[27]

Even though the switch to atonality coincided with modern, state sanctioned violence, Schoenberg and other atonal composers used atonality in purely instrumental music. It would be a mistake to assume that atonality was primarily a mirror of the surrounding horrors. In addition, Kandinsky was using abstraction in search for the spiritual rather than material world. Moreover, Adorno, who was a great admirer of Schoenberg, seemed willing to extend his criticism from lyrical art to all art. He noted that one could become morally culpable of enjoying Schoenberg's *Survivor of Warsaw*:

Atonality in Music and the Upheavals of High Modernity 213

> But even Schönberg's *Survivor of Warsaw* remains trapped in the aporia to which it, autonomous figuration of heteronomy raised to the intensity of hell, totally surrenders. The so-called artistic representation of the sheer physical pain of people beaten to the ground by rifle butts contains, however, remotely, the power to elicit enjoyment out of it. The moral of this art, not to forget for a single instant, slithers into the abyss of its opposite. The esthetic principle of stylization, and even the solemn prayer of the chorus, make an unthinkable fate appear to have had some meaning; it is transfigured, something of its horror is removed. This alone does an injustice to the victims. . . .When genocide becomes part of the cultural heritage in the themes of committed literature, it becomes easier to continue to play along with the culture which gave birth to murder.[28]

Adorno revived a known philosophical criticism against tragic art: it is unethical to make human suffering into something beautiful or entertaining. Even Schoenberg, a Jewish refugee, was "playing along" with Nazis, according to Adorno, by entering with them into a cultural/artistic dialogue.

What was implicit in Adorno's criticism of tragic art and nontragic art in a violent world, was that atonality, like other forms of harmony, constituted beauty. *Survivor of Warsaw* was unethical because it was beautiful. A similar criticism can be applied to Dante's Inferno or the Book of Revelations. Adorno saw the ethical problems of feeling edified from scenes of slaughter.

However, most philosophers disagreed with Adorno's condemnation of tragic art—or even all art during, or after, times of mass violence. Aristotle, Nietzsche, Schopenhauer, Hegel, Freud, Walter Kaufmann, and Terry Eagleton have found value in tragedy. And even George Steiner, who declared that tragedy was dead, devotes most of his book on praising the great tragedies.[29] Atonality was used in horror films and seemed to be more accepted by the spectators in this context. This may have been one of the reasons that Adorno rejected Schoenberg's tragic art. Yet, with the exception of *Survivor of Warsaw*, Schoenberg tended to avoid writing music to tragic texts, especially following his creation of the 12-tone method. Schoenberg's pupils would take atonality in different directions.

Of all Schoenberg's pupils, Alban Berg seemed willing to base his music on tragic texts and events. His most famous opera, *Wozzeck*, was based on George Büchner's tragedy, *Woyzeck*.[30] The opera depicted the real-life crime and death of the soldier Woyzeck. After a failed marriage he murdered his girlfriend Marie. Büchner's tragedy was notable for several reasons. One was that it was the first tragedy to focus on the poor. Tragedies from the ancient Greeks through Shakespeare focused on the nobility and upper class. Two, Woyzeck showed anti-Enlightenment themes. Both the tragedy and the opera show that Woyzeck was driven to murder by economic, social, and psychological forces: "It reverses the historical view of the Enlightenment philosophers. Where they saw the inevitable progress of man in the ascendancy of reason, Woyzeck enlarges upon injustice and suffering as a continual condition."[31] Leo Treitler also notes the apocalyptic setting of the opera:

> It is a common enough story, but a tragic irony emerges from the tension between that surface view of things and Wozzeck's perceptions. Although Marie, as an adulteress, and Wozzeck, as a murderer, have violated the moral order of their world, they are nevertheless presented to us as the only sympathetic inhabitants of that world, driven to their acts by the cruelty of circumstances and of their fellow men. . . . Beyond any causal analysis of the action, and quite outside the minds of any of the characters, there is an atmosphere of foreboding and doom that hangs like a pall over the drama as it unfolds to its seemingly inevitable conclusions.[32]

Most of *Wozzeck* is atonal. However, Berg was not as strict as Schoenberg and Webern. He did not avoid tonal-sounding rows. There is a remarkable tonal passage following the murder scene that brings the nostalgic past to the forefront. And in a certain sense this tonal passage emphasizes the tragedy more than the atonal passages.

The idea that atonal music was connected to disaster was perpetrated mostly from the Nazis, who targeted Schoenberg. Joseph Goebbels, the Nazi minister of Enlightenment and Propaganda, stated in a speech:

> National Socialism has produced change. In a great burst it has swept away the pathological products of Jewish musical intellectualism. . . . Our classical masters again appear before the public in pure and untarnished form. They will be brought before the broad masses of the People in large-scale concerts. In place of pure construction and desolate atonal expressionism, artistic intuition will again step forward as the source of musical creation.[33]

At the same year, the Nazis held a Degenerate Music Exhibition. When the Nazis came to power, Schoenberg was forced to leave Germany. His pupils stayed in Germany, and some became Nazis, although many continued to write in the 12-tone method. Winfried Zillig was one of Schoenberg's favorite pupils and helped Schoenberg with *Moses und Aron* and *Die Jakobsleiter*. Zillig, although becoming a Nazi and composing agrarian-themed operas reflecting Nazi values, remained faithful to Schoenberg's teachings.[34] Paul von Klenau defended the 12-tone method by claiming it conformed to the rigidity of Nazism.[35] Thus, there were atonal Nazi composers, with some even linking atonality to the new music of the Reich.

Atonal music has a complicated role in history. In some cases it reflects the apocalyptic landscapes of the German Expressionists. Yet atonality does not conform entirely to catastrophe. Dissonance may seem painful, but dissonance has only received this idea with the works of the Baroque composers, using it to emphasize Crucifixion scenes. Both Schoenberg and Kandinsky were not Dadaists. Their works show careful planning and sketches; nor were they Futurists who rejected the instruments of the past for mechanized noise. The 12-tone system seemed to coincide with the neoclassicism of the post-World War I years, when Dadaism split into Surrealism and Das Neue Sachlichkeit (The New Objectivity). Once tonality returned with 1960s minimalism, it did not replace atonality. There are still atonal composers today.

NOTES

1. See Plato, *Timaeus and Critias*, trans. Desmond Lee (New York: Penguin, 1965), 65. See also, James Leggio, "Kandinsky, Schoenberg, and the Music of the Spheres," in *Music and Modern Art*, ed. J. Leggio (New York: Routledge, 2002).

2. Jim Samson, *Music in Transition: A Study of Tonal Expansion and Atonality, 1900–1920* (New York: Norton, 1977), 155.

3. Ibid., 94.

4. Cited in Hal Foster, Rosalind Krauss, Yve-Alain Bois, and Benjamin Buchloh, *Art since 1900* (New York: Thames and Hudson, 2004), 1–86.

5. Carl Dahlhaus, *Schoenberg and the New Music*, trans. Derrick Puffett and Alfred Clayton (New York: Cambridge University Press, 1987), 88.

6. Dahlhaus, *Schoenberg*, 89.

7. For a good summary, see: Lynn Edward Bolland, "A Culture of Dissonance: Wassily Kandinsky, Atonality, and Abstraction" (Ph.D. diss., University of Texas at Austin, 2014), 59–89.

8. See Dahlhaus, *Schoenberg*, 81–85.

9. Cited in Dahlhaus, *Schoenberg*, 82.

10. Cited in Bryan R. Simms, *Music of the Twentieth Century: Style and Structure* (New York: Schirmer, 1986), 36.

11. Dahlhaus, *Schoenberg*, 62–72.

12. Friedrich Nietzsche, *The Birth of Tragedy*, trans. Walter Kaufmann (New York: Modern Library, 1992), 141.

13. See Arnold Schoenberg, *Theory of Harmony* (Berkeley: University of California Press, 1986), 46–50.

14. Bolland, "Culture of Dissonance," 28–30.

15. Cited in Bolland, "Culture of Dissonance," 225.

16. See Klaus Kropfinger, "Latent Structural Power versus the Dissolution of Artistic Material in the Works of Kandinsky and Schönberg," in *Schönberg and Kandinsky*, ed. Boehmer, 9.

17. Ibid.

18. Ibid., 10.

19. Ibid., 26.

20. Ibid., 31.

21. See H. Harvard Arnason, *History of Modern Art* (Upper Saddle River, NJ: Prentice-Hall, 2004), 136.

22. See Albrecht Dümling, "Public Loneliness: Atonality and the Crisis of Subjectivity in Schönberg's Opus 15," in *Schönberg and Kandinsky, An Historic Encounter*, ed. Konrad Boehmer (Amsterdam: Harwood Academic, 1997).

23. Bolland, "Culture of Dissonance," 212.

24. Wilhelm Worringer, "From *Abstraction and Empathy*," in *Art in Theory, 1900–1999* (Oxford: Blackwell, 1999), 71.

25. For a good discussion of Worringer's influence on the German Expressionists, see Foster, et al., *Art since 1900*, 1: 85–89.

26. Theodor Adorno, "From Commitment," in *Art in Theory 1900–2000: An Anthology of Changing Ideas*, ed. Charles Harrison and Paul Wood (Hoboken, NJ: Wiley, 1992), 761.

27. For a good review of the first decade of the 20th Century, see Martin Gilbert, *A History of the Twentieth Century* (New York: HarperCollins, 2001), 1–52.

28. Adorno, "From Commitment," 761.

29. See George Steiner, *The Death of Tragedy* (New Haven, CT: Yale University Press, 1996).

30. Berg changed the name to avoid the diphthong for musical reasons.

31. Leo Treitler, "*Wozzeck* and the Apocalypse: An Essay in Historical Criticism," *Critical Inquiry* 3, no. 2: 258.

32. Ibid., 255.

33. Joseph Goebbels, "Speech for the Düsseldorf Music Festival," [1938] in *Strunk's Source Readings in Music History*, ed. Oliver Strunk and Leo Treitler (New York: Norton, 1998), 1396.

34. See Erik Levi, "12-Tone Music and the Third Reich," *Tempo* 178 (September 1991): 19.

35. Ibid., 21.

BIBLIOGRAPHY

Adorno, Theodor. "From Commitment." In *Art in Theory 1900–2000: An Anthology of Changing Ideas*. Edited by Charles Harrison and Paul Wood. Hoboken, NJ: Wiley, 1992.

Arnason, H. Harvard. *History of Modern Art*. Upper Saddle River, NJ: Prentice Hall, 2004.

Bolland, Lynn Edward. "A Culture of Dissonance: Wasily Kandinsky, Atonality and Abstraction." Ph.D. dissertation, University of Texas at Austin, 2014.

Dahlhaus, Carl. *Schoenberg and the New Music*. Translated by Derrick Puffett and Alfred Clayton. New York: Cambridge, 1987.

Dümling, Albrecht. "Public Loneliness: Atonality and the Crisis of Subjectivity in Schonberg's Opus 15." In *Schonberg and Kandinsky, An Historic Encounter*, edited by Konrad Boehmer, 101–138. Amsterdam: Harwood Academic, 1997.

Foster, Hal, Rosalind Krauss, Yve-Alain Bois, and Benjamin Buchloh. *Art Since 1900*. New York: Thames and Hudson, 2004.

Goebbels, Joseph. "Speech for the Dusseldorf Music Festival." [1938] In *Strunk's Source Readings in Music History*, edited by Oliver Strunk and Leo Treitler, 1396. New York: Norton, 1998.

Gilbert, Martin. *A History of the Twentieth Century*. New York: Harper Collins, 2001.

Kropfinger, Klaus. "Latent Structural Power versus the Dissolution of Artistic Material in the Works of Kandinsky and Schonberg." In *Schonberg and Kandinsky, An Historic Encounter*, edited by Konrad Boehmer. Amsterdam: Harwood Academic, 1997.

Leggio, James. "Kandinsky, Schoenberg and the Music of the Spheres." in *Music and Modern Art*, ed. James Leggio. New York: Routledge, 2002.

Nietzsche, Friedrich. *The Birth of Tragedy*. Translated by Walter Kaufmann. New York: Modern Library, 1992.

Levi, Eric. "12-Tone Music and the Third Reich." *Tempo* 178 (September, 1991): 17–21.

Plato. *Timaeus* and *Critias*. Translated by Desmond Lee. New York: Penguin, 1965.

Samson, Jim. *Music in Transition: A Study of Tonal Expansion and Atonality, 1900–1920*. New York: Norton, 1977.

Schoenberg, Arnold. *Theory of Harmony*. Berkeley: University of California Press, 1986.

Simms, Bryan R. *Music of the Twentieth Century: Style and Structure*. New York: Schirmer, 1986.

Steiner, George. *The Death of Tragedy*. New Haven, CT: Yale University Press, 1996.

Treitler, Leo. "Wozzeck and the Apocalypse: An Essay in Historical Criticism." *Critical Inquiry* 3, no. 2: 251–270.

Worringer, Wilhelm. "From Abstraction to Empathy." In *Art in Theory 1900–1999*. Oxford: Blackwell, 1999.

Chapter 14

Toynbee and the World Wars Catastrophe

From the Philosophy of History to the Comparative Study of Civilizations

David Wilkinson

Arnold J. Toynbee (1889–1975) was a student of the classics, of ancient history, and later of Byzantine and Modern Greek history and of international affairs. He was also active in British intelligence, diplomacy, and diplomatic research in and after World Wars I and II. He was profoundly affected, in his personal and in his public life, by the catastrophes of the twentieth century, from World War I through World War II and the First Nuclear War; by future catastrophes he judged impending; and by the comparative study of catastrophe past, through time and across civilizations.

Toynbee's lifework made him a leading student of international affairs in the mid-twentieth century. His most noted accomplishment was his twelve-volume *A Study of History* (1934–1961, with a follow up 1972), which issued in the discipline known as the comparative study of civilizations. Among its other distinctions, the *Study* involved the construction of a philosophy of history, and, as inspired by the need to comprehend a colossal, evolving, global sociopolitical catastrophe, stands as an example of the historical relationship between catastrophic events and their philosophical consequences.

Toynbee defined as a central element of all these catastrophes what he labeled "General Wars." Toynbee's monumental Study of History seeks—among other things—to divine the meaning of "General Wars," treating the world wars as members of a class with earlier members in Western, Sinic, and Classical civilizations.

Toynbee's life path took him from a relatively placid early twentieth-century schoolboyhood through an epoch of extreme violence and to a less violent but still menacing Cold War era. Early Biblically based historico-scientific chronologies referred to three epochs centered on the supposed Noachian deluge—diluvian (from Lat. "diluvium," a flood, a deluge, a washing away), antediluvian, and postdiluvian, Toynbee's biography can, I think, also be usefully divided into three "epochs," centered on a catastrophic "Deluge": in this case, the Deluge is the entire world wars catastrophe, 1914–1945, culminating in the First Nuclear War moment (August 6–9, 1945, Hiroshima-Nagasaki).

TOYNBEE BEFORE THE DELUGE

Before this cascade of catastrophes, Arnold Joseph Toynbee was an ordinary, talented scholar. He was the son of a fairly well-off middle-class English family. His mother, Sarah Edith Marshall, had studied history at Cambridge, and had thereby made a historian of him.[1] Toynbee was born into a family whose religion was Christian, and was brought up by his family as orthodox Church-of-England Episcopalian Protestant Christian. However, Toynbee himself had reservations from an early age, first of all with respect to the doctrine of the Virgin Birth of Jesus: "I disbelieved instantaneously in the assertion that Jesus had been brought to birth without having a human father."[2]

TOYNBEE'S LIBERAL IDEOLOGY

Toynbee's political inclinations seem to have crystallized at an early age. As of 1967, Toynbee declares, "I was, and am, a Liberal of the Campbell-Bannerman school."[3] Henry Campbell-Bannerman (1836–1908) led the Liberal party, as Leader of the Opposition 1899–1905 and as Prime Minister 1905–1908. Campbell-Bannerman believed in the fundamental Liberal doctrines of Free Trade, "Peace, Retrenchment and Reform." "Peace" to a Liberal entailed the belief that war was both wrong and, in a world of trading states, obsolete; "Retrenchment" denoted a consequent inclination toward reduction in armaments spending; and "Reform" meant the widest extension of the right to vote, involving at that time women's suffrage.[4]

TOYNBEE AS A STUDENT

At Oxford, Toynbee had already somewhat edged toward dissent from the liberal-progressive "Whig Interpretation of History." This view of history as progress was perhaps best evinced in the work of the Marquis de Condorcet's *Sketch for a Historical Picture of the Progress of the Human Mind* ([1795] 1955). But Toynbee's questioning was only half-spirited at the time: while in no way fundamentally questioning the attainments of Western modernity, he had been aggrieved by the tendency of classical studies to look away from Greek history after the rise of Macedon and suicide of Demosthenes, and to turn away from Roman history after its second-century AD zenith of power, peace, philanthropy, and philosophy.[5]

Having read Edward Gibbon's *The History of the Decline and Fall of the Roman Empire* (1776–1788), Toynbee attended to the decline and fall of Greco-Roman civilization. He admired the work of the fourth-century historian of Roman decline Ammianus Marcellinus, and of the sixth-century historian Procopius (c. AD 500–554) on the wars, plague, glories and scandals of the Byzantine emperor Justinian (r. AD 527–565).[6] And the course of lectures by A.E. Zimmern, in 1909 the Ancient History tutor at New College, Oxford, had built "bridges over the time-gulf between the Greeks' history and ours."[7]

But, though thus acutely aware of classical decline and decay, and of bridges over time, Toynbee accepted Gibbon's verdict on the question of "whether Europe is still threatened with a repetition of those calamities which formerly oppressed the arms and institutions of Rome." The progress of the science of European war, and of the arts of peace, law, and policy, of trade and manufactures, of arts and sciences, and their diffusion through European colonization and schooling of the world led Gibbon to propose (c. 1781) that "We may therefore acquiesce in the pleasing conclusion that every age of the world has increased and still increases the real wealth, the happiness, the knowledge, and perhaps the virtue, of the human race."[8] Toynbee confessed that "Before August 1914 it never occurred to me to question Gibbon's judgment."[9]

TOYNBEE'S RELIGIOUS EVOLUTION

Toynbee's religious beliefs were greatly altered by his philosophical studies at Oxford. He became an "ex-Christian" agnostic.[10] Though able to accept the historicity of the Crucifixion, Toynbee became unable to believe in historicity of the Resurrection and bodily Ascension of Jesus into Heaven. Nor could he accept the tenets of the Adamic Fall of Man, the Incarnation of God in Jesus, the Redemption of the fallen creation by the self-sacrifice of God.[11]

Toynbee was likewise unable to believe in the key doctrines of other religions—a Chosen people, a final prophet, the "sorrowful round of rebirth," or a final victory of goodness in the war between good and evil.[12] He did reserve a belief in one elements of Christian theology: the concept of Original Sin, a built-in, inborn "sin of self-centredness," which he found repeatedly confirmed by experience. In 1912, wandering through Crete, he was kindly and hospitably treated by an old mule-driver, who however shocked him by exulting in his treasured memory of the hand he had taken in cutting the throats of his Muslim neighbors in 1897.[13]

TOYNBEE IN THE DELUGE

A Cascade of Catastrophes: The onset of World War I (1914 to 1918) was utterly unexpected in Toynbee's circle—except for the then Balliol undergraduate Lewis Bernstein (later Sir Lewis Namier), who in late 1912 or early 1913 declared "a European war is just around the corner now," at which point he was silenced when "most of the young Englishmen whom Bernstein was addressing in the Balliol front quad burst out laughing. . . . Within three years of this fantastic conversation in the quad, half of those unfortunate laughers were dead."[14]

The war's consequences—the destruction of German, Austro-Hungarian, and Russian regimes and empires, the near-destruction of the victorious British and French empires, and, most of all, the c. 17 million military and civilian death toll—justify the name of "catastrophe," in both the senses of "unexpected reversal" and "sudden disaster."

The onset of World War II (1939–1945, or, more accurately and less Eurocentrically, 1937–1945) was another sort of catastrophe, in that this "sudden disaster," with c. 50–80 million dead, was amply foreshadowed, and followed years of arduous preventive efforts that ultimately failed.

World War II of course contained, was capped by, gave birth to, and concluded with, the First Nuclear War (August 6–9, 1945, c. 100,000–300,000 dead), which, in Toynbee's eyes as in those of others, menaced an even more horrific sequel.

DEAD FRIENDS

World War I utterly reshaped Toynbee's life, most poignantly by destroying many of his schoolfellows from Winchester and Oxford: "half my contemporaries were killed on battlefields in France," "about half of my closest friends of my own age." This unearned loss—and his equally undeserved survival, spared active military service by dysentery—became an idée fixe, continually intruding on Toynbee's life and work.[15]

THE CLASSICAL SCHOLAR BECOMES THE RECORDER OF GENOCIDE

Toynbee's career path was radically altered by the catastrophe. Toynbee had been appointed a Balliol tutorial fellow for Ancient Greek and Roman history. But he left Balliol in 1915, to do war-work.[16] Having been medically exempted from experiencing the horrific death toll of the Western Front,

Toynbee was instead assigned to experience vicariously a different but associated massacre. He was detailed[17] to assist James Bryce, 1st Viscount Bryce (1838–1922) in compiling and publishing the "Blue Book," The Treatment of Armenians in the Ottoman Empire 1915–1916.[18] The "Blue Book" was a collection of documents on the deportations of Ottoman Armenians from the Russo-Turkish war zone, deportations that "were deliberately conducted with a brutality that was calculated to take the maximum toll of lives en route"; this, to Toynbee in 1967, qualified them as "the genocide that had been committed in Turkey in 1915."[19] even despite Toynbee's later conclusion that the purpose of His Majesty's Government in requesting the collection was political and propagandistic rather than innocently humanitarian.

Toynbee's philosophical and unorthodox theology was only fortified by such experiences. "My study of the genocide that had been committed in Turkey in 1915 brought home to me the reality of Original Sin. Human nature has in it an inherent vein of abominable wickedness; but then it also has in it an inherent vein of lovable goodness too. Each human soul is a battlefield on which these two irreconcilable spiritual forces are perpetually contending for the mastery."[20]

THE CLASSICAL SCHOLAR BECOMES THE WAR-ABOLITIONIST

Toynbee's life-plan was drastically altered in the long term as well as immediately by the World Wars catastrophe. He was "jolted" out of his acceptance of, and acquiescence in, the notion that war, "one of mankind's master institutions," was a permanent and ineradicable aspect of normal human life, and into the belief that it was a wicked, criminal institution that had come to menace that same human life; and he could no longer sustain the Whiggish belief that world wars had become mere "ancient history." Accordingly, from August 1914, he was "concerned above all . . . to do what I can in my lifetime toward bringing about the abolition of war."[21]

CYCLES OR PROGRESS?

Toynbee attended[22] two Paris peace conferences (January 1919–January 1920, for World War I; July–October 1946, for World War II). He found this iteration an "uncanny and disquieting experience." A Greek or Indian philosopher would not have seen "things coming around again in recurrent cycles" as disquieting, but much as might have been expected. "It is disquieting for a Muslim or a Christian or a Jew; and it upsets us, 'the people of the

Book,' because it suggests that, after all, the cyclic theory may be nearer the truth than our own ancestral faith that history moves, not in circles, but in a straight line which is running from a starting point toward a goal."[23]

A STUDY OF HISTORY

A Study of History was born of a sense of historical déjà vu, in this case the sense that what Toynbee was living through was not new. "The Western general war of A.D. 1914–18 ('World War One') opened my eyes to the historical and at the same time philosophic truth that my world in my generation was entering upon experiences which Thucydides, in his world in his generation, had already registered and recorded."[24] In the first instance, *A Study of History* is a ransacking of history for parallels to the Deluge, which was for Toynbee still evolving, but for others long ago had been reached its dramatic conclusion.

Objectivity and Subjectivity in *A Study of History*

Toynbee was far from unaware of at least some of the potentially biasing elements in his own life-circumstances. He acknowledged and considered the consequences of being born in 1889 in England and living into the twentieth century; of being a Westerner and a student of history; of having received an uncompromisingly "classical" Hellenic and humanistic education; of having traveled through a Laconian landscape of ruins remindful of repetitive disaster; and of being irreverent and disinclined toward scholarly caution. Were he writing the "Ad Hominem" chapter today, he would doubtless have inquired into the scholarly effect of his own race and gender. He recognized that it was all these influences that had led to ask whether the disasters that overtook the Greco-Roman world he studied and admired (most notably the Atheno-Peloponnesian War) were being paralleled in the Western world of his time, and whether the destruction of that former world was likewise to be paralleled in the coming history of the West.[25] Having so recognized his bias, Toynbee proceeded nonetheless to seek both objectivity in history—searching for patterns—and subjectivity—searching for meaning.

Thus, objectively, what recurrent or characteristic patterns are to be seen in the Deluge, in classical Greece and Rome, and elsewhere? And subjectively: what was the meaning of World War I—and the failure to anticipate it? What was the meaning of World War II—and the failure to prevent it? What was the meaning of the First Nuclear War? And what can we learn about their meanings from the meanings of their predecessors?

TOYNBEE AND THE PHILOSOPHERS OF HISTORY

If by the "philosophy of history" we understand the search for, and perhaps the discovery of, patterns and meanings in the course of human events, Toynbee's *Study* is unquestionably a work in that genre. Since historians have often served incidentally as philosophers of history, many precedents for Toynbee's undertaking could be cited. Among those whom he noticed in the Study, we may cite Oswald Spengler (1880–1936), Giambattista Vico (1668–1744), Ibn Khaldun (1332–1406), and Joachim of Floris or Fiore (c. 1132–1202).

Oswald Spengler's *Decline of the West* (1926–28) appeared in German (as *Der Untergang des Abendlandes* 1920–22) as Toynbee's lifework was just beginning. It posited a course of irretrievable disintegration for Western ("Faustian") culture and civilization. Recognizing the similarity of their concerns, Toynbee often cites Spengler, sometimes at length, but is at pains to draw contrasts between their ideas. He accepted the questions raised by Spengler, but not his answers. Toynbee rejects Spengler's ideas that a civilization is an organism,[26] and that each civilization has an absolute and all-pervasive qualitative individuality,[27] such that the world-views of other civilizations than our own are totally incomprehensible to us.[28] Toynbee considered Spengler's "Determinism" undocumented, and his ineluctable "Destiny" merely hypothetical; he rejected Spengler's dogma of the inevitability of social breakdown, disintegration and dissolution, and declared the question still open both in general and in the particular case of the West.[29]

Giambattista Vico, author of *The New Science* ([1725] 2002; [1744] 1961), Toynbee regards as "the most original and imaginative" of any of the Western explorers of the comparative study of civilizations.[30] Toynbee approves Vico's use of a civilizational "model" in his study,[31] shares with him the inclination to use myth as historical model[32] and the decision to use Hellenic civilization as the starting point and key-tool for a comparative study of civilizations.[33] He praises Vico for having brought to light the existence of a cyclic rhythm in the two civilizations (Hellenic and his own) that he studied.[34]

Ibn Khaldun, viewing the decline of the "Islamic Commonwealth" under the impacts of the Banu Hilal in North Africa and the Mongols in Southwest Asia, sought an understanding. He was led to write a universal history, discerned a cyclical rise and fall of empires and cultures, "an alternating rhythm in which the alternate periods of relative order and disorder were consequences of the successive rises and falls of a series of dynasties."[35] He "set out to explain the declines and falls of empires in sociological terms, but discovered that this would-be strictly scientific explanation did not account for all the phenomena."[36] He was compelled to add a religious element to the explanation, and this Toynbee found persuasive. "Ibn Khaldun, in his

Muqqadamāt (the Introduction to his *Universal History*) gave me a vision of a study of history bursting the bounds of this world and breaking through into an Other World."[37]

Joachim, a prophetic mystic, in his *Expositio in Apocalipsim* (Exposition of the Book of Revelation), saw the Christian Trinity as "an allegory of the history of mankind's progress of mankind toward spiritual enlightenment," that history being divided into three ages: the Age of the Father, and of the Old Testament; the Age of the Son, and of the New Testament; and the Age of the Holy Spirit, an imminent time of direct contact with God, total freedom, and universal love.[38] Toynbee speaks approvingly of Joachim's interpretation of the meaning of human religious history,[39] though without quite endorsing the Joachimite vision, inasmuch as he has a vision of his own, not Joachim's eternal gospel, but definitely a progressive millennialism, aiming toward universal love, but with no guarantee of reaching that destination.

Toynbee shared with Spengler a concern over the decline of the West, but not the conviction that this decline was irreversible. Like Spengler and Vico, he saw a classical parallel to the historical evolution of the West. Like Ibn Khaldun, he saw a pattern of decline in Islam, saw rhythms of decline and recovery, and considered that decline and recovery had spiritual dimensions. And like Joachim, he had hopes for the future as extreme as were the fears for the future he shared with Spengler.

TOYNBEE'S PHILOSOPHICAL PRESUPPOSITIONS

In addition to believing that he lived in an epoch of decline, parallel to epochs of decline in remote times and places, a decline which could be retrieved, but not by secular means alone, Toynbee made assumptions that may be styled "holist," "culturalist," and "endogenist."

Holism

Toynbee, having been persuaded by his classical education, and against the tendency of Western scholars to shred history into minute morsels, that "human affairs do not become intelligible until they are seen as a whole," was encouraged by the idea of "Holism" as advanced by the Boer farmer-guerrilla-statesman-philosopher Jan Smuts. Central to "holism" was the idea that chemical compounds, biological organisms, minds and personalities, families, churches, states, nations, societies, and human society, all have in common a property of "wholeness," such that they are at one and the same time composed of distinguishable "parts" and comprise more than the sum of those parts: each "whole" its own nature, character, inner relations, structure, function, and activities, attributable not to its parts but to itself as a whole, and needing to be viewed and understood as belonging to that whole.[40]

Culturalism

In seeking an understanding of general wars, Toynbee considered that nations were not the "wholes" in question, notwithstanding the proclivities of national historians. He sought more broadly for "an intelligible field of study independent of the local and temporary standpoints of historians."[41] However, in defining this field for his research, Toynbee made a choice that reflected his own standpoint. Despite noting the existence of the world-encompassing "Great War" and League of Nations Council and Assembly,[42] and despite acknowledging that the Industrial Revolution required a worldwide field of study, that the Anglo-Japanese Alliance of 1902 had brought Japan into the once-European balance of power,[43] and that there existed a worldwide society on the political plane,[44] Toynbee chose the cultural plane to demarcate the limit of the intelligible field of historical study.[45] There being no worldwide culture, the world was not an intelligible whole; but Toynbee judged that there did exist an intelligible "Western Society" or "Civilization," which coexisted with "Orthodox Christian," "Islamic," "Hindu," and "Far Eastern" societies.

Toynbee's focus upon culture, broadly defined but with strong emphasis upon religion and philosophy (vs. e.g. language or ethnicity) is unmistakable. His civilizations are cultural wholes; their most notable achievements and worthiest legacies are cultural creations—philosophies, religions, poetic works. Though he notes the existence of a worldwide economy and a global balance of power, he does not treat them as autonomously evolving, but as reflecting the moral and creative evolution of the cultures, the true social wholes of which economy and polity are activities, potentially useful, more often destructive, but in no sense of paramount importance.

By 1934, when *A Study of History* began to be published, Toynbee had already concluded that "general wars" were an activity of this cultural species, of "civilizations," and that to understand their function it was necessary to carry on a "comparative study of civilizations," sociocultural wholes which came into existence, grew, broke down, disintegrated, and left legacies behind them.

Endogenism

"Endogenous" phenomena are those produced or caused by factors within an organism or system. "Endogenism" we may then define as a philosophical or ideological inclination to explain the events in a system preferentially by reference to internal factors.

The World-Wars-era sense that "world wars" were both "ancient history" and "living reality"[46] led Toynbee to contemplate "general wars" as a class, with the twin objectives of understanding and abolishing that class. His philosophical presuppositions directed him toward finding the causation of general wars within whole cultures. His search for causation—and control—plays out at full length in *A Study of History*.

The Deluge is presupposed to be a property of Western civilization (although the vast majority of fatalities from violence, disease, and famine in World War II were suffered by the Soviet Union, China, the Dutch East Indies, Japan, and British India). The Deluge is presupposed to belong to and derive from Western culture as a whole—neither from Western economy nor from Western polity. The cascade of catastrophes is presupposed to be capable of termination and recovery. Studying the parallels known to exist, and locating others, might help the work of retrieval.

COMPARATIVE CIVILIZATIONS

Toynbee developed his list of civilizations through study and revision over time. Three main installments may be recognized: a set of twenty-three "full-blown" civilizations, plus four "arrested" and five "abortive" civilizations, developed in the first ten volumes of the *Study;*[47] a set of thirteen "full-blown" civilizations, plus twelve to fifteen "satellite" civilizations and six "abortive" civilizations;[48] and a set of fourteen or fifteen "full-blown" civilizations, fourteen to seventeen "satellite" civilizations, and six "abortive" civilizations, presented in the one-volume 1972 abridgement (70–72). The final list of "independent" civilizations included Middle American, Andean, Sumero-Akkadian, Egyptiac, Aegean, Indus, Sinic, Syriac, Hellenic, Indic, African, Orthodox Christian, Western, and Islamic.

Stages of Civilizations: Toynbee's Argument in A Study of History

Geneses

The insights of mythology and religion lead Toynbee to conclude that civilizations are born as responses to a strong, but not overpowering, "challenge." The concept of challenge-and-response is taken from the Old Testament.[49]

Civilizations are born as creative responses to such "challenges" as living in "hard countries," colonizing new ground, undergoing "blows" (sudden crushing defeats), "pressures" (of constant danger at frontiers), or "penalizations" (by dominant and oppressive ruling classes or races).[50] Creativity "means the conjuring of something out of nothing" and is observable but unintelligible.[51]

Under their challenges, some societies—Far Western Christians of Ireland and Far Northern Vikings of Scandinavia—that might have become full-blown civilizations suffer instead "infant mortality," while others reach a dead end and stay there: these are the "abortive" and "arrested" civilizations, respectively.

Growth

Civilizations display growth-phases, beginning with an "Epiphany," ending in a breakdown, and lasting on average about 300 years—though Hellenic Society's growth lasted ~700 years, and Western Society, not yet certainly broken down, will have lasted 875 years at least.[52] Civilizations "grow" by inventiveness in art, religion, or industry. Growth continues when a successful response to a challenge provokes a fresh challenge and a new response. Led by creative minorities and individuals, civilizations continue to grow as long—only as long as such culture leaders continue to create, and to inspire mimesis, or imitation, by the majority.[53]

Breakdown

Civilizations break down when those culture leaders suffer a spiritual demoralization—when their very success and achievement inspires laziness, self-satisfaction, conceit, or complacence.[54] Creative elites always need to innovate and to change, but the possibility always exists that that they may cease to create and begin merely to dominate, and so lose the allegiance of the majority. Breakdowns are not inevitable, nor are they irretrievable.[55]

Disintegration

Civilizations "disintegrate" in the sense of losing their common history—their common social and cultural existence. "The masses become estranged from their leaders, whom then try to cling to their position by using force as a substitute for their lost power of attraction."[56] Society falls into three parts: a "dominant minority" of rulers, and two "proletariats"—an alienated majority, a ruled "internal proletariat," and an "external proletariat" of barbarians on an armed frontier.[57] Each of these societies produces it's own culture, alien to the others.[58]

General Wars

As long as the civilization's dominant minority is itself divided among some number of "parochial" sovereign states, these tend to produce "fratricidal warfare of ever increasing violence,"[59] in cycles of routs and rallies. Further, the fracture of a disintegrating civilization also promotes civil wars, social revolutions, and barbarian invasions, again in the form of "rhythmic bouts of disorder."[60]

Western civilization has produced five such cycles, each with a breathing-space within and a "general peace" between: 1494–1559, 1568–1648, 1672–1763, 1792–1871, and 1914–1945.[61] Similar cycles are to be found in Hellenic and Sinic histories.[62]

Universal States, Universal Churches, and Barbarian War-Bands

Each of the three parts of a disintegrating civilization produces its own creative work, all positive achievements, though of unequal value.[63] The dominant minority produces a "universal state"; the ruled "internal proletariat" produces a "higher religion" and a "universal church";[64] and the peoples outside the frontier of the civilizations, its "external proletariat," produce "barbarian war-bands"[65] who create "heroic ages" and epics and sagas of human struggle,[66] in the process of sweeping the historical stage clear of the débris of a dead civilization."[67]

Universal States and Their Work

From within or without a disintegrating civilization, "universal states"[68] have been established after, and by, a prolonged "Time of Troubles." The universal state ends the general wars and Time of Troubles, and establishes a more or less durable "Pax Oecumenica/Universal Peace."[69] The universal state ends the general wars, and its peace and order, uniformity and conductivity, permit the spread of the higher religion produced by the internal proletariat.[70]

In his first ten volumes, Toynbee viewed the Roman Empire (in the years 31 BC–AD 378) as the universal state that brought a universal peace to Hellenic civilization; the "Ts'in and Han Empire" (in 221 BC–c. AD 172) served the same purpose for the "Sinic" civilization.[71] In his twelfth volume, *Reconsiderations* (1961), Toynbee further developed a "Helleno-Sinic Standard Model for Civilizations." These societies start as culturally united but politically divided. They make progress but fall increasingly into intense and devastating warfare, ended by the establishment of a universal state, which in turn periodically lapses into anarchy but is then re-established.[72] This means that civilizations' histories fall into a "Pre-universal-state phase" and a "Universal-state phase."[73] The pattern of growth, breakdown, and disintegration continues, but the universal state can re-integrate; there is no necessary end to the pattern of rallies and routs.

THE OPEN QUESTION OF A FUTURE WORLD ORDER: POLITICAL

Western civilization remains in the "Pre-universal state phase."[74] The West, still in its "Time of Troubles," has not yet found its Universal State (despite the efforts of the Napoleonic Empire and twentieth-century Germany to impose one).[75] Indeed, "international anarchy . . . prevails today all around the globe."[76]

By the time he wrote *Experiences*, Toynbee had become persuaded that there was a single "World Society" knit together by the progress of technology,[77] that "the establishment of an effective world state [was] the positive act that is required for enforcing the abolition of the institution of war," and that, absent nuclear war, "nationalism is going to be subordinated to world-government."[78]

Toynbee proposed that a "literally worldwide" universal state had been made imperative by nuclear weapons, the population explosion, and environmental destruction; that if this state were to be established by force, the result would be world tyranny and social collapse; that the only viable and durable world state would be a multicultural/multicivilizational voluntary political association, tolerant of diversity in language, religion and ideology, and maintaining peace through monopolizing nuclear weapons.[79] He styled this a "Future oecumenical civilization, starting in a Western framework and on a Western basis, but progressively drawing contributions from living non-Western civilizations embraced in it."[80]

To render it tolerable, the world state would have to be not only federal, but a voluntary federation of federations, with further devolutions down to the neighborhood level.[81] Toynbee was personally well acquainted[82] with the leading proponent of an alternative to international anarchy: Lionel Curtis (1872–1955). "Lionel's vision embraced the whole of mankind, and his objective was nothing less than the union of all the peoples of the earth in a federation that would enable mankind to liberate itself at last from the self-inflicted scourge of war. In the Atomic Age, the translation of Lionel's ideal into practice may well be our only alternative to destroying ourselves."[83] Toynbee followed in advocating a "world-wide federal union in which the local states would surrender their sovereignty while continuing to exist as subordinate parts of the whole."[84]

No definite path to this end, however, commended itself to Toynbee: leadership might come from the United States, the Soviet Union,[85] to China;[86] or not at all.

THE OPEN QUESTION OF A FUTURE WORLD ORDER: CULTURAL-RELIGIOUS

Toynbee had moved on from a youthful belief that justified many wars. He had thought that Greece, Bulgaria, Serbia and Montenegro had been justified in making war on the Ottoman Empire in 1912 to erase its rule over non-Turkish, non-Muslim populations; that Bismarck's warmaking for German unification and Cavour's for Italian unification were likewise justified; and that the American war of independence and Joan of Arc's war of liberation, both fought against Toynbee's own country, were also just. By 1968, he had ceased to believe in the justice of any war initiation, while retaining the sense that there could be just and violent resistance to aggression, for example, to German, Japanese and Italian aggression in World War II.[87]

He also observed that the revulsion from war which in his childhood he saw only in the Quakers,[88] had in his lifetime spread more widely, with Britain, France and Austria war-shy after the World War I, Japan and Germany seemingly joining them after the Second.[89] But the Turks and Russians had not, and Americans and Israeli Jews had as of 1968[90] moved in an opposite direction.

Having in his youth rejected religion on account of his study of philosophy, Toynbee gradually and through experience came to believe that "religion" of some form was an inseparable part of human consciousness, individual and collective.[91] Through experiencing and witnessing human love, Toynbee found his way to the evidenceless, unverifiable, indemonstrable, and thus religious—perhaps one may say meta-Christian—belief that "love is God." He could never accept the tenet that God was both infinitely powerful and infinitely loving, but he was able to attain the "unorthodox" belief that "God's love is unlimited but that his power is not."[92] Indeed, having rejected the belief in an omnipotent God, Toynbee rejected with it the belief that love is omnipotent, and the belief that any omnipotent power whatever governs and guides the universe.[93] He became able to hold "the Christian belief that God and love are identical,"[94] that "self-sacrificing love is both the best and the most powerful of all the spiritual impulses that are known to us."[95] "My creed consists of a single article: . . . 'For a human being, God is the act of helping another human being.'"[96]

This conversion, or reconversion, caused Toynbee to view the evolution of the higher religions as a cultural road away from Times of Troubles and

General War toward worldwide ecumenical peace. "The 'sorrowful round' of the recurrent vicissitudes of civilization has carried the higher religions forward in a spiritual movement that has been, not cyclical, but progressive."[97]

Toynbee's hopes as regards the possible contribution toward peace of progress in religion were lifted by his observation that the "historic religions" whose factiousness had seemed incurable in 1907–1911, had to some extent had a change of heart and replaced spitefulness and intolerance with a spirit of mutual charity, represented for him by the *aggiornamento* program of Pope John XXIII and the Muslim and Hindu welcomes then extended to visits by the Roman Catholic Pope Paul VI to Jordan and India, respectively.[98] But no certainty was possible: "it seems likely that in the Universe, as in our human world, love is perpetually striving to overcome hate, but that, on this larger spiritual battlefield too, love's victory is not assured."[99]

TOYNBEE'S LEGACY

Toynbee left no school of Toynbeean world-federalist or religious evolution activists to carry on his worldview. Accordingly, we may allow Toynbee to write his own coda to this essay: "Any scholar is sufficiently rewarded if his bucketful of water has not been lost in a whirlpool, but has gone to quicken a flowing stream."[100] Actually, we can ascertain two "flowing streams" of Toynbee's influence: The comparative study of civilizations has emerged as a discipline that has been carried forward on expressly Toynbeean lines—by J.W. Smurr (1990), Carroll Quigley (1961), Matthew Melko (1969; and with Leighton Scott, 1987), and Samuel P. Huntington (1996). The study of general or systemic wars has been carried forward by Jack S. Levy (1983), Manus I. Midlarsky (1988), Karen A. Rasler and William R. Thompson (1994), Matthew Melko (1973; 1990; 2001; and with John Hord, 1984); and with Richard D. Weigel, 1981), and others. Yet, ultimately, as with most penetrating theorists of human behavior and history, what is left of his work is more a considerable residue of questions rather than answers.

NOTES

1. Arnold J. Toynbee, *A Study of History*, 12 vols. (London: Oxford University Press, 1934–61), 10:213.

2. Arnold J. Toynbee, *Experiences* (London: Oxford University Press, 1969), 127; see also 132.

3. Arnold J. Toynbee, *Acquaintances* (London: Oxford University Press, 1967), 29.

4. Ronald B. McCallum, *The Liberal Party from Earl Grey to Asquith* (London: Victor Gollancz, 1963), 68–70.
5. Toynbee, *Experiences*, 200.
6. Ibid., 202.
7. Toynbee, *Acquaintances*, 49.
8. Toynbee, *A Study of History*, 4:112.
9. Toynbee, *Experiences*, 200–02.
10. Ibid., 138, 127.
11. Ibid., 130–34.
12. Ibid., 135–38.
13. Ibid., 36.
14. Toynbee, *Acquaintances*, 64–65.
15. Toynbee, *Acquaintances*, 35, 114; *Experiences*, 10, 37–40, 61, 82, 105, 114, 119.
16. Toynbee, *Experiences*, 4, 11, 18, 65–71, 197–98.
17. Toynbee, *Acquaintances*, chapter 11, 149–61.
18. James Bryce and Arnold J. Toynbee, *The Treatment of Armenians in the Ottoman Empire, 1915–1916: Documents Presented to Viscount Grey of Falloden by Viscount Bryce*, ed. and intro. Ara Sarafian (Princeton, NJ: Gomidas Institute, 2000).
19. Toynbee, *Acquaintances*, 242; see also *Experiences*, 341.
20. Toynbee, *Acquaintances*, 242.
21. Toynbee, *Experiences*, 82; cf. 61, 207–09, 214, 221, 240.
22. Ibid., 46–60.
23. Ibid., 49.
24. Toynbee, *A Study of History*, 10:233.
25. Ibid., 12:573–657; 10:91–98, 107–12; Arnold J. Toynbee, *A Study of History*, Abridgement of Volumes 7–10 by D.C. Somervell (New York and London: Oxford University Press, 1957), 350–54, 393.
26. Toynbee, *A Study of History*, 3:221–27.
27. Ibid., 3:379–80.
28. Ibid., 3:378n.
29. Ibid., 9:168, 296–97.
30. Ibid., 12:584.
31. Ibid., 12:161n.
32. Ibid., 12:252.
33. Ibid., 12:584, 586–87.
34. Ibid., 12:585.
35. Ibid., 12:205.
36. Ibid., 10:85.
37. Ibid., 10:85.
38. Joachim of Fiore, "The *Three Status*," in *Visions of the End: Apocalyptic Traditions in the Middle Ages*, ed. Bernard McGinn, rev. ed. (New York: Columbia University Press [1196–99] 1998).
39. Toynbee, *Experiences*, 177–78.

40. Jan C. Smuts, *Holism and Evolution* (New York: Macmillan, 1926), 86–87, 98, 103–04, 106–07, 119, 339–40, 344.
41. Toynbee, *A Study of History*, 1:16.
42. Ibid., 1:15, 31.
43. Ibid., 1:28.
44. Ibid., 1:30–31.
45. Ibid., 1:31.
46. Toynbee, *Experiences*, 61.
47. Toynbee, *A Study of History*, 12:546–47.
48. Ibid., 12:558–61.
49. Ibid., 12:254.
50. Arnold Toynbee with Jane Caplan, *A Study of History*, new abridgement (New York: Weathervane Books, 1972), 73–126.
51. Toynbee, *A Study of History*, 12:252–54.
52. Ibid., 9:374–76, 758–59.
53. Toynbee with Caplan, *A Study of History* (1972), 127–40.
54. Toynbee, *A Study of History*, 12:254.
55. Toynbee with Caplan, *A Study of History* (1972), 141–211, 222.
56. Ibid., 211.
57. Ibid., 211–54.
58. Ibid., 211–54.
59. Toynbee, *A Study of History*, 9:442.
60. Ibid., 9:283–84.
61. Ibid., 9:253–60.
62. Ibid., 10:260–87.
63. Toynbee with Caplan, *A Study of History* (1972), 56–57, 228.
64. Toynbee, *A Study of History*, Abridgement of Volumes 1–6 by D.C. Somervell (New York and London: Oxford University Press, 1946), 563; Toynbee with Caplan, *A Study of History* (1972), 319–50.
65. Toynbee, *A Study of History* (abridged 1946), 564–65.
66. Toynbee with Caplan, *A Study of History* (1972), 351–78.
67. Ibid., 351.
68. Toynbee, *A Study of History* (abridged 1946), 561.
69. Ibid., 561, 566.
70. Toynbee, *A Study of History* (abridged 1957), 378.
71. Toynbee, *A Study of History* (abridged 1946), 561, 566.
72. Toynbee, *A Study of History*, 12:197–209; Toynbee with Caplan, *A Study of History* (1972), 61.
73. Toynbee, *A Study of History*, 12:559; Toynbee with Caplan, *A Study of History* (1972), 72.
74. Toynbee with Caplan, *A Study of History* (1972), 72.
75. Toynbee, *A Study of History* (abridged 1946), 552, 566.
76. Toynbee with Caplan, *A Study of History* (1972), 316.
77. Toynbee, *Experiences*, 75, 183.
78. Ibid., 110.

79. Toynbee, *A Study of History*, 9:524–60; Toynbee, *A Study of History* (abridged 1957), 326–31; Toynbee with Caplan, *A Study of History* (1972), 316–18.
80. Toynbee, *A Study of History*, 12:559.
81. Toynbee, *Experiences*, 84, 377–78.
82. Toynbee, *Acquaintances*, chapter 10, 127–48.
83. Ibid., 180–81.
84. Toynbee, *Experiences*, 84–85.
85. Toynbee, *A Study of History*, 9:536–56.
86. Toynbee with Caplan, *A Study of History* (1972), 444.
87. Toynbee, *Experiences*, 209.
88. Ibid., 209–11, 239–40, 341.
89. Ibid., 203–39.
90. Ibid., 239.
91. Ibid., 322.
92. Ibid., 135; see also 168–69.
93. Ibid., 147–50.
94. cf. 1 John 4:8.
95. Toynbee, *Experiences*, 135.
96. Ibid., 146; cf. 369–70.
97. Toynbee with Caplan, *A Study of History* (1972), 350.
98. Toynbee, *Experiences*, 324–31.
99. Toynbee with Caplan, *A Study of History* (1972), 350.
100. Toynbee, *Acquaintances*, 97.

BIBLIOGRAPHY

Bryce, James, and Arnold J. Toynbee. *The treatment of Armenians in the Ottoman Empire, 1915–1916: documents presented to Viscount Grey of Falloden by Viscount Bryce*. Edited and with an introduction by Ara Sarafian. Princeton, NJ: Gomidas Institute, 2000.

Butterfield, Herbert. *The Whig Interpretation of History*. London: Bell, 1931.

Condorcet, Jean-Antoine-Nicolas de Caritat, Marquis de. *Sketch for a Historical Picture of the Progress of the Human Mind*. Translated by June Barraclough. Introduction by Stuart Hampshire. London: Weidenfeld and Nicolson, 1955.

Gibbon, Edward. *Decline and Fall of the Roman Empire*. London: J.M. Dent and Sons, Ltd., 1910.

Huntington, Samuel P. *The Clash of Civilizations and the Remaking of World Order*. New York: Simon & Schuster, 1996.

Joachim of Fiore. "The *Three Status*." In *Visions of the End: Apocalyptic Traditions in the Middle Ages*. Edited by Bernard McGinn. Revised ed. New York: Columbia University Press, [1196–99] 1998, 133–34.

Khaldūn, Ibn, and Franz Rosenthal. *The Muqaddimah: An Introduction to History*. Princeton, NJ: Princeton University Press, 1967.

Levy, Jack S. *War in the Modern Great Power System, 1495–1975*. Lexington, KY: University Press of Kentucky, 1983.
McCallum, Ronald B. *The Liberal Party from Earl Grey to Asquith*. London: Victor Gollancz, 1963.
McNeill, William Hardy. *Arnold J. Toynbee, a Life*. New York: Oxford University Press, 1989.
Melko, Matthew. *52 Peaceful Societies*. Oakville, ON: Child and Parent Resource Institute, 1973.
———. *General War among Great Powers in World History*. Lewiston, NY: Edwin Mellen, 2001.
———. *Peace in Our Time*. New York: Paragon, 1990.
———. *The Nature of Civilizations*. Boston: Porter Sargent, 1969.
Melko, Matthew, and John Hord. *Peace in the Western World*. Jefferson, NC: McFarland, 1984.
Melko, Matthew, and Richard D. Weigel. *Peace in the Ancient World*. Jefferson, NC: McFarland, 1981.
Melko, Matthew, and Leighton R. Scott. *The Boundaries of Civilizations in Space and Time*. Lanham, MD: University Press of America, 1987.
Midlarsky, Manus I. *The Onset of World War*. Boston: Unwin Hyman, 1988.
Oxford Dictionary of National Biography, s.v. "Curtis, Lionel George (1872–1955)" by Alex May. Oxford: Oxford University Press, 2004. Online ed., May 2006. http://www.oxforddnb.com/view/article/32678.
Oxford Dictionary of National Biography, s.v. "Bannerman, Sir Henry Campbell (1836–1908)" by A. J. A. Morris. Oxford: Oxford University Press, 2004. Online ed., Jan 2008. http://www.oxforddnb.com/view/article/32275.
Quigley, Carroll. *The Evolution of Civilizations: An Introduction to Historical Analysis*. New York: Macmillan, 1961.
Rasler, Karen A., and William R. Thompson. *The Great Powers and Global Struggle 1490–1990*. Lexington, KY: University Press of Kentucky, 1994.
Smurr, J. W. *Toynbee at Home*. Hanover, MA: Christopher Publishing House, 1990.
Smuts, Jan C. *Holism and Evolution*. New York: Macmillan, 1926.
Spengler, O. *The Decline of the West*. Translated by Charles Francis Atkinson. 2 vols. New York: A.A. Knopf, 1926–28.
Spengler, Oswald. *Der Untergang Des Abendlandes: Umrisse Einer Morphologie Der Weltgeschichte*. München: Beck, 1920–1922.
Toynbee, Arnold J. *Acquaintances*. London: Oxford University Press, 1967.
———. *A Study of History*. 12 vols. London: Oxford University Press, 1934–1961.
———. *A Study of History*. Abridgement of Volumes 1–6 by D.C. Somervell. New York and London: Oxford University Press, 1946.
———. *A Study of History*. Abridgement of Volumes 7–10 by D.C. Somervell. New York and London: Oxford University Press, 1957.
———. *Experiences*. London: Oxford University Press, 1969.
———. with Jane Caplan. *A Study of History*. New one-volume abridgement, with new material and revisions. New York: Weathervane Books, 1972.

Vico, Giambattista. *The First New Science*. Edited by Leon Pompa. Cambridge, UK: Cambridge University Press, [1725] 2002.

———. *The New Science of Giambattista Vico*. Edited by Fausto Nicolini. Translated by Thomas Bergin and Max Harold Fisch. 3rd ed. Garden City, NY: Doubleday, [1744] 1961.

Chapter 15

Catastrophe and Decadence in *The Great Gatsby*

Peter W. Wakefield

My goal in this chapter is to extract a philosophical analysis of an era of crisis through examination of a literary classic. While others have traditionally read F. Scott Fitzgerald's masterpiece as a modernist paradigm, one that reduces moral aspiration to distraction by luxury in the spirit of the Jazz Age that it supposedly epitomizes, this reading fails to account for the trouble at the center of the novel—Gatsby's beauty, even amid the persistent "valley of ashes," amidst the racial, sexual, colonialist, and classist outrages that the novel gazes at, painfully and unflinchingly. *The Great Gatsby* portrays, but does not linger or conclude in decadence. Gatsby's mansion and milieu are not presented as a nihilistic or necessary response to the crises of the early twentieth century in the United States, rather as a warning, possibly an antidote, to the captivating horror of American national identity. Fitzgerald, defying his personal aspirations, diagnoses an American politics of nostalgia, and reminds us, in the spirit of Plato, who is invoked in the text, of the need for difficult, embodied beauty and meaning in the face of material greed. But the hope held forth by the novel, the "romantic readiness" of Gatsby, is silhouetted against the ash of disillusionment, waste, and injustice. Fitzgerald takes up the consuming force of injustice as a burden, but one that he does not carry alone—for the novel establishes a human, moral community through its lucid prose, which makes its readers complicit in the nation's political future.

The most obvious reading of The Great Gatsby as a response to crisis would foreground the novel's excessive material excess and drunkenness. Jazz and recklessness might be seen as compensation for the political upheaval of World War I. My undergraduates come from high school armed with such an interpretation. But World War I has only a postcard presence in this text. Both Gatsby himself and our narrator, Nick Carraway, have seen action in Europe, but neither carries any obvious trauma. In the opening pages, Nick apostrophizes the experience: "[. . .] and a little later I participated in that delayed Teutonic migration known as the Great War. I enjoyed the counter-raid so thoroughly that I came back restless."[1] Gatsby, for his part, describes his war experiences in general heroic terms, and gleefully produces a medal from Montenegro that both he and Nick seem to treat as meretricious (a conspicuous adjective in this novel[2]): "Little Montenegro! He lifted up the words and nodded at them—with his smile."[3]

The crisis in this novel is bigger than the "Great War," and touches on principles of American identity that we deal with still today. Fitzgerald signals deliberately that the national essence is at stake. Gatsby is compared on page 2 to a seismograph "that register[s] earthquakes ten thousand miles away," and the book ends with another focus on the American continent, by telescoping us back in time to: "'the old island here that flowered once for Dutch sailors' eyes—a fresh, green breast of the new world."[4] In the intervening plot, the national crises that loom largest have to do with race, immigration, and the nation's foundational genocide of native Americans ("an aesthetic contemplation he [the Dutch sailor] neither understood nor desired, face to face for the last time in history with something commensurate to his capacity for wonder"[5]). As if to highlight these themes, the looming figure of Tom Buchanan gives full throat to an emergent, scientific White supremacy at the heart of the American upper class and its politics.

The catastrophe underlying the novel is that America itself has been built upon a number of holocausts such as the enslavement of African Americans, the destruction of the American Indian, and obscene inequalities of wealth. The fortunes and lifestyles of Gatsby and his ilk have been constructed on top of these gaping wounds in American civilization. Not only has this lifestyle built on top of these catastrophes; it has been fundamentally enabled by these existing unjust social, political, and economic structures. Indifference to these brutal episodes as exemplified in Gatsby's distractive lifestyle—as well as our collective "looking the other way"—are thus also a basic part of the underlying catastrophe of American life. These factors are still relevant today as the chasms of entrenched racism, increasing economic inequality, and a Capitalism unmasked as brutal social Darwinism have been increasingly opened up in the postmodern "Age of Trump."

Yet an abandonment of values in favor of the distractions of things and their empty showiness is not the end of the story. The novel relentlessly refuses redemption. Tom and Daisy survive, but their vivid portrayal in the text subverts all sympathy. Gatsby explicitly dismisses material decadence as soon as he sees that Daisy herself doubts it. Gatsby dies as a symbol of an elusive, delusional but compelling beauty, and as a strong warning against a national nostalgia for a past, purportedly more golden age.

I develop this argument now, with attention to specific passages, establishing first the text's problematization of modernity. The Platonic elements of Gatsby's character are then explored as a counterweight to modernist or psychoanalytic readings of this novel. I close by tracing the contemporary implications of Fitzgerald's implicit warnings about the dangers involved in American identity politics.

Briefly, in case a reminder of the setting and plot is needed: Given the setting of a hiatus of five years after a love's first spark, a war in Europe, a move of Midwesterners to the East—the reader now finds Gatsby still grasping at the only meaning of his life in Daisy, who lives across the bay, married to Tom Buchanan. Daisy's cousin Nick, in traumatized retrospect, takes up the story of the summer when they meet again.

UN-MODERN

The opening scene of F. Scott Fitzgerald's The Great Gatsby simmers with repressed desperation, embodied in the successful and malevolent character of Tom Buchanan. Fitzgerald writes:

Tom Buchanan, who had been hovering restlessly about the room, stopped and rested his hand on my shoulder.
 "What you doing, Nick?"
 "I'm a bond man."
 "Who with?"
 I told him.
 "Never heard of them," he remarked decisively.
 This annoyed me.
 "You will," I answered shortly. "You will if you stay in the East."[6]

Tom is positioned as the ideal American of his age. A college football star, Yale graduate, now an economic player with family money in the financial recovery of the country after World War I, Tom is perched atop the most influential and discreet circles of national culture, his significance magnified by the imaginary geographical centrality of New York City. He is aware of the most important Wall Street investment brokers, but never reveals his own corporate connections. Tom is a conservative savior in a time of national fear and crisis. He mouths family values, but applies them neither to himself in microcosm, nor macrocosmically to social classes beneath his own.

But, while Fitzgerald thus codes Tom as a reaction to the social crises of early 20th century America, the themes of the novel's opening scenes also link Tom to deeper, more universal turmoil—man's troubled relationship to nature, science, race, gender, and, in a word, change. By confronting his all-American male with existential notions, Fitzgerald begins a delicate construction of national identity that arcs across the novel, an identity at once beautiful and foul. Breaking the mold of modernism, the novel reads as a monitory reflection on American identity.

With Nick's arrival at Tom and Daisy's for dinner, American identity is immediately framed in tension with Europe. References to east and west, to France and King George, to Columbus and to restlessness abound in the novel's opening pages.[7] To put Tom's position in high relief, we must mine a longer literary tradition of relation to nature. The poet in Petrarch's 14th-century sonnet ("Una candida cerva sopra l'erba") announces a celebration of individual observation when, in fascination at the natural beauty of a sunlit doe, the poet splashes into the reflecting river waters, immersed in nature itself:

Et era 'l sol giá vòlto al mezzo giorno;
Gli occhi miei stanchi di mirar, non sazi,
Quand' io caddi ne l'acqua et ella sparve.

Already toward noon had climbed the sun,
My weary eyes were not sated to see,
When I fell in the stream and she was gone.[8]

Petrarch's poet flaunts greed and cannot get enough of his sensual experience of nature, which is elusive but holds a promise of human empirical advances.

Tom similarly bathes in nature, but reacts in sharp contrast to Petrarch's poet, and thus marks his break from European enlightenment. Nick describes the waves of natural growth that originate implicitly on the other side of the Atlantic and arrive at the very doors of Tom's sitting room:

> Their house was even more elaborate than I expected, a cheerful red-and-white Georgian Colonial mansion, overlooking the bay. The lawn started at the beach and ran toward the front door for a quarter of a mile, jumping over sun-dials and brick walks and burning gardens—finally when it reached the house drifting up the side in bright vines as though from the momentum of its run.[9]

The lawn's influx into the house itself is mirrored in the wind's invasion into the room, which pushes the ridiculously airy figures of Daisy and Jordan around the room. Definitively, Tom closes the French doors with a "boom," and the sensuality of the scene is cut. Tom's action symbolically casts America in a new world-historical light: the powers of perception and Renaissance empiricism stop at Tom's doors. His talk turns in immediate sequence to work and bonds and drink. The powers of the future are economic, material, and alcoholic for Tom.

But there is trouble in his arrogant confidence. In the emotional register, this scene reveals the violence and rage that seethe beneath changing gender, racial, and ethnic roles of the time—changes that are reflected later in the novel as Nick and Gatsby traverse the immigrant neighborhoods that lie between the Eggs and the city.

It is telling, in this first encounter of the novel, to track Daisy's voice, as Nick himself urges us to do;[10] we hear how torture speaks its name through mirth. Having not seen his cousin Daisy in years, Nick refers to Chicago. Daisy first wants to know if people there miss her. Then, "irrelevantly," she tells Nick he ought to see the baby. We barely note the fleeting nexus of longing and motherhood, when Tom cuts her off to talk about bonds.

Jordan enters the conversation briefly and speaks the name of "Gatsby," firing the first shot of the novel. Before Daisy can take up the question, Tom interrupts again. Daisy's defeated attentions then flit to the candles, to the summer solstice, then to the emptiness of plans:

She looked at us all radiantly. "Do you always watch for the longest day of the year and then miss it? I always watch for the longest day in the year and then miss it."

"We ought to plan something," yawned Miss Baker, sitting down at the table as if she were getting into bed.

"All right," said Daisy. "What'll we plan?" She turned to me helplessly: "What do people plan?"[11]

There is desperation in Daisy's train of thought that is nearly lost on Nick. We see it in the physical abuse that is breezily revealed. Daisy's knuckle is black and blue, and Tom did it, she tells us. A passing observation. But what causes a knuckle to bruise? This was no accident in a car door. Daisy is clear that Tom did it; there must have been cruelty involved. We suddenly glimpse him—enraged, twisting, forcing. Tom immediately explodes at Daisy's characterization of him as "hulking," as if to confirm these speculations about their troubled relationship.

And he doesn't stop. Tom next pounces on Nick's allusion to civilization, to launch into a racist, scientistic diatribe about Whiteness, citing an author—"this man Goddard." The crushing moment comes when Tom reveals that he has doubts about (dark-haired) Daisy's own purity:

"This idea is that we're Nordics. I am, and you are, and you are, and—" After an infinitesimal hesitation he included Daisy with a slight nod, and she winked at me again. "—And we've produced all the things that go to make civilization—oh, science and art, and all that. Do you see?"[12]

That hesitation, which reveals volumes about the failure of Tom's accomplishments and wealth to calm his emotional doubts about the world. He inwardly impugns even his own wife's racial purity. But this struggle is not Tom's alone. To the extent that Tom represents power within the American paradigm of New York, we also see here the doubts of a nation. Immigration, miscegenation, class inequity, and change can infiltrate even the married couple, a taint that Tom's science and technology seem alarmed about. Modernist production of "all the things that go to make civilization" haven't saved Tom; the novel shows us an entropic element of American identity that cannot rest in romance, nature, or things.

A second shot rings out in the form of the telephone—another technology that purports to integrate (infiltrate?) the home. Tom's mistress calls him during dinner, and the central dynamic of the novel is in place. Again, Daisy's voice leads us unfalteringly to her despair, something that Nick is slow to see, hearing only beauty, sexuality, and excitement. She falters, distracted by Tom's departure for the phone, recounts an absurd tidbit about the butler's nose. Then she breaks. Nick misreads her alteration, as nostalgic, beautiful: "[. . .] then the glow faded, each light deserting her with lingering regret, like children leaving a pleasant street at dusk."[13] It quickly becomes clear, however, that Daisy's carefree energies have no crossroad to return to on the morrow. Nick's feelings about the interaction he is part of change rapidly. He imagines the police and a dead body somewhere in the emotional mix: "To a certain temperament the situation might have seemed intriguing—my own instinct was to telephone immediately for the police."[14] Daisy walks Nick outside and unburdens her heart. She has had "a very bad time." Immediately, she recalls childbirth, where she wept for the fact of her daughter, hoping only that she'd be "a fool."[15]

The failures represented across the romance of Tom and Daisy can be usefully understood against a theoretical background of decadence and modernism. In an excellent volume that takes up the relation of Thomas Pynchon to Fitzgerald, Kathleen Fitzpatrick encapsulates the notion of decadence in a way that encompasses Tom: "A decadence . . . is a falling away from what is human, and the further we fall the less human we become. Because we are less human, we foist off the humanity we have lost on inanimate objects and abstract theories."[16] Modernism as a response to decadence attempts to measure, capture, and find meaning in the newness of things.[17]

Yet we would be wrong to read Gatsby as a modernist novel. Beyond his abuses of Daisy, the very point of Tom, even to Nick's clouded eyes, is that his material success is a disgrace; a fact that doesn't thereby diminish the spirit of the broader society that Tom surmounts. Tom's French doors exclude nature, his phone calls rip apart his domestic life, even the train that takes him to his mistress (providing, in its wide-windowed passage through the landscape, the original encounter with framed viewing screens that now consume our lives) must stop each time before the valley of ash.

Maureen Corrigan, in *And So We Read On*, nails this interpretation of Tom as the cautionary tale of the novel. We must look to the novel as a whole, argues Corrigan:

> Because Tom's tirade is played for laughs in the very first chapter of *The Great Gatsby*, it reassures us from the outset that the novel is inclusive, even progressive, in its politics. Then we run smack into Wolfsheim and watch in dismay as those speeding carloads of immigrants and African Americans roar past Gatsby and Nick on the Queensboro Bridge. What to think, what to think? [. . .] But, but, but . . . that antic automobile race—which dramatizes Goddard's and Tom's very fears—concludes on a note of anticipation, not dread. Nick thinks: "Anything can happen now that we've slid over this bridge . . . anything at all." Maybe the most accurate thing to say about the politics of Fitzgerald's novel is that, as a product of the early to mid-1920s, Gatsby doesn't know yet what's going to happen to America. The novel keeps its mind open, even if it's a conflicted one.[18]

I would argue, further, that the character of Jay Gatsby provides a crucial piece of the novel's implicitly un-modern analysis of American identity. But let me first briefly reject another critical reading—namely, one that would find in the novel as a whole a romantic response to Oedipal conflict, culminating in Nick's supposed retreat to the Midwest as a source of untainted meaning and beauty.

Also discussing *The Great Gatsby* in relation to Pynchon, Thomas Schaub splashes the novel with a powerful Freudian solvent. Not only is Jay Gatsby himself a failed Oedipal patricide for having run away from his birth family, Nick Carraway, for Schaub, provides the novel's coda to Gatsby's failure with Daisy, which is at the same time an abortive attempt to find reality in a return to the maternal breast that Daisy represents:

> Nick Carraway's narrative of Gatsby clearly reflects his own unresolved Oedipal conflicts. [. . .] It is Carraway, after all, who describes the shores of America as the "fresh, green breast of the new world" (180), Carraway who characterizes Gatsby's disillusionment as the loss of "the old warm world" (GG, 161), and it is Carraway who turns tail on the world before him and returns to "the warm center of the world," (GG, 3), the maternal place of origin. [. . .] For Carraway, retreat to the country's womb-like middle is embodied in memories of return [. . .] Unlike Gatsby, who has given up any hope of return well before he is shot by Wilson, Carraway imagines that he can leave the present behind by a physical retreat to Minnesota. Viewed in this way, *The Great Gatsby* represents the national ideology as the oedipal [*sic*] relation of the subject to the nation, a relation which Carraway, in his idealization of Gatsby and the tragic inevitability of failed romance (of embodied dreams), mystifies with a universal and tragic humanism: "So, we beat on, boats against the current." (180)[19]

One can't argue with Schaub's collection of breast imagery from Fitzgerald's prose. But, with Corrigan, I want to look at the novel as a whole, and in particular at the fact that Nick's retreat to the Midwest is in no way successful. The novel begins with Nick's rambling admission that he is still wanting for an understanding of what Gatsby has meant to him: "When I came back from the East last autumn I felt that I wanted the world to be in uniform and at a sort of moral attention forever [. . .]"[20] Neither is it clear that Gatsby ends his life and relationship with Daisy in disillusionment. The novel is silent on what thoughts might, in fact, have occupied Gatsby as he waited for Daisy's phone call. But he was still waiting. Schaub is correct on this point to observe that it is Nick's reading of Gatsby that suggests that Gatsby "shivered as he found what a grotesque thing a rose is."[21] But, to see the novel's challenge and creative act; to see the novel's closing words as neither mystical nor tragic, as Schaub's eloquent claim would have it—we must examine the Platonic framework against which Fitzgerald pointedly stretches the character of Gatsby.

GATSBY'S PLATONISM

The most haunting dimension of Jay Gatsby is his belief that that the past can be repeated. In chapter six, immediately after Gatsby has corrected Nick on the notion of time, and soon after Daisy has seen something ugly in the painted world of things on display at Gatsby's parties,[22] Nick breaks off his narration and takes the reader back to a moment of Gatsby and Daisy's first relationship. The scene is unmistakably patterned on Plato's *Symposium* (210a–211d), where the interlocutors hear from Socrates a tale about the priestess Diotima, who, he claims, has instructed him on love and beauty. Diotima's reflections culminate in a famous image of a ladder of love that takes the soul of a rational lover from love of a single person and of that person's body, though a love for many others, through love for laws, and beauty in all forms, until, finally, beauty itself bursts out into the soul of the lover—an unchanging, stable, abstract object of love that is not subject to the vulnerabilities and tragedy of contingent, fragile material bodies and people. Beauty itself, for Diotima, is timeless—just like the love that Gatsby knows he shared (albeit not abstractly) with Daisy.[23]

This is one thread in the fabric of Gatsby's love that Schaub sees as dreamlike and doomed to failure. But the novel's echoes of Plato do not stop with the *Symposium's* ladder of love. Gatsby rejects transcendence in favor of incarnation. In fact, many scholars see Plato's *Phaedrus* as a subsequent and apologetic reconsideration of the extreme abstraction of beauty advocated by the *Symposium*.[24] Aristotle criticized Plato's ethics as "too high for human beings" (*NE* X.7). The *Phaedrus*, while not abandoning the notion of transcendent reality, emphasizes the evocative connection between two lovers, an attraction that draws both of them to something better, larger than themselves—something shared, common, communal.[25]

> Out of the corner of his eye Gatsby saw that the blocks of the sidewalks really formed a ladder and mounted to a secret place above the trees—he could climb to it, if he climbed alone, and once there he could suck on the pap of life, gulp down the incomparable milk of wonder.
> His heart beat faster and faster as Daisy's white face came up to his own. He knew that when he kissed this girl, and forever wed his unutterable visions to her perishable breath, his mind would never romp again like the mind of God. So he waited, listening for a moment longer to the tuning-fork that had been struck upon a star. Then he kissed her. At his lips' touch she blossomed for him like a flower and the incarnation was complete.[26]

Gatsby, not unlike the Socrates who uncovers his head in the *Phaedrus*, reads a poem, and speaks of the melting and moisture in the soul that comes with seeing a beloved, chooses incarnation—in full understanding that eternity is thus left for the gods. Yet his choice is neither lustfully reckless nor tragic (as Schaub thinks). Nor does Gatsby make a decadent turn toward finding meaning in mere things. Gatsby, standing in for "national ideology" (as Schaub correctly suggests), chooses to make something bloom in the embodied, living world. The collective project of beating against the current is not vain or mystical—it is the active creation of meaning in an imperfect world. Such meaning comes from love, community, and the communities that are created by shared literary beauty. I would argue that Fitzgerald evokes the same striving in his readers,[27] even as he challenges them with his unflinching insights into the complexities and pitfalls of an American politics that would substitute nostalgia and fear for something that we can never quite articulate in advance. In *Phaedrus*, as in many of discussions of his trademark "theory of forms," Plato talks about the journey of the soul to a realm where the forms of beauty and justice can be grasped purely. But, then, after such a sublime vision, many souls, bound by attractions of the body (or just human, like Socrates), drop back into life and forget—even as they constantly strive for—a reality that they hold in confidence. The striving itself ennobles. This is where we see Nick at the end of chapter 6—sensing the reality of a beauty that he can neither define nor embody once and for all:

> Through all he said, even through his appalling sentimentality, I was reminded of something—an elusive rhythm, a fragment of lost words, that I heard somewhere a long time ago. For a moment a phrase tried to take shape in my mouth and my lips parted like a dumb man's, as though there was more struggling on

them than a wisp of startled air. But they made no sound, and what I had almost remembered was uncommunicable forever.[28]

The metaphysics of this beautiful passage, which is impossible to interpret apart from Platonism, provide a more hopeful key to the final words of the novel than either Schaub's Freudianism or Fitzpatrick's modernist interpretation.

POLITICS OF AN IMPOSSIBLE PAST

I write these reflections at a time when billboards along a Georgia freeway scream "Make America Great Again." There is surely a large component of coincidence in the fact that this slogan is bruited by another ostentatious, wealthy character from New York City—now the U.S. president. The parallel is limited, but the billboard's demand raises pertinent questions: can we repeat the past? Which past? And, at a more fundamental level, what does our national fascination with the past say about our moment in history and about ourselves, as defined in part by national identity?

The organizing questions for this presented volume also deserve an answer: How and why have important movements and shifts in the history of thought arisen out of times of crisis and catastrophe? How have these upheavals specifically played out in the history of ideas?

My own specific approach to these questions relies heavily on pedagogical experience with this novel. *The Great Gatsby* is a staple of high-school curricula in the United States, and (to judge from the testimony of my students of Chinese, Korean, and Indian extraction) increasingly of preparatory high schools around the world.[29] Students encounter this novel in college with a stock list of themes and take-always: Gatsby is about class privilege (fundamentally an issue of injustice); the novel is about the American Dream (by which students understand: hard work can lead to wealth and the realization of one's dreams); here we have also a tragic love story; finally, this is a tale of fate—Dr. T. J. Eckleburg's eyeglasses (to speak of billboards) symbolize the eyes of God—ever watchful, inescapable.

But the students have not been able to think about scenes, like that in the opening chapter, in terms of the violence—gender-based, racial, scientific—that Fitzgerald is able to crystallize for an emerging nation. Why doesn't Daisy just leave? What would the real possibilities be for divorce, or for a divorced woman in society at the time? What are the real possibilities for a divorced or single woman now? Have we changed so much? Are we repeating the past? What does it mean that Tom tars people by racial groupings, relying on an implicit notion of purity and Whiteness, vaguely grounded in science? Is White supremacy now really something we must evoke in more abashed terms, an aberration that will fade (like Lee's monument in Charlottesville), or is it intrinsic to our politics and epistemologies? At the most fundamental level, what does Tom Buchanan symbolize, in contrast to Gatsby, or even in contrast to Nick, especially when we realize that Fitzgerald consciously frames this novel as a lens for looking into national ideology?

In a word, the students don't see the trouble in this novel. There's trouble for the American Dream—because Gatsby makes his money illegally, in league with gangsters and thugs. There's trouble for the tragic love story—since, at the end of the novel, Daisy is no worse off in her marriage than before, and Gatsby's dies for reasons unrelated to his love affair.[30] There's trouble with Eckleburg's role as an angry God—for Wilson's deranged mumblings serve as a flimsy basis for religious interpretation of the novel as a whole. There's even trouble for classist injustice—since Daisy (a Midwesterner) does come to (another Midwesterner) Gatsby (in a sense, for a while), and since we constantly behold the valley of ash. Before anyone in this novel can reach "the city rising up across the river in white heaps and sugar lumps all built with a wish out of non-olfactory money,"[31] he must confront the valley that effectively consumes all—characters, relationships, symbols.

Surprisingly, the Great War, World War I, does not trouble this novel. I submit that the catastrophe at the heart of this novel is not particular to the early 20th century. Rather, the crisis that Fitzgerald senses lies at the level of national aspiration and hypocrisy about high ideals. The nation here is restless—a word much repeated.[32] The relationship to Europe; to Platonic ideals; to old ideas of nature and to new ideas of social science—this relationship carries a ghost in the form of the valley of ashes. This is not an essence that we will shed through simplifying our politics by building walls or by lumping people into religious categories, the easier to vent our hate (which is only an extreme form of fear). Rather, this is a catastrophe that we must courageously, painfully probe, acknowledge, and name. The response is a long project of incarnate community that benefits from the madness and ambiguity of inspired literature. Fitzgerald himself—climbing into Zelda's social circles in New York, and Asheville, and Paris—could have had little notion of where the country would head through immigration, racial justice, and world politics: "We passed Port Roosevelt, where there was a glimpse of red-belted ocean-going ships, and sped along a cobbled slum lined with the dark, undeserted saloons of the faded-gilt nineteen-hundreds."[33]

Fitzgerald looked at these elements of our character baldly. He evokes readers into the fray of national identity with his binding prose—prose whose power and troubles linger, not letting let us go, giving us something shared. He presents Gatsby as a hero, if only for his willingness to embrace the endless task of remaining, embodying an ideal, beating against the current. Still,

NOTES

1. F. Scott Fitzgerald, *The Great Gatsby* (New York: Scribner, [1925] pbk ed. 2004), 3.
2. Fitzgerald, *Gatsby*, 98: "The truth was that Jay Gatsby of West Egg, Long Island, spring from his Platonic conception of himself. He was the son of God—a phrase which, if it means anything, means just that—and he must be about His Father's business, the service of a vast, vulgar, and meretricious beauty."
3. Fitzgerald, *Gatsby*, 66.
4. Fitzgerald, *Gatsby*, 180.
5. Fitzgerald, *Gatsby*, 180.
6. Fitzgerald, *Gatsby*, 10.
7. Fitzgerald, *Gatsby*, 2–5: "When I came back from the East last autumn [. . .]" "Instead of being the warm center of the world, the Middle West now seemed like the ragged edge of the universe—so I decided to go East [. . .]" "[. . .] and after various delays I came East, permanently, I thought, in the spring of twenty-two." "Twenty miles from the city a pair of enormous eggs, identical in contour and separated only by a courtesy bay, jut out into the most domesticated body of salt water in the Western hemisphere, the great wet barnyard of Long Island Sound. They are not perfect ovals—like the egg in the Columbus story [. . .]."
8. "Poetic and Narrative Forms—Goucher," accessed August 18, 2016, http://faculty.goucher.edu/eng211/poetic.htm.
9. Fitzgerald, *Gatsby*, 6.
10. Fitzgerald, *Gatsby*, 9: "It was the kind of voice that the ear follows up and down, as if each speech is an arrangement of notes that will never be played again."
11. Fitzgerald, *Gatsby*, 11.
12. Fitzgerald, *Gatsby*, 13.
13. Fitzgerald, *Gatsby*, 14.
14. Fitzgerald, *Gatsby*, 16.
15. Fitzgerald, *Gatsby*, 16–17.
16. Kathleen Fitzpatrick, "The Clockwork Eye: Technology, Woman, and the Decay of the Modern in Thomas Pynchon's 'V'" in *Thomas Pynchon: Reading from the Margins*, ed. Niran Abbas (Madison, WI: Rosemount Publishing and Printing Co., 2003), 93, citing Pynchon's V.
17. Fitzpatrick, "Clockwork Eye," 92, cites Fredric Jameson: "Modernism, claims Jameson, 'thought compulsively about the New and tried to watch its coming into being (inventing for that purpose the registering and inscription devices akin to historical time-lapse photography) [. . .].'" Compare Fitzgerald, Gatsby, 2: "[. . .] as if he [Gatsby] were related to one of those intricate machines that register earthquakes ten thousand miles away."
18. Maureen Corrigan, *And So We Read On: How 'The Great Gatsby' Came to Be and Why It Endures* (New York: Little, Brown & Co., 2014), 101–02.
19. Thomas Schaub, "Influence and Incest: Relations between 'The Crying of Lot 49' and 'The Great Gatsby,'" in *Thomas Pynchon: Reading from the Margins*, ed. Niran Abbas (Madison, WI: Rosemount Publishing and Printing Co., 2003), 147–48, citing Fitzgerald, *Gatsby*.

20. Fitzgerald, *Gatsby*, 2.
21. Fitzgerald, *Gatsby*, 161.
22. Fitzgerald, *Gatsby*, 107: "She was appalled [. . .] by its raw vigor that chafed under the old euphemisms and by the too obtrusive fate that herded its inhabitants along a short-cut from nothing to nothing."
23. Fitzgerald, *Gatsby*, 109: "He wanted nothing less of Daisy than that she should go to Tom and say: 'I never loved you.' After she had obliterated four years with that sentence they could decide upon the more practical measures to be taken. One of them was that, after she was free, they were to go back to Louisville and be married from her house—just as if it were five years ago."
24. Martha Nussbaum, *The Fragility of Goodness: Luck and Ethics in Greek Tragedy and Philosophy* (Cambridge, UK: Cambridge University Press, 1986), 202: "I shall argue that the *Phaedrus* displays a new view of the role of feeling, emotion, and particular love in the good life, and that this change of view is explored inside the dialogue itself: Plato embodies important features of his own earlier view in the first two speeches, and then both 'recants' and criticizes those speeches. All this is given special immediacy by being set in the context of Phaedrus's personal erotic choice. And the conclusion about the passions will prove to have implications, as well, for Plato's understanding of the role of poetry and of the connections between poetry and philosophy."
25. Nussbaum, *Fragility*, 213, translating *Phaedrus*, in a chapter entitled "Madness, Reason, and Recantation in the 'Phaedrus'": "Similarly, the poet who is truly inspired and mad can instruct the tender soul of a young person, making it join the bacchic revels; with this madness 'he is imperfect, and he and his poetry, being that of a self-possessed (sôphronsountos) person, are eclipsed by the work of people who are mad' (245a). Finally, Socrates applies these observations to the case of erôs: the 'transported' (kekinêmenos) friend or lover (philos) should be preferred to the self-possessed (sôphrôn, 245b)."
26. Fitzgerald, *Gatsby*, 110–11.
27. Perhaps, Fitzgerald evokes this same striving in himself. The idea that this novel stood above even its author would help to explain the comment quoted from Corrigan that "the novel keeps its mind open, even if it's a conflicted one" (see fn. 11, above). I consciously resist interpretation of *Gatsby* through the biographical lens of Fitzgerald's own life. In part, this avoidance is because such biography bears many aching realizations about Fitzgerald's vanity. One episode involves Zelda's decline into mental illness, which was treated in the bucolic setting of Asheville, North Carolina, a city that even today preserves its role as a retreat for the rich, as I discovered when I first visited Ashville earlier this summer. Reading scholarly accounts of Zelda's hospitalization and Scott's boarding at the Grove Park Hotel, I had imagined a Fitzgerald who kept daily watch on his wife from some modest room in which he also tried to write. The fact, however, is captured by the lobby of the absurdly ornate Grove Park, where visitors today can see a blazing fire in the fireplace, even as the heat of a Carolina summer necessitates accompanying blasts of overpowered air-conditioning. It was in the industrialist Grove's monumental resort for the country's elite that Scott in fact stayed and plied his pages, keeping track of Zelda as best he could, separated as he was by a valley, several miles from her hospital. Both for what

it says about *The Great Gatsby* as literature, and about Fitzgerald himself, the most intriguing quotation I have found is cited by Corrigan, from one of Fitzgerald's letters to his editor, written while he was working on this novel: "And even [if] it takes me 10 times that long I cannot let it go out unless it has the very best I'm capable of in it or even as I feel sometimes, much better than I'm capable of" (quoted in Corrigan, *And So We Read On*, 116).

28. Fitzgerald, *Gatsby*, 111.

29. Maureen Corrigan again performs a valuable service on this point, tracing the rise of *Gatsby* in anthologies of literature through the late 50s and 60s, an increase in popularity that has much more to do with the questions of identity that arise in periods of political struggle than with the novel's short span of pages. See Corrigan, *And So We Read On*, 215–65.

30. In tipping off Wilson in where to find the death car, Tom may aim at revenge; but Wilson's revenge is mistakenly directed at Gatsby.

31. Fitzgerald, *Gatsby*, 68.

32. See Corrigan, *And So We Read On*, 89.

33. Fitzgerald, *Gatsby*, 68.

BIBLIOGRAPHY

Corrigan, Maureen. *And So We Read On: How 'The Great Gatsby' came to be and why it endures*. New York: Little and Brown and Co., 2014.

Fitzgerald, F. Scott. *The Great Gatsby*. New York: Scribner, [1925] pbk ed., 2004.

Fitzpatrick, Kathleen. "The Clockwork Eye: Technology, Woman, and the Decay of the Modern in Thomas Pynchon's 'V'." In *Thomas Pynchon: Reading from the Margins*, edited by Niran Abbas, 91–107. Madison, WI: Rosemount Publishing and Printing Co., 2003.

Nussbaum, Martha. *The Fragility of Goodness: Luck and ethics in Greek tragedy and philosophy*. Cambridge UK: Cambridge University Press, 1986.

Schaub, Thomas. "Influence and Incest: Relations between 'The Crying of Lot 49' and 'The Great Gatsby'" In *Thomas Pynchon: Reading from the Margins*, edited by Niran Abbas, 139–153. Madison, WI: Rosemount Publishing and Printing Co., 2003.

Chapter 16

Deep Silence in the Holocaust Stories of Tadeusz Borowski

Nancy M. Reale

"If my life ends—what will become of my diary?"[1] This succinct question, the final entry in Chaim Kaplan's *Warsaw Diary*, implies a presumed imminent death, a struggle to counterbalance the certainty of the termination of life with the creation of an ongoing personal history, and a complex relationship between a life lived and the words left behind. Perhaps the question further suggests an apparent paradox that the diary is more important than the life it documents precisely because it survives the writer's death. One also feels the desperation of a writer, himself without protection, who foresees a future in which he will not be present to protect his words, his best hope that his life might be recognized posthumously. The question is thus impossibly fraught: how can a writer who cannot be responsible for his own story once he has died ensure that anyone will know what he has experienced? How can someone whose death will be determined by external violent forces protect himself by putting himself into his words if he cannot protect his words? How can he act in the face of an irrational reality in which he is himself responsible for any ongoing acknowledgement that he suffered, thought—lived?

What we now call the Holocaust or *Shoah* involved a multiplication of individual situations like Chaim Kaplan's (and worse) so heinous in design and enormous in scope as to be virtually incomprehensible.[2] The brutality enacted to systematically exterminate European Jews and others who were "undesirable" according to Nazi ideology was a sustained barbarism of such proportion that it that simultaneously redefined modernity and called into question value systems (religious, philosophical, moral, historical, aesthetic) that had been previously assumed in the West. The "Final Solution" (*die Endlösung*) of the "Jewish Question" (*die Judenfrage*) proposed at the 1942 Wannsee Conference was enforced by the murderous atrocities of the *Einsatzgruppen* in eastern Europe, the establishment of ghettoes, the implementation of work and extermination camps, and other components of a genocidal campaign of unprecedented scale and efficiency. While genocide was hardly a novel concept in the mid-20th century, the magnitude and success of the Nazi death machine threatened most inherited notions of civilization and civility, and the seemingly gratuitous atrocities that regularly accompanied the "logical" requirements of the concerted extermination effort exposed a brutality inherent in human nature that shook the world. The sheer catastrophe—the *Shoah*—was utterly shocking, but equally appalling was the complicity of so many who, as Hannah Arendt famously noted, were precisely *not* acting out of deep conviction: "The sad truth of the matter is that most evil is done by people who never made up their minds to be or do either evil or good."[3] The world is still grappling with Nazi barbarism that was so unprecedented that a new term, "crimes against humanity," was used to refer to it, but many victims of the brutality were denied the luxury of time or possibility of reflection about the implications of the violence.[4] It remained for those who were not killed but had witnessed various aspects of the Nazi program to communicate to an uncomprehending world what they knew had happened. Many found that they were unable to meet this challenge that involved revisiting traumas of seemingly incalculable proportion, but some could speak not only of their own suffering but also of the catastrophic experiences of multitudes.

As survivor after survivor has made evident, the problem of *how* to talk about the Holocaust is fundamental to discussing what happened or how what did occur was apprehended, and the various contexts in which people recount the horrors they witnessed present distinct challenges for the intimately related projects of recollection and articulation. Lawrence Langer makes clear in *Holocaust Testimonies: The Ruins of Memory* that oral testimony differs considerably from written testimony and that the words of unlettered survivors must be understood differently from those of practiced writers who were victims and/or survivors.[5] Moreover, Langer notes, one must distinguish between personal accounts and whatever can be understood as becoming part of a collective inheritance, a public record that can be interrogated for various purposes.[6] Another complication with Holocaust accounts involves recognizing the monumental undertaking of returning in memory to the occasion(s) of one's traumatic suffering. Here Charlotte Delbo's term "deep memory" (*mémoire profonde*) is especially useful, as many working in Holocaust studies have noted. Langer seizes on Delbo's reflection that she seems to live "beside" rather than "with" Auschwitz; she experiences what happened to her in Auschwitz as having happened to someone else: "No, it's too unbelievable. And everything that happened to this other 'self,' the one from Auschwitz, doesn't touch me now, *me*, doesn't concern me, so distinct are deep memory (*mémoire profonde*) and common memory (*mémoire ordinaire*)."[7] For Langer, Delbo's "terms initiate a verbal breakthrough, a vital and refreshing departure from the familiar approach that tries to entice the Auschwitz experience, and others like it, into the uncongenial sanctuaries of a redeeming salvation."[8] Of course, a related problem for anyone who recounts first-hand Holocaust experiences is the burden of speaking not only for oneself, but also for those who have been silenced. Thus, intimate personal histories inevitably merge with larger political agendas whether this is intended or not.

Here I will consider the voice of the "poet," specifically a narrative strategy involving silence in two short stories by Tadeusz Borowski, a young (non-Jewish) Pole who was an aspiring poet when he was arrested and sent to Auschwitz. To imagine what possibilities for language Borowski might have felt were available to him after his "liberation," I begin with an early survivor story instrumental in shaping literary tradition in the West that takes as a central premise the ineffability of catastrophic suffering. I hope to demonstrate that in his two stories Borowski utilizes a literary technique that, following the model of Delbo's "deep memory," I will call "deep silence." He accomplishes this by applying a rhetorical device with a long pedigree in such a way that he bends it to conform to a post-Holocaust world in which the very project of communication is questioned and the value of the literary enterprise in which he is engaged is challenged if not altogether undermined by the very act of writing.

"Infandum, regina, jubes renouare dolorem"; "Sorrow too deep to tell, your majesty, / You order me to feel and tell once more."[9] Virgil's Aeneas speaks these words to Dido in *Aeneid* 2 when asked to recount the fall of Troy. The words are ironic because they themselves *are* spoken and because Aeneas will describe at length the destruction of his city and the violence of the enemy conquerors. He recalls Greek brutality in vivid detail, and he also speaks of his own violent response to the madness he saw in the streets of his beloved city. The *Aeneid* begins as a tale about a survivor whose mission to found a new world is determined in part by the loss and grief and uprootedness he experiences as the victim of the catastrophic destruction of his home, and it is significant that we come to know his ordeal through his own discourse. Subsequently, over the course of the poem, we see Aeneas transform into a model of a Roman hero, simultaneously drawing strength from his harrowing past and struggling to come to terms with it. As Virgil begins to shape the trajectory of Aeneas' journey from victim to hero, the poet brilliantly opens the Trojan's account of the fall of Troy with the potent "infandum," a word that refers to something so abominable that it is unspeakable, unutterable. Of course this is a trope for Virgil—and so too for Aeneas—but it is also a succinct recognition of the impossibility of making one's trauma real for another. Trauma is non-transferrable; deep suffering and loss can be expressed but not conveyed, articulated but not shared, spoken but not fully told.

Early in his foundational epic, then, Virgil asks us to consider how utter catastrophe can and cannot be revisited, whether in terms of the psychological processing of traumatic events or the means by which one evaluates, records, and communicates a mental return to past events. Virgil implicitly asks here (and elsewhere in the *Aeneid*) whether descriptions of horror experienced can ever be understood by those who have not themselves lived it and whether a profound shift in perspective is an inevitable consequence of catastrophe that even close examination cannot temper or prevent.[10] The poet also posits another question about the effects of trauma initially when Aeneas describes the destruction of Troy and again later in the work: is a person who experiences violence inevitably irremediably damaged and perhaps even consigned to repeat the violence he has witnessed?

This idea is introduced when Aeneas describes his state of mind as he sees his city collapsing around him: "To arm was my first maddened impulse" ("arma amens capio").[11] The reaction comes after he has been awakened by a dream of Hector that stirs him out of sleep in response to the chaos outside, and Aeneas tells Dido that he was driven by fury and anger ("furor iraque mentem praecipitat."[12] One noun is insufficient here; Aeneas underscores the depth of his emotional reaction by using two words, one of which ("ira") assumes an internal state and the other ("furor") an external stimulus (a Fury). Later in his discourse, he admits that he wanted to punish Helen for bringing catastrophe to his home:

Shall this one
Look untouched on Sparta and Mycenae
After her triumph, . . .
. . . . ?
Must Priam perish by the sword for this?
Troy burn, for this? Dardania's littoral
Be soaked in blood, so many times, for this?
Not by my leave. I know
No glory comes of punishing a woman,
The feat can bring no honor. Still, I'll be
Approved for snuffing out a monstrous life,
For a just sentence carried out. My heart
Will teem with joy in this avenging fire,
And the shades of my kin will be appeased.[13]

We shall see that this violent impulse is not anomalous; later in the poem, as the territorial struggle rages in Italy and Virgil's poem is nearing conclusion, Aeneas encourages his men with the following words:

Unless our enemies accept our yoke
And promise to obey us, on this day

> I shall destroy their town, root of this war,
> Soul of Latinus' kingdom. I shall bring
> Their smoking rooftops level with the ground.
> ....
>   Bring out your firebrands!
> Make terms, this time, with a town in flames![14]

The depth of Virgil's psychological portrait of his Trojan/Roman hero is remarkable, and we should attend to how the poet so deftly associates motivation for action with political turmoil. Indeed, Virgil is an early (and exceptional) example in Western literature of a writer who probes the psychic destruction caused by catastrophic events. Even the appearance of Hector in Aeneas' dream tells us that Virgil recognizes the psychological rending created by experienced horrors. At this late point in the poem, however, what Virgil suggests is that brutality once experienced is never unlearned; rather, it becomes so integral to the psyche that a victim of catastrophe, having learned its efficacy so well, can turn his own experiences outward, inflicting them upon others. Aeneas does not punish those who once hurt him and his community; rather, he borrows and repeats their violent tactics in dealing with his new enemy.

We must bear in mind that Virgil is not describing his own experiences; he is ascribing thoughts and behaviors to a fictional character (who, crucially, has another role as founder and hero), and in so doing he can utilize authorial distance to shape both the language of his narrative and the philosophical and political issues he uses it to engage. He is speaking to Rome, to Augustus, about the horrors of war and the consequences of brutality, but he is always at a remove from the events he describes. This allows him an artistic freedom that is likely not possible for an actual victim who must re-engage his past directly if he is to write about it even in a fictive form. As we consider the works produced by Borowski after his experiences in the camps, we must be mindful that they require a double kind of reading because he is both a trained, practiced author and a survivor. The capability and creativity of the former is enlisted in the service of the latter, but the two are not necessarily working in easy harmony. To read Borowski properly, we must read him simultaneously as a writer of fiction (and poetry) *and* as a writer of testimony, and if we are to evaluate his corpus, we must address both the quality of the literature as it stands on its own *and* whether or not the process of writing was for him an historical "service," a source of comfort if not liberation, an act of choice, or yet another act of compulsion determined by Nazi brutality.[15]

One can argue that the fundamental understanding of the relationship between external catastrophic events and the interior landscape of the psyche explored by Virgil held into modernity, shaken but not fully shattered by the enormity of the carnage of World War 1. Edith Wyschogrod asserts, however, that the concentration camps would change irreparably man's relation to the world around him, redefining the relationship between the individual psyche and the world assumed by Virgil. Her view is worth quoting at length:

> Human existence can no longer be interpreted as inserted into the world as an isolated subject, a consciousness that surveys the world . . . nor is the world a system of . . . objects whose existence can be described as *partes extra partes* with the individual as only another entity in the world. . . . Instead the person is a mode of activity that constitutes the phenomenal field in which he or she lives. . . .
>
> The life-world can be envisioned as a three-tiered field of experience: the inanimate world given in primary sensation; the vital world . . . given to us as living beings, self-motion, self-boundedness, and "inner" states experienced in their temporal flux; and an axiological . . . dimension in which other persons are apprehended as centers of value. . . . The ethical world cannot emerge without the existence of anterior levels, that is, of the vital and the inanimate as its ontological ground. Nevertheless, the ethical is given in its immediacy even if it presents itself in a . . . different manner from the inanimate and the vital. All socio-cultural forms of existence "live on" or express this fundament although no *specific* pattern of culture is endemic to the life-world as such. . . . Prior to . . . the concentration camp it was possible to imagine the destruction of all human life, but it was not possible to imagine the paradox: Life perdures but the life-world ceases to exist.
>
> Perhaps the concentration camp signals the emergence of a new and barren life-world but does not . . . spell the end of the life-world. . . . How would this coming to an end manifest itself? At this stage we can only . . . [bring] to light the aim . . . for which the camp provides the means. This . . . is the ultimate death of every inmate. Even if documentary evidence were lacking, the existence of the means themselves attest to this. Conversely, if we suppose the means as our starting point, we see that they cannot exist as *mere* means, as "implements" of death. Because death itself is a terminus, these means can lead to no further ends . . . foreclosing the possibility that they are merely instrumental. The camps are ends in themselves, uniquely designed death-worlds.[16]

This grotesque assumption—that death, not life, is the goal—changes everything.

Virgil utilized a sound rhetorical strategy of apparent avoidance of a subject to comment on the terrible cost of establishing what we see in retrospect as an empire—a *Reich*—and his critical method has been echoed by many Western literary voices responding to political oppression, imperial domination, and genocide. Literary reliance on preterition (placing emphasis on something by seeming to pass over it) or apophasis (the technique of pretending to deny something that is actually affirmed) for representing subjects that seemingly cannot be represented has also been part of the Greek and Jewish traditions, as William Franke notes when he refers to post-Holocaust use of apophasis:

Postmodern writers and artists of all sorts have evolved radical new poetics based preeminently on the secret resources of silence. Poets have focused particularly on silences become audible in the tearing of language and the rending of sense. To a significant degree, this is a rediscovery of the oftentimes-repressed resources in the Western tradition of apophatic discourse, a discourse about what cannot be said. *Apophasis* is the Greek word for negation, and it is used here, as it has been used since ancient times, initially in Neoplatonic ambiences, specifically to designate the negation, and especially the self-negation, of discourse. Jewish writers have been particularly important in this revival, partly because the biblical interdiction on representations of the divine, denounced as idolatrous ("graven images"), gave Jewish tradition a peculiar attunement to the limits of representation and an especially acute sensibility for the Unrepresentable. Furthermore, the Holocaust experience has become recognized as a cultural code for the unspeakable par excellence.[17]

Franke argues that two separate strands of the ineluctable weave through Western literature and philosophy:

From ancient times, there has been an apophaticism of existence, of the positively and absolutely existing that language cannot comprehend, which from Philo Judaeus to Wittgenstein registers in the fact *that* something is, even though *what* it is cannot in the least be expressed. But alongside this there is also an apophaticism of the divine Name. In this latter case, it is language, paradigmatically the unpronounceable Name of God, rather than existence, that emerges as the prime instance of what cannot be said.[18]

Perhaps for poets and other writers who sought to describe the events and effects of the Holocaust, there was a conjoining of these two different models of apophasis that rendered literary discourse especially challenging. If the history of the twentieth century required people to reflect on personal experiences that they themselves could not believe, it was inevitable that the vehicle of language used to convey those experiences would be deemed at best inadequate and at worst traitorous. Delbo describes her own aporia this way: "I am no longer sure that what I have written is true, but I am sure that it happened" ("Aujourd'hui, je ne suis pas sûre que ce que j'ai écrit soit vrai. Je suis sûre que c'est véridique").[19]

Shortly after the war, a young man from Poland was also coming to grips with how to articulate horrors he had witnessed. As Jan Kott so aptly puts it, Tadeusz Borowski had "received a full 'European education'."[20] He was born a Pole in the Soviet Ukraine, and his father was sent to a labor camp, after which Borowski, at the age of eight, joined his mother in Siberia.[21] The family was reunited in Warsaw in 1934, and Borowski was sixteen when World War II began. He continued his studies as part of an underground university, but he was arrested and sent to Auschwitz. After being evacuated from Auschwitz, he was eventually sent to Dachau, which was liberated on May 1, 1945.[22] After becoming a displaced person, Borowski finally returned to Poland, where he and his fiancée were reunited and married and he worked as a writer.[23] His suicide in 1951 came just days after the birth of his daughter.[24] In two of the shortest tales in the English collection of his short stories entitled *This Way for the Gas, Ladies and Gentlemen*, (originally known as *Pożegnanie z Marią, Farewell to Maria*), Borowski takes up the very question of the ability of language to address and/or communicate catastrophic experience, demonstrating with stunning directness and succinctness the incalculable distinction between those who have experienced torture and degradation and those who have not.

Fellow Pole and novelist Czeslaw Milosz speaks of the strength of the modern novel as deriving from "a curiosity about a reality that is veiled yet cognizable," and he sees the writer as "a reasonable human being. As such, he is confronted by a reality that resists his attempts at rational ordering, both in the sense of cognition and action. His feeling of impotence in the face of man-created absurdity makes him jealous of the great novelists of the past, who trusted their vocation as pathfinders."[25] Milosz puts Borowski's *Farewell to Maria* in the context of a pervasive impotence of fiction created by Polish history under the Nazis:

> There is no necessity to remind anyone of the country's fate in the years 1939–1945. In any event, it probably afforded more opportunities for experiencing "limit situations" than did any other area in Europe. Neither traditional forms inherited from realism nor a refined satirical investigation accessible only to an elite fitted a reality that was reduced to a naked choice between life and death. This is why, immediately after the war, a leading literary critic, Kazimierz Wyka, foresaw an impotence of fiction. Anything invented by fiction would be pale compared with what every reader had seen and touched. He advocated a "borderline" novel, and he was not mistaken. The most poignant images of concentration camps, guerrilla warfare, escapes, and migration came from the pens of writers who barely fictionalized events—balancing on the limit of artistic prose and factual report. The stories of Tadeusz Borowski (a former inmate of Auschwitz and Dachau), published in Poland under the title *Farewell to Mary*, are an example of this technique. Narrated in the first person, they are perhaps the most durable work in world literature on Nazi concentration camps.[26]

Milosz suggests that it is not coincidental that Borowski used a short narrative form in a new manner to try to capture the traumatic events he witnessed: "The crime of genocide committed by the Nazis upon three million Polish Jews has been one of the traumas marking the literature of postwar Poland. Here the inadequacy of traditional narrative again finds confirmation."[27] While Borowski also used poetry to speak of the Holocaust, it is fascinating to see in his collection of stories a strange narrative whole, a narrator's oddly "reliable" consciousness, a paradoxically reassuring presence of the "writer as a reasonable human being."[28] But how can a reasonable human being write reasonably about the unreasonable?

As Franke notes, the "unutterable" seems paradoxically intrinsic to language and literature; one need not consider only horror but also to the ineffability of beauty or divinity to find examples of apprehensions that seem beyond human linguistic capacity. One can think, for instance, of Dante's falling into silence at the conclusion of the *Commedia* or the Upanishadic *brahmodya*, a linguistic "contest in which the competitors tried to formulate the mystery of the brahman. The competition had always ended in silence, indicating that the reality lay beyond the grasp of speech and concepts."[29] For Franke, this movement into silence is part of the Western philosophical and religious tradition:

> This sort of discourse is best known in its theological expressions, particularly in the millenary discourse of negative theology that originates with Plotinus. It was, of course, anticipated by Plato, not to mention Pythagoreanism, Orphism, and mystery cults, all of which in various ways acknowledge the inexpressibility in language of some kind of divine transcendence.[30]

It is particularly interesting when those who use language most capably—the poets, novelists, and other gifted writers—find it insufficient, so we note Dante's use of the ineffability topos in the *Commedia* or the various ways in which rhetoricians and theologians utilize preterition and apophasis to deal with positive and negative extremes. What can one learn, then, from looking at some small examples of Borowski's struggle with his own art form in the wake of his internment? What do the remarkably controlled words of a young man who would commit suicide while still in his twenties tell us about what drove him to end his life? What connections can we posit between his act of putting pen to paper and the act of turning on a gas valve—and how might those connections have been overly determined by his Holocaust experience? Finally, what can we see in the trajectory of a single life riddled with tragedy that characterizes our collective post-Holocaust world?

To explore such questions, I turn now to two of Borowski's camp stories, "Silence" and "The Supper," both outstanding in his body of work because they speak of excruciating moral extremes without descriptions of physical violence present in so many of Borowski's other stories and accounts by others. In terms of the aporia occasioned by the Holocaust, "Silence" is not only one of the most succinct of Borowski's statements but also perhaps the most troubling—and the most far-reaching despite its paradoxical apparent tightness of focus. Similarly, "The Supper" reads as a vignette, a description of a single night of silent observation as inmates stand at attention for hours; the most disturbing and astounding information we are given about this vigil comes in the form of a seemingly offhand remark appended at the end of the narrator's description. In both stories Borowski has accomplished a remarkable narrative feat: he has expressed the inexpressible precisely by *not* saying it, something that more typical examples of preterition only aspire to do.

"Silence" opens with a brief account of the capture of an unidentified man:

> At last they seized him inside the German barracks, just as he was about to climb over the window ledge. In absolute silence they pulled him down to the floor and panting with hate dragged him into a dark alley. Here, closely surrounded by a silent mob, they began tearing at him with greedy hands.[31]

As we read this, we know nothing of the actors or circumstances except that the barracks are "German." The only other adjectives in the passage—"absolute," "silent," "greedy"—are ominous in tone, and we note the emphasis on stillness that is broken only by the panting. We do not know the relation of the narrator to the scene.

As the story progresses, scanty details provide just enough information to give us the context we need: sound enters as "a whispered warning was passed from one mouth to another."[32] The narrator gives us soldiers, rifles, "clusters of men in stripes," a crowd that "scattered and vanished inside the blocks."[33] The scene then shifts to the crowded and "noisy" barracks in which prisoners prepare food, play cards, and kill fleas. These signs of life with prisoners providing for themselves, stand starkly against the surreptitious silence of the initial scene.

Next comes another shift as a "young American officer with a tin helmet on his head enter[s] the block and look[s] with curiosity at the bunks and the tables."[34] He wears "a freshly pressed uniform" and is accompanied by a translator called an "interpreter" and the "chairman of the Prisoners' Committee, dressed in a white summer coat, a pair of tuxedo trousers and tennis shoes."[35] In response to this intrusion, the men in the barracks fall silent, eyes on the face of the officer. Again we see a silent crowd intent on a single figure.

The officer's words come to these waiting men through the interpreter, who translates "sentence after sentence":

> I know, of course, that after what you have gone through and after what you have seen, you must feel a deep hate for your tormentors. But we, the soldiers of America, and you, the people of Europe, have fought so that law should prevail over lawlessness. We must show our respect for the law. I assure you that the guilty will be punished, in this camp as well as in all the others. You have already seen, for example, that the S.S. men were made to bury the dead.[36]

These words are met only with whispered grumbling from the officer's audience, but once he assures the prisoners that "the criminals of the S.S." are to be punished, the response becomes "applause and shouts. In smiles and gestures they tried to convey their friendly approval of the young man from across the ocean."[37]

This strange discourse continues as the translator, "his voice turning somewhat hoarse," calls for patience, asking that the men "do not commit lawless deeds, which may only lead to trouble."[38] Another shout and "a friendly hum of voices" provide the background music of the officer's exit from the block. And then comes Borowski's chilling final paragraph, one that finally reveals the narrator's complicity in the scene he describes:

> Not until after he had visited all the blocks and returned with the soldiers to his headquarters did we pull our man off the bunk—where covered with blankets and half-smothered with the weight of our bodies he lay gagged, his face buried in the straw mattress—and dragged him on to the cement floor under the stove, where the entire block, grunting and growling with hatred, trampled him to death.[39]

Again there is silence: no discussion about rule of law or justice or even a plan of action; it is as though the members of this group act as one in their resolve. The captured man is also voiceless, gagged by this strangely silent crowd so that the collective and deliberate act of murder goes unspoken—until Borowski records it in his story.

The fact that the men ignore the words of the officer (or perhaps even actively defy them) makes their silence paradoxically loud and clear; the inmates speak of one accord, their actions the most extreme form of disregard for the rule of law invoked by the American officer that they can muster. Borowski does not describe any active decision to murder the unidentified man who must have been either a German or a Kapo; rather, the "mob" seems to act reflexively, even instinctively: one simply kills the enemy and/or oppressor if given the opportunity in the most extreme of circumstances that define camp life. Hiding and subsequently trampling a man to death are described so as to make them seem natural and inevitable to those involved, perhaps even to the narrator who is both part of the event and sufficiently detached from it after the fact to break the very silence he has captured in language.

The silent violence that follows the words of the young American underscores the fact that in more ways than one the officer is speaking a language that is incomprehensible to the inmates and vice versa. Indeed, the emphasis Borowski places on the "sentence by sentence" work of the "interpreter" is the paradoxical heart of this short tale that reflects the larger paradox of Borowski's own literary project; he seems by his very choice of subject here to be offering a profound post-internment "truth" that speaks simultaneously to trauma, to outrage so deep it confounds language, to complicity, guilt, confession, and to a profound despair of ever being understood. He is also documenting the fact that, like Aeneas, these actors have internalized the brutality they suffered such that they can themselves become perpetrators of violence.

In another of the shorter works in the *This Way for the Gas* entitled "The Supper," Borowski utilizes an emphasis on hunger that pervades his stories in a particularly grotesque manner. He begins with the pronoun "we," announcing from the beginning the participatory role of the narrator, yet here too Borowski uses paradox because, until the very end of the story, the principal act of the inmates in this tale seems to be forced observation. They are made to wait outside in a darkening cold night devoid of comprehensible language. The stillness is broken only by linguistic fragments that come from beyond the camp. The absence of sustained speech signals the absence of anything recognizably human, or at least of anything that attests to those values and experiences normally associated with human experience:

> We waited patiently for the darkness to fall. The sun had already slipped far beyond the hills. . . .
>
> A dark, gusty wind, heavy with the smells of thawing, sour earth, tossed the clouds about and cut through your body like a blade of ice. A solitary piece of tar-board, torn by a stronger gust, rattled monotonously on a rooftop; a dry but penetrating chill was moving in from the fields. In the valley below, wheels clattered against the rails and locomotives whined mournfully. Dusk was falling; our hunger was growing more and more terrible; the traffic along the highway had died down almost completely, only now and then the wind would waft a fragment of conversation, a coachman's call, or the occasional rumble of a cow-drawn cart; the cows dragged their hooves lazily along the gravel. The clatter of wooden sandals on the pavement and the guttural laughter of the peasant girls hurrying to a Saturday night dance at the village were slowly fading in the distance.[40]

Again we see Borowski's characteristic move: he says next to nothing about his true subject. If not for the mention of the growing hunger, this might almost be a peaceful bucolic evening scene. As he does in "Silence," Borowski establishes a perspectival dissonance crucial for understanding the story. There is a world "out there" beyond the camp that has not been mentioned, and that outside world does not (or cannot) recognize (much less validate) the consciousness of the narrator who knows far too much about where he is and the relation of his place in the world to what he describes. Borowski's strategy is to establish a void at the center of the story that both presents the reader with the sociopolitical insanity of the narrator's situation and reflects his recognition of his own absence. He is not a real person capable of free and spontaneous speech and action like those connected to the voices he hears; he is forced into immobile silence.

Small clue by small clue, Borowski reveals the scene: there are soldiers marching and searchlights and a Kommandant's driver. Next come "twenty Russian soldiers in camp stripes, their arms tied with barbed-wire behind their backs" who are lined up so as to face the "crowd that had been standing there for many silent hours, motionless, bareheaded, hungry."[41] A cascade of terrible detail follows, serving as a counterpoint to the normalcy of the world outside the prison walls:

> In the strong glare, the Russians' bodies stood out incredibly clearly. Every fold, bulge or wrinkle in their clothing; the cracked soles in their worn-out boots; the dry lumps of brown clay stuck to the edges of their trousers; the thick seams along their crotches; the white thread showing on the blue stripe of their prison suits; their sagging buttocks, their stiff hands and bloodless fingers twisted in pain, with drops of dry blood at the joints; their swollen wrists where the skin had started turning blue from the rusty wire cutting into their flesh; their naked elbows, pulled back unnaturally and tied with another piece of wire—all this emerged out of the surrounding blackness as if carved in ice.[42]

The Komandant, we are told, surveys and approves the scene, after which "matters proceeded [sic] quickly, though maybe not quite quickly enough for the freezing body and the empty stomach that had been waiting seventeen hours for a pint of soup."[43] He addresses those assembled, explaining that the Russians are criminals, that time is not to be wasted—and that the camp will go without dinner. The withdrawal of dinner is reiterated by the Camp Elder, and two ominous sentences follow: "A long, deep sigh went through the crowd. Slowly, slowly, the rear rows began pushing forward; the crowd near the road grew denser and a pleasant warmth spread along your back from the breath of men pressing behind you, preparing to jump forward."[44] The language here is disorienting because we do not know why the crowd is surging forward and because the "pleasant warmth" of close human contact here contrasted with the bitter cold of the night is anything but a reassuring testament to a common humanity, a physical manifestation of mankind's existential solidarity.

The Kommandant gives the order "without raising his voice":

> "*Achtung! Bereit, Feuer!*" . . . The rifles barked, the soldiers jumped back a step to keep from being splattered by the shattered heads. The Russians seemed to quiver on their feet for an instant and then fell to the ground like heavy sacks, splashing the pavement with blood and scattered chunks of brain.[45]

The German needs no translation; the rapid fire of the language mimetically recreates the murderous actions of the firing squad and the oversight of the officer. These Russians, whose bodies were described in such detail, are no longer human, falling like inanimate objects whose contents have been spilled and scattered. The corpses are dragged a slight distance away, the Kommandant departs, and there is a second abrupt piercing of the silent horror of the night: "No sooner was the greying, sunburned Kommandant out of sight than the silent crowd, pressing forward more and more persistently, burst into a shrieking roar, and fell in an avalanche on the blood-spattered pavement, swarming over it noisily."[46]

Perhaps we are naïve enough to wonder what this means, what isn't being said about the scene we are trying to see through the literal and metaphorical darkness, but Borowski quickly concludes the story by providing horrible clarity: "I had been standing some distance away from the place of execution so I could not reach the road. But the following day, when we were again driven out to work, a 'Muslimized' Jew from Estonia who was helping me haul steel bars tried to convince me all day that human brains are, in fact, so tender you can eat them absolutely raw."[47]

The effect is stunning, created by the discord between the subject matter and the nonchalance of the narrative tone and also by Borowski's saving the harsh cannibalistic reality for the very last words of the story. This is an experience that is at once captured by language and beyond it; it has been recorded and communicated, but the actual eating of the human brains by the famished inmates—the central truth of the story—is never directly described. Perhaps even more shocking here and in "Silence" is the absence of any affect communicated by the narrative voice. The matter-of-fact—almost casual—delivery makes behaviors that would "ordinarily" be judged as beyond any acceptable moral framework seem routine, unremarkable. The absence of both outrage and judgment (like that expressed by Aeneas) adds another level of paradoxical silence, perhaps the deepest of all, to these words that strive to communicate. At the center of this discourse we have no omniscient narrator. third-person narrator, or clearly defined first-person narrator with whom we can identify. Rather, the speaker seems an absence, a void around which events have transpired and out which words seem to spill. The critique lies not in what is written on the page but in the physical existence of the page. Thus, the literary work, even for someone like Borowski who wrote after Auschwitz, is like a diary of a dead man, a vestigial echo of someone who was once alive and who subsequently disappeared. The fact that *This Way for the Gas Ladies and Gentlemen*, taken as a whole, presents the reader with what appears to be a single narrator likely closely connected to Borowski himself (though nowhere does he make the claim that the stories are autobiographical) underscores this strange sensibility, this unnerving conflation of intimacy and profound distance.[48] Even as we read to attempt to understand what is being communicated, we recognize the chasm of silence that can never be breached and that ultimately must have contributed to driving to his death this young writer who valiantly and desperately tried to save his own voice.

We should linger on the hunger described in the story since it pervades Borowski's collection and since eating and speech stand in an interesting relation to one another, both activities performed with the mouth. Eating is both primitive and complex, a process that assures and asserts life through taking something in from the world outside. Speech also affirms and asserts existence, but by the process of emitting rather than ingesting. When speaking, one gives up something of the self to an exterior other, perhaps even an assumed community, as an act of self-preservation, self-reflection, or generosity. The silence of the inmates in the story is inversely connected to the eating of human brains toward which they are driven by the extremity—and absurdity—of circumstance.

According to Edith Wyschogrod, in Borowski's work "the meaning of food and death coalesce":

> Borowski depicts hunger as the omnipresent background of camp life. . . . For those camp workers who unloaded the human cargo that . . . was deposited at Auschwitz, access to food . . . was available. But relief from hunger depended upon unloading this human freight and hurrying the herded masses to their deaths in the gas chambers. Thus, . . . when the narrator of one of Borowski's stories expresses his fear of impending hunger, his cynical friend replies: "Stop talking nonsense. They can't run out of people."[49]

"The Supper" serves as an excellent example of this extraordinary "coalescence." Elsewhere, in "A Day at Harmenz," Borowski reduces the extremity of the hunger experienced by the inmates to a single sentence spoken by Becker, an "old, melancholy, silver-haired Jew": "Real hunger is when one man regards another man as something to eat."[50] This terrible truth is corroborated by survivor testimony; see, for example, Langer's report of an interview with a survivor named Moses S. who describes a moment when five people, having come upon a human hand after the English bombing of Mauthausen, divided it up and ate it.[51]

But perhaps even being driven to acts of cannibalism did not mark the most profound violation perpetrated by the Nazis. As numerous Holocaust survivors have reminded us, one of the most profound psychological assaults of time spent in the camps was the sustained loss of free will. Among the "inexplicable" absurdities recounted repeatedly by survivors were the instances in which prisoners were forced to make "choices" that were anything but choices; Langer's *Holocaust Testimonies* contains a painful abundance of examples of such situations, and there exist myriad other accounts of similar ordeals.[52]

There are silences imposed by censorship. There are silences imposed by gravitas. There are silences inspired by bliss. There are silences that result from the confrontation with death itself, as so many survivors can attest. And, as François Cheng rightly notes in *Five Meditations on Death*, any apprehension of death as an inextricable part of life that imbues life with meaning was made impossible by the Nazis who "carried out an industrialization of death with a coldblooded rationality, depriving death of all meaning: death no longer had anything to do with being human. . . . That death which [is] one of our most precious possessions died at Auschwitz."[53]

There are also some words that break through silences, even as they call attention to them. In *The Shriek of Silence*, Patterson sums up the literary project of the survivor: "So the Holocaust author moves one hand across the silence of the blank page, leaving a trail of words on the track of the word. And the other hand he holds over his mouth."[54] In "The World of Stone," a story that uses first-person narration to describe post-internment life, Borowski refers specifically to the onus of writing in the face of the immense weight of senselessness. Here, perhaps more profoundly than in the other two stories, Borowski faces that abyss of silence that he knows he must try to overcome with words. After his release from Dachau, he struggled to return to something like a "normal" life, but—like so many others—he was unable to do so. Part of that struggle is recorded in "The World of Stone," in which he speaks of a world dissolving into emptiness:

> For quite some time now, like the foetus inside a womb, a terrible knowledge has been ripening within me and filling my soul with frightened foreboding: that the Infinite Universe is inflating at incredible speed, like some ridiculous soap bubble. I become obsessed with a miser's piercing anxiety whenever I allow myself to think that the Universe may be slipping out into space, like water through cupped hands, and that, ultimately—perhaps even today, perhaps not till tomorrow or for several light years—it will dissolve for ever into emptiness, as though it were made not of solid matter but only of fleeting sound.[55]

Despite this foreboding, he struggles to attend to the details of life and, further, to continue his writing in the context of "normalcy" and the rebuilding of the world of the past:[56]

> And since today the world has not yet blown away, I take out fresh paper, arrange it neatly on the desk, and closing my eyes try to find within me a tender feeling for the workmen hammering the rails, for the peasant women with their ersatz sour cream, the trains full of merchandise, the fading sky above the ruins, for the passers-by on the street below and the newly installed windows, and even for my wife who is washing dishes in the kitchen alcove; and with a tremendous intellectual effort I attempt to grasp the true significance of the

events, things and people I have seen. For I intend to write a great, immortal epic, worthy of this unchanging, difficult world chiseled out of stone.[57]

David Patterson describes what must be faced if one is to accomplish this Herculean task:

> The silence of the word in exile is not a blank emptiness but an oppressive, stifling substance, a "rumbling," as Levinas characterizes it (*Ethics* 48), that rattles the soul and seizes the breath. Here silence emerges "as a spokesman for the invincible Nothingness. Thus Silence replaces the Word because Nothingness takes the place of Being" (Neher 63). Because nothingness overtakes being, the collision with silence belongs to no specific time; the Holocaust novel erases the distinctions of before, during, and after.[58]

Patterson's word "collision" speaks directly to what Borowski describes, for in Patterson's understanding the collision with silence is a collision with death itself. Thus, writing a Holocaust narrative is an act of simultaneously facing and describing the death that was the defining logic and condition of the camp and a breaking free—for oneself and on behalf of those who died—from the inevitability of death. Patterson offers a relevant observation:

> Wiesel posits silence, death, and slavery against word, life, and freedom, underscoring the dialectical connection between silence and freedom. Situating his character in this dialectic, the author reveals his own life-and-death, word-and-silence, freedom-and-slavery situation, which, of course, has existential implications for the reader's position. Freedom—for author, character, and reader—is born from a response capacity, from responsibility, the one thing that can bring the word out of exile and overcome the silence that kills. One recalls that for Levinas, only responsibility could "stop the anonymous and senseless rumbling of being" (*Ethics* 52). In responsibility the human being is no longer enslaved by silence or threatened by death; rather, the person becomes free for death through a responsibility for the other, like a mother liberated in her readiness to die for her child.[59]

If the literary sentence becomes a judgmental sentence, the sentence used by a Holocaust writer like Borowski to represent silence is perhaps a trace of an effort to circumvent if not deny the guilt associated with having—or trying to find—a voice. But if the effort is not successful, then the author must fall into the dreaded remembered experience of being beside him or herself that was the condition of those in the camps.[60] In such a case, as Joseph Brodsky has said, "a freed man is not a free man."[61]

Virgil was in full control of his political epic, but Borowski, a political victim, did not produce the "great immortal epic" he intended to write, at least not in a strictly literary sense. After the war, he worked as a journalist and identified as a Communist as he sought a renewed life in a new political landscape. He produced a body of Holocaust works that were small in form, but taken together they might indeed be seen as constituting an epic composed by the young former student whose "European education" symbolized that of a generation, whose life course was determined by political exigencies, and whose struggle for personal agency and for his fellow men surely eclipsed what Virgil imagined for his character Aeneas. For Borowski and other writers who tackled the Holocaust with words, the silence with which they had to grapple was of an existential order, and of this they were fully cognizant. As Patterson notes, "the collision with silence . . . is a collision with death; the struggle with the word in exile is a struggle with death, which is as palpable as silence."[62]

> What is made "real" in the Holocaust novel is not just the death camp but death itself; words that transmit silence transmit death. Death is not only, however, a force that overtakes life but also the thing that life struggles to overtake through the return of the word from its exile. The harsh cry of death that splits the heavens pours from the mouth of life. The author cries out to make heard the outcry of those who have been silenced. In that hearing he finds his own voice, and through that voice he regains life.[63]

This, it seems, is the best-case scenario, but there were many survivors whose voices could not fully return them to life.

Central to Borowski's literary process is a juxtaposition of exquisite detailed linguistic control and a lack of faith in that very craft, something Franke would no doubt see as emblematic of a contemporary crisis of faith in language such as he sees in the work of Paul Celan and Edmond Jabès:

> Our contemporary world and culture have been visited by a radical crisis of confidence in language and a concomitant resurgence of interest in apophatic modes of discourse. We have been ardently in search of alternatives to strictly rational speaking and logical expression, since in crucial ways the Logos has proved impotent to disclose our reality and to truly express things as we experience them.[64]

While Franke is primarily interested in "radical singularity or otherness"[65] in post-Holocaust writing as an impetus for a discursive strategy that points to the limits of language, an irreparable disjunction between a specific point of view and alterity is not the only such impetus; time itself, the unbearable ongoing presence of history, is a reason to lose faith in language, as Franke acknowledges in relation to the poetry of Paul Celan:

The Holocaust experience Celan's poetry revolves around stands as the incomparable "that which happened" that it is impossible to say or name. But this historical catastrophe is not really accessible as history, and it is not only an event in the past. In its very uniqueness and incomparability it becomes for Celan key to interpreting the situation of human beings at all times—that is, simply as in time, in time that is always catastrophic by its very nature.[66]

For Borowski, the negation of self in the experiences of the "Musselmänner," the survivors (among them, writers like himself), changed forever the functionality of language. If a survivor is to speak or write his experiences, language, by definition a system of order, rules, and explicative function, must be used in the service of the inexplicable, and Borowski repeatedly assures his reader throughout his stories that "the inexplicable actually happens."

> . . . you do miles of somersaults; spend hours simply rolling on the ground; you do hundreds of squat-jumps; you stand motionless for endless days and nights; you sit for a full month inside a cement coffin—the bunker; you hang from a post or a wooden pole extended between two chairs; you jump like a frog and crawl like a snake; drink bucketfuls of water until you suffocate; you are beaten with a thousand different whips and clubs, by a thousand different men.[67]

Given a catalog of such absurdities, there is grim assurance in the logical causality that Borowski evinces in the episodes discussed above: one is hungry, so he eats whatever food is available; one seeks justice, so he kills his tormentor. Borowski's words remind us of Langer's observation that those survivors who seek to describe what they have endured "are in the thrall of what Maurice Blanchot calls the 'impossible real.'"[68]

Borowski turns to the concept of justice elsewhere in his stories, underscoring the point he makes in "Silence." Perhaps the most complex treatment of the subject comes in "The People Who Walked On," where it is articulated with characteristic brevity. When a Block Elder muses about whether or not a man who "does evil" will—or should—be punished, the narrator (Borowski himself?) responds: "I think that for those who have suffered unjustly, justice alone is not enough. They want the guilty to suffer unjustly too. Only this will they understand as justice."[69] The crux is the illogic that characterizes a new morality that comes in the wake of catastrophic suffering: having been plunged violently into a world in which death and suffering are desired ends and any learned systems of moral accountability fail to apply, the victim is driven paradoxically—insanely—to acts that he himself deems immoral to accommodate any vestigial concept of morality that might be applicable to his experience.

How can one articulate such a deep rupture of the personality, the very concept of the human being as an integral, worthy, sentient creature? How can one speak of what has been lost when the mechanisms normally available for such a project have themselves been lost? A skilled writer, Borowski turned to a literary heritage reflective of an entire cultural apparatus; by drawing on the rhetorical strength of preterition and exposing its inadequacy to accommodate his subject, he left a "diary" of sorts, a written record of life experiences for which he had no words. We cannot know if he had any faith in his art or if he simply felt compelled to write. What we can see, however, is his artistic mastery over and against a world in which he had (or felt he had) no control and the skill with which he crafted language to convey the enormity of the silence that divides those who were there from those who were not.

NOTES

1. *Scroll of Agony: The Warsaw Diary of Chaim A. Kaplan*, trans. and ed. Abraham I. Katsh (New York: Macmillan, 1965), 340, quoted in Barbara Foley, "Fiction, Fascism: Testimony and Mimesis in Holocaust Narratives," *Comparative Literature* 34, no. 4 (Autumn 1982): 330–60. http://www.jstor.org/stable/1771153.

2. "Holocaust" is derived from Greek: "holos" means "whole, entire," and the verb "kaiein" means "to burn." The term originally referred to burnt religious offerings. While "Holocaust" is frequently used in English to refer to the Nazi genocide, the Hebrew term "shoah," whose etymological meaning is tied to destruction and catastrophe, was widely used before "Holocaust" was accepted. "Shoah" is perhaps the better term for the subject of this chapter and the volume in which it appears, but for the purposes of clarity, I have elected to use the more familiar "Holocaust."

3. Hannah Arendt, *Life of the Mind, Vol. 1: Thinking* (New York and London: Harcourt Brace Jovanovich, 1977, 1978), 180. In the original text, this sentence appears in parentheses. The sentence often appears in a misquoted form on the Internet.

4. See Hannah Arendt, *Eichmann in Jerusalem: A Report on the Banality of Evil* (New York: Penguin 1977, 1994), 255ff. Arendt also makes the important observation that Eichmann was not unusual in his complicity with Nazi policy:

The trouble with Eichmann was precisely that so many were like him, and that the many were neither perverted nor sadistic, that they were, and still are, terribly and terrifyingly normal. From the viewpoint of our legal institutions and of our moral standards of judgment, this normality was much more terrifying than all the atrocities put together, for it implied—as had been said at Nuremberg over and over again by the defendants and their counsels—that this new type of criminal, who is in actual fact *hostis generis humani*, commits his crimes under circumstances that make it well-nigh impossible for him to know or to feel that he is doing wrong (276).

5. Lawrence L. Langer, *Holocaust Testimonies: The Ruins of Memory* (New Haven, CT and London: Yale University Press, 1991). Finding an appropriate term

for those who experienced the Nazi camps and/or other Nazi barbarism is a problem that much Holocaust literature has addressed. Is someone always a victim having once been one? Is living through an experience equivalent to having survived it? What is the relation of the survivor to those who did not survive, and what is his or her responsibility to them?

6. Ibid., 39.

7. Charlotte Delbo, *La mémoire et les jours* (Paris: Berg International, 1985), 11. Langer's translation, quoted in Lawrence L. Langer, *Holocaust Testimonies: The Ruins of Memory*, 5. Delbo's work was published posthumously in 1985; there is an English translation by Rose C. Lamont (Northwestern University Press). See Delbo's earlier volumes published as the trilogy *Auschwitz and After*, trans. Rose C. Lamont (New Haven: Yale University Press, 1985). See also Inga Clendinnen, *Reading the Holocaust* (Cambridge, UK: Cambridge University Press, 1999), 50–55 on Delbo.

8. Langer, *Holocaust Testimonies*, 5.

9. Virgil, "Aeneidos" 2.3 in *P. Vergili Maronis Opera*, ed. R. A. B. Mynors (Oxford: Oxford University Press, 1969, 1977); *The Aeneid of Virgil*, trans. Robert Fitzgerald (New York: Random House, 1981–83), 33.

10. On this subject, see Langer, *Holocaust Testimonies*.

11. Virgil, *Aeneid* 2.314; Fitzgerald, 44.

12. Ibid., 2.316–17.

13. Ibid., 2.577–87; Fitzgerald, 53–54.

14. Ibid., 12.567–73; Fitzgerald, 388.

15. I would like to distinguish between "horror experienced" and descriptions of horrific acts. Virgil proves himself skilled at representing violence in quite distinct ways; consider, for instance, the difference between the extended description of the fall of Troy with all its brutality and the extraordinarily succinct way Virgil later describes various types of violence, among them the manner in which Mezentius yokes together the living and the dead (*Aen.* 8.485–88; Fitzgerald 247). We shall return later to such chilling descriptions of depravity when we consider Borowski.

16. Edith Wyschogrod, "Concentration Camps and the End of the Life-World," in *Echoes from the Holocaust: Philosophical Reflections on a Dark Time*, ed. Alan Rosenberg and Gerald E. Myers, (Philadelphia: Temple University Press, 1988), 328–29. http://www.jstor.org/stable/j.ctt14bt4nf.20.

17. William Franke, "The Singular and the Other at the Limits of Language in the Apophatic Poetics of Edmond Jabès and Paul Celan," *New Literary History* 36, no. 4; "On Exploring Language in Philosophy, Poetry, and History" (Autumn 2005): 621–38. http://www.jstor.org/stable/20057916.

18. Ibid., 635.

19. Charlotte Delbo, *None of Us Will Return*, trans. John Githens (New York: Grove, 1968), 128, quoted in Langer, *Testimonies*, 42.

20. Jan Kott, Introduction. Trans. Michael Kandel. In Tadeusz Borowski, *This Way for the Gas, Ladies and Gentlemen*. Trans. Barbara Vedder (New York: Penguin Books, 1967, 1976), 12.

21. Ibid., 12–13.

22. Ibid., 14–16.

23. Ibid., 16–18.

24. http://culture.pl/en/artist/tadeusz-borowski. Accessed February 13, 2017. Borowski's suicide suggests that he did not feel liberated and that he was disturbed by the apparent failure of art in the face of the political realities generated by the Nazi atrocity.

25. Czeslaw Milosz, "The Novel in Poland," 1005–06. *Daedalus* 95, no. 4, Fiction in Several Languages (Fall 1966), 1004–20. http://www.jstor.org/stable/20027015.

26. Ibid., 1010–11.

27. Ibid., 1012.

28. Ibid., 1006.

29. Karen Armstrong, *The Great Transformation* (New York: Anchor Books, 2007), 149. Armstrong notes that in the 14th century, "Greek Orthodox theologians developed a principle about theology that takes us to the heart of the Axial Age. Any statement about God, they said, should have two qualities: it must be *paradoxical*, to remind us that the divine cannot fit into our limited human categories, and *apophatic*, leading us to silence. A theological discussion, therefore, should not answer all our queries about the ineffable deity, but should be like a *brahmodya*, which reduced contestants to speechless awe" (469).

30. Franke, 622.

31. Borowski, 161.

32. Ibid., 161.

33. Ibid., 161.

34. Ibid., 162.

35. Ibid., 162.

36. Ibid., 162.

37. Ibid., 163.

38. Ibid., 163.

39. Ibid., 163.

40. Ibid., 152–53.

41. Ibid., 153.

42. Ibid., 153.

43. Ibid., 154.

44. Ibid., 154–5.

45. Ibid., 155.

46. Ibid., 155.

47. Ibid., To be "Muslimized" was to be nearly without will, ready for death. Much has written about the *Musselmänner*, about why some people gave up when others continued to struggle to survive. Borowski uses the term in the story "This Way for the Gas, Ladies and Gentlemen," in which the narrator speaks somewhat condescendingly of the way the "Muslims scurry in fright to the safety of their bunks" when they hear a commotion (32). The fellow inmates' disdain for the *Musselmänner* was no doubt a consequence of their fear of becoming like them.

48. On Borowski's narrative voice, see Foley, "Fiction, Fascism," 352–53. See also "Representing the Holocaust" in Clendinnen, *Reading the Holocaust*, especially pp. 168–69, which explicitly refer to Borowski's "studiously offhand style" to describe action that takes place within a "moral void"; for Clendinnen, the fact that

Borowski wrote from experience "supplies an undertext of intimate moral implication never present in 'pure' fiction" (169).

49. Wyschogrod, 332–3.

50. Borowski, 54. Near the end of the story, we learn that the narrator Tadek (Borowski himself?) gives Becker something to eat as he is on his way to the "cremo" (80).

51. Langer, 117.

52. On the subject of choice (and absence of choice), see Jerome Kohn, "Arendt's Concept and Description of Totalitarianism," *Social Research* 69, no. 2, "Hannah Arendt's 'The Origins of Totalitarianism': Fifty Years Later" (Summer 2002): 621–56. http://www.jstor.org/stable/40971564. See also Foley, who argues that the Nazi philosophy is that truth is relative and determined by force, not by reason (358).

53. François Cheng, *Five Meditations on Death*, trans. Jody Gladding (Rochester, VT and Toronto: Inner Traditions, 2016), 59.

54. David Patterson. *The Shriek of Silence: A Phenomenology of the Holocaust Novel* (University Press of Kentucky, 1992), 30. http://www.jstor.org/stable/j.ctt13 0j86j.5. Patterson argues that those who write must "collide" with the silence of those victims who did not survive or otherwise have voices (33–34).

55. Borowski, 177.

56. See Michael J. Martin. "The Ethics of After: Melvin Jules Bukiet, Holocaust Fiction, and the Reemergence of an Ethical Sense in the Post-Holocaust World." *Shofar*, Vol. 22, no. 3 [Special Issue]: Unfinalized Moments in Jewish American Narrative (Spring 2004) (Purdue UP), 44. Stable URL: http://www.jstor.org/stable/42943677, accessed January 20, 2017 20:59 UTC.

57. Borowski, 180.

58. Patterson, 31.

59. Ibid., 33.

60. See Sharon B. Oster, "Impossible Holocaust Metaphors: The Muselmann," in *Prooftexts*, Vol. 34, no. 3 (Fall 2014) (Indiana UP), 302–48. Stable URL: http://www.jstor.org/stable/10.2979/prooftexts.34.3.02, accessed January 20, 2017.

61. Joseph Brodsky. "The Condition We Call Exile," *New York Review of Books*, January 18, 1990, 6 quoted in Langer, 170. Wyschogrod speaks to this from a slightly different angle in "Concentration Camps and the End of the Life-World": "the life-world now and in the future includes . . . the death-world of the camp. *Once the death-world has existed it continues to exist . . . for it becomes part of . . . the irrevocable past*" (335). She makes the important point that survival in the camps and after was an ethical choice beyond the frameworks intended by those who inflicted the horrors. Patterson is instructive as well:

> "As the man—both character and author—collides with silence, he is invaded with silence; those who were robbed of their cemeteries, reduced to smoke and ash, make the survivor into the cemetery of their silence. The more that silence is articulated, the deeper it runs; the more the author bespeaks the silence of the word in exile, the greater becomes his need to speak. The debt increases in the measure that it is paid; thus the silence of the other that cuts into me becomes

the judgment I pronounce upon myself. The Holocaust novelist, therefore, lives in an "accusative that derives from no nominative" (Levinas, *Otherwise*, 11). The author is accused not of survival but of silence; the author's responsibility for the exile of the word demands response. The sentence for the failure to respond is the death that lurks in the silence" (34).

62. Patterson, 32.
63. Ibid., 33.
64. Franke, 622.
65. Ibid., 624.
66. Ibid., 626.
67. Borowski, 118–9.
68. See Langer, 39.
69. Borowski, 90.

BIBLIOGRAPHY

Arendt, Hannah. *Eichmann in Jerusalem: A Report on the Banality of Evil*. New York: Penguin, 1977, 1994.

Arendt, Hannah. *Life of the Mind. Volume One: Thinking*. New York and London: Harcourt Brace Jovanovich, 1977, 1978.

Armstrong, Karen. *The Great Transformation*. New York: Anchor Books, 2007.

Borowski, Tadeusz. *This Way for the Gas, Ladies and Gentlemen. Translated by Barbara Vedder*. Introduction by Jan Kott, Translated by Michael Kandel. New York: Penguin Books, 1967, 1976.

Cheng, François. *Five Meditations on Death*. Translated by Jody Gladding, Rochester, VT and Toronto: Inner Traditions, 2016.

Clendinnen, Inga. *Reading the Holocaust*. Cambridge, UK: Cambridge University Press, 1999.

Culture.pl. "Tadeusz Borowski." Accessed February 13, 2017. http://culture.pl/en/artist/tadeusz-borowski.

Delbo, Charlotte. *Auschwitz and After*. Translated by Rose C. Lamont. New Haven, CT: Yale University Press, 1985.

Delbo, Charlotte. *La mémoire et les jours*. Paris: Berg International, 1985.

Foley, Barbara. "Fiction, Fascism: Testimony and Mimesis in Holocaust Narratives." *Comparative Literature* 34, no. 4 (Autumn, 1982): 330–360. http://www.jstor.org/stable/1771153.

Franke, William. "The Singular and the Other at the Limits of Language in the Apophatic Poetics of Edmond Jabès and Paul Celan." *New Literary History* 36, no. 4, On Exploring Language in Philosophy, Poetry, and History (Autumn, 2005): 621–638. http://www.jstor.org/stable/20057916.

Kohn, Jerome. "Arendt's Concept and Description of Totalitarianism." *Social Research* 69, no. 2 "Hannah Arendt's 'The Origins of Totalitarianism': Fifty Years Later" (Summer 2002): 621–656. http://www.jstor.org/stable/40971564.

Langer, Lawrence L. *Holocaust Testimonies: The Ruins of Memory*. New Haven and London: Yale University Press, 1991.

Martin, Michael J. "The Ethics of After: Melvin Jules Bukiet, Holocaust Fiction, and the Reemergence of an Ethical Sense in the Post-Holocaust World." *Shofar* 22, no. 3, Special Issue: Unfinalized Moments in Jewish American Narrative (Spring 2004): 43–55. http://www.jstor.org/stable/42943677.

Milosz, Czeslaw. "The Novel in Poland," 1005–6. *Daedalus* 95, no. 4, Fiction in Several Languages (Fall, 1966): 1004–1020. http://www.jstor.org/stable/20027015.

Oster, Sharon B. Impossible Holocaust Metaphors: The Muselmann." *Prooftexts* 34, no. 3 (Fall 2014): 302–348. http://www.jstor.org/stable/10.2979/prooftexts.34.3.02.

Patterson, David. *The Shriek of Silence: A Phenomenology of the Holocaust Novel*. Lexington, KY: University Press of Kentucky, 1992. http://www.jstor.org/stable/j.ctt130j86j.5.

Virgil. "Aeneidos" in *P. Vergili Maronis Opera*, ed. R. A. B. Mynors. Oxford, UK: Oxford University Press, 1969, 1977.

Virgil. *The Aeneid of Virgil*. Translated by Robert Fitzgerald. New York: Random House, 1981–83.

Wyschogrod, Edith. "Concentration Camps and the End of the Life-World." In *Echoes From The Holocaust: Philosophical Reflections on a Dark Time*. Alan Rosenberg and Gerald E. Myers, editors. Philadelphia: Temple University Press, 1988. http://www.jstor.org/stable/j.ctt14bt4nf.20.

Part V

POST-MODERNITY

Preface

Postmodernity

Postmodernity, beginning around the time of the cultural revolutions of the 1960s, is a complicated phenomenon, one that brought into sharp relief the rejection of long-standing social assumptions. During this time, and on a number of different fronts, many "traditional values" and established ways of seeing were replaced more or less with different forms of skepticism and relativism. On the academic front, this is borne out in the writings of many postmodern literary critics, for example, Derrida, according to whom there is not and perhaps never was a way to ascertain the true meaning of texts and events.[1]

This "new relativism" can be seen as a double-edged sword. On the cultural front, we have witnessed a number of transformations arising in the late 1960s, including a loosening of moral strictures and traditional roles. These developments opened up new vistas of understanding, heralded new ideas and attempts at social and political equality, and brought about more in the way of multiculturalism and inclusiveness, with greater tolerance of difference. Yet these transformations have also revealed aspects of a deeper anomie, in which generally secular cultures now witness segments of their population turning toward more intolerant forms of nationalism, populism, and religious fundamentalism. Regarding this return to religious fundamentalism, many now deem postmodernity as somehow now being secular and postsecular at once. Perhaps this is the "second religiousness" Spengler wrote of in *Decline of the West*. We are now witness to a general confusion regarding which values are tenable and which are not.

A related new darker phenomenon has also appeared on the horizon at the crossroads of international politics, economics, and religion—the age of terror. This phenomenon has become particularly acute within the world of Islam, but the other Abrahamic faiths have shown themselves to be not completely immune from this sort of trajectory. We have grown accustomed to a state of heightened, regulated anxiety, a state in which air travel alone now requires hours of security detail. Diverse thinkers such as Schmitt, Benjamin, and Agamben have argued, in different contexts, that we are living in a state of emergency, in which the "state of exception" "has now become the rule."[2] This current state of exception has, at least in the United States, resulted in the proliferation of practices—travel bans, surveillance, detentions, profiling, even torture—that may in some cases constitute basic human rights violations—yet they have now deemed justifiable on Utilitarian grounds. This situation has raised questions (now hotly debated) about the political and spiritual future of our country, and the implications of such measures on the current state of American Democracy.

From a larger standpoint, the entire human race is currently facing an unprecedented catastrophe right now. Overpopulation, climate change, environmental degradation, and nuclear proliferation have combined to form a Damocles' sword hanging ominously over the entire world. These problems are severely testing the limited resources of the planet.

If such patterns continue, the future does not look promising. It is human nature to not want to think too much about such depressing things, and to "kick the can down the road" as problems to be confronted later. Of course, there are climate change and other rehabilitative initiatives underway now to try and solve these problems. These initiatives are laudable and progress has been made, but the question is whether at this point it is "too little, too late." What sort of world will our children and grandchildren inherit? Can we try as a species to work collectively, to minimize local conflicts, and to prioritize this larger picture, so as to cooperatively undertake the sort of global initiatives necessary to save civilization? Or is this too optimistic a picture given human nature? Thinkers such as Karl Lorenz have argued that conflict and opposition are fundamental to humanity—more basic to our makeup than the more pleasant sounding attributes of cooperation and mutual understanding. The answer to these questions remains open.

NOTES

1. See Jacques Derrida, *Aporias* (Palo Alto, CA: Stanford University Press, 1993).
2. Giorgio Agamben, *State of Exception* (Chicago: University of Chicago Press, 2005).

BIBLIOGRAPHY

Agamben, Giorgio. *State of Exception*. Chicago: University of Chicago Press, 2005.
Derrida, Jacques. *Aporias*. Palo Alto, CA: Stanford University Press, 1993.

Chapter 17

States of Exception and the Problem of Detention in Post-9/11 American Jurisprudence

David A. Chalfin

The coordinated terrorist attacks perpetrated by the radical militant Sunni Islamist group al-Qaeda on September 11, 2001, are now permanently emblazoned on the American consciousness. Four commercial airplanes were hijacked and used as giant missiles, bringing down the World Trade Center's Twin Towers, and partially collapsing part of the Pentagon. Three thousand people were killed and six thousand more were injured. These were neither radical Islam's first lethal attacks on Western interests nor the first ones to take place on American soil. But the magnitude of the damage and the chaos caused, the shocking success of the coordinated plan, and the toppling of the West's great symbols of achievement highlighted the country's vulnerability to a new and different threat. "9/11" is not so much a date as a turning point in Western civilization's understanding of a novel and persistent challenge to normalcy, a simmering low-grade emergency.

As with catastrophes and crises more generally, long-standing existential securities were suddenly uprooted. In fact, since the disaster of 9/11 and the beginning of America's "war on terror," there has been a widespread questioning of a number of basic political assumptions in the United States. Some of these questions have been prompted by actions taken by the Trump administration (but not all, as some of the actions in question originated earlier under the authority of Presidents Obama and George W. Bush). Under what conditions, if any, could it be morally permissible during "states of exception" to ban members of a certain group from entering the country? Similar questions have been raised about such practices as phone surveillance of target populations, searches of targeted populations in transportation hubs, the treatment of incarcerated prisoners involved in terrorist acts, "waterboarding," and so on. Can such actions be justified, particularly during states of exception? There are certainly utilitarian and deontological arguments that have been offered on both sides of these issues. Writ large, these questions addressed in the context of the U.S. Constitution, precipitate debates about the current state of democracy in the United States, the values we hold as a nation based on the writings of the founding fathers, and our collective vision about the sort of country we wish to be.

DETENTION POST 9/11

This chapter explores the American reaction to the challenge of 9/11 by analyzing a narrow part of the legal system's response. The U.S. Patriot Act,[1] which was signed into law by President George W. Bush on October 26, 2001, provides law enforcement officials with expanded "search and seizure" tools to fight terrorism, and facilitates coordination among government agencies.[2] Other counter-terrorism measures enacted post 9/11 restructured government itself—the establishment of the Transportation Security Administration and the Department of Homeland Security.

Notwithstanding the practical importance of these wide-ranging legal responses in fighting terrorism, and the constitutional friction they create, the narrow focus here is on the constitutional law of detention post 9/11. Detention of persons by the government embodies the *ultimate conflict* between the state's goal of *maintaining order* during times of crisis, and the individual's *right to freedom* from state activity. It is one thing to have one's communications monitored and one's meta-data taken, stored, and analyzed by the state. It is quite another to be detained—imprisoned and held by force against one's will. There is virtually no greater imposition of power by the state and no greater detriment to the individual. The focus here is on the government's exercise of that power to maintain security in times of perceived emergency.

EMERGENCIES, THE STATE OF EXCEPTION, AND LEGAL THEORY

Agamben and Schmitt

Though the crisis of 9/11 is unique, governmental suspension of legal rules in times of crisis is not. Giorgio Agamben's *State of Exception*[3] is a sweeping historical and philosophical study of just this phenomenon—the imposition by government of "states of exception" to legal rules in exigent circumstances. Agamben's study reaches back to events across Europe and to concepts in medieval and Roman legal philosophy. He takes as his prime interlocutor Carl Schmitt and his concept of the state of exception. Schmitt is the political theorist most often associated with the defense of the exceptions in the Weimar Constitution that led to the rise of Nazism, and also, by extension, of dictatorship itself. Agamben's and Schmitt's concept of the State of Exception is a useful jumping off point.

Agamben begins *State of Exception* with Schmitt's famous definition of the sovereign as "he who decides on the state of exception" and posits the key paradox of State of Exception (SOE) legal theory—how can a legal scheme itself suspend the legal scheme in an internally consistent manner. If law suspends itself, to the point of claiming that law does not govern, then what authoritative basis can such suspension have? It cannot be legal authority, as the authority of the suspension, which would otherwise have been legal, has been suspended. The self-referential nature of the action leaves a gap. The authority behind the suspension, Schmitt claims, is the definition of sovereignty. The suspender necessarily is operating *outside of law*.

EXIGENCIES AND THE LIBERAL LEGAL PARADOX

But why does a legal scheme necessarily need to be suspended? Why do there need to be exceptions? Schmitt's critique of the liberal legal tradition is based on the premise that there inevitably are non-normal circumstances, call them emergencies, for which normal rules are not applicable. Such emergencies, or states of exception, exist because a system of legal rules can not anticipate all exigent circumstances, particularly circumstances that threaten the legal system itself. Schmitt critiques liberal legal theory for pretending to be a complete, comprehensive normative system when it cannot be. Liberal legal theory, the claim is, is intellectually dishonest. The self-proclaimed virtue of Schmitt's theory is that it is open and transparent. It unmasks the inevitable truth: ultimately the foundation for legal authority is extra-legal.

The liberal legal paradox goes further. If the essential goal of the liberal rule of law is to constrain the ruler (as well as the ruled), then the ruler cannot be the one empowered to declare an exception to the rules. Allowing such an exception would vitiate the essence of the rule of law itself. If there needs to be a *decider (outside of law)* of when and which rules are to be suspended, and if the decider is the ruler, the result is non-rule constrained power—call it dictatorship.[4]

The baseline framework, for both Schmitt and Agamben, is that legal systems are designed for normal, ordinary states of affairs, not emergencies, which are different in kind. War is the clearest example of an emergency. According to the baseline framework, *emergencies are, by definition, the exception*. They are temporary, sporadic, and nonordinary. The power of the state to react to emergencies, it follows, is also supposed to be temporary and exceptional. The goal is to restore normalcy. As Oren Gross states, "the 'normalcy-rule, emergency-exception' paradigm has been adopted as normatively desirable by most . . . legal and political thinkers."[5] It is this paradigm to which both Schmitt and Agamben are reacting. For Schmitt, Agamben and Gross, "claims that *emergency government has become the norm* can no longer be dismissed."[6] Agamben's and Schmitt's work are self-conscious reactions to the reversal of the baseline framework. Put otherwise, their focus is on exceptions subordinating rules.

Internalism and Externalism

Like Schmitt, Agamben distinguishes between legal traditions that attempt to ground authority for the imposition of exceptions to law within law and those where the ultimate grounding is outside of law. "The differences in the legal traditions correspond in scholarship to the division between those who seek to *include the state of exception within the sphere of the juridical order* [which we will call the "Internal" perspective] and those who consider it something *external*, that is, an *essentially political*, or in any case extrajuridical, phenomenon [which we will call the "External" perspective].[7] To restate the paradox in these terms,

> "if the state of exception's characteristic property is a (total or partial) suspension of the juridical order, how can such a suspension still be contained within it? . . . And if the state of exception is instead only a de facto situation, and is as such unrelated or contrary to law, how is it possible for the order to contain a lacuna precisely where the decisive situation is concerned? And what is the meaning of this lacuna? . . . Hence the interest of . . . theories . . . like Schmitt's . . . in which the very limit of the juridical order is at issue."[8]

State of Exception and 9/11

Agamben's overall project in *State of Exception* is to give meaning to what he describes as the illogical anomie that results from the "state of exception" being neither internal nor external to law, and to situate this "lacuna" within his larger philosophy. "The essential task of a theory of the state of exception is not simply to clarify whether it has a juridical nature or [i.e., whether the theory of legal exception is at root legal, the Internal perspective], but to define the meaning, place and modes of its relation to the law."[9] The project here is to elucidate the reaction to the crisis of 9/11 in SOE terms: how were legal rules adapted; are the foundations of the response within or external to the legal scheme; and what does the legal methodology imply?

Notwithstanding the projects' differences, Agamben is a useful foil. He is well-known for his criticism of the United States' response to 9/11, which he sees as evidence for his theory that the state of exception is becoming the rule—"a paradigm shift echoing through the din of the 'war on terror.'"[10] He highlights the plight of the Taliban captured in Afghanistan falling between the cracks—they are not POWs covered by the Geneva Convention, and do not have the status of persons charged with a crime according to American laws. They are "'simply detainees,' . . . the object of a pure de facto rule, of detention that is indefinite temporally and by nature, as they are entirely removed from judicial oversight."[11] He then compares and conflates the status of such detainees to the legal situation of Jews in Nazi concentration camps.

Moreover, Agamben has been criticized for "his minimal and inconclusive discussion of the separation of powers" and not discussing the importance of the judiciary.[12] He correctly identifies the paradigmatic SOE concept in the U.S. Constitution, the Suspension Clause to the privilege of the Writ of Habeas Corpus—the exception to the right of the accused to be charged and tried in court, not to be detained indefinitely without charges.[13] In his short gloss on the history of invocation of the Suspension Clause, he correctly highlights Lincoln's "dictatorial" suspension of the Writ in 1861 at the outset of the American Civil War as the quintessential example of the American executive invoking the state of exception.[14] But he passes over the judiciary's role. In *Ex Parte Merryman*, Chief Justice Taney rejected Lincoln's unauthorized suspension.[15] What better example could one find of the executive asserting power by invoking the exception! Agamben understands that separation of powers principles are a bulwark against the imposition of SOEs,[16] but ignores the judicial details.

Similarly, Agamben is correct to highlight the importance of the gulf between the regimes of criminal law and the law of war. But he glosses over the actual legal principles that fill in the gulf. Equating the status of the Taliban detainees and the Jews in concentration camps, and claiming that the U.S. war on terror is an example of the exception becoming the rule, is a gross and inaccurate generalization. But, post-9/11 and related case law does expose aspects of American jurisprudence that are subject to the paradox of SOE theory and Schmitt's critique of liberal legalism. Talking about the paradox of a legal scheme suspending itself sounds like a flighty theoretical topic. Analyzing a small, but important, snippet of case law roots these concepts in practice. It also leads back to theory—can a legal scheme be comprehensive or must it rely on systems, like politics or morality, external to itself?

POST-9/11 DETENTION JURISPRUDENCE

Detention of Enemy Combatants—*Hamdi*

One week after 9/11, Congress passed the Authorization for Use of Military Force Act (AUMF), authorizing the president to "use all necessary and appropriate force against those nations, organizations or persons he determines planned, authorized, committed, or aided the terrorist attacks" or "harbored such organizations or person, in order to prevent any future acts of international terrorism against the United States by such nations, organizations of persons." U.S. armed forces were deployed to Afghanistan to subdue al-Qaeda and quell the Taliban regime that harbored it.[17] Yaser Esam Hamdi was born in Louisiana, grew up in Saudi Arabia, and by 2001, resided in Afghanistan. His father claimed that he went to Afghanistan in the summer of 2001 as a relief worker. Hamdi was seized by a group opposed to the Taliban and turned over to the U.S. military. He was accused of fighting for the Taliban and transferred to Guantanamo Bay. When it was learned that he was a U.S. citizen, he was transferred to a military prison in Virginia.

In June, Hamdi's father filed a petition for a writ of habeas corpus, the procedural petition requiring the military to justify Hamdi's detention in court, claiming that his son had gone to Afghanistan to do relief work and was not fighting with the Taliban. The petition argues 1) that, as a U.S. citizen, he is entitled to the protections of the U.S. Constitution and 2) that his detention without charges, access to an impartial tribunal or assistance of counsel violates his Fifth Amendment right to due process of law [notwithstanding exigent circumstances]. On that basis, the habeas corpus petition demanded that the court release him from unlawful custody. The Government countered that Hamdi was captured while fighting with the Taliban. It argued 1) that the Executive Branch has the right in wartime to declare those who fight against the United States "enemy combatants," and 2) therefore that it is justified in detaining him indefinitely without formal charges or proceedings [which would be prohibited in normal circumstances].

In the American legal system, cases often wind their way through the courts slowly, as the mosaic of legal issues are appealed. *Hamdi* reached the Supreme Court after the Fourth Circuit Court of Appeals reversed an evidentiary ruling of the District Court requiring the government to produce evidence justifying its initial claims that Hamdi was fighting with the Taliban. The Fourth Circuit declared that because Hamdi was captured in a combat zone, the president was justified by his war powers in declaring Hamdi an enemy combatant and in detaining him, and, as a separation of powers matter, that such an executive decision was not reviewable by the judiciary.

In 2004, the Supreme Court reversed the Fourth Circuit, addressing the threshold question on the Executive's authority to detain citizens who qualify as enemy combatants.[18] Justice Sandra Day O'Connor held that, though Hamdi's detention was authorized as a "necessary and appropriate" use of force incidental to war under the AUMF,[19] *as a Constitutional matter, Hamdi's Fifth Amendment due process rights were violated.* The Fifth Amendment provides that no person shall be deprived of liberty without "due process of law." On that basis, O'Connor held that "a citizen-detainee seeking to challenge his classification as an enemy combatant must receive notice of the factual basis of the classification, and a fair opportunity to rebut the Government's factual assertions before a neutral decision maker."[20] The President's congressionally granted power to detain enemy combatants is not absolute; the power cannot be exercised in a way that abrogates a citizen-detainee's right to contest that determination before a neutral arbitrator.

SEPARATION OF POWERS, JUDICIAL REVIEW, AND SOE

At root, *Hamdi* is a forceful assertion of constitutional separation of powers principles. Even under exigent circumstances, the executive does not have unilateral powers to declare citizen-detainees to be enemy combatants and on that basis to detain them indefinitely. Rather, constitutional due process requires that the judiciary plays a role. As O'Connor puts it,

> We necessarily reject the Government's asserting that separation of powers principles mandate a heavily circumscribed role for the courts in such [exigent] circumstances. Indeed, the position that the courts must forgo any examination of the individual case and focus exclusively on the broader detention scheme cannot be mandated by any reasonable view of separation of powers, as this approach serves only to *condense power* into a single branch of government. We have long since made clear that [the exigent circumstance of] a state of war is not a blank check when it comes to the rights of the Nation's citizens.[21]

O'Connor's defense of the judiciary against the attempt of the executive branch to declare an exception to normal legal rules in *Hamdi* is a counterexample to the assertion that post-9/11 constitutional detention jurisprudence is exemplified by the impositions of states of exception to normal rules in emergency circumstances. O'Connor's rejection of the executive's attempt to assert unconstrained power is itself an assertion of power. The very fact that the Supreme Court issues a legal opinion, and that action is taken on that basis, demonstrates that the executive does not have unchecked power. Under the U.S. constitutional system, the Supreme Court typically has the last word as the ultimate arbiter of constitutional super-principles.[22]

EXPLICIT INTERNALISM AND EXIGENT CIRCUMSTANCES

O'Connor's jurisprudence does not on its face require her to go outside of the law itself to address emergency or non-normal situations. This is true from both an explicitly self-conscious perspective and also from a more implicit perspective. Per O'Connor, the beauty of the Constitution is that it can, and should, apply in emergencies. "It is during our most challenging and uncertain moments that our Nation's commitment to due process is most severely tested; and it is in those times that we must preserve our commitment at home to the principles for which we fight abroad."[23] O'Connor cites a line of prior Supreme Court cases for the applicability of the Constitution in exigent circumstances, thereby finding authority for this general claim within law—that is, as an Internalist.

O'Connor also finds authority for the Supreme Court's assertion of its role in reviewing actions of the Executive branch (within the Constitution) in the fact that the Constitution's SOE assertion mechanism, the Suspension Clause, was not invoked—as long as the Writ of Habeas Corpus has not been suspended, normal separation of powers principles apply.[24] The flip side of the reasoning is that only if the privilege of the writ of habeas corpus were suspended, could the judiciary's role (in balancing the government's interest in jailing people against the value of the procedural rights of those people to require the government to justify the detention) constitutionally be curtailed. The Suspension Clause provides that the fundamental habeas corpus right may be suspended "in cases of Rebellion or Invasion [when] the Public Safety may require it."[25] But, Congress had not invoked the suspension mechanism and no one had claimed that these conditions had been met. To date, the Suspension Clause has not invoked in response to the events of 9/11.

BALANCING AND COMPREHENSIVENESS—
IMPLICIT INTERNALISM

Hamdi has a second part. Having determined that constitutional due process rights are applicable, O'Connor sets forth a due process scheme to which detainees, like Hamdi, are entitled. Under exigent circumstances, due process rights are not suspended, but they are different. The scheme is based on a methodical application of a calculus that balances the *grave harm* of erroneous and potentially indefinite detention and the *threat to security* of the country, due to handicapping the military and the law enforcement community in allowing detainees to challenge the propriety of their detention. The interest of the government is in *maximizing its success* in combating terrorism without being hampered by having to participate in legal proceedings intended to provide detainees a *fair opportunity* to challenge the propriety of the detention. The detainee's interest is in having procedural due process rights to rebut facts on the basis of which detention is based.[26]

A balancing test is used to address the tension between legitimate interests—the government's interest in fighting terrorism and the detainee's interest in due process rights to rebut erroneous detention. Justice Souter, in his concurring opinion in *Hamdi*, calls this constant tension between security and liberty: "the defining character of American constitutional government."[27] In a certain respect, internalism is implicit in this balancing methodology, as the two values being weighed, individual liberty and state security, are internal to the Constitution. Values external to the legal system are not referenced. Particularly under exigent circumstances balancing is at the crux: "Striking the proper constitutional balance here is of great importance to the Nation during this period of ongoing combat. But it is equally vital that our calculus not give short shrift to the values that this country holds dear or the privilege of American citizenship."[28]

O'Connor's methodology, based on balancing multiple values *internal* to the system, also enables a certain comprehensiveness. Recall Schmitt's criticism that liberal legal theory claims to be a comprehensive normative system; but inevitably there are circumstances, typically extreme emergencies, that cannot be anticipated and that are so different that "normal" rules do not work; therefore there must be a *decision based on justifications or values outside the legal system as to when to suspend the system*. Contra Schmitt, insofar as O'Connor's balancing methodology incorporates multiple values internal to the legal system, it is better able to accommodate exigencies without explicit reference to extralegal principles.

SHORTCOMINGS OF BALANCING AND OF INTERNALISM

The due process system appropriate for *Hamdi*-like exigencies that emerges from Justice O'Connor's Internalist balancing methodology has been criticized for being a watered down version of the normal constitutional concept of due process of law.[29] Specifically, *Hamdi* holds that due process requires that "a citizen-detainee seeking to challenge his classification as an enemy combatant must receive notice of the factual basis of the classification, and be afforded a fair "opportunity to rebut the Government's factual assertions before a neutral decision maker."[30] The neutral decision maker need not be a "normal" court applying "normal" evidentiary rules that allow the detainee to contest facts, and the burden of proof may be on the detainee, not the government, unlike "normal" rules. Military tribunals may be sufficient.[31]

O'Connor's conclusion is subject to challenge based both on narrow (internal) considerations and broad (external) grounds. Ronald Dworkin, in his article "What the Court Really Said," claims that the neutral arbiter and procedural rules that O'Connor comes up with (based on balancing the due process versus military efficiency) are lacking as a matter of due process: for example, flipping the normal burden of proof from the government to the detainee is a factor that favors the government enormously. "O'Connor is no doubt right that it would be unduly burdensome to require the military to prepare elaborate dossiers describing and justifying the capture of every prisoner it takes. But her methods of protecting the military from such burdens do not give much protection to detainees."[32]

That may be correct, but on what basis is Dworkin criticizing O'Connor for favoring the government over the detainee? Has Dworkin simply undertaken the same balancing test, but weighed the factors differently? If so, is the basis for the difference simply *his* value preferences? And is the basis for his preference for one legal value over another one *external to law*? In three articles on post-9/11 detention practices, Dworkin argues that: 1) the Bush administration's post-9/11 detention of suspected terror suspects is wrong on moral grounds (though until 2003 the practices had been upheld as legal)[33]; 2) O'Connor's due process system is flawed in giving inadequate protection to detainees[34]; and 3) certain detention practices are unconstitutional, based on a narrow balancing methodology, internal to law.[35]

Dworkin clearly understands the difference between claims based on moral values *outside of the Constitution* and legally cognizable arguments *within the American constitutional scheme*. In his pre-*Hamdi* article, "Terror and the Attack on Civil Liberties,"[36] Dworkin argues that prisoners detained by the Bush administration, even though not entitled to prisoner of war status under the Geneva Convention itself (because they are part of a fighting force independent of a government, which does not wear uniforms or respect the laws of war) are entitled to the protections of the Geneva Convention on moral grounds:

> *a decent respect for human rights* requires . . . choos[ing] between prosecuting . . . prisoners as criminals, with the normal safeguards of the criminal process [more robust than the safeguards O'Connor later promulgates in *Hamdi*], and treating them as prisoners of war [within the Geneva Convention], which would mean an end to round-the-clock interrogation, sensory deprivation, humiliation and other forms of coercion. . . . [which reflect] an impermissible *contempt for the rights and dignity of its victims.*[37]

Dworkin explicitly admits that this critique is founded only on moral concepts—rights and dignity—not necessarily legal ones.[38] Indeed his overall critique of the Bush administration's strategy is laced with moral arguments, based on "principles of shared humanity." He spends considerable effort arguing that putting American safety not only first, but absolutely first, an even timelier topic in 2017, is morally impermissible.[39]

In "What the Court Really Said," Dworkin moves his argument more explicitly to applying legal balancing tests, which are essential under the Constitution. The mere fact of due process rights necessitates balancing: "No doubt police would be more efficient in preventing crime and we would all be safer . . . if there were no due process rights."[40] On the basis of O'Connor's own balancing test, Dworkin argues that legally, terror suspect detainees must not be tortured or coercively interrogated. Using O'Connor's language, he balances two considerations. On one hand, there is the government's interest in avoiding the *burdens* that might compromise its efficiency in promoting security and "the *weighty and sensitive* governmental interests in ensuring that those who have in fact fought with the enemy do not return to battle against the United States." Yet there is also the fact that "commitment for any purpose constitutes a *significant deprivation of liberty*" [and] "the *magnitude of the harm* that an erroneous determination would inflict on the detainee who was not in fact an enemy combatant." Dworkin then observes that the governmental interests are "no better served when the government holds detainees under . . . harsh conditions than the less fearsome conditions of conventional prisoners of war." Based on this subtle balancing, he concludes that detention marked by coercion and torture is not justified. That is, even though the detainees may not be entitled to the protections of the Geneva Convention as prisoners, they are entitled to such protections (including the prohibition of coercive interrogation) *as if* they were prisoners, since the governmental purpose is "no better served when the protections of the Geneva Convention are ignored."[41]

Perhaps, as a matter of risk-balancing, Dworkin is simply more willing than O'Connor to take the risk of impeding the government because he values individual rights more. The difference between what O'Connor and Dworkin think is constitutionally required in terms of due process could be based on different factual analyses, the application of personal preferences or principles (which in each case could be internal or external to the legal system), or some combination of these factors.

In "Why it was a Great Victory,"[42] Dworkin describes his difference with O'Connor even more narrowly, as internal to O'Connor's own explicitly internalist test, almost as if there need be no difference between himself and O'Connor on personal preferences or foundational values, whether internal or external. For example, Dworkin refers to applying O'Connor's balancing test "in retrospect," that is, at a later time. "It is worth noticing . . . that O'Connor's standards of due process . . . in *Hamdi* . . . do not appear, *at least in retrospect,* to satisfy the test she herself proposed: any procedure for classifying citizens as enemy combatants . . . must *balance* the *grave harm* done to someone *unjustly detained* against the *risk* of releasing someone who would *rejoin a terrorist group*."[43] Dworkin's opposing views as to what constitutes a violation of constitutional procedural due process appear to be based only on his consideration of subsequent facts (which were not available to O'Connor four years before when *Hamdi* was written), as if Dworkin and O'Connor differ in no other respects.

LESSONS FROM KOREMATSU

The Hollowness of Internalist Balancing

One virtue of the narrow fact-specific balancing tests of the sort O'Connor employs in *Hamdi,* is that they are better suited to survive the Schmittian critique that liberal legal systems cannot be comprehensive. The cost, however, is that situation and fact-specific balancing is prone to being unprincipled. For example, as we saw, Dworkin and O'Connor may come out with opposite conclusions based on differing considerations of the same finely grained facts. Overemphasis on a balancing methodology, where slight analytical differences can end up justifying opposite conclusions, can lead to substantive hollowness.

This hollowness can be understood by comparing O'Connor's method to that of Justice Murphy (in his dissent) and Justice Black (writing for the majority) in *Korematsu,* and then comparing Murphy's dissent to that of Justice Jackson. *Korematsu* is the famous Supreme Court case on the internment of persons of Japanese descent in California during World War II. The military issued a series of seemingly inconsistent orders, which in effect required all such persons, U.S. citizens and non-citizens, to report to internment camps. Justice Murphy dissented from the Supreme Court's holding that the military orders that required persons of Japanese descent to report to internment camps were constitutional.

Murphy's reasoning is just like O'Connor's. First, he states that, in matters relating to the prosecution of war the Supreme Court must be deferential to the "judgments of the military authorities . . . who have full knowledge of the military facts. The scope of their discretion must . . . be wide." Overturning such judgments by judges without training in military matters ought not to be taken lightly. However, "it is essential that there be definite limits to military discretion, especially where martial law has not been declared [i.e., where the Writ of Habeas Corpus has not been suspended]." "The military claim must subject itself to the judicial process of having its reasonableness determined and it conflicts with other interests reconciled." In *Hamdi ,* O'Connor cites this very sentence.[44] As long as the Writ of Habeas Corpus has not been suspended, the judiciary has a role to play—balancing.

States of Exception and Post-9/11 Jurisprudence 295

Murphy proceeds to determine "whether the Government, on a plea of military necessity, can deprive an individual of any of his constitutional rights [by analyzing] whether the *deprivation* is *reasonably related to a public danger that is so 'immediate, imminent and impending'* as not to admit of delay and not to permit the intervention of ordinary constitutional process to alleviate the danger."[45]

Murphy notes that there were very real fears of invasion of the Pacific Coast and of sabotage and espionage, but finds that internment of all persons belonging to a racial group bore no reasonable relation to such fears: The assumption that all persons of Japanese ancestry may have a dangerous tendency to aid the enemy and be disloyal, was factually unsupported. The military asserted the need for protective custody due to episodes of violence, but did not provide evidence of such episodes. No evidence was marshaled of immediate, immanent, or impending danger. No evidence was offered that subversive persons had not previously been detained, prior to the group detention orders. The fact that the Suspension Clause had not been invoked supports the lack of urgency or military necessity. No adequate basis was provided for not treating the detainees on an individual basis. Based on these narrow fact-specific determinations, Murphy deduces that the true rationale for the detention orders, are racial and sociological factors—racism! Military judgments based principally on racism, Murphy concludes, are not entitled to deference by the judiciary because they are not reasonably related to an immediate, immanent, and impending threat of public danger.[46]

Justice Black's majority opinion in *Korematsu*, holding the detention of persons of Japanese descent constitutional, is similarly based on a narrow finely tuned balancing method (ironically, Black applied a stricter standard of review than the "reasonably related" test.) To be constitutional, legal restrictions curtailing civil rights based on race must pass a "rigid scrutiny" test: there must pressing public necessity. Black explicitly recognized the severity of the hardship of internment, stating that such *severe* hardship could be justified based only upon the military's apprehension of the *gravest* imminent danger. Black's balancing calculus highlights different facts and assesses the likelihood and severity of the danger differently than Murphy does. He notes that 5000 American citizens of Japanese ancestry refused to swear loyalty oaths; several thousand evacuees requested repatriation to Japan; the number of disloyal Japanese could not be ascertained; it was not possible to hold individual loyalty hearings. He deferred to the military's judgment that it was not feasible to address the risk of sabotage and espionage except by segregating people based on their being members of a group. On these narrow bases, Black deferred to the judgment of the military and held that the exclusion of all persons of Japanese ancestry from a designated military area was constitutional. He limits the holding to "circumstances of direct emergency and peril."[47]

The *Korematsu* majority and dissent reach diametrically opposed rulings, based on subtle differences in their balancing calculus, not based on applying different or opposing rules. To the contrary, there is one general rule that both majority and dissent purport to support—that detention based on *racial prejudice* cannot be the basis for group detention, not that detention based on race cannot be the basis for detention.[48] The *Korematsu* decision is now generally thought to have been incorrectly decided and is often cited as an example of bad law, but not because it violates a legal rule—for example, that detention based on race is unconstitutional or that group ethnicity or race cannot be the basis for curtailing due process rights. Indeed, though *Korematsu* has been criticized by the courts and other branches of government, it has never been judicially overruled. If there is no violation of a subsequent legal rule, to deny the case precedential legal authority, it must be distinguished by narrowing its applicability, for example, claiming that Justice Black erred in incorrectly perceiving the nature of the danger presented by the Japanese, quite a circumscribed error. Such a narrow criticism leaves open the possibility that in other cases it could be constitutional to curtail due process based on racial or ethnic identity, for example, if the nature of the danger is in good faith thought to be real. Even Dworkin's own criticism of *Korematsu*, which he calls an "episode of great national embarrassment," is at least in part based on narrow balancing: "the benefit to security of that wholesale detention was minimal and the damage it inflicted on its victims was enormous."[49]

Externalism in Korematsu

Though they come up with opposite conclusions on the constitutionality of racially based detention orders, Black and Murphy, like O'Connor are Internalists. They apply legal analysis to exigent circumstances, and do not invoke extralegal values or norms. Justice Jackson's bold dissent in *Korematsu* is the rare counterexample.

Like Murphy, he dissents, but he does so based on explicit extralegal grounds. Unlike O'Connor and Murphy, Jackson disclaims a role for the judiciary. Rather, he in effect declares a state of exception, segregating the legal realm from the military realm and refusing to evaluate the expediency of military's orders. Even if the military orders were expedient, he asserts, that does not mean they are constitutional. More harm than good is done when the judiciary normalizes responses to emergencies by stretching constitutional principles. "If we cannot confine military expedients by the Constitution, neither would I distort the Constitution to approve all that the military may deem expedient."[50]

Like Schmitt's claim underlying his criticism of liberal legal theory, Jackson implicitly agrees that there are extreme circumstances that normal constitutional rules can and should not address. Like Agamben, he asserts that there is a realm of matters that are and should be non-justiciable, outside of law. This is a case of legal authority declaring the existence of a zone outside itself.

> Much is said of the danger to liberty from the Army program for deporting and detaining these citizens of Japanese extraction. But a judicial construction of the due process clause that will sustain this order is a far more subtle blow to liberty than the promulgation of the order itself. A military order will not last longer than the emergency itself. But once a judicial opinion rationalizes such an order to show that it conforms to the Constitution, or rather rationalizes the Constitution to show that the Constitution sanctions such an order, *the Court for all time has validated the principle of racial discrimination* in *criminal procedure and of transplanting American citizens. The principle then lies about like a loaded weapon, ready for the hand of any authority that can bring forward a plausible claim of an urgent need.*[51]

Understood narrowly, Jackson is highlighting a distinctively legal problem: due to the important role that legal precedent has as a basis for legal authority, a judicial opinion that limits rights in emergency situations may improperly be relied upon in normal times or under different exigent circumstances. The danger from holding the use of race in criminal procedure to be constitutional is that it creates a legal principle that "lies about like a loaded weapon." Moreover, the principle is subject to abuse—plausible claims of urgent need may be mistaken claims. There are a wide variety of potential abusers, including, for example, populist demagogues— "the hand of *any authority* that can bring forward a *plausible* claim."

But, the problem is not merely legal. Jackson is unmasking the damage caused by the perpetuation of a false veneer—the justificatory foundation of the military order (which is at root military) being falsely held out as being legal (which, per Jackson, it is not and should not be). Seen as what it is, a military order, not falsely cloaked in the legitimacy of law, the damage will be temporary—"it will last no longer than the emergency itself." Creating a false veneer subverts systemic democratic values, including the capacity of citizens to understand the nature of political action and react appropriately.

Jackson is, contra liberal legal theory, explicitly countenancing a subset of the realm of politics for non-normal exigent circumstances that is unregulated by law, a state of exception, in Agamben's terms. Military power, as instantiated in detention orders like those in *Korematsu*, according to Jackson, exists in such a realm. But, if not law, what regulates unvarnished military orders? For Jackson, as an externalist, politics, and morality. "The chief restraint upon those who command the physical forces of the country, in the future as in the past, must be their responsibility to the political judgments of their contemporaries and to the moral judgments of history."[52]

CONCLUSION—PROBLEMS WITH POST-9/11 DETENTION JURISPRUDENCE

Jackson treats the internment of persons of Japanese descent during World War II as a state of exception. His intent is to curtail the systemic political and legal damage that he believes legitimizing race-based detention orders would cause. In his judicial capacity, he explicitly countenanced a realm beyond law, based on a foundation external to law. Contra Agamben, 9/11 has not, to date, elicited a similar full-throated declaration of a state of exception. In what circumstances should it? In what respects is O'Connor's facial internalism preferable? In what ways has the jurisprudential response to 9/11 demonstrated a need to resort to extralegal justifications? It is beyond the scope of this chapter to provide a comprehensive and systematic defense of one approach. But we can highlight deficiencies. Sometimes it is easiest to say what is right by seeing what is wrong.

The Danger of Jackson's Black Hole

Some have lauded Jackson's dissent, arguing "it is better to have emergency powers exercised in an extra-constitutional way, so that everyone understands that the actions are extraordinary," than to normalize emergencies.[53] But it would not have been preferable in *Hamdi* for O'Connor to have thrown up her hands and refused to assert the role of the judiciary in protecting due process rights. Democratic government based on constitutional principles of separation of powers requires an independent and assertive judiciary. Unopposed executive detention power is the hallmark of a police state; it enshrines totalitarianism. As Justice Souter explains in his concurring opinion,

> In a government of separated powers deciding finally on what is a reasonable degree of guaranteed liberty whether in peace or war (or some condition in between) is not well entrusted to the Executive Branch of Government, whose particular responsibility is to maintain security. For reasons of inescapable human nature, the branch of Government asked to counter a serious threat is not the branch on which to rest the Nation's entire reliance in striking the balance between the will to win and cost to liberty. . . . The responsibility for security will naturally amplify the claim that security legitimately raises. A reasonable balance is more likely to be reached on the judgment of a different branch.[54]

It has not been necessary to declare a Jacksonian state of exception, to respond to the potential problem of the loaded gun or to unmask the false veneer of the Supreme Court cloaking unchecked military power in legal legitimacy. The closest we come is Justice Thomas's dissent in *Hamdi*, where, like Jackson, he asserts no role for the judiciary. As an extreme Schmittian, Thomas claims that, as a legal matter, the judiciary should *completely defer* to the executive all national security powers, including the power to declare a person to be an enemy combatant and subject to detention without charges. Judicial balancing has no place. Moreover, with respect to detaining post-9/11 terror suspects, like Hamdi, Thomas supports the executive taking action that could only be taken if the writ of habeas corpus were suspended, *but without having to suspend it*. His rationale is that even if post-9/11 terrorism does not satisfy the constitutional requirement of there being an invasion or rebellion, deferring to the military is necessary to protect the nation.[55]

If the Supreme Court's post-9/11 *majority* opinions were to adopt such excessively deferential Schmittian positions, thereby cloaking raw unchecked executive power in judicial legitimacy, invoking a Jacksonian state of exception might be warranted. The danger of the veneer of legal legitimacy is that it disrupts the potential for self-corrective democratic action. Post-9/11 detention jurisprudence has not been so extreme and veneer-laden as to make carving a path for democratic self-corrective action desirable.

The Danger of Declaring Exceptions

The Constitution includes a mechanism for suspending the habeas corpus right "in cases of Rebellion or Invasion, where the Public Safety may require it." Both O'Connor and Murphy are properly hesitant to effectively broaden the constitutional provision, extra-constitutionally as Justice Thomas in effect would. There is a tendency to overestimate the direness of an emergency to justify the need for expanded exceptions to the habeas corpus right. Sticking close to the Constitution, including its provisions on exceptions and amendments, helps to check such temptations. If Schmitt is right that he who declares the exception is the sovereign, and sovereigns in the end are not bound by rules, declaring exceptions too soon and too often threatens democracy and enables dictatorship.

A declaration of a state of exception by the executive is ripe for abuse. As U.S. presidential politics in 2016 and 2017 has shown, the risk of a political demagogue quick to discard constitutional protections in the name of "plausible claims of an urgent need" is not as remote as many had assumed. O'Connor's forceful defense of a role for the judiciary, founded on the separation of powers, constitutes a necessary bulwark against the dangers of the executive attempting to usurp unilateral detention powers.

The Benefits of Narrowness

Regarding the second part of O'Connor's opinion, the "watered down due process scheme," we noted that the narrow, fact-specific methodological foundation on which the scheme is based can be used to justify opposing conclusions and is in that sense hollow. There are also virtues of such a narrow scheme. One of the many interpretations of the maxim "great and hard cases make bad law,"[56] is that it is challenging to make general rules from extreme scenarios. Yet narrow fact-specific rulings are preferable, and for many reasons. One is that if a judicial ruling based on a finely tuned balancing calculus justifies a result that, in hindsight, appears wrong (like *Korematsu*), the precedential impact of the ruling can be minimized if subsequent courts limit the scope of the ruling to the facts and specific considerations of the balancing calculus.

If there is no constitutional basis for a general rule that detention based on race or ethnicity is impermissible, it is preferable that the holding *not* be construed broadly as a general rule (e.g., that detention based on race or ethnicity is permissible when there is a perceived threat to security). Rather, to deny *Korematsu* precedential authority, the case can be said to stand for the proposition that detention based on race is justified only in response to a factually specific threat to security that is unlikely to arise in the future. The problem with *Korematsu* is that there is no guarantee that future courts will choose to limit the scope of the holding in this way. As Bruce Ackerman said, in 2004, we hope not presciently, in light of *Korematsu* not having been overruled, "What will the Supreme Court say if Arab-Americans are herded into concentration camps? Are we certain any longer that the wartime precedent of *Korematsu* will not be extended to the 'war on terrorism?'"[57]

The Inevitability of Extralegal Considerations and the Need for Rules

But why would it be preferable to render *Korematsu powerless* as authority? On what basis would it be a *problem* if the holding were construed broadly? If using race as the basis for detention is so bad, why is there no general legal prohibition against it? Combating terrorism accentuates a deep and unavoidable conflict between liberty and security. Using normal balancing tests, and without a general rule outlawing the use of race or ethnicity as a basis or detention, if a threat to security is enormous, a threat to liberty necessary to contain the enormity of the security threat can be similarly enormous. But there is no general rule in the Constitution that outlaws the use of race or ethnicity; rather, the Constitution is tilted toward procedural rules for adjudicating conflicting values, like balancing tests and standards of what must be balanced, like compelling state interests, and standards for the review of the relation between the threat and the remedy, such as "strict scrutiny."

Therefore, the foundation for a rule that prohibits the use of race or ethnicity as a basis for detention must be extrajudicially based. Analogously, Dworkin might build an argument for more robust due process protections for terror suspects using accepted modes of legal argument and legal concepts—appeals to precedent, application of holdings from prior cases, references to the Constitution, and its legislative history. He may even attempt to apply O'Connor's own rules and standards and legal thinking, as he does. But ultimately, his difference with O'Connor on the rights a terror suspect like Hamdi is constitutionally entitled to, must rest, at least in part, on moral and political considerations outside of law.

The rule of law is in some respects superior to moral schemes—it is more objective and neutral. Moral and political considerations are, by nature more subjective and personal, less objectively justifiable. It is human nature to be tempted to choose which rules to apply and when, depending on whether their particular application favors our political or moral convictions. The rule of law necessitates subjugating one's own personal desires, moral values and political convictions to a system of rules that are affirmed prior to our knowing whether they favor a particular desired outcome, or whether in a given case, we are in the majority or the minority.[58] But ultimately, legal systems exist within, and must rely on, political and moral foundations. Nevertheless, it is often desirable to delay as long as possible admitting this. When people acknowledge that law inevitably ultimately depends on moral and political considerations, political power is asserted too soon. This may promote a premature destruction of the legal system itself.

Constitutional super-principles such as due process rights protect those in a minority (the accused) against the tyranny of majority rule. From a game theory perspective, without such super-principles, it is natural that the majority would succeed: by definition, most of the time, most people are in the majority and are therefore not subject to its tyranny. Detaining terror suspects because they are members of an ethnic or racial minority is just one example of the danger unchecked majority rule presents. As long as one cannot be assured that one will not, in some context, be in a minority (such as the accused), super-principles, like the right to due process, are valuable as a matter of rational self-interest.

But what if one can be assured that one will not be in the relevant minority? Post- 9/11 terrorism is overwhelmingly perpetuated by radical Islamic militants. It follows that the class of people who are at risk of being detained are Muslims. As Dworkin presciently put it in 2003, commenting on the balance between security and liberty, "with hardly any exceptions, no American who is not a Muslim and has no Muslim connections actually runs the risk of being labeled an enemy combatant and locked up in military jail. The only balance in question is the balance between the majority's security and *other* people's rights, and we must think about that as a matter of moral principle, not of our own self-interest."[59] Ultimately, the justification of a decision to affirm a constitutional principle prohibiting the use of race or ethnicity as the basis for detention is a moral one. In Justice Jackson's words, the chief restraint upon us "must be our responsibility to the political judgments of our contemporaries and to the moral judgments of history."

POSTSCRIPT

Constitutional Limitations

Terrorism, as we have come to know it in the fifteen years since 9/11, uproots many assumptions about emergencies: it is not temporary, so justifications of exceptions based on restoring normalcy fit poorly. As experienced to date, terrorism has not called into question the viability of the state itself. Harm to public safety has been quantitatively circumscribed. Exceptions that might be justified on existential grounds, such as defending the state itself, would be overkill. On the other hand, the possibility of cataclysmic harm caused by radical Islamic terrorists (whether al-Qaeda, ISIS, or some future variant) to the Western world is omnipresent. The concern that terrorists gain access to, and use, weapons of mass destruction (WMD)—nuclear, radiological, chemical, or biological—is very real. While ascertaining how close terrorists are to gaining access to WMD is rife with uncertainty, the magnitude of possible destruction is not. Multiplying an uncertain number by a very large number creates confusion, making balancing state security and individual liberty, and tailoring adaptations internal to the Constitution, uniquely difficult.

The problem is compounded if we consider the vulnerability of our constitutional democracy itself to less potent weapons, like commercial airplanes acting as giant guided missiles. As Lawrence Tribe and Patrick Gudridge point out, "Should terrorists ever succeed in doing what the September 11 hijackers evidently intended to do, and hit the Capitol or the Supreme Court while Congress or the Court is in session, it doesn't take a world-class imagination to read the Constitution and figure out that, unfortunately, the document offers only an incomplete blueprint for what comes next."[60] In the first few years after 9/11 this unique quagmire gave rise to commentary in the academic legal community on the need to amend or supplement the Constitution. Tribe and Gudridge reference the bi-partisan work of the Continuity of Government Commission (CGC) on constitutional amendments to address governmental succession issues. The CGC issued three reports and dissolved in 2011.

Unlike constitutions of other democracies, the U.S Constitution's mechanism for declaring a state of exception is limited both in the emergencies it enumerates and in the procedures it enunciates for addressing them. Bruce Ackerman's *The Emergency Constitution*[61] is the most prominent attempt to address the limitations of the Suspension Clause. Like Schmitt, Ackerman believes that that the emergency circumstances posed by terrorism post-9/11, are not adequately addressed by the Constitution. His particular response is to design a separate, supplemental Emergency Constitution that expands governmental power (authorizing widespread preventive detention) but that has built-in, self-limiting and self-executing rule-bound processes, intended to bolster civil liberties in the long run by making the Emergency Constitution temporary and subordinate to the normal Constitution. The project can be seen as an attempt to fill in the legal gap that Jackson leaves behind in *Korematsu* with an extra-constitutional legal scheme. Ackerman in effect resists Schmitt's claim that the justification for the imposition of exceptions to normal legal rules must be extralegal.[62] At first glance, Ackerman's intricately designed procedural mechanisms (with super-majoritarian escalator clauses intended to increasingly limit the duration of the extra-constitutional scheme) appear like the product of an informal brainstorming session. It is enlightening and surprising to learn that many aspects of Ackerman's scheme are modeled on the actual constitutions of countries like Germany, South Africa, and Canada. The modern German Constitution, for example, was designed in response to the catastrophic role that the Weimar Constitution played in the Nazi ascent to power.

Ackerman's particular proposal may or may not be efficacious in enabling the government to fight terrorism with unconstitutional tactics short-term, while protecting civil rights long-term. But, insofar as Ackerman's Emergency Constitution attempts to respond to the unique challenges that post-9/11 terrorism presents, it prompts us to consider whether the Constitution itself needs to be amended or supplemented with a more fulsome, extra-constitutional, but legal scheme.

NOTES

1. An acronym standing for "Uniting and Strengthening America by Providing Appropriate Tools Required to Intercept and Obstruct Terrorism Act."

2. For a full-length description and analysis of the PATRIOT Act, see Kim Lane Scheppele, "Law in a Time of Emergency: States of Exception and the Temptations of 9/11," *Journal of Constitutional Law* 6, no. 5 (2004): 1034–47.

3. Giorgio Agamben, *State of Exception*, trans. Kevin Attell (Chicago: The University of Chicago Press, 2005).

4. Based on Schmitt's theory, there is more than one type of dictatorship. If the suspender's justification is the defense of the constitutional scheme itself, to which the emergency is a threat, commissarial dictatorship is the result. If the threat that constitutes the state of emergency is to the sovereign itself, the result is a pure dictatorship. The dictatorship that has its roots in the Weimar Constitution is commissarial, at least to begin.

5. Oren Gross, "The Normless and Exceptionless Exception: Carl Schmitt's Theory of Emergency Powers and the 'Norm-Exception Dichotomy'" *Cardozo Law Review* 21 (2000): 1825.

6. Ibid. (See footnote 23, which provides empirical support for the claim about expansion of emergency regimes, with statistics on the number of countries operating under states of emergency.)

7. Agamben, *State of Exception*, 23.

8. Agamben, *State of Exception*, 23.

9. Agamben, *State of Exception*, 51.

10. Stephen Humphreys, "Legalizing Lawlessness: On Giorgio Agamben's *State of Exception*," *The European Journal of International Law* 17, no. 3 (2006): 677.

11. Agamben, *State of Exception*, 3–4.

12. Humphreys, "Legalizing Lawlessness," 684. "The place— both logical and pragmatic—of a theory of exception in the American constitution is in the dialectic between the powers of the president and those of Congress."

13. "The privilege of the Writ of Habeas Corpus shall not be suspended, unless when in Cases of Rebellion or Invasion, the public Safety may require it." U.S. Const. Art. I, §9, cl.2.

14. Agamben, *State of Exception*, 19–21.

15. 17 F. Cas 144, 151–52 (CD Md. 1861). The dominant historical view of *Merryman* is that President Lincoln defied the Chief Justice's judicial order. But see Randy Barnett, "Did President Lincoln Defy a Court Order by Chief Justice Taney," *Washington Post*, October 8, 2016, highlighting Seth Barrett Tillman's emerging minority view, that Lincoln's actions were ambiguous.

16. Agamben, *State of Exception*, 7. "One of the essential characteristics of the state of exception . . . [is] the provisional abolition of the distinction among legislative, executive *and judicial powers*" (emphasis added).

17. *Hamdi v. Rumsfeld* 542 U.S. 2–3 (2004) (plurality opinion).

18. Ibid., 8.

19. Ibid., 10.

20. Ibid., 26.

21. Ibid., 29 (citing *Youngstown Sheet & Tube*, 343 U.S. 587).

22. This is an example of the constitutional principle of judicial review *Marbury v Madison* 5 U.S. 137 (1803).

23. *Hamdi*, note 17, 25 (citing *Kennedy v Mendoza-Martinez*, 372 U.S. 144, 164–65 (1963)). "The imperative necessity for safeguarding these rights to procedural due process under the gravest of emergencies has existed throughout our constitutional history, for it is then, under the pressing exigencies of crisis, that there is the greatest temptation to dispense with guarantees which, it is feared, will inhibit government

action" (internal quotes omitted) and *United States v. Robel*, 389 U.S. 258, 264 (1967).

24. Ibid., 30. "Unless Congress acts to suspend it, the Great Writ of habeas corpus allows the Judicial Branch to play a necessary role in maintaining this delicate balance of governance, serving as an important judicial check on the Executive's discretion in the realm of detentions. See St. Cyr, 533 U.S., at 301 . . . The writ of habeas corpus has served as a means of reviewing the legality of Executive detention, and it is in that context that its protections have been strongest."

25. U.S. Const. Art. I, §9, cl.2.
26. *Hamdi*, 22.
27. Ibid., 6–7 (Souter J., concurring).
28. Ibid., 25.
29. See for example, Ronald Dworkin, "What the Court Really Said," *NY Review of Books*, August 12, 2004 and Sanford Levinson, "Constitutional Norms in a State of Permanent Emergency," *Georgia Law Review* 40, no. 3 (2006), 699, 747. Justice Scalia is similarly critical. To curtail Hamdi's due process rights, Congress has to have suspended the writ of habeas corpus. "If civil rights are to be curtailed during wartime, it must be done openly and democratically, as the Constitution requires, rather than by silent erosion through an opinion of this Court." *Hamdi*, 26 (Scalia, J., dissenting).
30. *Hamdi*, note 17, 26 (emphasis added).
31. Ibid., 26.
32. Dworkin, "What the Court Really Said," 3.
33. Ronald Dworkin, "Terror and the Attack on Civil Liberties," *The New York Review of Books*, November 6, 2003.
34. Dworkin, "What the Court Really Said."
35. Ibid. and Ronald Dworkin, "Why It Was a Great Victory," *The New York Review of Books*, August 14, 2008.
36. Dworkin, "Terror and the Attack on Civil Liberties."
37. Dworkin, "What the Court Really Said," 6.
38. Ibid.
39. Dworkin, "Terror and the Attack on Civil Liberties," 6–8, 11, 13.
40. Dworkin, "What the Court Really Said," 7.
41. Ibid., 6 (emphasis added).
42. Dworkin, "Why It Was a Great Victory."
43. Ibid., 4 (emphasis added).
44. *Hamdi*, note 17, 29.
45. *Korematsu v. United States* 323 U.S. 214, 235 (Murphy, J., dissenting) (1944).
46. Ibid., 242.
47. *Korematsu v. United States* 323 U.S. 214, 220 (1944).
48. Ibid. at 216; Ibid. at 240 (Murphy, J., dissenting).
49. Dworkin, "Terror and the Attack on Civil Liberties," 5.
50. *Korematsu v. United States* 323 U.S. 214, 244 (Jackson, J., dissenting) (1944).
51. Ibid. (emphasis added).
52. Ibid., 244–45.

53. Mark Tushnet, "Defending Korematsu? Reflections on Civil Liberties in Wartime," *Wisconsin Law Review* (2003): 273, 306.
54. *Hamdi*, 7 (Souter, J., concurring).
55. *Hamdi*, 1, 7–8, 12, 16 (Thomas, J., dissenting).
56. *Northern Securities Co. v. United States*, 193 U.S. 197,400 (1904) (Holmes, J., dissenting).
57. Bruce Ackerman, "The Emergency Constitution," *Yale Law Journal* 113, no. 5 (2003): 1043. (See footnote 31 on the nature and status of the legal criticism.) Note that the precise legal status of *Korematsu* changed since this paper was initially submitted for publication. On June 26, 2018 the Supreme Court handed down the "Travel Ban" decision, *Trump v. Hawaii* 585 U.S. __ (2018) holding that the Executive Order prohibiting persons from predominately Muslim countries from entering the United States was within the president's authority and did not violate the Constitution's Establishment Clause. The case raises anew the question as to whether *Korematsu* has been overruled or repeated. Justice Sotomayor, in dissent, likens the Court's reasoning to that in *Korematsu*, invoking a national security threat to justify an exclusionary policy motivated by animus against a religious group, re-raising Ackerman's concern (slip op at 26). Chief Justice Roberts, writing for the Court, responded: "Whatever rhetorical advantage the dissent may see in [invoking *Korematsu*] *Korematsu* has *nothing to do with this case*. . . . The dissent . . . affords this Court the opportunity to make express what is already obvious: *Korematsu* was gravely wrong the day it was decided, has been overruled *in the court of history*, and—to be clear—*'has no place in law under the Constitution.'*" (emphasis added; quoting Jackson's *Korematsu* dissent, slip op at 38.) Whether that constitutes "overruling" is a matter of debate. In an odd twist, Justice Sotomayor construed those words to constitute overruling: "Today the Court takes the important step of finally overruling *Korematsu*, denouncing it as 'gravely wrong the day it was decided'" (slip op at 28). But, Roberts's opinion did not explicitly overrule *Korematsu* as *having precedential legal authority* which is the essence of what it means for a case to be overruled. Roberts says the case has been overruled "in the court of history," not in the Supreme Court. Moreover, disagreeing with Sotomayor, Roberts says that the "morally repugnant order" in *Korematsu* is unlike the "facially neutral policy denying certain nationals the privilege of admission" (slip op at 38). Saying that *Korematsu* "has no place in law under the Constitution," comes closest to denying *Korematsu*'s precedential authority, as Roberts is telling future litigants not to cite *Korematsu* as justification for a national security policy that discriminates on the basis of race or religion. Still, Roberts's rejection of *Korematsu* is best understood as dicta—a statement of opinion or pronouncement of a rule by a court that is *not necessary the court's actual ruling*, and, therefore, not as overruling *Korematsu*. Specifically, the Court's rejection of *Korematsu* was not necessary to its ruling upholding the Executive Order.
58. Of course, perhaps the most comprehensive and compelling political theory of justice of the twentieth century is built on a similar procedure—a single social contractor, choosing rules to govern the basic structure of society from the "original position" behind a "veil of ignorance," not knowing his or her particular characteristics—class

position, fortune, or the results of the natural lottery. John Rawls, *A Theory of Justice* (Cambridge, MA: Harvard University Press, 1971).

59. Dworkin, "Terror and the Attack on Civil Liberties," 5.

60. Lawrence H. Tribe and Patrick O. Gudridge, "The Anti-Emergency Constitution," *Yale Law Journal* 113 no. 8 (2004): 1801, 1839 (a response to Ackerman's *The Emergency Constitution, Op. cit.*, note 57).

61. Ackerman, note 57.

62. For Ackerman's Emergency Constitution to itself not be unconstitutional, it would need to either fit within the Suspension Clause's rebellion-invasion-public safety provision, or be adopted as a constitutional amendment.

BIBLIOGRAPHY

Ackerman, Bruce. "The Emergency Constitution." *Yale Law Journal* 113, no. 5 (2003): 1029–1091.

Agamben, Giorgio. *State of Exception*. Translated by Kevin Attell. Chicago: The University of Chicago Press, 2005.

Barnett, Randy. "Did President Lincoln defy a court order by Chief Justice Taney," *Washington Post*, October 8, 2016.

Dworkin, Ronald. "Terror and the Attack on Civil Liberties," *The New York Review of Books*, November 6, 2003.

———. "What the Court Really Said," *The New York Review of Books*, August 12, 2004.

———. "Why it was a Great Victory," *The New York Review of Books*, August 14, 2008.

Gross, Oren. "The Normless and Exceptionless Exception: Carl Schmitt's Theory of Emergency Powers and the 'Norm-Exception Dichotomy.'" *Cardozo Law Review* 21 (2000): 1825.

Humphreys, Stephen. "Legalizing Lawlessness: On Giorgio Agamben's *State of Exception*." *The European Journal of International Law* 17, no. 3 (2006): 677.

Levinson, Sanford. "Constitutional Norms in a State of Permanent Emergency." *Georgia Law Review* 40, no. 3 (2006): 699-752.

Rawls, John. *A Theory of Justice*. Cambridge, MA: Harvard University Press, 1971.

Scheppele, Kim Lane. "Law in a Time of Emergency: States of Exception and the Temptations of 9/11." *University of Pennsylvania Journal of Constitutional Law* 6, no. 5 (2004): 1001-1083.

Schmitt, Carl. *Political Theology: Four Chapters on the Concept of Sovereignty*, George Schwab, trans. Cambridge, MA: MIT Press, 1985.

Tribe, Lawrence and Patrick O. Gudridge. "The Anti-Emergency Constitution." *Yale Law Journal* 113, no. 8 (2004): 1801-1870.

Tushnet, Mark. "Defending Korematsu? Reflections on Civil Liberties in Wartime." *Wisconsin Law Review* (2003): 273-307.

Cases

Ex Parte Merryman 17 F. Cas 144 (CD Md. 1861).
Hamdi v. Rumsfeld 542 U.S. 507 (2004).
Korematsu v. United States 323 U.S. 214 (1944).
Northern Securities Co. v. United States, 193 U.S. 197,400 (1904).

Chapter 18

Swords of Damocles

An Essay on Catastrophe and Globalization

Pedro Geiger

This chapter will develop the relation between catastrophe and the present era of globalization. The Greek myth of Damocles' sword represents the ominous threat of permanent destruction of the planet. We will look at impending global catastrophes in terms of the impending threats of nuclear conflagration, ecological disaster, and economic breakdown. These three threats recall the myth of the three beggars announcing the Apocalypse[1] representing suffering, pain, and despair, a subject represented in the 2009 film *The Antichrist*.[2] We will also discuss the role of contingency in human affairs, how this relates to the threats currently facing the planet, and whether our present age calls for an attitude of pessimism, optimism, or some middle ground between the two.

WAR AND THE NEW TECHNOLOGIES

World War II was the first manifestation of "globalization," as for the first time in history we witnessed an event where all of humanity was involved, battling on all seas and on almost all the Earth's lands. World War II caused the deaths of more than 60,000,000 people and an amount of material destruction calculated in trillions of dollars. It was the overarching catastrophe of the 20th century.

The relation between the catastrophe of World War II and our current globalized situation lies in the new technologies developed during the war, which introduced a faster rhythm in all social practices that supported the globalization movement. The war began without a formal declaration, for example, the invasion of Poland in 1939 and the Pearl Harbor attack on December 7, 1941. The initial attack was followed by the blitzkrieg in which cities and civilian populations become military targets. The conceptions of "preventive wars" and of "just wars" were thus ideas created only recently. Among the inventions made during the war, one may count the computer, radar, turbo and jet airplanes, atomic energy, antibiotics, and others.

At the end of the war in the Pacific in summer 1945, there occurred a monumental event: the dropping of atomic bombs on Japan, on Hiroshima (August 6) and Nagasaki (August 9). Each Japanese city received only one bomb, yet this single bomb not only totally razed each city, killing almost all its population of about 80,000, but left a completely radiated environment destroying all life for years to come.

After the war, the USSR built its own atomic bombs. The United States and the USSR, involved in a competition for world hegemony which took the form of a *cold war*, also developed their capacities for dropping the A bomb by way of ballistic vehicles. They also developed the nuclear hydrogen bomb (which explodes by fusion, as the A bomb explodes by fission) and the nuclear neutron bomb. There now exists a number of countries with nuclear capacity. Beside the United States and Russia, one can count England, France, Israel, North Korea, China, India, and Pakistan.

Because a mere fraction of the world's present atomic weapons could destroy the entire planet, the atomic weapon became an effective deterrent between the great world powers. During the 1961 Cuban Missile Crisis, when American president John F. Kennedy threatened to take out the atomic missiles posed in Cuba, the world witnessed the most extreme possibility of World War III. However, Nikita Khruschev, the Soviet leader, blinked first, and the threat was removed.

We have since seen a sequence of measures orchestrated by the United States and by the former Soviet Union, which continue today with Russia, seeking to avoid nuclear war. These measures include agreements controlling the number of atomic weapons and ballistic missiles held by the two powers, and actions taken by them through the Organization of the United Nations to prohibit new atomic tests and to stop the proliferation of atomic capacities. An international treaty between nation states was created—the "nonproliferation" treaty—which involves collaboration of the nuclear powers toward developing peaceful uses for nuclear energy.

While some catastrophes present the "end of the line" for the involved countries or civilizations, as happened with Pompeii during ancient times, in the present globalized era, new technologies allow for quicker recoveries. By the end of the 20th century, Japan, which was hit by two A bombs, and Germany, also routed in World War II, appear as major world powers as measured by their gross domestic product. China is now joining Russia and the United States as a military superpower and has reached second place in GDP; which indicates the contemporary value for the countries of their geographic scale in area and population. The current GDP is estimated in 17 trillion dollars for the United States, 11 trillion for China, 5 trillion for Japan, and 4 trillion for Germany.

The Damocles' sword of nuclear conflagration has lessened since the years of the *Cold War* (1946 to 1991), raising the level of optimism about the outbreak of a new world war. It could be argued that a policy of shared nuclear deterrence has forestalled a predicted World War III, though there were other relevant reasons as well, such as a higher political consciousness within civilian national societies. In any case, while the danger of a direct military confrontation between the nuclear powers seems to have lessened, the danger now lies in the multiplication of armed conflicts between, or inside, the less powerful countries and their capacity to involve the big powers. The current multiplication of local armed conflicts, as in the Middle East, and the rise and spread of terrorism around the world is thus now again raising the Damocles' sword over our global civilization. At the time of this writing, a new threat has emerged and has brought with it new and pronounced dangers. North Korea has been working feverishly to develop and test nuclear weapons and intercontinental ballistic missiles. The United States and North Korea have been involved in increased episodes of saber rattling, use of threatening language, military drills, and so on. The outcome of all this is still unclear and frightening as well, owing to a number of radical contingencies. But what exactly is the nature of the relationship between causality and contingency, and how does it make itself manifest in dark times?

CAUSALITY AND CONTINGENCY

It is difficult to present a definite cause for the eruption of catastrophes, because while there certainly are objective conditions of causes and effects, human reactions to these conditions can vary, and it is sometimes challenging to sort out these objective and subjective factors. Consider again World War II and its aftermath. A Marxist interpretation might have considered the war as an objective determination of the capitalist system. The destruction of people and goods would solve the problems of overpopulation and overproduction, by reestablishing the equilibrium between supply and demand, and by reducing unemployment. But during the *Cold War*, while the world feared World War III as a consequence, this disaster never occurred. This is because the relevant leaders of that time, for a number of reasons, were not inclined in that direction. But it could have been otherwise if other leaders had been in power. Neo-Marxist thinking added new theories of *determination* and *dominance*[3] through which the eruption of war could further be interpreted. According to this doctrine, history is guided by these movements.

Determination, implying a relation between causes and effects, is expressed in actions of objective forces, as in the formation of merchandise values; while dominance includes the subjective choices of men that leads to contingencies, such as the formation of prices.

Contingency can also be observed with regard to natural occurrences. For instance: heat causes evaporation from the ocean and the formation of clouds, which produce rain. However, often the sky fills up with clouds, and people leave their homes with umbrellas, but the rain does not fall. Economic and political crises were objective causal conditions for World War II, but its eruption originated from the Nazi leaders' decisions, a human contingency. It could have happened the way it did, or otherwise, depending on whom was in power at the time.

The accumulation of causes may indicate strong tendencies in a particular direction, but the human creative capacity of opening new *clearings* [4] and making new choices can dissipate these tendencies and offer new possibilities. It is easier to preview causal effects then to preview contingency options, as the latter depend upon subjective factors and the complex vagaries of human nature. One sees the dangers of the catastrophes facing us, as in the case of the global warming—the scientific conditions are objective, but one for a number of reasons cannot predict the human social capacity to solve these problems.

THE ENVIRONMENTAL CRISIS

We now turn to the Damocles' sword of global environmental degradation. The Earth has always been exposed to natural environmental cycles. There have been ages of glaciations and ages of warming, and the current period constitutes a moment of warming; this has been accompanied both by the marked melting of glaciers and the elevation of sea levels. During the remote past the continents formed a united space and they were separated by sea elevation. One theory regarding the human settlement of America considers a migration from Asia when it was possible to cross by foot through the area now called the Bering Strait. The Earth's warming now also contains a human component, responsible for an acceleration of the process, confirmed by data measurements during the last decades. It is represented by the emission in the atmosphere of dioxide of CO_2 and of methanol (CH_4), which provoke a *stove effect*. The reader can find long and increasing lists of scholarly sources indicating the mean temperature average rising over lands and oceans.[5] The current warming is documented by meteorological measures and observed effects of the continuous melting of the North Pole glacier cover and the invasion of ocean waters over the continents. The annual average temperature rose almost 1 degree Centigrade, between 1880 and 2012.

A set of political measures have been undertaken favoring *clean* sources of energy that do not provoke the emission of gases mentioned above, which occurs with fossil combustibles such as coal and oil. Clean energy is energy obtained from waterfalls, tides, winds, the sun, and so on, also identified as energies produced by *renewable resources,* thus avoiding those elements vulnerable to eventual depletion. This is in fact another face of the environmental crisis—the possibility of the depletion of nonrenewal resources due to the acceleration of their exploration by the current economy. But the use of clean energy sources does not exempt the user from taking a number of safety precautions, for example, when handling nuclear reactors. A disaster such as occurred in Chernobyl, Ukraine, killed thousands and left a large region inhabitable for dozens of years.

In the case of creating huge deepwater reservoirs for the production of electricity, two kinds of problems have been also created, one environmental and the other social. The creation of a big lake implies displacing the former residents of this area. New technologies are now being introduced which consist of capturing energy from the flow of large rivers with new kinds of generators, acting at their surface, without waterfalls, barrages, and reservoirs.[6]

The environmental crisis, in the same way as some of the aforementioned wars, brought a collective orchestrated reaction, uniting the world's countries through formal written agreements. This increase of governmental responsibilities regarding the environment resulted from strong pressures inside national civilian societies, where a new kind of organization appeared and multiplied in current times, nongovernmental organizations, or NGOs. The NGOs also play an important role as civilian campaigns resulting from wars or economic disasters. They favor international peace, help for refugees of local wars and their acceptance as immigrants, for example, by European countries when refugees fled from the Middle East and Africa because of war or economic reasons.

In Rio de Janeiro, in 1992, the United Nations Convention of Climatic Changes was established. Later, in Kyoto, Japan, a protocol was established fixing goals for countries regarding gas emissions, but it was never ratified by the United States or China. In December 2015, in Paris, fifty-five of the most powerful and influential countries produced the Paris Treaty, replacing the Kyoto Protocol. This time the United States and China already ratified the agreement and other nations are doing the same at a pace faster than before. One of the goals is to limit the present warming to less than 2 degrees Celsius.

A number of developments thus express the collaborative world effort to deal with environmental degradation. During the first part of 2016 alone, China installed impressive 20.000 MW capacity of electricity through solar generation, and the United States started production of a new kind of wider batteries. Can such collective global measures ultimately stem the time of current environmental crisis? Should we be optimistic or pessimistic about the state of the environment and its future? Human behavior gives us reasons for both attitudes. Can nations rise about their seemingly endless conflicts with each other and cooperate on larger issues like the environment for the greater good of the planet? This is a question about human nature and the answer remains to be seen.

ECONOMIC AND FINANCIAL CATASTROPHES

One may also include severe economic recessions as catastrophes, as they involve heavy losses of capital and high levels of unemployment, which in turn impact millions in the labor force. Such a depression in current times started in 2008, beginning in the United States, as a financial crisis impacting the housing sector spread over the world, and remained until 2012.

The financial crises in the housing sector began when the Federal Reserve elevated basic interest taxes. The costs of paying for houses became much higher than their market value and the owners became unable to pay their debts. In the capitalist system the goods not paid return to the bank, which sells it to another client. But with the amount of houses returned there was no way to circulate the capital. On the other side, the business of housing, as all the other sectors, was linked to the system of *derivatives* introduced by the *neoliberal* economy. The system of derivatives consists of speculative games, in which people were betting against the betting of other people, over the price trajectories of all kinds of goods, currencies, gold, wheat, houses, and so on. Thus the crisis in the housing sector affected the derivative sector, the banks, and quickly, as a domino effect, impacted economic systems around the world.

The reaction to this catastrophe differed from that following the 1929 crash of the Wall Street stock market. Then, each country tried in its own way to escape from the Depression. Franklin Roosevelt in the United States faced the crisis by introducing the *Social Security* system and a number of regional planning efforts, such as the Tennessee Valley Agency. Under Hitler, Germany turned to the rebuilding of the weapons industry that animated the steel sector (and others) and by conquering territories and their goods. In our current globalized times, the 2008 Depression triggered increasing international cooperation to face the crisis in an integrated way. A special role was played by China, which had started a growth cycle founded in a planned economy.

The need for a collective and articulated state action to fight recession increased the role of the G20, a group of the world's wealthiest states, founded in 1999, which started to replace the functions of the older G7+1. The G7+1, instituted after the Cold War and before China's growth, united the seven richest countries, the United States, Japan, Germany, France, the

United Kingdom, Italy, Canada, and Russia. The G20, installed in 1999, included the same countries, plus China, India, México, Brazil, Argentina, Turkey, Saudi Arabia, South Africa, South Korea, Indonesia, Australia, and a representative for Europe as a whole. Since then the collective lost Russia and a European representative, but added other countries—Egypt, Nigeria, Chile, Philippines. Currently the so-called G20 represents 85 percent of the world GDP and two-third of the world population. The 2016 conference was held in September, in China.

Thus, the state of the present economy is constantly monitored and controlled by collective, international actions. However other political drives may intervene negatively in the patterns of the global economy. This tension reflects the role of contingency in human affairs and thus renders outcomes difficult to predict. In the European Union the introduction of a unified currency, the euro, was not accompanied by unified budget obligations for the member countries, which lost the capacity of setting a value of their money, now actually in the hand of a European Central Bank. The United Kingdom, having maintained its pound, saw the country decide by a miscalculated national referendum in 2016 to exit the European Union.

The oil markets also present a contradictory picture. There is a general positive feeling about the decline of the use of oil, based in part upon the global desire to replace fossil fuels with renewal sources of energy. On the other hand, the fall of oil prices presents contradictory results, negatively affecting countries and producers, yet positively affecting consumers. One might say that in the long term this kind of situation is positive, but in the short term it leaves contradictory effects in Middle East politics.

The most dangerous economic Damocles' sword today, however, is the growing inequality of wealth distribution in the world's most developed countries. In the United States, estimates are that 10 percent of its population owns 50 percent of the monetary goods, the same as the other 90 percent of the population. This issue recently received recently attention in the studies of the French economist Thomas Piketty who considers not only income distribution, but also the role of inherited wealth in its statistics of social distribution.[7] The problem of skewed income and wealth distribution may bring economic troubles not only inside the system, but may also hasten political change, most likely accompanied by violence, if history is to be considered a reliable guide.

CONCLUSION

The three swords of Damocles of the postmodern era appear in the form of threats of world war, a world economic disaster, and extreme planetary warming. In the face of these threats have come preventive measures taken by nations and by international organizations, under growing pressure from world civilian societies. Those social, national, and international movements are also directed to help vulnerable populations located in areas already hit by the abovementioned calamities. This raises larger questions about human nature itself: Are human beings naturally cooperative, or are they hardwired for conflict? Or both? This question has been debated for centuries.

Throughout history, the human race has sought hope of redemption, arising from many different sources. Some of these sources include biblical prophecies about a time of peace between nations, with swords being replaced by ploughshares; or by the idea of the Greek Olympic Games, which were peaceful competitions between the Greek cities, often at war otherwise. During modernity, these kinds of discourses and actions took international forms. After World War I came the installment of the League of Nations, renewed as the United Nations Organization, UNO, after World War II. The Olympiad Games were also reestablished after the mentioned wars.

The formal political sessions of the UNO occur in closed rooms, *spaces of representation*[8] gathering national politicians in power by vote or by force, while the Olympic Games occur in a variety of open and closed spaces, *lived spaces (idem)*, with people competing by their merits. To watch the Olympic Games, the public has to pay, which means a formal direct involvement with their ideology. Televised transmission, in real time, of events of international interest, such as the sessions of the Security Council of the UNO, or of the Olympic competitions, is a contemporary phenomenon that characterizes the cultural side of globalization. In postmodern times, culture became the "strategy of the late capitalism,"[9] and all historical events are transformed into spectacles. Catastrophes have also become spectacles.

At the same time, however, new technologies, having developed the ideographic language—the others being the verbal and the quantitative[10]—are offering the possibility of creating stronger synergetic effects for efforts to prevent catastrophes. The importance acquired by visual information was well observed during the sequence of catastrophes related to the Vietnam War. When a nude Vietnamese girl appeared in front of the TV camera, horribly burned by napalm, this picture accelerated the clamor around the world and especially inside the United States, demanding an end to the war, which actually occurred shortly thereafter. One may suppose that if TV had existed during World War II, it would performed a similar role and that the Holocaust, if watched on real time, would have been stopped before the murder of so many millions.

New technologies however, have always reflected aspects of dialectical contingency. They may produce redemptive effects, or, on the contrary, introduce disasters, as in riots. The use of atomic energy is viewed as a form of using clean energy, but in Chernobyl, Ukraine it ended in a tragedy, when the reactor started to melt. The question lies in the human difficulty of driving the synthesis only to a positive end. Freud described this dialectic in terms of the drives of Eros and Thanatos coexisting inside the human psyche forever.[11]

During the period known as "modernity," enormous scientific and technological progress together with social revolutions, exalted the power of human reasoning based in mathematical language. This reinforced an optimistic belief in the human capacity to guide civilization to a positive end. Yet many of the developments analyzed in this chapter do not suggest an optimistic conclusion. It is necessary to strike a balanced approach to the future, between the moods of optimism and pessimism.

Artists, the first to signal the changes of human moods, have since the last quarter of the past century brought new styles breaking the lines of modernity. Postmodernity emphasizes the melting of the different historical ages into a whole complexity, the absence of symmetries, the coexistence of perfections and of errors.[12] An extraordinary film, *Adieu*, deals with the current dialectic of optimism versus pessimism.[13] The French word *adieu* is composed by a, to, and *dieu*, God, and means goodbye—goodbye for a moment, for a long period, or forever. In the film the word adieu appears in some moments entire, in others divided, representing the dialectic of continuous aggregations, or constructions, and of deconstructions of the world. Catastrophes express form of deconstruction.

Meantime, one witnesses the human adventure of developing interplanetary flights and planning the colonization of the moon and of the planet Mars. There is not a direct relation between the origins of this adventure and the world's existing catastrophic menaces, but future human settlement of other planets could be one of the weapons for maintaining human survival in the face of overwhelming catastrophe. Another planet may thus become a new Noah's ark.

NOTES

1. 2, Peter, 3:10.
2. Lars von Trier, *The Anti-Christ*, directed by Lars von Trier (Denmark, Germany, France, Sweden, Italy, Poland: Zentropa Entertainment, 2009).
3. See Alain Badiou and Louis Althusser *Materialismo Histórico e Materialismo Dialético* (São Paulo: Global Editorial Distribuidora, 1979).
4. Martin Heidegger, *Tempo e Ser*, I Parte, 4ª edição (Petrópolis, BR: Vozes, 1993).
5. See King's College *Select Bibliography of Books on Global Warming* (Cambridge, UK: Cambridge University Press, 2013).

6. Rolf Sternberg, "Hydropower's Future, the Environment, and Global Electricity Systems," *Renewable and Sustainable Energy Reviews* 14, no. 2 (2010): 713–23.

7. Thomas Piketti, *Capital in the Twenty First Century* (Cambridge, MA: Harvard University Press, 2014).

8. Henri Lefebvre, *La Production de L'Espace* (Paris: Anthropos, 1974).

9. Frederic Jameson, *Pós Modernismo, a lógica cultural do capitalismo tardio* (São Paulo: Áttica, 1996).

10. Paul Valery, *Introdução ao Método Leonardo da Vinci* (São Paulo: Editora 34, 1998).

11. Sigmund Freud, *O mal estar da cultura, Vol. XXI: Obras Completas* (Rio de Janeiro: Imago, 1975).

12. Robert Atkins, *Art Speak* (New York: Abbeville Press, 1990).

13. Jean-Luc Godard, *Adieu au Langage*. Directed by Jean-Luc Godard (France: Wild Bunch, 2014).

BIBLIOGRAPHY

Atkins, Robert. *Art Speak*. New York: Abbeville Press, 1990.

Badiou, Alain, and Louis Althusser. *Materialismo Histórico e Materialismo Dialético*. São Paulo: Global Editorial Distribuidora, 1979.

Fleischer, Richard, Kinji Fukusaku, and Toshio Masudo (Directors). *Tora! Tora! Tora!* USA and Japan: 20th Century Fox, 1970.

Freud, Sigmund. *O mal estar da cultura*, volume XXI, *Obras Completas*. Rio de Janeiro: Imago, 1975.

Goddard, Jean-Luc. *Adieu au Langage*. Directed by Jean-Luc Godard. France: Wild Bunch, 2014.

Heidegger, Martin. *Tempo e Ser*, I Parte, 4ª edição. Petrópolis, BR: Vozes, 1993.

Jameson, Frederic. *Pós Modernismo, a lógica cultural do capitalismo tardio*. São Paulo: Áttica, 1996.

King's College. *Select Bibliography of Books on Global Warming*. Cambridge, UK: Cambridge University Press, 2013.

Lefebvre, Henri. *La Production de L`Espace*. Paris: Anthropos, 1974.

Piketti, Thomas. *Capital in the Twenty First Century*. Cambridge, MA: Harvard University Press, 2014.

Sternberg, Rolf. "Hydropower's future, the environment, and global electricity systems." *Renewable and Sustainable Energy Reviews* 14, no. 2 (2010): 713-723.

Valery, Paul. *Introdução ao Método Leonardo da Vinci*. São Paulo: editora 34, 1998.

von Trier, Lars. *The Anti-Christ*. Directed by Lars von Trier. Denmark, Germany, France, Sweden, Italy, Poland: Zentropa Entertainment, 2009.

Part VI

CONCLUSION

Concluding Postscript

COPING WITH CATASTROPHE: DEVELOPING PATHWAYS TOWARD RESILIENCE

Hopefully the reader will view this book not merely in terms of the individual papers contained within, but also in more holistic, cumulative terms. The book details many different responses thinkers have offered in the wake of catastrophe over many times and places. But can we find any commonalities among all these responses? We have seen, for example, how Voltaire proposed a kind of fatalistic withdrawal as the response to catastrophe, while Machiavelli proposed a more assertive, political reaction. Boccaccio wrote a cautionary tale describing a descent into nihilism in times of plague, while others advocated a return to traditional values to provide a needed sense of stability. Some Holocaust writers like Borowski and Celan suggested that silence is the only authentic response we can give to a catastrophe so far reaching that it lies beyond the realm of linguistic and rational understanding.

All these thinkers reacted to different catastrophic situations in different ways, but perhaps one commonality among the responses is that no one response can ultimately be adequate to the task. All of these responses in their own way are attempts to render intelligible particular aspects of the world and of human existence that may be (or may have to remain to us) simply unintelligible. This may even constitute a paradox of philosophy itself. Sense-making is what human beings, as rational animals, are somehow "programmed to do." We try to make sense out of the world as best we can, given all the information we have at our disposal at the time and the limitations of our finite minds, but we are often left with more questions than answers. Some might find this frustrating or futile; others might find it humbling or even strangely liberating. In any case, aporia in the face of life's most difficult questions is a large part of what it means to be human.

Given the foregoing, is there a way we can learn to develop a perspective of resilience and hope regarding life's negative events, rather than falling into despair or cynicism? While this volume has so far confronted some depressing aspects of our world, we now consider a perspective that, while realistic, could also be seen as more forward-looking and life-affirming.

Chapter 19

Primary Life Orientations and Philosophical Response to Catastrophe

Marek J. Celinski

This chapter will discuss the path to resilience in the wake of catastrophe. The chapter will outline both the relevant psychological mechanisms and the underlying philosophical questions involved in this path.

CRISIS AND COPING

The human mind is structured to make sense out of diverse and conflicting ideas, and to establish consistency and continuity over time, even when people acknowledge that they have little control over reality and the outcomes of their plans. As we mature, we may find purpose in our lives if we engage courageously with life's challenges, while also accepting its fundamental unpredictability and our lack of control.

The Biblical story of the Tower of Babel highlights the opposition between the strength of collective unity versus the chaos of diversity without consensus or mutual understanding. Cohesiveness implies common understanding as well as sustained, goal-oriented efforts. However, without common ground or values to bind people, disorder develops from an inability to work together for a common purpose. Individual and collective lives reflect a continuous exploration and testing of the limits of growth, expansion, and our control over events. Our efforts are successful as long as we recognize what is changeable and malleable, yet also respect what is permanent and steady.[1] Catastrophe provides insights into reality's complexity, and the degree to which it is controllable. In everyday life these opposite forces are hidden, as they are superficially masked by conventions, rules, and societal laws, as well as the support of others who help us sustain our goal-oriented efforts and maintain some continuity. All these disguises give us an illusion of control until the everyday routine is broken down.

The Babel story foresaw humanity's struggle with its own nature. The ancient Greeks recognized as hubris that which attempts "to overstep just bounds" which keep "every person and every thing . . . in its appointed place and . . . function"—boundaries to which even Zeus is subjected. According to the Greek view, "some kind of impersonal super-Olympian law punishes *hubris,* and restores the eternal order which the aggressor sought to violate."[2] Concepts of unity and diversity are also reflected in the different ways in which people visualize their role and mission in life. People may view themselves as self-made and restrictions as temporary until the way is found to reach the sky with their ambitions; on the other hand, we are subjected to restrictions which, if violated, lead to disastrous consequences. There is an imminent danger related to both sides of the dichotomy—represented in Figure 19.1 below by hubris on one side and by helplessness on the other (which is typically the state of mind experienced when people feel isolated and abandoned in difficult situations). We call this the "Bipolarity of Catastrophic Response."

The difficulty is finding the right balance in the larger scheme of things. If we believe that we were created and are to some degree dependent on our creator, and moreover recognize that much of life is not under our direct control, then we need to continuously review our perspectives to reconcile them with a more perfect source. Bertrand Russell stated: "the search for something permanent is one of the deepest of the instincts leading men to philosophy."[3] We have an intuitive appreciation of the freedom to act compassionately and in solidarity with others.[4] The alternative approach is based on the assumption that we are self-reliant in our ability to progressively engage with reality and each other.

Furthermore, if we believe that we create ourselves as free agents of social evolution and that we are solely in control of our lives and our moral norms, we ultimately view humanity as the master of its destiny.[5] These contrary visions of human nature and agency, addressed in various religious and philosophical contexts, play an important role in our dealing with reality and setting an agenda for future development.

Crisis—and especially a crisis of a catastrophic proportion—represents a disruption in the flow of routine activities[6] and a breakdown in the cohesive social structure, which forces us to change our behavior. Such disruptions are inevitable, but are there ways we could benefit psychologically from learning how the crisis developed? As a crisis manifests itself as the destruction of the existing order, people are forced to find a new axiomatic understanding of reality and review their own roles; otherwise it results in the continuation of the crisis.[7]

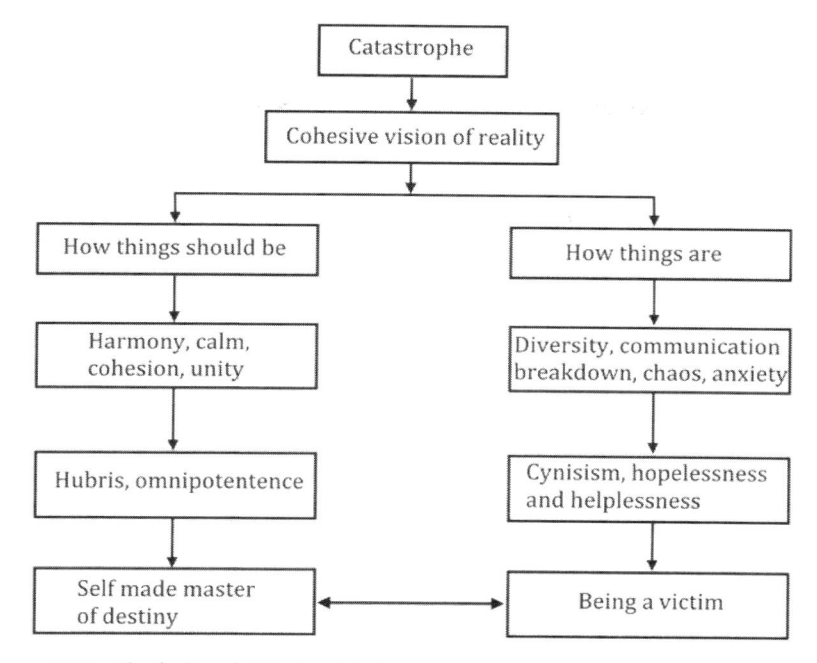

```
                    ┌──────────────┐
                    │ Catastrophe  │
                    └──────┬───────┘
                           ▼
              ┌────────────────────────┐
              │Cohesive vision of reality│
              └────────────┬───────────┘
                ┌──────────┴──────────┐
                ▼                     ▼
    ┌──────────────────┐    ┌──────────────────┐
    │How things should be│   │  How things are  │
    └─────────┬────────┘    └─────────┬────────┘
              ▼                       ▼
    ┌──────────────────┐    ┌──────────────────────┐
    │  Harmony, calm,  │    │Diversity, communication│
    │  cohesion, unity │    │breakdown, chaos, anxiety│
    └─────────┬────────┘    └─────────┬────────────┘
              ▼                       ▼
    ┌──────────────────┐    ┌──────────────────────┐
    │Hubris, omnipotentence│ │Cynicism, hopelessness│
    │                  │    │  and helplessness    │
    └─────────┬────────┘    └─────────┬────────────┘
              ▼                       ▼
    ┌──────────────────┐    ┌──────────────────┐
    │ Self made master │◄──►│  Being a victim  │
    │   of destiny     │    │                  │
    └──────────────────┘    └──────────────────┘
```

Figure 19.1   Bipolarity of Catastrophic Response.

Crisis often causes us to regress in the emotional, cognitive and spiritual domains. We feel anxious and confused, unable to understand reality and lacking direction. This state of mind causes a sense of alienation and abandonment, and people become fearful, aggressive, and helpless.

Such regressive behavior may become adaptive if it causes us some discomfort and motivates us to review the fundamentals of our engagement with reality. Our psychological apparatus consists of components such as cognitions, instincts, and emotions. We need to identify those characteristics in each domain which are helpful in dealing with crisis and those which reflect the negative consequences of being a witness to or a victim of such events. The major options involve trying to exercise control on the one hand and a spirituality-based coping on the other, which represents "rational "versus "irrational" (or perhaps "nonrational") ways of dealing with events.

When dealing with crisis and catastrophe, people apply basic assumptions and assess the relevant situational demands. Have we dealt with similar circumstances previously with a known methodology or do they require a novel and creative response?[8] Catastrophe reminds us that our understanding of reality was inadequate to prevent it. Another aspect of the adaptive response to catastrophe is reflected in the discovery of our strengths: physical strengths, creative intellectual abilities, social support networks, and understanding the laws of nature. For religious people, it is the relationship with God as the ultimate source of power that gives us wisdom[9] and the awareness of our freedom to choose. Our primary response should manifest itself in resilience,[10] a decision to face the situation truthfully and to empower ourselves to match our perceived threats with the most appropriate resources available in order to engage more effectively. These responses are illustrated in Figure 19.2.

Therefore, crisis (and even more so catastrophe) creates a new reality, forcing us to review our ways of understanding and general comportment. It prompts us to either seek inspiration for coping or be crushed by the circumstances. There are two ways of dealing with such tasks—reflected in the two primary philosophical approaches to reality: materialism and idealism. Activities inspired by a materialistic orientation allow people to achieve a measure of control over physical reality based on the notion of causality. By causality, we mean the discovered laws governing physical, biological, social and economic events. According to Bandura (1997 and 2001) our individual and collaborative efforts become successful when we regard ourselves as agents capable of achieving the desired outcome (self-efficacy), and utilize procedures and resources that match our level of resilience.[11] An inspiration derived from the Aristotelian view of reality as interconnected by causality[12] is especially fruitful in sciences that deal with the material and physical domains. Nature needs to be first explored and subject to experiment so that we may find causal relations between events. Control refers to choosing the most effective way of creating a mechanism and a reliable pathway for achieving a particular goal.

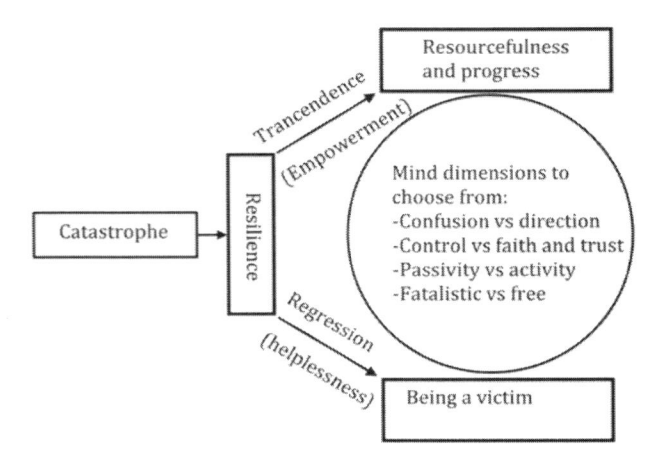

Figure 19.2 Progressive vs Regressive Responses to a Catastrophic Event.

The idealistic approach primarily refers to intuition, faith, and the hope that our activities will make a difference, without our knowing the outcome. This attitude is grounded in the Platonic view that the physical reality as we are able to perceive it is only a faint reflection of unchangeable, eternal ideas to which we only have partial access and understanding.[13] The tension between the attitudes inspired by the Aristotelian and Platonic inspirations is reflected in various attempts to close the gap (cognitive dissonance) between these two worlds.[14]

Every new piece of information is filtered through the individual's fundamental understanding of oneself, which basically tends in either of these directions. We use this mental framework to create a sense of familiarity and to manage life situations. Both approaches are necessary to successfully deal with life and all it's vicissitudes. Ideally they should be combined to reinforce each other. However, when an approach based on causality and control is not possible, resorting to faith is the only option.

There are further consequences of adapting one approach or the other. Either we change according to the circumstances, recognizing our present capabilities and relying on what is convenient and appears achievable, or we distance ourselves from the present and seek guidance in what is stable and eternal. These two streams of our involvement should not be confused. We should not apply the spiritual principle of unpredictability to the physical world where we assume that events are linked by causal factors, even though in the physical domain there are also situations when relationships cannot be understood in deterministic terms. Heisenberg's "Uncertainty Principle"[15] specifies that particles on the subatomic level "no longer have defined position and velocities that could be observed," which has profound implications for our scientific understanding of the world in terms of deterministic relationships.[16] Similarly, as in the physical world where there are a number of possible outcomes and we may know only the likelihood of each to occur,[17] in the social, psychological and spiritual domains there is no linear process or solitary causation behind unfolding events. We assume that people act freely, inspired by their fundamental belief systems. However, there is a continuous temptation to impose control over events, applying various coercive measures to achieve the expected results.

A catastrophe forces us to seek causes but also to find ways of coping with how chaotic reality has become. If we accept the situation as a challenge, it may lead us to rediscover our resourcefulness and prevent us from regressing into cynical and destructive behavior. A catastrophe forces us to review various assumptions[18] which we have about ourselves and the world.

Considering that what we believe will manifest in our daily life, philosophy can help us view our options and seek wise choices. We need to submerge ourselves in the breadth of human experience with courage and hope in order to develop the wisdom that could integrate these discoveries into a cohesive pattern of sustained involvement. From a clinical perspective, post-traumatic stress disorder is a good example of what matters when we are facing tragic circumstances: if we focus narrowly, we are crushed by the experience, but if we expand our awareness, we may find resources to cope. Even though our social advancement may depend separately on ourselves, on the forces of nature or on some spiritual power, it is a combination of these that reflects our humanity. We have to implement both science and intuition to integrate the contradictory aspects of reality and of our own nature. This should discourage us from acting impulsively or routinely, allowing us to become resilient so as to withstand the pressure of reality choose resources to act wisely.

Crises and catastrophes thus may have both positive and negative impacts. Human evolution occurs through the recognition that we must engage with life, try to find truth, accept truth regardless how painful it is, express our understanding and values, and find the ways to successfully cope with those tasks we regard as worthy of our involvement.[19]

SENSEMAKING IN A "RATIONAL" VERSUS "IRRATIONAL" WAY

"Sense-making" is the human brain's attempt to seek order where apparent randomness rules. Our minds are constantly absorbing information and organizing our experiences into cohesive *gestalts*. Whereas reality continuously threatens the return to chaos, we continue attempting to establish sense and order in spite of entropic pressure. This is possible only if we strive to understand the deeper meaning of events by integrating increasingly greater amounts of information to establish more complex images of reality.[20] Yet, this process is never complete or accurate, as reality constantly threatens the breakdown of these images and constructs.

When the routine breaks down and the outcomes of our activity turn out to be different than expected, our fundamental assumptions reveal themselves. In some instances it triggers curiosity, in others fear or amazement when reality presents something unknown and unexpected. Our "rational" approach to dealing with life's unpredictability is based on the assumption that the world is intelligible. Its intelligibility need only be discovered and this knowledge will make reality potentially manageable.[21] We achieve our goals in satisfying our basic instinctual needs but, more importantly, we simultaneously engage in co-creation by revising our life vision. We impose on this continuously changing reality a network of ideas, which allows us to recognize events as random and unpredictable, or we organize separately observable events into a structure we believe is linked by unifying principles (i.e., we assume they are governed by the law of causality). In such a case we believe that mechanistic, biological, physical or spiritual forces cause changes in the material world, social environments and ultimately in ourselves. If we extend our inquiry, we may ask about the origin of the world and our self-identity. We inevitably reach the realization that we were only partially created through our own efforts and experiences; much else was given to us through our genes, pre-existing social arrangements and the educational efforts controlled by others. We may ask further if what is changeable both outside and inside of us allows us to gain reliable knowledge, and whether what we know reveals an intelligible pattern behind these changes or the unexpected, unexplainable disruption of continuity. If we accept that these changes make sense as expected outcomes based on known assumptions, we may ask if the recognized pattern behind past events helps us understand present events and whether these events can lead us to some sort of final understanding. Furthermore, we may seek to clarify whether we can have any impact on the events or if they are simply beyond our control.

The alternative is to look to the spiritual domain. Whereas the rational approach necessitates making decisions based on likely outcomes from known facts, the spiritual motivates us to rely on the transforming powers of eternal virtues such as justice, freedom, etc. This spiritual perspective does not rely on a need to control. Rather, we do things because they are right and we do not ask for immediate results. We have an ability to recognize the fundamental order of things, and we reinforce stability in our lives by remembering it at the moment of crisis. This process is governed by the assumption that what is eternal and permanent was temporarily hidden from us but our efforts may restore the right perspective. With this intention, we look for intellectual insights and apply our moral sensitivity and social intelligence as guiding inspirations.[22]

Even though a reliance on spirituality is not based on an understanding of causal or probabilistic links between events, its merit stems from the belief that goodness (a virtue which is permanent and eternal) will ultimately prevail, even though we do not know when and in which form. This approach requires that we engage faithfully with the world, even though the outcome is unknown. This assumes the belief that life is worth living, that our efforts matter regardless of the circumstances, and that the values we express through our actions are worthy of our sacrifices. Without going into controversies surrounding such assumptions, it is sufficient to say that the majority of people are guided by these principles. As we engage the world without knowing the consequences, we are still motivated by compassion and solidarity with others.[23] Such an attitude is considered "irrational" because there is no assurance based on the established probability that what we hope for will be achievable. Nonetheless, history teaches us that ideas once considered "irrational" materialized simply because they were eventually recognized as good. A steadfast commitment to a vision liberated people from slavery, brought freedom to many nations and created sufficient social pressure to entrench the principles of human rights, social order, and cooperation.

Philosophy deals with questions the mind naturally generates when encountering a complicated reality. To make sense out of these complexities, we try to develop networks of ideas and explanations that could begin to articulate a cohesive, though necessarily incomplete, view of reality, and our direction in life.

Relationships between catastrophe and philosophy described in Figure 19.3 below refer to the changes occurring in people's mental states when unexpected, undesirable situations cause a breakdown in the continuity of the established worldview. A catastrophe reveals a basic incongruence between how we believe things should be and how they are. A conflict develops between a previously established routine and the new situation for which previous thought patterns, emotions, and ethical considerations no longer apply. This forces the mind to reconcile the apparent tension to establish some direction for further functioning.

Consider the mental condition of a man who enjoyed a happy relationship with his brother, a senior partner in a family business. Unexpectedly, he was informed that a contract on which their financial survival depended had been cancelled. His brother asked him to be patient and continue working on reduced or little pay until the situation improves; thus the new situation requires that the man's plans and his lifestyle be changed. As a result, the various domains of his mind need to be activated to process the new situation; if he intends to stay in the business, his sense of wellbeing needs to refocus from hedonistic enjoyment to a more holistic appreciation of happiness as

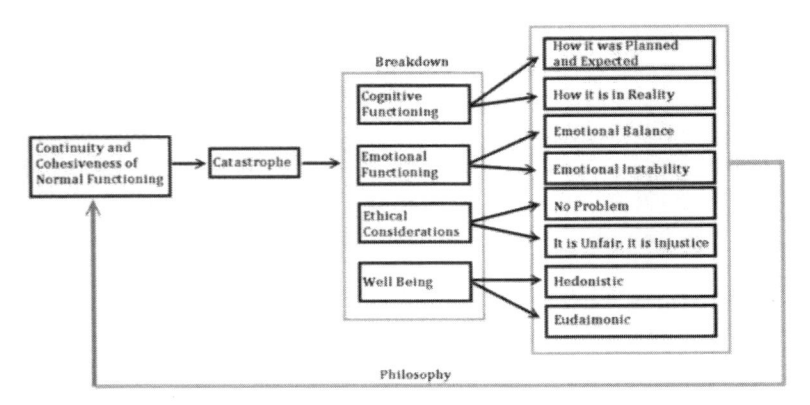

Figure 19.3 Catastrophe and Philosophy.

being specifically the human expression of virtues and wisdom.[24] If initially succeeds in changing his orientation in at least one domain, this may create an opportunity for him to implement other cognitive and emotional domains in a cohesive manner to help his brother out of trouble. This capacity to change our worldview helps us deal with new and disruptive situations. For this, we need to nurture our sensitivity to the issues related to social relations and to understanding what it means to be human. Zautra, Palucka and Celinski state:

> "Social evolution was due to a special human capacity to acknowledge and value the humanity in one another for its own sake, and not just as a means to an end. Such an attitude is rooted in the natural capacity and inclination to be broadly connected emotionally with others through empathy that is especially manifesting when other suffer.... The findings that are presented in this chapter illustrate the link between social attitudes and socially intelligent interactions on one hand, and cognitive abilities on the other along with the consequences when humanity of others is ignored or denied."[25]

Similarly, McMartin[26] states that courageous engagement in life accompanied by the pursuit of wisdom promotes perseverance through difficulty, and opens our minds to creative solutions.

Our fundamental assumptions are to be empirically or logically tested which offers direction for our life. When traumatized by a catastrophe, we experience tension in our attempts to make sense out of conflicting dimensions: order versus chaos, randomness versus direction, activity versus passivity, orientation to time (now or the past versus future and eternity), sense of control either within individuals or outside,[27] and trust and faith versus fatalistic, pessimistic visions. These dichotomies represent our freedom and our uniqueness among species.

Within the cognitive domain a question arises: can we even accurately understand the reality in which we are forced to live? There are both pessimistic and optimistic perspectives to consider. The pessimistic one argues that our perception is subjectively influenced by our mind's way of processing information; the extreme Berkeleyian view is that the material world only exists when we perceive it.[28] The optimistic belief is derived from the Aristotelian postulate[29] that to achieve an accurate understanding of reality we need to strive to match our mental images with a preexisting reality, which leads to the development of the principles of scientific methodology that are consistently revised and refined.

We either choose to impact on our world, or disengage from life into a shelter (physical, emotional or spiritual) that offers us a sense of protection from a hostile environment we cannot understand or manage. In this respect, there is a split between Judeo-Christianity which promotes engagement through determination and hope to achieve a higher level of moral development, and the Buddhist orientation which views people's minds as contaminated by untamed desires for power, control, wealth, lust, and so on—illusions to which, nevertheless, many commit their efforts.[30] From the Buddhist perspective the appropriate path toward the enlightened life is to purify the mind of all these false desires.

The alternative to withdrawing from reality or giving up on our desires is transcendence—an ability to go beyond our habitual existence and mobilize ourselves to face reality.[31] Facing life's enormity and complexity, we may put our trust in spiritual values of which we may not have immediate understanding. We need to believe in something which impacts us, even though we do not know how, such as a belief in God, in freedom, justice, etc. which would unite humanity across diverse ethnic, cultural, and religious barriers.[32]

Humans are the only creatures capable of transcending the most powerful mechanism of evolution—conditioning that utilizes punishment and reward to establish interactions with the environment. Humans overcome this process by developing an ability to decide what is or should be worth rewarding and what should be the reward, which becomes an evolutionary locomotive for individual development. Humans are able to free themselves from the hedonistic calculus by discovering themselves what is important or valuable. However, during times of stress, regressive behavior occurs. People lose touch with this freedom and act based on instinctual compulsion. The mental state associated with helplessness is an extreme condition when perceived losses and restrictions prevent individuals from their usual manner of self-expression based on broader views of their identity and moral sensitivity. Nevertheless, even in extreme conditions some are capable of understanding the essence of humanity and utilizing their freedom to express this. Even in concentration camps, we witnessed human solidarity, a will to survive, and forgiveness, as documented by Frankl and others. From this perspective, the purpose of human life is to express values and virtues, especially in harsh circumstances especially created to reduce individuals to instinctual reactions. A human capacity to do the opposite of what the pressure of circumstances compels is a manifestation of freedom, transcendence, and resilience, which advances humanity to higher cognitive and moral levels.

PHILOSOPHY, RESILIENCE, AND WISDOM

What is the purpose of life and our mission? Achieving happiness? Could the meaning of life be the fulfillment of our human potential, overcoming mental and societal constraints and becoming more resilient in order to confront

Primary Life Orientations and Philosophical Response to Catastrophe 333

life's challenges, to reduce suffering, and to act toward greater happiness for all? In order to answer these questions, it is necessary to further explain the difference between hedonistic versus eudaimonic happiness.

The difference between the both types of happiness may be illustrated by yet another example: a young man enjoyed the company of his girlfriend of several months when he suddenly learned that she is seriously ill. The choice he faced was to leave her, as her illness will disrupt their previous lifestyle, or to stay with her, which would require that he put all his efforts into helping her, without certainty that these efforts will bring her back to health. If he stays with her, chances are that his awareness of himself as a partner will be broadened and eventually their relationship will become stronger. In essence we need both types of happiness to function in society and establish relationships, but we need to individually establish the balance between them (see Figure 19.4 below).

How can we master our courage to face reality resiliently, aiming at a complete and truthful understanding thereof?[33] While it is tempting to be in charge of our lives and in control of the environment, it is also necessary to maintain our values and virtues regardless of the immediate results. Our minds need to process reality in a double track: acknowledging negativity but trying to do as much good as possible.[34] This is the basic mechanism of coping: to understand the challenge and withstand the pressure to regress, to become resilient and apply the right resources to advance.

The primary difficulty in dealing with catastrophic events and losses is a sense of entitlement. This belief manifests itself when we lose or do not get what we want in spite of our efforts and complain that "life is not fair." A sense of entitlement is a powerful force that only augments our suffering.

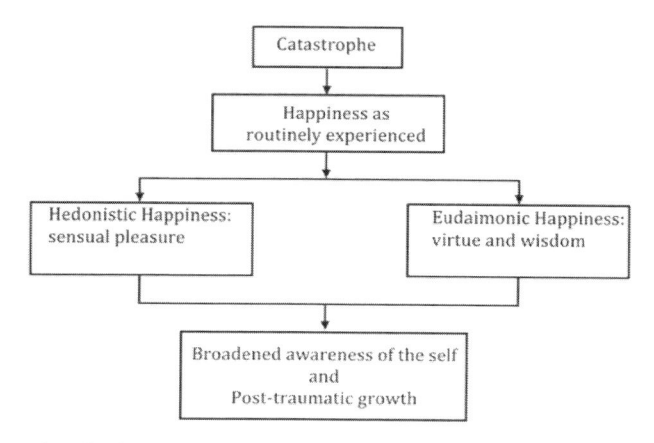

Figure 19.4 The Bipolar Nature of Happiness as Revealed by Catastrophe.

Buddhist teaching recognized that we need to overcome a sense of entitlement based on the belief that life or a society owes us happiness, satisfaction, fulfillment of our expectations, or replacement of valuable things we have lost. For a Buddhist, the ultimate answer to this is to aim at the cessation of passion and desire in order to achieve a condition of emptiness and peace.[35]

The results of clinical work validate such teaching and warn against excessive craving of possessions, control, power, and sensual pleasures. If we do not distance ourselves from such things, the losses and frustrations we will inevitably face will trigger disappointment, anger, or depression. Yet we need to overcome the tendency to withhold our energy and withdraw from life. Knowing that happiness is not our entitlement, and that nothing we aim to achieve is certain, what is left is a courageous involvement in life with curiosity, open-mindedness, creativity, and compassion. These methods may occasionally bring us satisfaction and even happiness through the fulfillment of our human potential.

CONCLUDING REMARKS

The major purpose of philosophy is sense-making, but it is valid to ask whether this sense and order actually exists or is merely the projection of our ideas on reality. Unfortunately, this is not a question we can answer because of the limitations of our finite minds. We do know that belief in the sense and order of things is the condition of our mental and possibly our physical health. Catastrophes fundamentally challenge this sense of order as well as basic human "sense-making" capabilities. Resilience develops when we patiently continue our efforts at understanding while being constantly surprised by our inadequacies.

Discovering and establishing order and finding meaning in life are the most important features of human nature, and philosophy is one very basic and natural expression of how we going about trying to do this.[36] The value of these philosophical activities is measured by how helpful they are to understanding ourselves and life in general, how they unite seemingly conflicting aspects of nature, and how much they help promote our quality of life. Yet we always need to recognize the limits of the enterprise: whenever we theorize about such large and complicated questions, it may not be possible to embrace everything that may be important and to package it within the framework of simple assumptions.

NOTES

1. See Rollo May, *Freedom and Destiny* (New York: Norton, 1981).

2. Bertrand Russell, *A History of Western Philosophy* (New York: Simon & Schuster, 1945), 114.

3. Ibid., 45.

4. See Jozef Tischner, *The Spirit of Solidarity* (San Francisco: Harper and Row, 1984).

5. See Jean Paul Sartre, *Existentialism Is a Humanism* (New Haven: Yale University Press, 2007).

6. George Mandler, *Human Nature Explored* (New York: Oxford University Press, 1997).

7. Jenny W. Rudolph and Nelson P. Reppenning, "Disaster Dynamics: Understanding the Role of Quantity in Organizational Collapse," *Administrative Science Quarterly* 47, no. 1 (2002): 1–32.

8. Ibid.

9. Andrew Targowski, *Harnessing the Power of Wisdom: From Data to Wisdom* (Hauppauge, NY: Nova Science Publishers, 2013).

10. Marek J. Celinski, "Framing Resilience as Transcendence and Resourcefulness as Transformation," in *Continuity versus Creative Response to Challenge: The Primacy of Resilience and Resourcefulness in Life and Therapy*, ed. Marek. J. Celinski and Kathryn M. Gow (Hauppauge, NY: Nova Science Publishers, 2011), 11–30.

11. Ibid.

12. Garth Kemmerling, "The Philosophy Pages" last modified November 12, 2011. http://www.philosophypages.com/hy/2n.htm.

13. Plato, *Republic*, trans. G. M. A. Grube, rev. C. D. C. Reeve (Indianapolis: Hackett Publishing Company, 1992).

14. Leon Festinger, *A Theory of Cognitive Dissonance* (Palo Alto, CA: Stanford University Press, 1957).

15. Steven Hawking, *A Brief History of Time: From the Big Bang to Black Holes* (New York: Bantam Books, 1988), 54–56.

16. Ibid., 55.

17. Ibid.

18. Frank J. Lucatelli and Rhonda C. Messinger, "Using Axioms to Unblock Civilization's Progress," in *Crisis and Renewal of Civilizations: The 21st Century Crisis of Ideas and Character*, ed. Marek J. Celinski (Hauppauge, NY: Nova Science Publishers, 2015), 161–85.

19. See Aaron Antonovsky, *Unravelling the Mystery of Health. How People Manage Stress and Stay Well* (San Francisco: Jossey-Bass, 1987) and "Complexity, Conflict, Chaos, Coherence, Coercion and Civility," *Social Science and Medicine* 37, no. 8 (1993): 969–74.

20. See Lucatelli and Messinger, "Using Axioms."

21. Antonovsky, *Unravelling the Mystery* and "Complexity, Conflict, Chaos."

22. Alex J. Zautra, Anna M. Palucka and Marek J. Celinski, "Social Connectedness and Creativity: Two Mutually Influencing Processes that Promote Human Evolution," in *Crisis and Renewal of Civilizations: The 21st Century Crisis of Ideas and Character*, ed. Marek. J. Celinski (Hauppauge, NY: Nova Science Publishers, 2015), 211.

23. Tischner, *Spirit of Solidarity*.

24. Brent Dean Robbins and Harris L. Friedman, "Resilience as Virtue: Contributions from Humanistic and Positive Psychology," in *Continuity versus Creative Response to Challenge: The Primacy of Resilience and Resourcefulness in Life and Therapy*, ed. Marek J. Celinski and Kathryn M. Gow (Hauppauge, NY: Nova Science Publishers, 2011), 93–104.

25. Zautra, Palucka and Celinski, "Social Connectedness and Creativity," 211–23.

26. Jason McMartin, "The Virtues of Resilience and Resourcefulness in the Western Philosophical Tradition" in *Continuity versus Creative Response to Challenge: The Primacy of Resilience and Resourcefulness in Life and Therapy*, ed. Marek J. Celinski and Kathryn M. Gow (Hauppauge, NY: Nova Science Publishers, 2011), 155–73.

27. Cecily J. Partridge and Marie Johnston, "Perceived Control of Recovery from Physical Disability: Measurement and Prediction" *British Journal of Psychology* 28, Part 1 (1989): 53–59.

28. See Russell, *History of Western Philosophy*, 647.

29. plato.stanford.edu/entries/truth/.

30. Peter Bishop and Michael Darton, eds., *The Encyclopedia of the World Faiths. An Illustrated Survey of the World's Living Religions* (London and Sydney: Macdonald & Co., Ltd., 1987).

31. Marek Celinski, "Framing Resilience," 11–30.

32. Andrew Targowski, "Universal Spirituality as a Condition for a Sustainable Civilization," in *Spirituality and Civilization Sustainability in the 21st Century*, ed. Andrew Targowski and Marek J. Celinski (Hauppauge, NY: Nova Science Publishers, 2013), 319–45.

33. See McMartin, "Virtues of Resilience."

34. John W. Reich, Alex J. Zautra, and John Stuart Hall, "Resilience Science and Practice: Current Status, Future Directions," in *Continuity versus Creative Response to Challenge: The Primacy of Resilience and Resourcefulness in Life and Therapy*, ed. Marek J. Celinski and Kathryn M. Gow (Hauppauge, NY: Nova Science Publishers, 2011), 33–50.

35. See Bishop and Darton, *Encyclopedia of World Faiths*, 226.

36. Søren Ventegodt, Trine Flensborg-Madsen, Niels Jørgen Andersen and Joav Merrick, "The Life Mission Theory VII. Theory of Existential (Antonovsky) Coherence: A Theory of Quality of Life, Health and Ability for Use in Holistic Medicine," *Scientific World Journal*, 2005, 6, 377–89.

BIBLIOGRAPHY

Antonovsky, Aaron. *Unravelling the Mystery of Health. How People Manage Stress and Stay Well.* San Francisco: Jossey-Bass, 1987.

———. "Complexity, Conflict, Chaos, Coherence, Coercion and Civility." *Social Science and Medicine* 37, no. 8 (1993): 969–974.

Aristotle—definitions of causality (http://www.philosophypages.com/hy/2n.htm).

Aristotle—definition of truth (plato.stanford.edu/entries/truth/).

Bandura, Albert. "Self-efficacy: Toward a Unifying Theory of Behavioural Change." *Psychological Review* 84, no. 2 (1977): 191–215.

———. "Social Cognitive Theory: An Agentic Perspective." *Annual Review of Psychology* 52, no. 1 (2001): 1–26.

Bishop, Peter and Michael Darton, eds. *The Encyclopedia of the World Faiths: An Illustrated Survey of the World's Living Religions.* London and Sydney: Macdonald & Co., Ltd., 1987.

Borthwick, Stephen M. "Dieu et Mon Droit." In *Spirituality and Civilization Sustainability in the 21st Century,* edited by A. Targowski and Marek J. Celinski, 59–77. Hauppauge, NY: Nova Science Publishers, 2015.

Celinski, Marek J. "Framing Resilience as Transcendence and Resourcefulness as Transformation." In *Continuity versus Creative Response to Challenge: The Primacy of Resilience and Resourcefulness in Life and Therapy,* edited by Marek J. Celinski and Kathryn M. Gow, 11–30. Hauppauge, NY: Nova Science Publishers, 2011.

———. "The Trauma of Time and the Development of Cognition and Morality." In *Crisis and Renewal of Civilizations: The 21st Century Crisis of Ideas and Character,* edited by Marek J. Celinski, 139–160. Hauppauge, NY: Nova Science Publishers, 2015.

Diener, Edward and Seligman, Martin E. "Very Happy People" *Psychological Science* 13, no. 1 (2002): 81–84.

Festinger, Leon. *A Theory of Cognitive Dissonance.* Palo Alto, CA: Stanford University Press, 1957.

Frankl, Viktor E. *Man's Search for Meaning: Introduction to Logotherapy.* New York: Washington Square Press, 1966.

———. *Man's Search for Ultimate Meaning.* Cambridge, MA: Perseus Publishing, 2000.

Freud, Sigmund. *Beyond the Pleasure Principle.* Translated by C. J. M. Hubback. London and Vienna: International Psycho-Analytical, 1922. https://www.bartleby.com/276/.

Hawking, Stephen. *A Brief History of Time: From the Big Bang to Black Holes.* New York: Bantam Books, 1988.

Kemmerling, Garth. "The Philosophy Pages" last modified November 12, 2011. http://www.philosophypages.com/hy/2n.htm.

Lucatelli, Frank J., and Rhonda C. Messinger. "Using Axioms to Unblock Civilization's Progress." In *Crisis and Renewal of Civilizations: The 21st Century Crisis of Ideas and Character,* edited by Marek J. Celinski, 161–185. Hauppauge, NY: Nova Science Publishers, 2015.

Mandler, George. *Human Nature Explored.* New York: Oxford University Press, 1997.

May, Rollo. *Freedom and Destiny.* New York: Norton and Co., 1981.

McMartin, Jason. "The Virtues of Resilience and Resourcefulness in the Western Philosophical Tradition." In *Continuity versus Creative Response to Challenge: The Primacy of Resilience and Resourcefulness in Life and Therapy,* edited by Marek J. Celinski and Kathryn M. Gow, 155–173. Hauppauge, NY: Nova Science Publishers, 2011.

Nazaretyan, A. P. "Non-Linear Future: Global Crises in View of Mega-History." In *Crisis and Renewal of Civilizations: The 21st Century Crisis of Ideas and Character,* edited by Marek J. Celinski, 51–70. Hauppauge, NY: Nova Science Publishers, 2015.

Partridge, Cecily J. and Marie Johnston. "Perceived Control of Recovery from Physical Disability: Measurement and Prediction." *British Journal of Psychology* 28, pt. 1 (1989): 53–59.

Plato, *Republic.* Translated by G. M. A. Grube and Revised by C. D. C. Reeve. Indianapolis: Hackett Publishing Company, 1992.

Reich, John W., Alex J. Zautra and John Stuart Hall. "Resilience Science and Practice: Current Status, Future Directions." In *Continuity versus Creative Response to Challenge: The Primacy of Resilience and Resourcefulness in Life and Therapy,* edited by Marek J. Celinski and Kathryn M. Gow, 33–50. Hauppauge, NY: Nova Science Publishers, 2011.

Robbins, Brent Dean, and Harris L. Friedman. "Resilience as Virtue: Contributions from Humanistic and Positive Psychology." In *Continuity versus Creative Response to Challenge: The Primacy of Resilience and Resourcefulness in Life and Therapy,* edited by Marek J. Celinski and Kathryn M. Gow, 93–104. Hauppauge, NY: Nova Science Publishers, 2011.

Rudolph, Jenny W. and Nelson P. Reppenning. "Disaster Dynamics: Understanding the Role of Quantity in Organizational Collapse." *Administrative Science Quarterly* 47, no. 1 (2002): 1–32.

Russell, Bertrand. *A History of Western Philosophy.* New York: Simon and Schuster, 1945.

Sartre, Jean Paul. *Existentialism is a Humanism.* Translated by C. Macomber. New Haven: Yale University Press, [1946] 2007.

Sorokin, Pitirim. *Social and Cultural Dynamics.* New York: MacMillan, 1937.

Targowski, Andrew. *Harnessing the Power of Wisdom: From Data to Wisdom.* Hauppauge, NY: Nova Science Publishers, 2013.

———. "Universal Spirituality as a Condition for a Sustainable Civilization." In *Spirituality and Civilization Sustainability in the 21st Century,* edited by Andrew Targowski and Marek J. Celinski, 319–345. Hauppauge, NY: Nova Science Publishers, 2013.

Genesis 11:1–9, *The New American Bible.* Chicago: J. G. Ferguson Publishing Company, 1971.

Tischner, Jozef. *The Spirit of Solidarity.* San Francisco: Harper & Row, 1984.

Ventegodt, Søren, Trine Flensborg-Madsen, Niels Jørgen Andersen, and Joav Merrick. "The Life Mission Theory VII. Theory of Existential (Antonovsky) Coherence: A Theory of Quality of Life, Health and Ability for Use in Holistic Medicine." *Scientific World Journal* 5 (2005), 377–389.

Zautra, Alex. J., Anna M. Palucka, and Marek J. Celinski. "Social Connectedness and Creativity: Two mutually influencing processes that promote human evolution." In *Crisis and Renewal of Civilizations: The 21st Century Crisis of Ideas and Character,* edited by Marek J. Celinski, 211–223. Hauppauge, NY: Nova Science Publishers, 2015.

Index

absolutism, 147
Adorno, T., 212–13
Agamben, G., xvii, 284*ff*
Alaric, 62
Amorality, 79, 97, 105,106
anomie, 43, 61, 142
Aporia, xiii, xiv, xix, 49, 78, 82,129, 147, 213, 319
Appearance vs. Reality, 96
Arendt, H., 143, 169, 254, 272nn3, 4
assumptions, xiii, xviii, 78, 81, 82, 141, 326, 327, 329, 332
Athens, 3, 43*ff*, 109–12
Augustine, 57, 61*ff*
Auschwitz, 83, 169, 212, 254*ff*

Bacon, F., 140, 141
Baudrillard, J., 96
Benjamin, W., 282
Berg, A., 213, 214
Berger, P., xiii
Black Death, 71*ff*, 106
Boccaccio, G., 58, 71*ff*, 321
Borowski, T., 253*ff*, 321
Braudel, F., 62
Broch, H., 80
Brueggemann, W., 25
Buddha, Buddhist thought, 7*ff*, 332, 334

Cantwell-Smith, W., 13
catharsis, xviii, 73, 77
Celan, P., 270–71, 321
certainty, 139–41
Cheng, F., 268
Christianity, 9, 57, 58*ff*, 63, 73*ff*, 173
Cold War, 310–12
compassion, 148
Confucius, Confucianism, 4, 31*ff*
conservatism, 34,145
contingency, 311–12
control, 323, 324, 329, 331, 333
Corrigan, M., 245

Dahlhaus, C., 207
Darwin, C., 171–75, 178, 180–85
Dawkins, R., 181
decadence, 57, 58, 63, 239 ff
decline, 225
Degenerate Music Exhibition, 214
Delbo, C., 254
deluge, 220–22, 228
De Sanctis, F., 77
Descartes, R., 137, 139–41
disintegration, 72, 77, 78, 229
Donne, J., 83, 139
doubt, 63, 84, 142 ff
Durkheim, E., 14

Dworkin, R., 289*ff*

Ebola, 82
economics, 314–15
Eliade, M., xiii
Emmanuel, S., 10
English Civil Wars, 107, 115–20
environment, 282, 312–14
epistemology, xiv, 78, 147
Epstein, M., xv,
explanation, xii, xiv, 78–79, 82

Fenn, M., 7, 8, 14
filial piety, 35
Franke, W., 258–59, 261, 270
Freud, S., 67, 168, 184, 195, 317

Galileo, 138
Geertz, C., xiii, xv
Gibaldi, J., 72, 84n9
Gibbon, E., 65, 221
Goths, 57, 63
Gottfried, R., 78, 80
Griffin, R., 142

Hamdi (legal case of), 287*ff*
Hastings, R., 75
Heidegger, M., xxiin36, 58
heretics, 83, 137
Herlihy, D., 76, 80
Heschel, A. J., 26
Hesse, H., xvi
Hiroshima and Nagasaki, 169
Hitler, A., xvi, 195, 314
Hobbes, T., xix, 107*ff*
Hoffer, E., 67, 69
Holocaust, xv, 25 152,168–69, 253*ff*
Homer, 4, 48, 51
hope, 320, 325
humility, 147

Ibn Khaldun, 225–26
ISIS, 83, 142, 145–46

James, W., 65, 66

Janoff-Bulman, R., xiii
Jedan, C., 76
Jews, 65, 85n39, 168, 194, 201, 208, 212, 223, 232, 253*ff*
Joachim of Floris, 225–26
Job, 14, 79
Jost, J., 145

Kandinsky, W., 206*ff*
Kaufmann, J., xiii
Kermode, F., xviii
Korematsu (legal case of), 294*ff*
Kraus, K., 195*ff*
Kruglianski, A., 145

Lamine, A. S., 143, 144
Laozi, 35, 36
legalism, 31, 33
Leibniz, G. W., 105, 52*ff*. *See also* Pangloss
Lisbon Earthquake, xv, xix, 25, 105, 151*ff*
Loos, A., 195, 197
Loy, D., 12

Machiavelli, N., 58, 89*ff*
MacIntyre, A., xiv, 78
Magnan, A., 153
Mahler, G., 206
Manichaeanism, 147, 153, 158
Marx, K., 311
McBride, P., 72, 81
McBrien, J., 143
meaning, xi, 81–83, 334
Melian Dialogue, 3, 45, 51
Milocz, C., 260
More, T., 94
Mozi (Mohism), 31, 33
Musil, R., 81, 167, 195
Mytilene debate, 45

nature, 36–37, 75
Nietzsche, F., 81, 106, 168, 171*ff*, 209
Nihilism, 81, 176*ff*
Nock, A. D., 66

Index

Nuclear War, 130, 280, 282, 309–11

O'Connor, K., 25
optimism, 154, 322, 331

Pangloss, 105, 155*ff*
Patterson, D., 269, 270, 275nn54, 58, 61
Pelkmans, M., 143
Peloponnesian War, 3, 43, 44, 107–13, 224
Pericles, 3, 43–44
Piaget, J., xiv
Plato, 3, 43*ff*, 57, 63, 205, 246, 247, 327
Popper, K., 51
positivism, 196, 200
prediction, predictability, viv, 328
progress, 223
proprieties, 35, 37

Rahula, W., 11
Reale, N., 74, 253
realism vs idealism, 94, 99
reason (and rationality), 140, 328*ff*
reformation, 80, 83, 139
relativism, 47, 49, 281
resilience, 321*ff*
Rome, 57, 58, 62 ff, 146, 221
Russell, B., 64, 198, 199, 324

Samson, J., 206
Schaub, T., 245, 246
Schmitt, C., 282, 284*ff*
Schoenberg, A., 205*ff*
scientific revolution, 105, 138–39
sensate cultures, 74
September 11, 2001, 283*ff*
Seven Years War, 152, 154, 161
Shenefelt, M., 137, 138, 140
silence, 253*ff*
Simmel, G., 144
Skinner, Q., 108, 118, 120, 121, 124
slave morality, 175*ff*

Sorokin, P., 72–74, 77–78, 80
Spencer, H., 173
Spengler, O., 225–26, 281
stability, xx, 90*ff*
State of Nature, xix, 115, 118, 130
States of Exception, 282*ff*
stoicism, 58
suffering, xv, 7*ff*, 25

Taoism, 31, 34*ff*
Taylor, C., 144
terrorism, xvii, 281, 283*ff*
theodicy, 9, 153
Thirty Tyrants, 43
Thirty Years War, 113–15
Thrasymachus, 49–50
Thucydides, 3, 43–46, 51, 107–13, 224
Tillyard, E., 139
Toynbee, 84n9, 90, 130, 219*ff*
trauma, xii, xv, 71, 78, 323*ff*

Vico, G., 225
Virgil, 255–58, 269
Voltaire, F., 151*ff*

Wagner, R., 205, 209
Warring States Period, 31*ff*
Webern, A., 210
Weil, S., 51
Wittgenstein, L., 191*ff*
World War I, xv, xvi, 168, 194, 201–202, 210, 219*ff*, 232, 239, 240, 249
World War II, xvi, 83, 168–69, 201–202, 212–14, 219*ff*, 232, 253*ff*, 309–10, 316
Worringer, W., 211
Wozzeck, 213–14
Wyschograd, E., 258, 267

Xenophanes of Colophon, 147

Zhuangzi, 36

Contributor Bios for *Catastrophe and Philosophy*

David J. Rosner

Marek Celinski, PhD, is a psychologist in private practice, and has published more than fifty papers and book chapters on the subjects of clinical psychology, rehabilitation, neuropsychology, and hypnosis. He is also coeditor of a four-book series on Resilience and Resourcefulness and Individual and Mass Trauma, coeditor of book on spirituality for sustainable civilization, and sole editor of a book on civilization, crisis, and renewal.

David A. Chalfin received an AB and a MA in philosophy from Brown University and a J.D. from Stanford Law School. David practiced law at Debevoise & Plimpton in New York City and has been a financial executive for more than twenty years. Currently he is Chief Financial Officer of The Roosevelt Investment Group, Inc.

Sarah Katerina Corrigan is a PhD student in the Department of Comparative Literature at Harvard University. She has a Master's in Divinity from Candler School of Theology in Atlanta, Georgia. Sarah graduated from Emory University with a Bachelor of Arts with Highest Honors in German and interdisciplinary studies. Her interests include religion, literature, and philosophy.

Steven Cresap obtained his PhD from Cornell University, is an Emeritus at Metropolitan College of New York, has authored many articles on nineteenth- and twentieth-century philosophy, aesthetics, and cultural studies.

Pedro Geiger earned a license in geography and in history from the Federal University of Rio de Janeiro in 1943. He served as geographer at the Brazilian Institute of Geography and Statistics, IBGE, 1942–1984. Other credits include: Invited Professor of Graduate Studies at Columbia University,

NY, 1967; at Paris Sorbonne, 1967; at the Texas State University at Austin, 1984; and others. He is also a member of the American Geographers Association, AAG; the International Society of Comparative Studies of Civilizations, ISCSC; and others. He is the author of *Estudos Rurais da Baixada Fluminense* (Rio de Janeiro, IBGE, 1956), *Evolução da Rede Urbana do Brasil* (Rio de Janeiro, Ministry of Education and Culture, 1963), and many scholarly articles. He is an honorary member of the Societé De Geography de Paris, and recipient of prizes such as the CLAG's proze Enlace.

Carsten Meiner holds a PhD from the University of Paris VIII. He is Professor of French Literature in the Department of English, Germanic and Romance Studies at the University of Copenhagen. He is coeditor (with K. Veel) of *Cultural Life of Catastrophes and Crises.*

Diana Prokofyeva holds a PhD (2012) from Bashkir State University, Ufa, Russia. She is currently senior lecturer in the Bashkir State University Department of Philosophy. She has interests in personalism, existentialism. and the history of philosophy.

Robert Quist is a professor of humanities at Ferris State University in Michigan. He holds a PhD in humanities from Florida State University and a MA in musicology at Brigham Young University. He has published several articles and books on twentieth-century music and other subjects.

Nancy M. Reale holds a PhD in comparative literature from New York University. She is clinical professor of liberal studies at NYU, where she has taught since 1985. Her primary scholarly interests include epic poetry and late medieval and early Renaissance short prose fiction. She has written numerous essays on Italian and English medieval literature and is coeditor, with Ruth Sternglantz, of *Satura: Studies in Medieval Literature in Honour of Robert R. Raymo* (2001).

David J. Rosner holds a PhD in philosophy from Brown University. He is currently associate professor of values and ethics, School for Business, Metropolitan College of New York. He is the author of *Conservatism and Crisis: The Anti-Modernist Perspective in Twentieth Century German Philosophy* (Lexington, 2012), as well as numerous papers on the philosophy of education, business ethics, existential thought, and political philosophy. He is also Past President of the International Society for the Comparative Study of Civilizations.

John Ross received his PhD in philosophy from Fordham University. His research interests include Ludwig Wittgenstein's philosophy of psychology and Classical Western Philosophy. For the past fifteen years he has been teaching in the Liberal Studies Program at New York University.

Jeidong Ryu is a research professor at the Theological Institute, Sungkonghoe University, South Korea, with a LittD in religious studies from Sogang University, a Jesuit University in South Korea. His studies are mainly focused on the comparison of Buddhism and Christianity in their metaphysical visions and social engagements. His books include *God and One Mind: An Encounter between Wilfred Cantwell Smith and The Awakening of Faith in Mahayana* (in Korean, (c) Korean Studies Information: Paju, 2007), *Religion and Justice: A Study of the Holistic Concept of Justice in the Perspective of the Fourth Generation* (in Korean, in collaboration with others, Dongyeon: Seoul, 2015), and his articles including "Baqa and One Mind" (in English, *The Journal of Korean Association for Buddhist Studies*, vol. 55, pp. 301–324, 2009).

Peter W. Wakefield is professor of pedagogy and director of undergraduate studies at Emory University's Institute for the Liberal Arts. His training in ancient Greek philosophy (PhD Brown) has served him over twenty five years in a career of undergraduate teaching. F. Scott Fitzgerald's *The Great Gatsby* figures centrally in an interdisciplinary class Wakefield teaches on the nature of evidence, where students analyze Fitzgerald's novel as a late response to empiricism in the form of nascent and skeptical nationalism.

Phil Washburn holds a PhD in philosophy from Columbia. He is the author of *Philosophical Dilemmas: A Pro and Con Introduction to the Major Questions and Philosophers, The Vocabulary of Critical Thinking*, and the editor of *The Many Faces of Wisdom: Great Philosophers' Visions of Philosophy*.

David Wilkinson, PhD, is professor of political science at the University of California, Los Angeles, and author of more than fifty scholarly articles as well as several books, the latter including *Malraux: An Essay in Political Criticism* and *Deadly Quarrels: Lewis F. Richardson and the Statistical Study of War*.

Kwon Jong Yoo is professor of philosophy, Chung-Ang University, Korea. He graduated from Korea University with a PhD of East Asian Philosophy. He has published articles and books about Confucianism, Taoism, ethics, and philosophy of mind, with an interdisciplinary focus.